118(D)   JUL - 6 2017

SACRED TEXTS

THE

KORAN

The Holy Book of Islam with
Introduction and Notes

Translated by E. H. Palmer

Introduction to this edition
by R. A. Nicholson

WATKINS
Sharing Wisdom Since
1893

This translation of The Koran by E. H. Palmer
was first published in 1900

First published in 2007
This edition first published in 2017 by Watkins,
an imprint of Watkins Media Limited
19 Cecil Court
London WC2N 4EZ

3 5 7 9 10 8 6 4 2

Designed in Great Britain by Jerry Goldie
Typeset in Great Britain by Dorchester Typesetting Group
Printed and bound in Thailand by Imago

British Library Cataloguing-in-Publication data available

ISBN: 978-1-90585-702-9

www.watkinspublishing.com

CONTENTS

CONTENTS

INTRODUCTION

At the beginning of the seventh century of our era Arabian paganism was showing signs of decay. The influence of Judaism and Christianity, if seldom deep, was not confined to the numerous clans which had embraced one or other of these religions, but had made itself felt, as pre-Islamic poetry bears witness, amongst those who were still attached by custom and tradition to their tribals gods. We hear much of Christian hermits and also of a few persons known as *hanîfs*, who had rejected idolatry for a religion of their own, ascetic and monotheistic; Mohammed appears to have been in touch with some of them before his call. In a word, acquaintance with higher and purer ideas had shaken faith in the old order of things, and shadows cast by the coming event were already visible.

For us, Mohammed's earlier life is almost a blank, since on this subject the Qur'ân gives little information, while the accounts of Muslim writers contain far more fable than fact. It may be taken as certain that he came of humble stock, passed his youth in poverty, and gained a respectable position through his marriage to Khadija. His journeys with the trading caravans of Mecca afforded opportunities for conversation with Jews and Christians, of which the Qur'ân preserves the result. If prophets are like poets, then what made Mohammed a prophet will never be known. Whether we regard it as 'a pathological case' or a grand example of mystical ecstasy, the thing is essentially inexplicable, though at the outset of his mission a dominating *motive* can be discerned in his conviction that the Last Judgement was near and that he must at all costs warn his countrymen of the doom impending. That he believed himself to be the Messenger of Allah seems to me beyond doubt. Any other view involves the paradox that a world religion claiming at the present day over a hundred million adherents was founded by one who, not being peculiarly religious, was nevertheless capable of simulating religious enthusiasm so perfectly that his first essays in that style constitute for all Muslims and even for many who are not Muslims the clearest possible evidence of his prophetic genius. 'He was first and foremost a *revealer*, who uttered, by inspiration, truths which lay beyond the ken of his listeners, but which came with a conviction of reality when they were heard. The prophet's chief qualification was *vision* rather than logical power or learning . . . His speaking was apparently unpremeditated—a rapturous utterance, as though a power not himself were using him as a vehicle of communication.' Those who read in Arabic the chapters of the Qur'ân revealed at Mecca and now placed at the end of the sacred volume will have no difficulty in applying the above description of the New Testament prophet to Mohammed. To say that the rest of the Qur'ân is, on the whole, uninspired does not mean that its author was conscious of fraud when he gave out all sorts of regulations and instructions in Allah's name. When, by force of circumstances, the prophet in him had grown into the ruler and legislator, it was a psychological necessity that he should still feel himself to be the chosen medium for the divine message: 'The Child is father of the Man.'

He was addicted to the practice of solitary prayer, especially during the night, and may well have cultivated it for the purpose of inducing the abnormal states which caused his enemies to describe him as possessed by the jinn. It is important to observe that this practice was associated in his mind with the idea of Revelation. The opening verses of Surah LXXIII—'O thou who art enwrapped! rise (stand up in prayer) by night except a little—the half, or deduct therefrom a little, or add thereto, and chant the Qur'ân chanting. Verily we will cast on thee a heavy speech (a weighty word)'—surely depict the process by which many of the early revelations came. According to tradition, Mohammed was keeping vigil on a night of Ramadan, in or about the year 610, when he saw the vision of an Angel who seized him with a strong grasp, crying, 'Recite!' (iqra'), and after the Prophet had thrice refused to obey, himself recited the words that now stand at the beginning of Surah XCVI. This is said to have been the first 'recital' (qur'ân), a term applicable to each of the succeeding revelations known collectively as 'the Recital' (al-Qur'ân), Although Mohammed could not presume to think that what he heard was the voice of Allah, he never doubted its divine origin or believed that he himself had any part in shaping the form of the revelations as they were brought to him by 'the Spirit', whom he afterwards identified with Gabriel. On the contrary, he conceived them as excerpts, communicated in the Arabic tongue, from a Heavenly Book inscribed on 'a preserved tablet', whence are derived all prophetic revelations, including the Jewish, Christian, and Zoroastrian scriptures. Between these and the Qur'ân there is no essential difference. The Qur'ân 'is in the scriptures of yore' and confirms their truth. As Allah is One, so his Revelation is One. This idea, momentous for the future of Islam, raised some awkward questions. Is the divine original fixed and unalterable? Obviously not; the Qur'ân often contradicts itself as well as other scriptures. Allah, then, changes his mind and alters the text of the Heavenly Book accordingly (Surah XIII, 39). Such is the famous doctrine of 'abrogation' as stated in Surah II, 100: 'Whatever verse we may annul or cause thee to forget, we will bring a better one than it, or one like it; dost thou not know that Allah is mighty over all?' To the Prophet, of course, this solution presented none of the difficulties which occur to ordinary men. His belief in a pre-estab-lished harmony of the Qur'ân with the ancient scriptures was maintained, with but slight reservations, even at Medina, where both Jews and Christians criticized his statements regarding books which he confessed himself unable to read; but as he was not in a position to fall back upon Dr. Johnson's plea of 'sheer ignorance', he countered their attack by alleging that they and their co-religionists had corrupted and falsified the Pentateuch, Psalms, and Gospels for their own ends.

One of the most disconcerting features of the Qur'ân—its lack of connexion and continuity—is partly due to the way in which the existing text was compiled. During the

Prophet's lifetime the revelations followed each other at brief intervals, and some of his hearers would learn them by heart or perhaps write them down on any material that came to hand, but neither he nor any one else seems to have thought of collecting them in a form that would secure their permanence. Only after his death, when disputes arose concerning the text, and when the number of those who carried it in their memories was rapidly decreasing, was the need for a complete and accurate recension of the Qur'ân felt to be urgent. The details are uncertain, but we know that in the Caliphate of Othmân an authorized edition was prepared by Zaid ibn Thâbit, the Prophet's amanuensis, with the assistance of three colleagues. This edition, which contains the Qur'ân in its present form, soon gained universal currency. While its value as a genuine record of the Prophet's teaching and preaching cannot be impugned, the contents are in such a state of confusion that to read the book through from beginning to end is to miss all its significance as an historical document. Granting that the editors could not possibly have arranged the whole series of revelations in the exact order in which they were delivered, we must accuse them of ignoring chronology entirely. The plan they adopted was very simple, the place of each surah being determined by its length, and the longer ones preceding the shorter. Had this principle been reversed, readers would have less cause to complain, for in the earliest surahs the words are few and strong, contrasting strangely with the copious but somewhat pedestrian eloquence of those revealed at Medina, four of which come immediately after the opening prayer and occupy more than a hundred pages in the present translation. In attempting to restore the original order, European critics have divided the surahs into groups. The following table may be found useful, though the reader should bear in mind that many passages of diverse date and provenance remain embedded in surahs which have been assigned to a particular period:

MECCAN SURAHS
(*circa* AD 610–22)

First Period: I, LI–LIII, LV, LVI, LXVIII–LXX, LXXIII–LXXV, LXXVII–XCVII XCIX–CIX, CXI–CXIV.

Second Period: XV, XVII–XXI, XXIII, XXV–XXVII, XXXVI–XXXVIII, XLIII, XLIV, L, LIV, LXVII, LXXI, LXXII, LXXVI.

Third Period: VI, VII, X–XIV, XVI, XXVIII–XXXII, XXXIV, XXXV, XXXIX–XLII, XLV, XLVI.

MEDINA SURAHS
(AD 622–32)

II–V, VIII, IX, XXII, XXIV, XXXIII, XLVII–XLIX, LVII–LXVI, XCVIII, CX.

Apart from its preposterous arrangement, the Qur'ân is not so much a book as a collection of manifestoes, diatribes, harangues, edicts, discourses, sermons, and suchlike occasional pieces. No subject is treated systematically, and the surprising omissions even in matters affecting the public worship of the Muslims show that Mohammed did not regard the revelations as chapters of a book, but rather as divine messages which had served their purpose when the emergency that produced them was past. From that point of view there was little reason why he or his audience should care what became of them.

At Mecca the Prophet concentrates on his fundamental doctrines—monotheism, resurrection, and retribution. These pages of the Qur'ân abound in weird oaths and terrible imprecations mingled with strains of sublime poetry. One sees that the preacher has lost control of himself and is speaking like a man possessed. Towards the close of the Meccan period the thunders die away into a stillness broken, now and then, by reverberations powerful enough to exalt, though they no longer alarm. Logic of a sort, argument, illustration, and narrative begin to prevail, and after the Hijrah or migration to Medina the contents of the Muslim scripture become exceedingly miscellaneous. Stories of the ancient prophets are repeated again and again, but Mohammed with his excitable temperament does not shine as a raconteur; he brings his predecessors on to the stage in order that they may enact for the benefit of his own stiff-necked generation a drama of which the real hero is always himself. His fortune had turned, he was fighting on favourable ground, and his chief adversaries in Medina—the Jews and the so-called Hypocrites—were unable to unite their forces against him. The revelations are now addressed mainly to the Faithful and deal to a large extent with matters of legal, social, and political interest, or comment on the news of the day. Meanwhile Islam was being nationalized. By this time Mohammed knew the Christian doctrine concerning Jesus to be incompatible with the unity of Allah, and, when his overtures to the Jews, based on their recognition of the Qur'ân as the Book of Abraham and Moses, were received with mockery and scorn, he looked back to Mecca. Henceforth every Muslim was to pray with his face towards the Kaabah, while the Pilgrimage, stripped if not completely purged of superstition, was installed as one of the five pillars of Islam.

That the Qur'ân, the literal Word of Allah, is in all respects unique and inimitable is an article of faith which Western students approaching the subject without religious prepossessions are not likely to endorse; on the other hand, they will do the Qur'ân less than justice if they measure it by common standards. Considered as a literary work it has many defects, but clearly it is not a literary work in the sense that the Bible is. It was addressed to the ear, not to the critical eye; it was uttered by a living voice that impressed those who heard it with the power and enthusiasm of the speaker: it made a *personal* appeal. Moreover, its doctrines were new to the great majority of Mohammed's countrymen and were in very truth a 'revelation' of things they had never dreamed of and could hardly believe or understand. In order to judge the Qur'ân fairly, we must see the time and the place and the Prophet all together. He sought to convert, by imbuing them with Jewish and Christian theology, a people who had only the dimmest and vaguest conceptions of a future life, and whose language therefore furnished no religious terms for the conveyance of such ideas. The poverty of Arabic in this domain may have stimulated his poetic invention. It has been pointed out that the descriptions of Paradise in the Qur'ân resemble passages in which the heathen bards that depicted earthly scenes of carousal and merrymaking; whether the Prophet drew from this source or not, in the Meccan surahs especially he uses the most vivid and striking imagery to describe the terrors of the Last Judgement and the tortures of the damned. If his hearers found the subject novel, the style at any rate was true to tradition. Its parent, however, it not the highly developed and artificial poetry which embodies the ideals of the pre-Islamic age and for the most part is thoroughly pagan in sentiment. Mohammed lacked the skill to make metrical verses, while his opinion of those who practised the art may be learned from Surah XXVI, 224–6: 'And the poets do those follow who go astray! Dost thou not see that they wander distraught in every vale? and that they say that which they do not do?' But the Arabs had long been acquainted with profession-al exponents of supernaturalism—wizards and soothsayers, whose oracles were couched in a sort of rhymed prose (saj'). There was no other model available for the first book in Arabic prose, and Mohammed inevitably adopted it. The Qur'ân, as regards its literary form, is a link between the old epoch and the new. An author who fashioned a style for himself out of rude jingling oracles may be excused for worse faults than any that modern critics have discovered in his work. They sometimes forget that he never wrote it and that the most effective speeches are seldom flawless in diction or taste, not to mention grammar. Though its abruptness and incoherence may offend, these qualities belong to the character of Arabian eloquence, which bursts out in flashes and refuses to burn with a steady flame. In the later surahs the style often sinks into a flatness and monotony tiresome to us, though not unexampled in our own scriptures. By comparing the Qur'ân with these we place ourselves in the least suitable attitude for judging it rightly. Any one can see how little its claim 'to confirm and perfect the teaching of the former prophets' is worth. Mohammed picked up all his knowledge of this kind by hearsay, and he makes a brave show with such borrowed trappings—largely consisting of legends from the Haggada and the Apocrypha. But we must get behind that. The essential truth about the Qur'ân is not that it is a garbled version of the old scriptures, but that the whole work bears the stamp of a creative personality in conflict with traditional ideas. Only against the background of Arabian heathendom, from which it sprang, can it be viewed in its true proportions. Unless we keep in mind the abominations, as Mohammed deemed them, of the system he was sent to overthrow, we shall fail to recognize the original and distinctive form which he imposed on his revolutionary doctrine. That doctrine is neither Judaism nor Christianity: it is Islam. The product was national, though most of the ingredients were imported. As an eminent Orientalist has remarked, 'The character of the new religion was very powerfully influenced by the manly spirit of some of its first confessors and champions; both the good and the bad qualities of the Arabs, among whom it arose and for whom it was in the first instance promulgated, have stamped their unmistakable impress upon it.'

So long as the Prophet lived, his personality was all that mattered; and afterwards when his followers were forced to turn for guidance to the Qur'ân alone, their first care was the Holy War which he had preached and inaugurated; for, whatever weight we may attach to such motives as hunger and rapacity, the wretchedly armed Bedouins who hurled themselves against the empires of Rome and Persia must have felt that Allah was fighting for them and that death was a sure passport to Paradise. Ere a century had elapsed, the Qur'ân was being recited in Samarcand and Toledo.

Since the verbal inspiration of the Bible has been maintained by some theologians even in this country till comparatively recent days, we need not wonder that Muslim reverence for the Qur'ân culminated, about two hundred years after the Hijrah, in the dogma that it is the eternal and uncreated Word of Allah. The absolute authority which it exercises, as such, in every department of Muslim life and thought was gradually modified in practice by the development of various supplementary sources and principles which enable it to move with the times sooner or later, while so much of the 'perspicuous' Book is equivocal or obscure that it has been quoted on both sides in all the great historical controversies of Islam and will be, no doubt, in those that are to come. Amongst the orthodox there are signs of discontent with traditional methods of interpretation; yet the critics hold fast to their belief in the divine nature of the text: here, indeed, all Muslims are united. If we do not share that belief, we can still acknowledge the extraordinary importance of the Qur'ân for students of history and religion, its vast influence upon the minds and lives of peoples widely different in culture, and its peculiar interest as the work in which the last of the great Semitic prophets gave his message to the world.

R. A. NICHOLSON

BIOGRAPHIES

E.H.Palmer (1840–1882) was an English orientalist and Professor of Arabic at Cambridge University. He was also a government negotiator in the area of Suez and Gaza. His brilliant scholarship, extraordinary linguistic range and versatile talent are displayed in the many books he wrote in Persian and other Eastern languages. His works include *The Desert of the Exodus, Arabic Grammar, History of Jerusalem* and *Persian Dictionary*.

R.A.Nicholson (1868–1945) was an eminent orientalist who is widely regarded as the greatest Rumi scholar in the English language. He was Professor of Arabic at Cambridge University, dedicating his life to the study of Islamic mysticism, studying and translating major Sufi texts in Arabic, Persian and Ottoman Turkish.

THE QUR'ÂN

THE OPENING CHAPTER

I (*Mecca*)

In the name of the merciful and compassionate Allah.

Praise *belongs* to Allah, the Lord of the worlds, the merciful, the compassionate, the ruler of the day of judgement! Thee we serve and Thee we ask for aid. [5] Guide us in the right path, the path of those Thou art gracious to; not of those Thou art wroth with; nor of those who err.

THE CHAPTER OF THE HEIFER

II (*Medina*)

In the name of the merciful and compassionate Allah.

A. L. M.¹ That² is the book! there is no doubt therein; a guide to the pious, who believe in the unseen, and are steadfast in prayer, and of what we have given them expend in alms; who believe in what is revealed to thee, and what was revealed before thee, and of the hereafter they are sure. These are in guidance from their Lord, and these are the prosperous. [5] Verily, those who misbelieve, it is the same to them if ye warn them or if ye warn them not, they will not believe. Allah has set a seal upon their hearts and on their hearing; and on their eyes is dimness, and for them is grievous woe. And there are those among men who say, 'We believe in Allah and in the last day'; but they do not believe. They would deceive Allah and those who believe; but they deceive only themselves and they do not perceive. In their hearts is a sickness, and Allah has made them still more sick, and for them is grievous woe because they lied. [10] And when it is said to them, 'Do not evil in the earth,' they say, 'We do but what is right.' Are not they the evil-doers? and yet they do not perceive. And when it is said to them, 'Believe as other men believe,' they say, 'Shall we believe as fools believe?' Are not they themselves the fools? and yet they do not know. And when they meet those who believe, they say, 'We do believe'; but when they go aside with their devils, they say, 'We are with you; we were but mocking!' Allah shall mock at them and let them go on in their rebellion, blindly wandering on.

[15] Those who buy error for guidance, their traffic profits not, and they are not guided. Their likeness is as the likeness of one³ who kindles a fire; and when it lights up all around, Allah goes off with their light, and leaves them in darkness that they cannot see. Deafness, dumbness, blindness, and they shall not return! Or like a storm cloud from the sky, wherein is darkness and thunder and lightning; they put their fingers in their ears at the thunderclap, for fear of death, for Allah encompasses the misbelievers. The lightning well-nigh snatches off their sight, whenever it shines for them they walk therein; but when it is dark for them they halt; and if

Allah willed He would go off with their hearing and their sight; verily, Allah is mighty over all.

O ye folk! serve your Lord who created you and those before you; haply ye may fear! [20] who made the earth for you a bed and the heaven a dome; and sent down from heaven water, and brought forth therewith fruits as a sustenance for you; so make no peers for Allah, the while ye know!

And if ye are in doubt of what we have revealed unto our servant, then bring a chapter like it, and call your witnesses other than Allah if ye tell truth. But if ye do it not, and ye shall surely do it not, then fear the Fire whose fuel is men and stones,[4] prepared for misbelievers. But bear the glad tidings to those who believe and work righteousness, that for them are gardens beneath which rivers flow; whenever they are provided with fruit therefrom they say, 'This is what we were provided with before,' and they shall be provided with the like;[5] and there are pure wives for them therein, and they shall dwell therein for aye.

Why, Allah is not ashamed to set forth a parable of a gnat,[6] or anything beyond; and as for those who believe, they know that it is truth from the Lord; but as for those who disbelieve, they say, 'What is it that Allah means by this as a parable? He leads astray many and He guides many';—but He leads astray only the evil-doers; [25] who break Allah's covenant after the fixing thereof, and cut asunder what Allah has ordered to be joined, and do evil in the earth;—these it is who lose.

How can ye disbelieve in Allah, when ye were dead

and He made you alive, and then He will kill you and then make you alive again, and then to Him will ye return? It is He who created for you all that is in the earth, then he made for the heavens and fashioned them seven heavens; and He knows all things.

And when thy Lord said unto the angels, 'I am about to place a vicegerent in the earth,' they said, 'Wilt Thou place therein one who will do evil therein and shed blood? [30] we celebrate Thy praise and hallow Thee.' Said (the Lord), 'I know what ye know not.' And He taught Adam the names, all of them; then He propounded them to the angels and said, 'Declare to me the names of these, if ye are truthful.'7 They said, 'Glory to be to Thee! no knowledge is ours but what Thou thyself hast taught us, verily, Thou art the knowing, the wise.' Said the Lord, 'O Adam declare to them their names'; and when he had declared to them their names He said, 'Did I not say to you, I know the secrets of the heavens and of the earth, and I know what ye show and what ye were hiding?' And when we said to the angels, 'Adore Adam,' they adored him save only Iblîs, who refused and was too proud and became one of the misbelievers. And we said, 'O Adam dwell, thou and thy wife, in Paradise, and eat therefrom amply as you wish; but do not draw near this tree or ye will be of the transgressors.' And Satan made them backslide therefrom and drove them out from what they were in and we said, 'Go down, one of you the enemy of the other, and in the earth there is an abode and a provision for a time.' [35] And Adam caught certain words from his Lord, and He turned towards him, for He is the compassionate one easily turned. We said, 'Go down therefrom altogether and haply there may come from me a guidance, and whoso follows my guidance, no fear is theirs, nor shall they grieve. But those who misbelieve, and call our signs lies, they are the fellows of the Fire, they shall dwell therein for aye.

O ye children of Israel! remember my favours which I have favoured you with; fulfil my covenant and I will fulfil your covenant; me therefore dread. Believe in what I have revealed, verifying what ye have got, and be not the first to disbelieve in it, and do not barter my signs for a little price, and me do ye fear. Clothe not truth with vanity, nor hide the truth the while ye know. [40] Be steadfast in prayer, give the alms, and bow down with those who bow. Will ye order men to do piety and forget yourselves? Ye read the Book, do ye not then understand? Seek aid with patience and prayer, though it is a hard thing save for the humble, and who think that they will meet their Lord, and that to Him will they return.

O ye children of Israel! remember my favours which I have favoured you with, and that I have preferred you above the worlds. Fear the day wherein no soul shall pay any recompense for another soul, [45] nor shall intercession be accepted for it, nor shall compensation be taken from it, nor shall they be helped.

When we saved you from Pharaoh's people who sought to wreak you evil and woe, slaughtering your sons and letting your women live; in that was a great trial for you from your Lord. When we divided for you the sea and saved you and drowned Pharaoh's people while ye looked on. When we treated with Moses forty nights, then ye took the calf after he had gone and ye did wrong. Yet then we forgave you after that; perhaps ye may be grateful. [50] And when we gave Moses the Scriptures and the Discrimination; perhaps ye will be guided. When Moses said to his people, 'O my people! Ye have wronged yourselves in taking his calf; repent unto your Creator and kill each other;[8] that will be better for you in your Creator's eyes; and He turned unto you, for He is the compassionate one easily turned.' And when ye said to Moses, 'O Moses! we will not believe in thee until we see Allah manifestly,' and the thunderbolt caught you while ye yet looked on. Then we raised you up after your death; perhaps ye may be grateful. And we overshadowed you with the cloud, and sent down the manna and the quails; 'Eat of the good things we have given you.' They did not wrong us, but it was themselves they were wronging. [55] And when we said, 'Enter the city[9] and eat therefrom as plentifully as ye wish; and enter the gate worshipping and say 'hittatun'.[10] So will we pardon you your sins and give increase unto those who do well.'

But those who did wrong changed it for another[11] word than that which was said to them: and we sent down upon those who did wrong, wrath from heaven for that they had so sinned.

When Moses, too, asked drink for his people and we said, 'Strike with thy staff the rock,' and from it burst forth twelve springs; each man among them knew his drinking place. 'Eat and drink of what Allah has provided, and transgress not on the earth as evil-doers.'

And when they said, 'O Moses, we cannot always bear one kind of food; pray then thy Lord to bring forth for us of what the earth grows, its green herbs, its cucumbers, its garlic, its lentils, and its onions.' Said he, 'Do ye ask what is meaner instead of what is best? Go down to Egypt,—there is what ye ask.' Then were they smitten with abasement and poverty, and met with wrath from Allah. That was because they had misbelieved in Allah's signs and killed the prophets undeservedly; that was for that they were rebellious and had transgressed.

Verily, whether it be of those who believe, or those who are Jews or Christians or Sabæans, whosoever believe in Allah and the last day and act aright, they have their reward at their Lord's hand, and there is no fear for them, nor shall they grieve.

[60] And when we took a covenant with you and held the mountain over you;[12] 'Accept what we have brought you with strong will, and bear in mind what is therein, haply ye yet may fear.'

Then did ye turn aside after this, and were it not for Allah's grace towards you and His mercy, ye would have been of those who lose. Ye know too of those among you who transgressed upon the Sabbath, and we said, 'Become ye apes, despised and spurned.'[13]

Thus we made them an example unto those who stood before them, and those who should come after them, and a warning unto those who fear.

And when Moses said to his people, 'Allah bids you slaughter a cow,'[14] they said, 'Art thou making a jest of us?' Said he, 'I seek refuge with Allah from being one of the unwise.' They said, 'They pray thy Lord for us to show us what she is to be.' He answered, 'He saith it is a cow, nor old, nor young, of middle age between the two; so do as ye are bid.' [65] They said, 'Pray now thy Lord to show us what her colour is to be.' He answered, 'He saith it is a dun cow, intensely dun, her colour delighting those who look upon her.'

Again they said, 'Pray thy Lord to show us what she is to be; for cows appear the same to us; then we, if Allah will, shall be guided.' He answered, 'He saith, it is a cow, not broken in to plough the earth or irrigate the tilth, a sound one with no blemish on her.' They said, 'Now hast thou brought the truth.' And they slaughtered her, though they came near leaving it undone.

When too ye slew a soul and disputed thereupon, and Allah brought forth that which ye had hidden, then we said, 'Strike him with part of her.' Thus Allah brings the dead to life and shows you His signs, that haply ye may understand.

Yet were your hearts hardened even after that, till they were as stones or harder still, for verily of stones are some from which streams burst forth, and of them there are some that burst asunder and the water issues out, and of them there are some that fall down for fear of Allah; but Allah is never careless of what ye do.

[70] Do ye crave that they should believe you when already a sect of them have heard the word of Allah and then perverted it[15] after they had understood it, though they knew?

And when they meet those who believe they say, 'We

believe,' but when one goes aside with another they say, 'Will ye talk to them of what Allah has opened up to you, that they may argue with you upon it before your Lord? Do ye not therefore understand?' Do they not then know that Allah knoweth what they keep secret and what they make known abroad?

And some of them there are, illiterate folk, that know not the Book, but only idle tales; for they do but fancy. But woe to those who write out the Book with their hands and say 'this is from Allah'; to buy therefore with a little price! and woe to them for what their hands have written, and woe to them for what they gain!

And then they say, 'Hellfire shall not touch us save for a number of days.'[16] Say, 'Have ye taken a covenant with Allah?' but Allah breaks not His covenant. Or do ye say of Allah that which ye do not know?

[75] Yea! whoso gains an evil gain, and is encompassed by his sins, those are the fellows of the Fire, and they shall dwell therein for aye! But such as act aright, those are the fellows of Paradise, and they shall dwell therein for aye!

And when we took from the children of Israel a covenant, saying 'Serve ye none but Allah, and to your two parents show kindness, and to your kindred and the orphans and the poor, and speak to men kindly, and be steadfast in prayer, and give alms'; and then ye turned back, save a few of you, and swerved aside.

And when we took a covenant from you, 'shed ye not your kinsman's blood, nor turn your kinsmen out of their homes':[17] then did ye confirm it and were witnesses thereto. Yet ye were those who slay your kinsmen and turn a party out of their homes, and back each other up against them with sin and enmity. But if they come to you as captives ye ransom them!—and yet it is as unlawful for you to turn them out. Do ye then believe in part of the Book and disbelieve in part? But the reward of such among you as do that shall be nought else but disgrace in this worldly life, and on the day of the resurrection shall they be driven to the most grievous torment, for Allah is not unmindful of what ye do.

[80] Those who have brought this worldly life with the Future, the torment shall not be lightened from them nor shall they be helped.

We gave Moses the Book and we followed him up with other apostles, and we gave Jesus the son of Mary manifest signs and aided him with the Holy Spirit. Do ye then, every time an apostle comes to you with what your souls love not, proudly scorn him, and charge a part with lying and slay a part?

They say, 'Our hearts are uncircumcised'; nay, Allah has cursed them in their unbelief, and few it is who do believe. And when a book came down from Allah confirming what they had with them, though they had before prayed for victory over those who misbelieve, yet when that came to them[18] which they knew, then they disbelieved it,—Allah's curse be on the misbelievers.

For a bad bargain have they sold their souls, not to believe it what Allah have revealed, grudging because Allah sends down of His grace on whomsoever of His servants He will; and they have brought on themselves wrath after wrath and for the misbelievers is there shameful woe.

[85] And when they are told to believe in what Allah has revealed, they say, 'We believe in what has been revealed to us'; but they disbelieve in all beside, although it is the truth confirming what they have. Say, 'Wherefore did ye kill Allah's prophets of yore if ye were true believers?'

Moses came to you with manifest signs, then ye took up with the calf when we had gone and did so wrong. And when we took a covenant with you and raised the mountain over you, 'Take what we have given you with resolution and hear'; they said, 'We hear but disobey'; and they were made to drink the calf down into their hearts for their unbelief.[19] Say, 'An evil thing is it which your belief bids you do, if ye be true believers.' Say, 'If the abode of the future with Allah is yours alone and not mankind's: long for death then if ye speak the truth.' But they will never long for it because of what their hands have sent on before; but Allah is knowing as to the wrong doers.

[90] Why, thou wilt find them the greediest of men for life; and of those who associate others with Allah one would fain live for a thousand years,—but he will not be reprieved from punishment by being let live, for Allah seeth what they do.

Say, 'Who is an enemy to Gabriel?'[20] for he hath revealed to thy heart, with Allah's permission, confirmation of what had been before, and a guidance and glad tidings to believers. Who is an enemy to Allah and His angels and His apostles and Gabriel and Michael?—Verily, Allah is an enemy to the unbelievers. We have sent down to thee conspicuous signs, and none will disbelieve therein except the evil-doers. Or every time they make a covenant, will a part of them repudiate it? Nay, most of them do not believe.

[95] And when there comes to them an apostle confirming what they have, a part of those who have received the Book repudiate Allah's book, casting it behind their backs as though they did not know. And they follow that which the devils recited against Solomon's kingdom;—it was not Solomon who misbelieved,[21] but the devils who misbelieved, teaching men sorcery,—and what has been revealed to the two angels at Babylon, Hârût and Mârût;[22] yet these taught no one until they said, 'We are but a temptation, so do not misbelieve.' Men learn from them only that by which they may part man and wife; but they can harm no one therewith, unless with the permission of Allah, and they learn what hurts them and profits them not. And yet they knew that he who purchased it would have no portion in the future; but sad is the price at which they have sold their souls, had they but known. But had they believed and feared, a reward from Allah were better, had they but known.

O ye who believe! say not 'râ'hinâ', but say 'unthurnâ',[23] and harken; for unto misbelievers shall be grievous woe.

They who misbelieve, whether of those who have the Book or of the idolaters, would fain that no good were sent down to you from your Lord; but Allah specially favours with His mercy whom He will, for Allah is Lord of mighty grace.

[100] Whatever verse we may annul or cause thee to forget, we will bring a better one than it, or one like it; dost thou not know that Allah is mighty over all? Dost thou not know that Allah's is the kingdom of the heavens and the earth? nor have ye besides Allah a patron or a help.

Do ye wish to question your apostle as Moses was questioned aforetime? but whoso takes misbelief in exchange for faith has erred from the level road.

Many of those who have the Book would fain turn you back into misbelievers after ye have once believed, through envy from themselves, after the truth has been made manifest to them; but pardon and shun them till Allah brings His command; verily, Allah is mighty over all.

Be ye steadfast in prayer, and give alms; and whatsoever good ye send before for your own souls, ye shall find it with Allah, for Allah in all ye do doth see.

[105] They say, 'None shall enter Paradise save such as be Jews or Christians'; that is their faith. Say thou, 'Bring your proofs, if ye be speaking truth.'

Aye, he who resigns[24] his face to Allah, and who is kind, he shall have his reward from his Lord, and no fear shall be on them, and they shall not grieve.

The Jews say, 'The Christians rest on nought'; and the Christians say, 'The Jews rest on nought'; and yet they read the Book. So, too, say those who know not, like to what these say; but Allah shall judge between them on the resurrection day concerning that whereon they do dispute.

But who is more unjust than he who prohibits Allah's mosques,[25] that His name should not be mentioned there, and who strives to ruin them? 'Tis not for such to enter into them except in fear, for them is disgrace in this world, and in the future mighty woe.

Allah's is the east and the west, and wherever ye turn there is Allah's face; verily, Allah comprehends and knows.

[110] They say, 'Allah takes unto Himself a son.' Celebrated be His praise![26] Nay, His is what is in the heavens and the earth, and Him all things obey. The Originator of the heavens and the earth, when He decrees a matter He doth but say unto it, 'BE', and it is.

And those who do not know (the Scriptures) say, 'Unless Allah speak to us, or there comes a sign.' So spake those before them like unto their speech. Their hearts are all alike. We have made manifest the signs unto a people that are sure.

We have sent thee with the truth, a bearer of good tidings and of warning, and thou shalt not be questioned as to the fellows of Hell.

The Jews will not be satisfied with thee, not yet the Christians, until thou followest their creed. Say, 'Allah's guidance is the guidance'; and if thou followest their lusts after the knowledge that has come to thee, thou hast not then from Allah a patron or a help.

[115] They to whom we have brought the Book and who read it as it should be read, believe therein; and whoso

disbelieve therein, 'tis they who lose thereby.

O children of Israel! remember my favours with which I favoured you, and that I have preferred you over the worlds. And fear the day when no soul shall pay a recompense for a soul, nor shall an equivalent be received therefrom, nor any intercession avail; and they shall not be helped.

And when his Lord tried Abraham with words, and he fulfilled them, He said, 'Verily, I will set thee as a high priest[27] for men.' Said he, 'And of my seed?' Allah said, 'My covenant touches not the evil-doers.'

And when we made the House[28] a place of resort unto men, and a sanctuary, and (said) take the station of Abraham[29] for a place of prayer; and covenanted with Abraham and Ishmael, saying, 'Do ye two cleanse my house for those who make the circuit, for those who pay devotions there, for those who bow down, and for those too who adore.'

[120] When Abraham said, 'Lord, make this a town of safety, and provide the dwellers there with fruits, such as believe in Allah and the last day!' (Allah) said, 'And he who misbelieves, I will give him but little to enjoy, then will I drive him to the torment of the Fire, an evil journey will it be.'

And when Abraham raised up the foundations of the House with Ishmael, 'Lord! receive it from us, verily, thou art hearing and dost know. Lord! and make us too resigned[30] unto Thee, and of our seed also a nation resigned unto Thee, and show us our rites, and turn towards us, verily, Thou art easy to be turned and merciful. Lord! and send them an apostle from amongst themselves, to read to them Thy signs and teach them the Book and wisdom, and to purify them; verily, Thou art the mighty and the wise.'

Who is averse from the faith of Abraham save one who is foolish of soul? for we have chosen him in this world, and in the future he is surely of the righteous.

[125] When his Lord said to him, 'Be resigned,' he said, 'I am resigned[31] unto the Lord of the worlds.'

And Abraham instructed his sons therein, and Jacob (saying), 'O my sons! verily, Allah has chosen for you a religion, do not therefore die unless ye be resigned.'[32]

Were ye then witnesses when Jacob was facing death, when he said to his sons, 'What will ye serve when I am gone?' They said, 'We will serve thy Allah, the Allah of thy fathers Abraham, and Ishmael, and Isaac, one Allah; and we are unto Him resigned.'

That is a nation that has passed away, theirs is what they gained; and yours shall be what ye have gained; ye shall not be questioned as to that which they have done.

They say, 'Be ye Jews or Christians so shall ye be guided.' Say, 'Not so! but the faith of Abraham the Hanîf,[33] he was not of the idolaters.'

[130] Say ye, 'We believe in Allah, and what has been revealed to us, and what has been revealed to Abraham, and Ishmael, and Isaac, and Jacob, and the Tribes, and what was brought to Moses and Jesus, and what was brought unto the Prophets from their Lord; we will not distinguish between any one of them, and unto Him are we resigned.'

If they believe in that in which ye believe, then are they guided; but if they turn back, then are they only in a schism, and Allah will suffice thee against them, for He both hears and knows.

The dye[34] of Allah! and who is better than Allah at dyeing? and we are worshippers of Him.

Say, 'Do ye dispute with us concerning Allah, and He is our Lord and your Lord? Ye have your works and we have ours, and unto Him are we sincere.'

Do ye say that Abraham, and Ishmael, and Isaac, and Jacob, and the Tribes were Jews or Christians? Say, 'Are ye more knowing than Allah? Who is more unjust than one who conceals a testimony that he has from Allah?' But Allah is not careless of what ye do.

[135] That is a nation that has passed away; theirs is what they gained, and yours shall be what ye have gained; ye shall not be questioned as to that which they have done.

The fools among men will say, 'What has turned them from their qiblah,[35] on which they were agreed?'

Say, 'Allah's is the east and the west, He guides whom He will unto the right path.'[36] Thus have we made you a middle nation, to be witnesses against men, and that the Apostle may be witness against you.

We have not appointed the qiblah on which thou wert agreed, save that we might know who follows the Apostle from him who turns upon his heels; although it is a great thing save to those whom Allah doth guide. Both Allah will not waste our faith, for verily, Allah with men is kind and merciful.

We see thee often turn about thy face in the heavens, but we will surely turn thee to a qiblah thou shalt like. Turn then they face towards the Sacred Mosque;[37] wherever ye be, turn your faces towards it; for verily, those who have the Book know that it is the truth from their Lord;—Allah is not careless of that which ye do.

[140] And if thou shouldst bring to those who have been given the Book every sign, they would not follow your qibla; and thou art not to follow their qiblah; nor do some of them follow the qibla of the others: and if thou followest their lusts after the knowledge that has come to thee then art thou of the evil-doers.

Those whom we have given the Book now him[38] as they know their sons, although a sect of them do surely hide the truth, the while they know.

The truth (is) from thy Lord; be not therefore one of those who doubt thereof.

Every sect has some one side to which they turn (in prayer); but do ye hasten onwards to good works; wherever ye are Allah will bring you all together;[39] verily, Allah is mighty over all.

From whencesoever thou comest forth, there turn thy face towards the Sacred Mosque, for it is surely truth from thy Lord; Allah is not careless about what ye do. [145] And from whencesoever thou comest forth, there turn thy face towards the Sacred Mosque, and where-soever ye are, turn your faces towards it, that men may have no argument against you, save only those of them who are unjust; and fear them not, but fear me and I will fulfil my favours to you, perchance ye may be guided yet.

Thus have we sent amongst you an apostle of yourselves, to recite to you our signs, to purify you and teach you the Book and wisdom, and to teach you what ye did not know; remember me, then, and I will remember you; thank me, and do not misbelieve.[40]

O ye who do believe! seek aid from patience and from prayer, verily, Allah is with the patient. And say not of those who are slain in Allah's way[41] (that they are) dead, but rather living; but ye do not perceive.

[150] We will try you with something of fear, and hunger and loss of wealth, and souls and fruit; but give good tidings to the patient, who when there falls on them a calamity say, 'Verily, we are Allah's and, verily, to Him do we return.'[42] These, on them are blessings from their Lord and mercy, and they it is who are guided.

Verily, Zafâ and Merwah[43] are of the beacons of Allah, and he who makes the pilgrimage unto the House, or visits it, it is no more crime for him to compass them both about; and he who obeys his own impulse to a good work,— Allah is grateful and doth know.

Verily, those who hide what we have revealed of manifest signs and of guidance after we have manifested it to men in the Book, them Allah shall curse, and those who curse shall curse them too. [155] Save those who turn and do right and make (the signs) manifest; these will I turn to again, for I am easy to be turned and merciful.

Verily, those who misbelieve and die while still in misbelief, of them is the curse of Allah, and of the angels, and of mankind altogether; to dwell therein for aye; the torment shall not be lightened for them, nor shall they be looked upon.[44]

Your Allah is one Allah; there is no Allah but He, the merciful, the compassionate.

Verily, in the creation of the heavens and the earth, and the alternation of night and day, and in the ship that runneth in the sea with that which profits man, and in what water Allah sends down from heaven and quickens therewith the earth after its death, and spreads abroad therein all kinds of cattle, and in the shifting of the winds, and in the clouds that are pressed into service betwixt heaven and earth, are signs to people who can understand.

[160] Yet are there some amongst mankind who take to themselves peers[45] other than Allah; they love them as they should love Allah; while those who believe love Allah more. O that those who are unjust could only see, when they see the torment, that power is altogether Allah's! Verily, Allah is keen to torment.

When those who are followed[46] clear themselves of those who followed them, and see the torment, and the cords[47] are cut asunder, those who followed shall say, 'Had we but another turn,[48] then would we clear ourselves of them as they have cleared themselves of us.' So will Allah show them their works; for them are sighs, and they shall not come forth from out the Fire.

O ye folk! eat of what is in the earth, things lawful and things good, and follow not the footsteps of Satan, verily, to you he is an open foe. He does but bid you evil and sin, and that ye should speak against Allah what ye do not know.

[165] When it is said to them, 'Follow what Allah has revealed,' they say, 'Nay, we will follow what we found our fathers agreed upon.' What! and though their fathers had no sense at all or guidance—?

The likeness of those who misbelieve is as the likeness of him who shouts to that which hears him not, save only a call and a cry;[49] deafness, dumbness, blindness, and they shall not understand.

O ye who do believe! eat of the good things wherewith we have provided you, and give thanks unto Allah if it be Him ye serve. He has only forbidden for you what is dead, and blood, and flesh of swine, and whatsoever has been consecrated to other than Allah;[50] but he who is forced, neither revolting nor transgressing, it is in no sin for him; verily, Allah is forgiving and merciful.

Verily, those who hide what Allah has revealed of the Book, and sell it for a little price, they shall eat nothing in their bellies save fire; and Allah will not speak to them on the day of resurrection, nor will He purify them, but for them is grievous woe.

[170] They who sell guidance for error, and pardon for torment, how patient must they be of fire!

That (is), because Allah has revealed the Book with truth, and verily those who disagree about the Book are in a wide schism.

Righteousness is not that ye turn your faces towards the east or the west, but righteousness is, one who believes in Allah, and the last day, and the angels, and the Book, and the prophets, and who gives wealth for His love to kindred, and orphans, and the poor, and the son of the road,⁵¹ and beggars, and those in captivity; and who is steadfast in prayer, and gives alms; and those who are sure of their covenant when they make a covenant; and the patient in poverty, and distress, and in time of violence; these are they who are true, and these are those who fear.

O ye who believe! Retaliation is prescribed for you for the slain: the free for the free, the slave for the slave, the female for the female; yet he who is pardoned at all by his brother, must be prosecuted in reason, and made to pay with kindness.⁵²

That is an alleviation from your Lord, and a mercy; and he who transgresses after that for him is grievous woe.

[175] For you in retaliation is there life, O ye possessors of minds! It may be ye will fear.

It is prescribed for you that when one of you is face to face with death, if he leave (any) goods, the legacy is to his parents, and to his kinsmen, in reason. A duty this upon all those that fear.

But he who alters it⁵³ after that he has heard it,—the sin thereof is only upon those who alter it; verily, Allah doth hear and know.

And he who fears from the testator a wrong intention, or a crime, and doth make up the matter between the parties, it is no sin to him; verily, Allah is forgiving and merciful.

O ye who believe! There is prescribed for you the fast as it was prescribed for those before you; haply ye may fear. [180] A certain number of days, but he amongst you who is ill or on a journey, then (let him fast) another number of days. And those who are fit to fast⁵⁴ may redeem it by feeding a poor man; but he who follows an impulse to a good work it is better for him; and if ye fast it is better for you, if ye did but know.

The month of Ramadân, wherein was revealed the Qur'ân, for a guidance to men, and for manifestations of guidance, and for a Discrimination. And he amongst you who beholds this month[55] then let him fast it; but he who is sick or on a journey, then another number of days;—Allah desires for you what is easy, and desires not for you what is difficult,—that ye may complete the number, and say, 'Great is Allah,' for that He has guided you; haply ye may give thanks.

When my servants ask thee concerning me, then, verily, I am near; I answer the prayer's prayer whene'er he prays to me. So let them ask me for an answer, and let them believe in me; haply they may be directed aright.

Lawful for you on the night of the fast is commerce with your wives; they are a garment unto you, and ye a garment unto them. Allah knows that ye did defraud yourselves, wherefore He has turned towards you and forgiven you; so now go in unto them and crave what Allah has prescribed for you, and eat and drink until a white thread can be distinguished by you from a black one at the dawn. Then fulfil the fast until the night, and go not in unto them, and yet at your devotions in the mosques the while. These are the bounds that Allah has set, so draw not near thereto. Thus does Allah make manifest His signs to men, that haply they may fear.

Devour not your wealth among yourselves vainly, nor present it to the judges that ye may devour a part of the wealth of men sinfully, the while ye know.

[185] They will ask thee about the phases of the moon; say, 'They are indications of time for men and for the pilgrimage.' And it is not righteousness that ye should enter into your houses from behind them,[56] but righteousness is he who fears; so enter into your houses by the doors thereof and fear Allah; haply ye may prosper yet.

Fight in Allah's way[57] with those who fight with you, but transgress[58] not; verily, Allah loves not those who do transgress.

Kill them wherever ye find them, and drive them out from whence they drive you out; for sedition is worse than slaughter; but fight them not by the Sacred Mosque until they fight you there; then kill them, for such is the recompense of those that misbelieve.

But if they desist, then, verily, Allah is forgiving and merciful.

But fight them that there be no sedition and that the religion may be Allah's; but, if they desist, then let there be no hostility save against the unjust.

[190] The sacred month for the sacred month;[59] for all sacred things demand retaliation;[60] and whoso transgress against you, transgress against him like as he transgressed against you; but fear ye Allah, and know that Allah is with those who fear.

Expend in alms in Allah's way and be not cast by your own hands into perdition; but do good, for Allah loves those who do good.

And fulfil the pilgrimage and the visitation to Allah; but if ye be beseiged, then what is easiest for you by way of gift. But shave not your heads until your gift shall reach its destination; and he amongst you who is sick or has a hurt upon his head, then the redemption is by fasting or by alms or by an offering. But when ye are safe again, then let him who would enjoy the visitation until the pilgrimage[61] (bring) what is easiest as a gift. And he who cannot find (anything to bring), then let him fast three days on the pilgrimage and seven when ye return; these make ten days complete. That is, for him whose family are not present in the Sacred Mosque; and fear Allah and know that Allah is keen to punish.

The pilgrimage is (in) well-known months; whosoever then makes it incumbent on himself (let him have neither) commerce with women, nor fornication, nor a quarrel on the pilgrimage; and whatsoever of good ye do, Allah knoweth it; then provide yourself for your journey; but the best provision is piety. Fear ye me ye who possess minds.

It is no crime to you that ye seek good[62] from your Lord; but when ye pour forth from Arafât, remember Allah by the sacred beacon. Remember Him how He guided you, although ye were surely before of those who err.

[195] Then pour ye forth from whence men do pour forth and ask pardon of Allah; verily, Allah is forgiving and merciful.

And when ye have performed your rites, remember Allah as ye remember your fathers, or with a keener memory still.

There is among men such as says, 'Our Lord! give us in this world'; but of the future life no portion shall he have.

And some there be who say, 'Our Lord! give us in this world good and in the future good; and keep us from the torment of the Fire!'

These,—they have their portion from what they have earned; for Allah is swift at reckoning up.

Remember Allah for a certain number of days; but whoso hastens off in two days, it is no sin to him, and he who lingers on it is no sin to him,—for him who fears. So fear ye Allah and know that unto Him shall ye be gathered.

[200] There is among men one[63] whose speech about the life of this world pleases thee, and he calls on Allah to witness what is in his heart; yet is he most fierce in opposition unto thee. And when he turns away, he strives upon the earth to do evil therein, and to destroy the tilth and the stock; verily; Allah loves not evil-doing. And when it is said to him, 'Fear Allah,' then pride takes hold upon him in sin; but Hell is enough for him! surely an evil couch is that.

And there is among men one who selleth his soul,[64] craving those things that are pleasing unto Allah; and Allah is kind unto His servants.

O ye who believe! enter ye into the peace,[65] one and all, and follow not the footsteps of Satan; verily, to you he is an open foe. [205] And if ye slip after that the manifest signs have come to you, then know that Allah is the mighty, the wise.

What can they expect but that Allah should come unto them in the shadow of a cloud, and the angels too? But the thing is decreed, and unto Allah do things return.

Ask the children of Israel how many a manifest sign we gave to them; and whoso alters Allah's favours after that they have come to him, then Allah is keen at following up.

Made fair to those who misbelieve is this world's life; they jest at those who do believe. But those who fear shall be above them on the resurrection day. Allah gives provision unto whom He will without account.

Men were one nation once, and Allah sent prophets with good tidings and with warnings, and sent down with them the Book in truth, to judge between men in that wherein they disagreed; but none did disagree therein save those who had been given it after that manifest signs had come to them, through greed amongst themselves; and Allah guided those who did believe to that truth concerning which they disagreed by His permission, for Allah guides whom He will unto the right path.

[210] Did ye count to enter Paradise, while there had nothing come to you like those who passed away before you; there touched them violence and harm, they were made to quake, until the Apostle and those who believed with him said, 'When (comes) Allah's help? Is not Allah's help then surely nigh?'

They will ask thee what they are to expend in alms: say, 'Whatsoever good ye expend it should be for parents and kinsmen, and the orphan and the poor, and the son of the road; and whatsoever good ye do, verily, of it Allah knows.'

Prescribed for you is fighting, but it is hateful to you. Yet peradventure that ye hate a thing while it is good for you, and peradventure that ye love a thing while it is bad for you; Allah knows, and ye,—ye do not know!

They will ask thee of the sacred month,—of fighting therein. Say, 'Fighting therein is a great sin; but turning folks off Allah's way, and misbelief in Him and in the Sacred Mosque, and turning His people out therefrom, is a greater in Allah's sight; and sedition is a greater sin than slaughter.'

They will not cease from fighting you until they turn you from your religion if they can; but whosoever of you is turned from his religion and dies while still a misbeliever; these are those whose works are vain in this world and the next; they are the fellows of the Fire, and they shall dwell therein for aye.

[215] Verily, those who believe, and those who flee,[66] and those who wage war[67] in Allah's way; these may hope for Allah's mercy, for Allah is forgiving and merciful.

They will ask thee about wine[68] and *el mâisar*,[69] say, 'In them both is sin and profit to men; but the sin of both is greater than the profit of the same.'

They will ask thee what they shall expend in alms: say, 'The surplus.' Thus goes Allah manifest to you His signs; haply ye may reflect on this world and the next! They will ask thee about orphans: say, 'To do good to them is best.' But if ye interfere with them—they are your brethren, and Allah knows the evil-doer from the well doer; and if Allah will He will surely trouble you.[70] Verily, Allah is mighty, wise.

[220] Wed not with idolatrous women until they believe, for surely a believing handmaid is better than an idolatrous women, even though she please you. And wed

not to idolatrous men until they believe, for a believing slave is better than an idolater, even though he please you.

Those invite you to the Fire, but Allah invites you to Paradise and pardon by His permission, and makes clear His signs to men; haply they may remember.

They will ask thee about menstruation: say, 'It is a hurt.' So keep apart from women in their menstruation, and go not near them till they be cleansed; but when they are cleansed come in to them by where Allah has ordered you; verily, Allah loves those who turn to Him, and those who keep themselves clean.

Your women are your tilth, so come into your tillage how you choose; but do a previous good act for yourselves,[71] and fear Allah, and know that ye are going to meet Him; and give good tidings unto those who do believe.

Make not Allah the butt of your oaths, that ye will keep clear and fear and make peace amongst men, for Allah both hears and knows.

[225] He will not catch you up for a casual word in your oaths, but He will catch you up for what your hearts have earned; but Allah is forgiving and clement.

Those who swear off from their women, they must wait four months; but if they break their vow Allah is forgiving and merciful.

And if they intend to divorce them, verily, Allah hears and knows.

Divorced women must wait for themselves three courses; and it is not lawful to them that they hide what Allah has created in their wombs, if they believe in Allah and in the last day. Their husbands will do better to take them back in that (case) if they wish for reconciliation; for, the same is due to them as from them; but the men should have precedence over them. Allah is mighty and wise.

Divorce (may happen) twice; then keep them in reason, or let them go with kindness. It is not lawful for you to take from them anything of what you have given them, unless both fear that they cannot keep within Allah's bounds. So if ye fear that ye cannot keep within Allah's bounds there is no crime in you both about what she ransoms herself with.[72] These are Allah's bounds, do not transgress them; and whoso transgresses Allah's bounds, they it is who are unjust.

[230] But if he divorce her (a third time) she shall not be lawful to him after that, until she marry another husband; but, if he divorce her too, it is no crime in them both to come together again, if they think that they can keep within Allah's bounds. These are Allah's bounds which He explains to a people who know.

When ye divorce women, and they have reached the prescribed time, then keep them kindly, or let them go in reason, but do not keep them by force to transgress; for whoso does that, he is unjust to his own soul: and do not take Allah's signs in jest; and remember Allah's favours to you, and what He has sent down to you of the Book and wisdom, to admonish you thereby; and fear Allah, and know that Allah doth all things know.

When ye divorce women, and they have reached their prescribed term, do not prevent them from marrying their (fresh) husbands, when they have agreed with each other reasonably. That is what he is admonished with who amongst you believes in Allah and in the last day. That is more pure for you and cleaner. But Allah knows, and ye know not.

Mothers must suckle their children two whole years for one who wishes to complete the time of suckling; and on him to whom it is born its sustenance and clothing are incumbent; but in reason, for no soul shall be obliged beyond its capacity. A mother shall not be forced for her child; nor he to whom it is born for his child. And the same (is incumbent) on the heir (of the father). But if both parties wish to wean, by mutual consent and counsel, then it is no crime in them. And if ye wish to provide a wet nurse for your children, it is no crime in you when you pay what you have promised her, in reason. Fear Allah, and know that Allah on what ye do doth look.

Those of you who die and leave wives behind, let these wait by themselves for four months and ten days; and when they have reached their prescribed time, there is no crime in them for what they do with themselves in reason; for Allah of what ye do is well aware.

[235] Nor is there any crime in you for that ye make them an offer of marriage, or that ye keep it secret, in your minds. Allah knows that ye will remember them; but do not propose to them in secret, unless ye speak a reasonable[73] speech; and resolve not on the marriage tie until the Book shall reach its time;[74] but know that Allah knows what is in your souls; so beware! and know that Allah is forgiving and clement.

It is no crime in you if you divorce your women ere you

have yet touched them, or settled for them a settlement. But provide maintenance for them; the wealthy according to his power, and the straitened in circumstances according to his power, must provide, in reason;—a duty this upon the kind.

And if ye divorce them before ye have touched them, but have already settled for them a settlement; the half of what ye have settled, unless they remit it, or he in whose hand is the marriage tie remits it;[75] and that ye should remit is nearer to piety, and forget not liberality between you. Verily, Allah on what ye do doth look.

Observe the prayers, and the middle prayer,[76] and stand ye attendant before Allah.

[240] And if ye fear, then afoot[77] or on horseback; but when ye are in safety remember Allah, how He taught you while yet ye did not know.

Those of you who die and leave wives, should bequeath to their wives maintenance for a year, without expulsion (from their home); but if they go out, there is no crime in you for what they do of themselves, in reason; but Allah is mighty and wise.

And divorced women should have a maintenance in reason,—a duty this on those that fear. Thus does Allah explain to you His signs; haply ye may understand.

Dost thou not look at those who left their homes by thousands, for fear of death; and Allah said to them 'Die', and then He quickened them again?[78] Verily, Allah is Lord of grace to men, but most men give no thanks.

[245] Fight then in Allah's way, and know that Allah both hears and knows.

Who is there that will lend to Allah a good loan? He will redouble it many a double; Allah closes His hand and holds it out, and unto Him shall ye return.

Dost thou not look at the crowd of the children of Israel after Moses' time, when they said to a prophet of theirs,[79] 'Raise up for us a king, and we will fight in Allah's way?' He said, 'Will ye perhaps, if it be written down for you to fight, refuse to fight?' They said, 'And why should we not fight in Allah's way, now that we are dispossessed of our homes and sons?' But when it was written down for them to fight they turned back, save a few of them, and Allah knows who are evil-doers. Then their prophet said to them, 'Verily, Allah has raised you for you Tâlût[80] as a king'; they said, 'How can the kingdom be his over us; we have more right to the kingdom than he, for he has not an amplitude of wealth?' He said, 'Verily, Allah has chosen him over you, and has provided him with an extent of knowledge and of form. Allah gives the kingdom unto whom He will; Allah comprehends and knows.'

Then said to them their prophet, 'The sign of his kingdom is that there shall come to you the ark with the *shechina*[81] in it from your Lord, and the relics of what the family of Moses and the family of Aaron left; the angels shall bear it.' In that is surely a sign to you if ye believe.[82]

[250] And when Tâlût set out with his soldiery, he said, 'Allah will try you with a river, and he who drinks therefrom, he is not of mine; but whoso tastes it not, he is of mine, save he who laps it lapping with his hand.'[83]

And they drank from it save a few of them, and when he crossed it, he and those who believed with him, they said, 'We have no power this day against Jâlût[84] and his soldiery,' those who thought that they should meet their Lord said, 'How many a small division of men have conquered a numerous division, by the permission of Allah, for Allah is with the patient.'

And when they went out against Jâlût and his soldiery, they said, 'Lord, pour out patience over us, and make firm our steps, and help us against the misbelieving people!'

And they put them to flight by the permission of Allah, and David killed Jâlût, and Allah gave him the kingdom and wisdom, and taught him of what He willed. And were it not for Allah's repelling men one with another the earth would become spoiled; but Allah is Lord of grace over the worlds.

These are the signs of Allah, we recite them to thee in truth, for, verily, thou art of those who are sent.

These apostles have we preferred one of them above another. Of them is one to whom Allah spake;[85] and we have raised some of them degrees; and we have given Jesus the son of Mary manifest signs, and strengthened him by the Holy Spirit. And, did Allah please, those who came after them would not have fought after there came to them manifest signs. But they did disagree, and of them are some who believe, and of them some who misbelieve, but, did Allah please, they would not have fought, for Allah does what He will.

[255] O ye who believe! expend in alms of what we have bestowed upon you, before the day comes in which is no barter, and no friendship, and no intercession; and the misbelievers, they are the unjust.

Allah,[86] there is no god but He, the living, the self-subsistent. Slumber takes Him not, nor sleep. His is what is in the heavens and what is in the earth. Who is it that intercedes with Him save by His permission? He knows what is before them and what behind them, and they comprehend not aught of His knowledge but of what He pleases. His throne extends over the heavens and the earth, and it tires Him not to guard them both, for He is high and grand.

There is no compulsion in religion; the right way has been distinguished from the wrong, and whoso disbelieves in Tâghût[87] and believes in Allah, he has got hold of the firm handle in which is no breaking off; but Allah both hears and knows.

Allah is the patron of those who believe, He brings them forth from darkness into light. But those who misbelieve, their patrons are Tâghût, these bring them forth from light to darkness,—fellows of the Fire, they dwell therein for aye.

[260] Do you not look at him who disputed with Abraham about his Lord, that Allah had given him the kingdom?[88] When Abraham said, 'My Lord is He who giveth life and death,' he said, 'I give life and death.' Abraham said, 'But verily, Allah brings the sun from the east, do thou then bring it from the west?' And he who misbelieved was dumbfounded, for Allah does not guide unjust folk.

Or like him who passed by a village,[89] when it was desolate and turned over on its roofs, and said, 'How will Allah revive this after its death?' And Allah made him die for a hundred years, then He raised him, and said, 'How long hast thou tarried?' Said he, 'I have tarried a day, or some part of a day.' He said, 'Nay, thou hast tarried a hundred years; look at thy food and drink, they are not spoiled, and look at thine ass; for we will make thee a sign to men. And look at the bones how we scatter them and then clothe them with flesh.' And when it was made manifest to him, he said, 'I know that Allah is mighty over all.'

And when Abraham said, 'Lord, show me how thou wilt revive the dead,' He said, 'What, dost thou not yet believe?' Said he, 'Yea, but that my heart may be quieted.' He said, 'Then take four birds, and take them close to thyself; then put a part of them on every mountain; then call them, and they will come to thee in haste; and know that Allah is mighty, wise.'[90]

The likeness of those who expend their wealth in Allah's way is as the likeness of a grain that grows to seven ears, in every ear a hundred grains, for Allah will double unto whom He pleases; for Allah both embraces and knows.

Those who expend their wealth in Allah's way, then do not follow up what they expend by taunting with it and by annoyance, these have their hire with their Lord, and no fear is on them, neither shall they grieve.

[265] Kind speech and pardon are better than almsgiving followed by annoyance, and Allah is rich and clement.

O ye who believe! make not your alms giving vain by taunts and annoyance, like him who expends what he has for the sake of appearances before men, and believes not in Allah and the last day; for his likeness is as the likeness of a flint with soil upon it, and a heavy shower falls on it and leaves it bare rock; they can do nought with what they earn, for Allah guides not the misbelieving folk.

But the likeness of those who expend their wealth craving the goodwill of Allah, and as an insurance for their souls, is as the likeness of a garden on a hill. A heavy shower falls on it, and it brings forth its eatables twofold; and if no heavy shower falls on it, the dew does; and Allah on what ye do doth look.

Would one of you fain have a garden of palms and vines, with rivers flowing beneath it, in which is every fruit; and when old age shall reach him, have weak seed, and there fall on it a storm wind with fire therein, and it gets burnt?

Thus does Allah manifest to you His signs, mayhap ye will reflect.

O ye who believe! expend in alms of the good things that ye have earned, and of what we have brought forth for you out of the earth, and do not take the vile thereof to spend in alms,—[270] what you would not take yourselves save by connivance at it;[91] but know that Allah is rich and to be praised.

The devil promises you poverty and bids you sin, but Allah promises you pardon from Him and grace, for Allah both embraces and knows. He bringeth wisdom unto whom He will, and he who is brought wisdom is brought much good; but none will remember save those endowed with minds.

Whatever expense ye expend, or vow ye vow, Allah knows it; but the unjust have no helpers. If ye display your alms giving, then well is it; but if ye hide it and bring it to the poor, then is it better for you, and will expiate for you your evil deeds; for Allah of what ye do is well aware.

Thou[92] art not bound to guide them; but Allah guides whom He will; and whatever good ye expend it is for yourselves, and do not expend save craving for Allah's face.

And what ye expend of good, it shall be repaid you, and ye shall not be wronged,—unto the poor who are straitened in Allah's way, and cannot knock about[93] in the earth. The ignorant think them to be rich because of their modesty; you will know them by their mark, they do not beg from men importunately; but what ye spend of good Allah knows.

[275] Those who expend their wealth by night and day, secretly and openly, they shall have their hire with their Lord. No fear shall come on them, nor shall they grieve.

Those who devour usury shall not rise again, save as he riseth whom Satan hath paralyzed with a touch; and that is because they say 'selling is only like usury', but Allah has made selling lawful and usury unlawful; and he to whom the admonition from his Lord has come, if he desists, what has gone before is his:[94] his matter is in Allah's hand. But whosoever returns (to usury) these are the fellows of the Fire, and they shall dwell therein for aye. Allah shall blot out usury, but shall make alms giving profitable, for Allah loves not any sinful misbeliever.

Verily, those who believe, and act righteously, and are steadfast in prayer, and give alms, theirs is their hire with their Lord; there is no fear on them, nor shall they grieve.

O ye who believe! fear Allah, and remit the balance of usury, if ye be believers; and if ye will not do it, then harken to the proclamation of war from Allah and His Apostle; but if ye repent, your capital is yours. Ye shall not wrong, nor shall ye be wronged.

[280] And if it be one in difficulties, then wait for easy circumstances; but that ye remit it as alms is better for you, if ye did but know.

Fear the day wherein ye shall return to Allah; then shall each soul be paid what it has earned, and they shall not be wronged.

O ye who believe! if ye engage to one another in a debt for a stated time, then write it down, and let a scribe write it down between you faithfully; nor let a scribe refuse to write as Allah taught him, but let him write, and let him who owes dictate; but let him fear Allah his Lord, and not distinguish therefrom aught; but if he who owes be a fool, or weak, or cannot dictate himself, then let his agent dictate faithfully, and let them call two witnesses out from amongst their men; or if there be not two men, then a man and two women, from those whom he chooses for witnesses, so that if one of the two should err, the second of the two may remind the other; and let not the witnesses refuse when they are summoned; and let them not tire of writing it, be it small or great, with its time of payment. That is more just in the sight of Allah, and more upright for testimony, and brings you nearer to not doubting.

Unless, indeed, it be a ready-money transaction between you, which ye arrange between yourselves, then it is no crime against you that ye do not write it down; but bring witnesses to what ye sell one to another, and let not either scribe or witness come to harm, for if ye do it will be abomination in you; but fear Allah, for Allah teaches you, and Allah knows all things. But if ye be upon a journey, and ye cannot find a scribe, then let a pledge be taken. But if one of you trust another, then let him who is trusted surrender his trust, and let him fear Allah his Lord, and conceal not testimony, for he who conceals it, verily, sinful is his heart: Allah knows what ye do.

Allah's is what is in heaven and in the earth, and if ye show what is in your souls, or hide it, Allah will call you to account; and He forgives whom He will, and punishes whom He will, for Allah is mighty over all.

[285] The Apostle believes in what is sent down to him from his Lord, and the believers all believe on Allah, and His angels, and His Books, and His apostles,—we make no difference between any of His apostles,—they say, 'We hear and obey, Thy pardon, O Lord! for to Thee our journey tends. Allah will not require of the soul save its capacity. It shall have what it has earned, and it shall owe what has been earned from it. Lord, catch us not up, if we forget or make mistake; Lord, load us not with a burden, as Thou hast loaded those who were before us. Lord, make us not to carry what we have not strength for, but forgive us, and pardon us, and have mercy on us. Thou art our Sovereign, then help us against the people who do not believe!'

THE CHAPTER OF IMRÂN'S FAMILY

III (*Medina*)

In the name of the merciful and compassionate Allah.

A. L. M. Allah, there is no god but He, the living, the self-subsistent. He has sent down to thee the Book in truth, confirming what was before it, and has revealed the law, and the gospel before for the guidance of men, and has revealed the Discrimination.

Verily, those who disbelieve in the signs of Allah, for them is severe torment, for Allah is mighty and avenging.

Verily, Allah, there is nothing hidden from Him in the earth, nor in the heaven; He it is who fashions you in the womb as He pleases. There is no Allah but He, the mighty, the wise.

[5] He it is who has revealed to thee the Book, of which there are some verses that are decisive, they are the mother¹ of the Book; and others ambiguous; but as for those in whose hearts is perversity, they follow what is ambiguous, and do crave for sedition, craving for (their own) inter-pretation of it; but none know the interpretation of it except Allah. But those who are well grounded in knowledge say, 'We believe in it; it is all from our Lord; but none will remember save those who possess minds.

'O Lord! pervert not our hearts again when Thou hast guided them, and grant us mercy from Thee, for Thou art He who grants. O Lord! Thou shalt gather together men unto the day wherein is no doubt. Verily, Allah will not depart from His promise.'

Verily, those who misbelieve, their wealth shall not help them, nor their children, against Allah at all; and they it is who are the fuel of the Fire.

As was the wont of Pharaoh's people, and those before them, they said our signs were lies, and Allah caught them up in their sins, for Allah is severe to punish.

[10] Say to those who misbelieve, 'Ye shall be overcome and driven together to Hell, an ill couch will it be.

'Ye have had a sign in the two parties who met; one party fighting in the way of Allah, the other misbelieving; these saw twice the same number as themselves to the eyesight,² for Allah aids with His help those whom He pleases.' Verily, in that is a lesson for those who have perception. Seemly unto men is a life of lusts, of women, and children, and hoarded talents of gold and silver, and of horses well bred, and cattle, and tilth;—that is the provision for the life of this world; but Allah, with Him is the best resort.

Say, 'But shall we tell you of a better thing than this?' For those who fear are gardens with their Lord, beneath which rivers flow; they shall dwell therein for aye, and pure wives and grace from Allah; the Lord looks on His servants, who say, 'Lord, we believe, pardon Thou our sins and keep us from the torment of the Fire,' [15]—upon the patient, the truthful, the devout, and those who ask for pardon at the dawn.

Allah bears witness that there is no god but He, and the angels, and those possessed of knowledge standing up for justice. There is no Allah but He, the mighty, the wise.

Verily, (the true) religion in Allah's sight is Islam, and those to whom the Book was given disagreed not until after that there was given to them knowledge, through mutual envy. But whoso disbelieves in Allah's signs, truly Allah is quick at reckoning up.

And if they would dispute with thee, then say, 'I turn my face with resignation unto Allah, and whoso follows me.'

And say to those who have been given the Book, unto the Gentiles,³ 'Are ye, too, resigned?'⁴ and if they are resigned, then are they guided. But if they turn their backs, then thou hast only to preach, and Allah looks on his servants.

[20] Verily, those who disbelieve in Allah's signs, and kill the prophets without right, and kill those from among men, who bid what is just,—to them give the glad tidings of grievous woe! These are they whose works are void in this world and the next, and helpers have they none.

Did ye not see those who have been given a portion of the Book? They were called unto the Book of Allah to decide between them; and then a sect of them turned their backs and turned away;—that is because they say the Fire shall not touch us save for a certain number of days. But that deceived them in their religion which they had invented. How will it be when we have gathered them together for a day whereof there is no doubt, when each soul shall be paid what it has earned, and they shall not be wronged?

[25] Say, 'O Allah, Lord of the kingdom! Thou givest the kingdom to whomsoever Thou pleasest, and strippest the

kingdom from whomsoever Thou pleasest; Thou honourest whom Thou pleasest, and abasest whom Thou pleasest; in Thy hand is good. Verily, Thou art mighty over all. Thou dost turn night to day, and dost turn day to night, and dost bring forth the living from the dead, and dost provide for whom Thou pleasest without taking count.'

Those who believe shall not take misbelievers for their patrons, rather than believers, and he who does this has no part with Allah at all, unless, indeed, ye fear some danger from them. But Allah bids you beware of Himself, for unto Him your journey is.

Say, 'If ye hide that which is in your breasts, or if ye show it, Allah knows it: He knows what is in the heavens and what is in the earth, for Allah is mighty over all.'

The day that every soul shall find what it has done of good present before it; and what it has done of evil, it would fain that there were between itself and that a wide interval. 'Allah bids you beware of Himself, but Allah is gentle with His servants.'

Say, 'If ye would love Allah then follow me, and Allah will love you and forgive you your sins, for Allah is forgiving and merciful.'

Say, 'Obey Allah and the Apostle; but if ye turn your backs Allah loves not misbelievers.'

[30] Verily, Allah has chosen Adam, and Noah, and Abraham's people, and Imrân's[5] people above the world,— a seed, of which one succeeds the other, but Allah both hears and knows.

When Imrân's wife said, 'Lord! I have vowed to Thee

what is within my womb, to be dedicated unto Thee, receive it then from me. Verily, Thou dost hear and know.' And when she brought it forth she said, 'Verily, I have brought it forth a female'—but Allah knew best what she brought forth; and a male is not like a female—'I have called her Mary, and I seek a refuge in Thee for her and for her seed from Satan the pelted.'[6]

And her Lord received her with a good reception, and made her grow up with a good growth, and Zachariah took care of her. Whenever Zachariah entered the chamber to her he found beside her a provision, and said, 'O Mary, how hast thou this?' She said, 'It is from Allah, for Allah provides for whom He pleases without count.' Therefore prayed Zachariah to his Lord, and said, 'Lord, grant me from Thee a good seed. Verily, Thou hearest prayer.' And an angel cried out to him as he was standing praying in the chamber (and said) that 'Allah gives thee the glad tidings of John, to confirm the Word from Allah,—of a chief and a chaste one, and a prophet from amongst the righteous.'

[35] He said, 'My Lord, how can there be to me a boy when old age has reached me, and my wife is barren?' Said he, 'Thus Allah does what He pleaseth.' He said, 'My Lord, make for me a sign.' He said, 'Thy sign is that thou shalt not speak to men for three days, save by gesture; but remember thy Lord much, and celebrate His praises in the evening and the morning.'

And when the angels said, 'O Mary! verily, Allah has chosen thee, and has purified thee, and has chosen thee above the women of the world. O Mary! be devout unto thy Lord, and adore and bow down with those who bow. That is (one) of the declarations of the unseen world which we reveal to thee, though thou wert not by them when they threw their lots⁷ which of them should take care of Mary, nor were ye by them when they did dispute.'

[40] When the angel said, 'O Mary! verily, Allah gives thee the glad tidings of a Word from Him; his name shall be the Messiah Jesus the son of Mary, regarded in this world and the next and of those whose place is nigh to Allah. And he shall speak to people in his cradle, and when grown up, and shall be among the righteous.' She said, 'Lord! how can I have a son, when man has not yet touched me?' He said, 'Thus Allah creates what He pleaseth. When He decrees a matter He only says, 'BE', and it is; and He will teach him the Book, and wisdom, and the law, and the gospel, and he shall be a prophet to the people of Israel (saying), that I have come to you, with a sign from Allah, namely, that I will create for you out of clay as though it were the form of a bird, and I will blow thereon and it shall become a bird by Allah's permission; and I will heal the blind from birth, and lepers; and I will bring the dead to life by Allah's permission; and I will tell you what you eat and what ye store up in your houses. Verily, in that is a sign for you if ye be believers. And I will confirm what is before you of the law, and will surely make lawful for you some of that which was prohibited from you. I have come to you with a sign from your Lord, so fear Allah and follow me, for Allah is my Lord, and your Lord, so worship Him:—this is the right path.'

[45] And when Jesus perceived their unbelief, He said,

'Who are my helpers for Allah?' Said the apostles,[8] 'We are Allah's helpers. We believe in Allah, so bear witness that we are resigned.[9] Lord, we have believed in what Thou hast revealed, and we have followed the Apostle, so write us down with those which bear witness.' But they (the Jews) were crafty, and Allah was crafty, for Allah is the best of crafty ones!

When Allah said, 'O Jesus! I will make Thee die and take Thee up again to me[10] and will clear thee of those who misbelieve, and will make those who follow thee above those who misbelieve, at the day of judgement, then to me is your return. I will decide between you concerning that wherein ye disagree. And as for those who misbelieve, I will punish them with grievous punishment in this world and the next, and they shall have none to help them.' [50] But as for those who believe and do what is right, He will pay them their reward, for Allah loves not the unjust.

That is what we recite to thee of the signs and of the wise reminder.[11] Verily, the likeness of Jesus with Allah is as the likeness of Adam. He created him from earth, then He said to him, 'BE', and he was;—the truth from thy Lord, so be thou not of those who are in doubt. And whoso disputeth with thee after what has come to thee of knowledge, say, 'Come, let us call our sons and your sons, and our women and your women, and ourselves and yourselves: then we will imprecate and put Allah's curse on those who lie.'

[55] Verily, those are the true stories, and there is no god but Allah, and, verily, Allah He is the mighty, the wise; but if they turn back, Allah knows the evil-doers.

Say, 'O ye people of the Book, come to a word laid down plainly between us and you, that we will not serve other than Allah, nor associate aught with him, nor take each other for lords rather than Allah.' But if they turn back then say, 'Bear witness that we are resigned.'

O people of the Book, why do ye dispute about Abraham, when the law and the gospel were not revealed until after him? What! do ye not understand? Here ye are, disputing about what ye have some knowledge of; why then do ye dispute about what ye have no knowledge of? Allah knows and ye know not.

[60] Abraham was not a Jew, nor yet a Christian, but he was a *hanîf*¹² resigned, and not of the idolaters. Verily, the people most worthy of Abraham are those who follow him and his prophets, and those who believe;—Allah is the patron of the believers.

A sect of the people of the Book would fain they could lead you astray, but they only lead themselves astray, and they do not perceive.

O people of the Book! why do ye disbelieve in the signs of Allah, the while ye witness them? O people of the Book! why do ye clothe the truth with falsehood and hide the truth the while ye know? [65] A sect of the people of the Book say, 'Believe in what was revealed to those who believed at the first appearance of the day, and disbelieve it at the end thereof,'—that (others) may perchance go back (from their faith)¹³—'do not believe save one who followeth your religion.'

Say, 'Verily, the (true) guidance is the guidance of Allah, that one should be given like what ye are given.' Or would they dispute with you before your Lord, say, 'Grace is in the hand of Allah, He gives it to whom he pleases, for Allah both comprehends and knows. He specially favours with his mercy whom he pleases, for Allah is Lord of mighty grace.'

And of the people of the Book, there are some of them who, if thou entrust them with a talent give it back to you; and some of them, if thou entrust them with a dinar,[14] he will not give it back to thee except so long as thou dost stand over him. That is because they say, 'We owe no duty to the Gentiles'; but they tell a lie against Allah, the while they know.

[70] Yea, whoso fulfils his convenant and fears,—verily, Allah loves those who fear. Those who sell Allah's covenant and their oaths for a little price, these have no portion in the future life. Allah will not speak to them, and will not look upon them on the resurrection day, and will not purify them; but for them is grievous woe.

And, verily, amongst them is a sect who twist their tongues[15] concerning the Book, that ye may reckon it to be from the Book, but it is not from the Book. They say, 'It is from Allah,' but it is not from Allah, and they tell a lie against Allah, the while they know.

It is not right for a man that Allah should give him a Book, and judgement, and prophecy, and that then he should say to men, 'Be ye servants of mine rather than of Allah'; but be ye rather masters[16] of teaching the Book and of what ye learn.

He does not bid you take the angels and the prophets

for your lords; shall He bid you misbelieve again when you are once resigned?

[75] And when Allah took the compact from the prophets '(this is) surely what we have given you of the Book and wisdom. Then shall come to you the Apostle confirming what is with you. Ye must believe in him and help him.' He said, moreover, 'Are ye resolved and have ye taken my compact on that (condition)?' They say, 'We are resolved.' He said, 'Then bear witness, for I am witness with you; but he who turns back after that, these are sinners.'[17]

What is it other than Allah's religion that they crave? when to Him is resigned whosoever is in the heavens and the earth, will he or nill he, and to him shall they return!

Say, 'We believe in Allah, and what has been revealed to thee, and what was revealed to Abraham, and Ishmael, and Isaac, and Jacob, and the tribes, and what was given to Moses, and Jesus, and the prophets from their Lord,— we will make no distinction between any of them,—and we are unto Him resigned. Whosoever craves other than Islam for a religion, it shall surely not be accepted from him, and he shall, in the next world, be of those who lose.'

[80] How shall Allah guide people who have disbelieved after believing and bearing witness that the Apostle is true, and after there come to them manifest signs? Allah guides the unjust folk.

These, their reward is, that on them is the curse of Allah, and of the angels, and of men together; they shall dwell therein for aye—the torment shall not be alleviated from them, nor shall they be respited; save those who repent after that, and act aright, for verily, Allah is forgiving and merciful.

Verily, those who misbelieve after believing, and then increase in misbelief, their repentance shall not be accepted; these are those who err.

[85] Verily, those who misbelieve and die in misbelief, there shall not be accepted from any one of them the earthful of gold, though he should give it as a ransom. For them is grievous woe, and helpers have they none.

Ye cannot attain to righteousness until ye expend in alms of what ye love. But what ye expend in alms, that Allah knows.

All food was lawful to the children of Israel save what Israel made unlawful to himself before that the law was revealed. Say, 'Bring the law and recite it, if ye speak the truth.' But whoso forges against Allah a lie, after that, they are the unjust. Say, 'Allah speaks the truth, then follow the faith of Abraham, a *hanîf*, who was not of the idolaters.'

[90] Verily, the first House founded for men was surely that at Bekkah,[18] for a blessing and a guidance to the worlds. Therein are manifest signs,—Abraham's station, and whosoever enters in is safe. There is due to Allah from man a pilgrimage unto the House, for whosoever can find his way there. But whoso misbelieves—Allah is independent of the worlds.

Say, 'O people of the Book! why do ye misbelieve in Allah's signs, while Allah is witness of what ye do?'

Say, 'O people of the Book! why do ye turn from the

way of Allah him who believes, craving to make it crooked, while ye are witnesses? But Allah is not careless of what ye do.'

[95] O ye who believe! if ye obey the sect of those to whom the Book was brought, they will turn you, after your faith, to unbelievers again. How can ye misbelieve while unto you are recited the signs of Allah, and among you is His Apostle? But whoso takes tight hold on Allah, he is guided into the right way.

O ye who believe! fear Allah with the fear that He deserves, and die not save ye be resigned.

Take tight hold of Allah's rope altogether, and do not part in sects; but remember the favours of Allah towards you, when ye were enemies and He made friendship between your hearts, and on the morrow ye were, by His favour, brothers. Ye were on the edge of a pit of fire, but he rescued you therefrom.¹⁹ Thus does Allah show to you His signs, perchance ye may be guided; [100] and that there may be of you a nation who shall invite to good, and bid what is reasonable, and forbid what is wrong; these are the prosperous.

Be not like those who parted in sects and disagreed after there came to them manifest signs; for them is mighty woe, on the day when faces shall be whitened and faces shall be blackened. As for those whose faces are blackened,—'Did ye misbelieve after your faith, then taste the torment for your misbelief!' But as for those whose faces are whitened, they are in Allah's mercy, and they shall dwell therein for aye.

These are the signs of Allah. We recite them to you in

truth, for Allah desires not wrong unto the worlds.

[105] Allah's is what is in the heavens and what is in the earth, and unto Allah affairs return.

Ye were the best of nations brought forth unto man. Ye bid what is reasonable, and forbid what is wrong, believing in Allah. Had the people of the Book believed, it would have been better for them. There are believers among them, though most of them are sinners.

They shall surely not harm you save a hurt;[20] and if they fight you, they shall show you their backs, then they shall not be helped.

They are smitten with abasement wherever they be found, save for the rope of Allah and the rope of man;[21] and they draw on themselves wrath from Allah. They are smitten, too, with poverty; that is because they did disbelieve in Allah's signs, and kill the prophets undeservedly. That is because they did rebel and did transgress.

They are not all alike. Of the people of the Book there is a nation upright, reciting Allah's signs throughout the night, as they adore the while. [110] They believe in Allah, and in the last day, and bid what is reasonable, and forbid what is wrong, and vie in charity; these are among the righteous.

What ye do of good surely Allah will not deny, for Allah knows those who fear.

Verily, those who misbelieve, their wealth is of no service to them, nor their children either, against Allah; they are the fellows of the Fire, and they shall dwell therein for aye.

The likeness of what they expend in this life of the world, is as the likeness of wind wherein is a cold blast that falls upon a people's tilth who have wronged themselves and destroys it. It is not Allah who wrongs them, but it is themselves they wrong.

O ye who believe! take not to intimacy with others than yourselves; they will not fail to spoil you; they would fain ye came to trouble,—hatred is shown by their mouths; but what their breasts conceal is greater still. We have made manifest to you our signs, did ye but understand.

[115] Ye it is who love them, but they love not you; and ye believe in the Book, all of it. But when they meet you they say, 'We believe'; and when they go aside they bite their fingertips at you through rage. Say, 'Die in your rage, for Allah doth know the nature of men's breasts.'

If good luck touch you it is bad for them, but if bad luck befall you they rejoice therein; yet if ye are patient and fear, their tricks shall not harm you, for what they do Allah comprehends.

When thou didst set forth early[22] from thy people to settle for the believers a camp to fight;—but Allah both hears and knows;—when two companies of you were on the point of showing cowardice; but Allah was their guardian, for on Allah surely the believers do rely. Why! Allah gave you victory at Bedr when ye were in a poor way; fear Allah, then, haply ye may give thanks. [120] When thou didst say unto the believers, 'Is it not enough for you that your Lord assists you with three thousand of the angels sent down from on high? Yea, if ye are patient and fear Allah, and they come upon you on a sudden, now, your Lord will assist you with five thousand of His angels, (angels) of mark. Allah only made this as glad tidings for you to comfort your hearts withal,—for victory is but from Allah, the mighty, the wise;—to cut off the flank of those who misbelieve, or make them downcast, that they may retire disappointed.'

Thou has nothing to do with the affair at all, whether He turn towards them again or punish them; for, verily, they are unjust.

Allah's is what is in the heavens and in the earth. He forgives whom He pleases, and punishes whom He pleases; for Allah is forgiving and merciful.

[125] O ye who believe! devour not usury doubly doubled, but fear Allah, perchance ye may be prosperous; fear the Fire which is prepared for the unbelievers, and obey Allah and His Apostle, perchance ye may get mercy. And vie with one another for pardon from your Lord, and for Paradise, the breadth of which is as the heaven and the earth, prepared for those who fear;—for those who expend in alms, in prosperity and adversity, for those who repress their rage, and those who pardon men; Allah loves the kind. Those who when they do a crime, or wrong themselves, remember Allah, and ask forgiveness for their sins,—and who forgives sins save Allah?—and do not perservere in what they did, the while they know;—[130]—these have their reward:—pardon from their Lord, and gardens beneath which rivers flow, dwelling therein for aye; for pleasant is the hire of those who act like this.

Incidents have passed before your time, go on then in

the earth, and see what was the end of those who called (the prophets) liars.

This is an explanation unto men, and a guidance and a warning unto those who fear. Do not give way nor grieve, for ye shall have the upper hand if ye but be believers.

If a sore touch you, a sore like it has touched people: these are days[23] which we make to alternate amongst mankind that Allah may know who it is that believe, and may take from you witnesses,[24] for Allah loves not the unjust; [135] and that Allah may assay those who believe, and blot out the misbelievers. Do ye think that ye can enter Paradise and Allah not know those of you who have fought well, or know the patient? Why, ye longed for death before ye met it! Now ye have looked upon it and ye halt!

Mohammed is but an apostle; apostles have passed away before his time; what if he die or is killed, will ye retreat upon your heels? He who retreats upon his heels does no harm to Allah at all; but Allah will recompense the thankful. It is not for any soul to die, save by Allah's permission written down for an appointed time; but he who wishes for the reward of this world we will give him of it, and he who wishes for the reward of the future we will give him of it, and we will recompense the grateful.

[140] How many prophets have myriads fought against! yet they did not give way at what befel them in Allah's way! Nor were they weak, nor did they demean themselves:—Allah loves the patient. And their word was only to say, 'Lord, forgive us our sins and our extravagance in our affairs; and make firm our footing, and help

us against the misbelieving folk!' and Allah gave them the reward of this world, and good reward for the future too, for Allah doth love the kind.

O ye who believe! if ye obey those who misbelieve, they will turn you back upon your heels, and ye will retreat the losers. Nay, Allah is your Lord, He is the best of helpers. We will throw dread into the hearts of those who misbelieve, for that they associate that with Allah which He has sent down no power for; but their resort is fire, and evil is the resort of the unjust.

[145] Allah has truly kept His promise, when ye knocked them senseless by His permission, until ye showed cowardice, and wrangled, and rebelled, after he had shown you what ye loved. Amongst you are those who love this world, and amongst you are those who love the next. Then He turned you away from them to try you; but He has pardoned you, for Allah is Lord of grace unto believers,—when ye went up and looked not round upon any one, although the Apostle was calling you from your rear. Therefore did Allah reward you with trouble on trouble that ye should not grieve after what ye had missed,[25] nor for what befell you, for Allah is well aware of what ye do. Then He sent down upon you after trouble safety,—drowsiness creeping over one company of you, and one company of you getting anxious about themselves, suspecting about Allah other than the truth, with the suspicion of the ignorant,[26] and saying, 'Have we any chance in the affair?' Say, 'Verily, the affair is Allah's.' They conceal in themselves what they will not show to thee, and say, 'If we had any chance in the affair

we should not be killed here.' Say, 'If ye were in your houses, surely those against whom slaughter was written down, would have gone forth to fight even to where they are lying now; that Allah may try what is in your breasts and assay what is in your hearts, for Allah doth know the nature of men's breasts.'

Verily, those of you who turned your backs on that day when the two armies met, it was but Satan who made them slip for something they had earned. But Allah has now pardoned them; verily, Allah is forgiving and clement.

[150] O ye who believe! be not like those who misbelieve, and say unto their brethren when they knock about in the earth, or are upon a raid, 'Had they but been at home, they had not died and had not been killed.' It was that Allah might make a sighing in their hearts, for Allah gives life and death; and Allah on what ye do doth look.

And if, indeed, ye be killed in Allah's way or die, surely forgiveness from Allah and mercy is better than what ye gather; and if ye die or be killed it is to Allah ye shall be assembled. It was by a sort of mercy from Allah thou didst deal gently with them, for hadst thou been rough and rude of heart they had dispersed from around thee. But pardon them, and ask forgiveness for them, and take counsel with them in the affair. As for what thou hast resolved, rely upon Allah; verily, Allah loves those who do rely. If Allah help you, there is none can overcome you; but if He leave you in the lurch, who is there can help you after Him? Upon Allah then let believers rely.

[155] It is not for the prophet to cheat; and he who cheats shall bring what he has cheated on the resurrection

day. Then shall each soul be paid what it has earned, and they shall not be wronged. Is he who follows the pleasure of Allah, like him who has drawn on himself anger from Allah, whose resort is Hell? An evil journey shall it be! These are degrees with Allah, and Allah sees what ye do.

Allah was surely very gracious to the believers, when He sent amongst them an apostle from themselves, to recite to them His signs, and purify them, and teach them the Book and wisdom, although they surely were before his time in manifest error. Or when an accident befalls you, and ye have fallen on twice as much, ye say, 'How is this?'[27] Say, 'It is from yourselves. Verily, Allah is mighty over all.'

[160] And what befell you the day when the two armies met, it was by Allah's permission; that He might know the believers, and might know those who behaved hypocritically; for it was said to them, 'Come, fight in Allah's way,' or 'repel (the foe)'; they said, 'If we knew how to fight we would surely follow you.' They were that day far higher unto misbelief than they were to faith. They say with their mouths what is not in their hearts, but Allah doth know best what they hid. Those who said of their brethren, whilst they themselves stayed at home, 'Had they obeyed us they would not have been killed.' Say, 'Ward off from yourselves death, if ye do speak the truth.'

Count not those who are killed in the way of Allah as dead, but living with their Lord;—provided for, rejoicing in what Allah has brought them of His grace, and being glad for those who have not reached them yet,—those left behind them; there is no fear for them, and they shall not be grieved; [165] glad at favour from Allah and grace, and that Allah wasteth not the hire of the believers. Whoso answered to the call of Allah and of His prophet after sorrow had befallen them, for those, if they do good and fear Allah, is a mighty hire. To whom when men said, 'Verily, men have gathered round you, fear then them,' it only increased their faith, and they said, 'Allah is enough for us, a good guardian is He.' Then they retired in favour from Allah and grace; no evil touched them; they followed the pleasure of Allah, and Allah is Lord of mighty grace.

It is only that Satan who frightens his friends. Do not ye fear them, but fear me, if ye be believers.

[170] Let them not grieve thee who vie with each other in misbelief. Verily, they cannot hurt Allah at all. Allah wills not to make for them a portion in the future life; but for them is mighty woe.

Verily, those who purchase misbelief for faith, they do not hurt Allah at all, and for them is grievous woe.

Let not those who misbelieve reckon that our letting them range is good for themselves. We only let them have their range that they may increase in sin. And for them is shameful woe. Allah would not leave believers in the state which ye are in, until He discerns the vile from the good. And Allah would not inform you of the unseen, but Allah chooses of His apostles whom He pleases. Wherefore believe ye in Allah and His Apostle; and if ye believe and fear, for you is mighty hire.

[175] And let not those who are niggard of what Allah has given them of His grace, count that it is best for them;—nay, it is worse for them. What they have been

niggard of shall be a collar round their necks upon the resurrection day. And Allah's is the heritage of the heavens and the earth, and Allah of what ye do is well aware.

Allah heard the speech of those who said, 'Verily, Allah is poor[28] and we are rich.' We will write down what they said, and how they killed the prophets undeservedly, and say, 'Taste ye the torment of burning'; this shall they suffer for what their hands have sent on before;—for, verily, Allah is no unjust one to His servants,—who say, 'Verily, Allah has covenanted with us that we should not believe in an apostle until he gives us a sacrifice which fire devours.'[29]

[180] Say, 'There have come to you apostles before me with manifest signs, and with what ye talk about; why then did ye kill them, if ye speak the truth?'

And if they did call thee a liar, apostles before thee have been called liars too, who came with manifest signs, and with scriptures, and with the illuminating Book.

Every soul must taste of death; and ye shall only be paid your hire upon the resurrection day. But he who is forced away from the Fire and brought into Paradise is indeed happy; but the life of this world is but a possession of deceit. Ye shall surely be tried in your wealth, and in your persons, and ye shall surely hear from those who have had the Book brought them before you, and from those who associate others with Allah, much harm. But if ye be patient and fear,—verily, that is one of the determined affairs.

When Allah took the compact from those who have had

the Book brought them that 'Ye shall of a surety manifest it unto men, and not hide it', they cast it behind their backs, and bought therewith a little price,—but evil is what they buy.

[185] Count not that those who rejoice in what they have produced, and love to be praised for what they have not done,—think not that they are in safety from woe,—for them is grievous woe!

Allah's is the kingdom of the heavens and the earth, and Allah is mighty over all!

Verily, in the creation of the heavens and the earth, and in the succession of night and day, are signs to those possessed of minds; who remember Allah standing and sitting or lying on their sides, and reflect on the creation of the heavens and the earth. 'O Lord! thou hast not created this in vain. We celebrate Thy praise; then keep us from the torment of the Fire! Lord! verily, whomsoever Thou hast made to enter the Fire, Thou hast disgraced him; and the unjust shall have none to help them.

[190] 'Lord! verily, we heard a crier calling to the faith, "Believe in your Lord," and we did believe. Lord! forgive us our sins and cover our offences, and let us die with the righteous. Lord! and bring us what Thou hast promised us by Thy apostles, and disgrace us not upon the resurrection day; for, verily, Thou dost not break Thy promises!' And the Lord shall answer them, 'I waste not the works of a worker amongst you, be it male or female,—one of you is from the other.[30]

'Those who fled, and were turned out of their houses, and were harmed in my way, and who fought and were killed, I will cover their offences, and I will make them enter into gardens beneath which rivers flow.' [195] A reward from Allah; for Allah, with Him are the best of rewards.

Let it not deceive you that those who misbelieve go to and fro in the earth. It is a slight possession, and then their resort is Hell; an evil couch shall it be. But those who fear their Lord, for them are gardens beneath which rivers flow, and they shall dwell therein for aye,—an entertainment from Allah; and that which is with Allah is best for the righteous.

Verily, of the people of the Book are some who do believe in Allah, and in what has been revealed to you, and what was revealed to them, humbling themselves before Allah, and selling not the signs of Allah for a little price. These shall have their reward with their Lord; verily, Allah is quick at reckoning up.

[200] O ye who believe! be patient and vie in being patient,[31] and be on the alert, and fear Allah, that haply ye may prosper.

THE CHAPTER OF WOMEN

IV (*Medina*)

In the name of the merciful and compassionate Allah.

O ye folk! fear your Lord, who created you from one soul, and created therefrom its mate, and diffused from them twain many men and women. And fear Allah, in whose name ye beg of one another, and the wombs; verily, Allah over you doth watch.[1]

And give unto the orphans their property, and give them not the vile in exchange for the good, and devour not their property to your own property; verily, that were a great sin. But if ye fear that ye cannot do justice between orphans, then marry what seems good to you of women, by twos, or threes, or fours; and if ye fear that ye cannot be equitable, then only one, or what your right hands possess.[2] That keeps you nearer to not being partial.

And give women their dowries freely; and if they are good enough to remit any of it of themselves, then devour it with good digestion and appetite.[3]

But do not give up to fools[4] their property which Allah has made you to stand by; but maintain them from it, and clothe them, and speak to them with a reasonable speech. [5] Prove orphans until they reach a marriageable age, and if ye perceive in them right management, then hand over to them their property, and do not devour it extravagantly in anticipation of their growing up. And he who is rich, let him abstain; but he who is poor, let him devour in reason, and when ye hand over to them their property, then take witnesses against them; but Allah sufficeth for taking account.

Men should have a portion of what their parents and kindred leave, and women should have a portion of what their parents and kindred leave, whether it be little or much, a determined portion. And when the next of kin and the orphans and the poor are present at the division, then maintain them out of it, and speak to them a reasonable speech. [10] And let these fear lest they leave behind them a weak seed, for whom they would be afraid; and let them fear Allah, and speak a straightforward speech. Verily, those who devour the property of orphans unjustly, only devour into their bellies fire, and they shall broil in flames.

Allah instructs you concerning your children; for a male the like of the portion of two females, and if there be women above two, then let them have two-thirds of what (the deceased) leaves; and if there be but one, then let her have a half; and as to the parents, to each of them a sixth of what he leaves, if he has a son; but if he have no son, and his parents inherit, then let his mother have a third, and if he have brethren, let his mother have a sixth after payment of the bequest he bequeaths and of his debt.

Your parents or your children, ye know not which of them is nearest to you in usefulness:—an ordinance this from Allah; verily, Allah is knowing and wise! And ye shall have half of what your wives leave, if they have no son; but if they have a son, then ye shall have a fourth of what they leave, after payment of the bequests they bequeath or of their debts. And they shall have a fourth of what ye leave, if ye have no son; but if ye have a son, then let them have an eighth of what ye leave, after payment of the bequest ye bequeath and of your debts.

[15] And if the man's or the woman's (property) be inherited by a kinsman who is neither parent nor child,[5] and he have a brother or sister, then let each of these two

have a sixth; but if they are more than that, let them share in a third after payment of the bequest he bequeaths and of his debts, without prejudice,[6]—an ordinance this from Allah, and Allah is knowing and clement!

These be Allah's bounds, and whoso obeys Allah and the Apostle He will make him enter into gardens beneath which rivers flow, and they shall dwell therein for aye;—that is the mighty happiness.

But whoso rebels against Allah and His Apostle, and transgresses His bounds, He will make him enter into fire, and dwell therein for aye; and for him is shameful woe.

Against those of your women who commit adultery, call witnesses four in number from among yourselves; and if these bear witness, then keep the women in houses[7] until death release them, or Allah shall make for them a way.

[20] And if two of you commit it, then hurt them both;[8] but if they turn again and amend, leave them alone, verily, Allah is easily turned, compassionate.

Allah is only bound to turn again towards those who do evil through ignorance and then turn again. Surely, these will Allah turn again to, for Allah is knowing, wise. His turning again is not for those who do evil, until, when death comes before one of them, he says, 'Now I turn again'; nor yet for those who die in misbelief. For such as these have we prepared a grievous woe.

O ye who believe! it is not lawful for you to inherit women's estates against their will; nor to hinder them,[9] that ye may go off with part of what ye brought them, unless they commit fornication manifestly; but associate with them in reason, for if ye are averse from them, it may be that ye are averse from something wherein Allah has put much good for you.

But if ye wish to exchange one wife for another, and have given one of them a talent,[10] then take not from it anything. What! would you take it for a calumny and a manifest crime?[11]

[25] How can ye take it when one of you has gone in unto the other, and they have taken from you a rigid compact?

And do not marry women your fathers married,—except bygones,—for it is abominable and hateful, and an evil way; unlawful for you are your mothers, and your daughters, and your sisters, and your paternal aunts and maternal aunts, and your brother's daughters, and your sister's daughters, and your foster mothers, and your foster sisters, and your wives' mothers, and your step daughters who are your wards, born of your wives to whom ye have gone in; but if ye have not gone in unto them, then it is no crime in you; and the lawful spouses of your sons from your own loins, and that ye form a connexion between two sisters,—except bygones,—verily, Allah is forgiving, merciful; and married women, save such as your right hands possess,—Allah's Book against you!—but lawful for you is all besides this, for you to seek them with your wealth, marrying them and not fornicating; but such of them as ye have enjoyed, give them their hire as a lawful due; for there is no crime in you about what ye agree between you after such lawful due, verily, Allah is knowing and wise.

But whosoever of you cannot go the length of marrying marriageable women who believe, then take of what your right hands possess, of your maidens who believe;—though Allah knows best about your faith. Ye come one from the other; then marry them with the permission of their people, and give them their hire in reason, they being chaste and not fornicating, and not receivers of paramours.

[30] But when they are married, if they commit fornication, then inflict upon them half the penalty for married women; that is for whomsoever of you fears wrong; but that ye should have patience is better for you, and Allah is forgiving and merciful.

Allah wishes to explain to you and to guide you into the ordinances of those who were before you, and to turn towards you, for Allah is knowing, wise. Allah wishes to turn towards you, but those who follow their lusts wish that ye should swerve with a mighty swerving! Allah wishes to make it light for you, for man was created weak.

O ye who believe! devour not your property amongst yourselves vainly, unless it be a merchandise by mutual consent. And do not kill yourselves; verily, Allah is compassionate unto you.

But whoso does that maliciously and unjustly, we will broil him with fire; for that is easy with Allah.

[35] If ye avoid great sins from which ye are forbidden, we will cover your offences and make you enter with a noble entrance.

And do not covet that by which Allah has preferred one of you over another. The men shall have a portion of what they earn, and the women a portion of what they earn; ask Allah for His grace, verily, Allah knows all.

To every one have we appointed kinsfolk as heirs of what parents and relatives and those with whom ye have joined right hands leave; so give them their portion, for, verily, Allah is over all a witness.

Men stand superior to women in that Allah hath preferred some of them over others, and in that they expend of their wealth: and the virtuous women, devoted, careful (in their husbands') absence, as Allah has cared for them. But those whose perverseness ye fear, admonish them and remove them into bedchambers and beat them; but if they submit to you, then do not seek a way against them; verily, Allah is high and great.

And if ye fear a breach between the two,[12] then send a judge from his people and a judge from her people. If they wish for reconciliation, Allah will arrange between them; verily, Allah is knowing and aware.

[40] And serve Allah, and do not associate aught with Him; and to your parents show kindness, and to kindred, and orphans, and the poor, and the neighbour who is akin, and the neighbour who is a stranger, and the companion who is strange, and the son of the road, and what your right hands possess,[13] verily, Allah loves not him who is proud and boastful; who are miserly and bid men be miserly too, and who hide what Allah has given them of His grace;—but we have prepared for the misbelievers shameful woe.

And those who expend their wealth in alms for appearance sake before men, and who believe not in Allah nor in the last day;—but whosoever has Satan for his mate, an evil mate has he.

What harm would it do them if they believed in Allah and in the last day, and expended in alms of what Allah has provided them with? but Allah knows about them.

Verily, Allah would not wrong by the weight of an atom; and if it's[14] a good work, He will double it and bring from Himself a mighty hire.

[45] How then when we bring from every nation a witness, and bring thee as a witness against these on the day when those who misbelieve and rebel against the Apostle would fain that the earth were levelled with them? But they cannot hide the news from Allah.

O ye who believe! approach not prayer while ye are drunk, until ye well know what ye say; nor yet while polluted,—unless ye be passing by the way,—until ye have washed yourselves. But if ye are sick, or on a journey, or one of you come from the privy, or if ye have touched a woman, and ye cannot find water, then use good surface sand and wipe your faces and your hands therewith; verily, Allah pardons and forgives.

Do ye not see those who have been given a portion of the Book? They buy error, and they wish that ye may err from the way! But Allah knows best who your enemies are, and Allah suffices as a patron, and sufficient is Allah as a help.

And those who are Jews, and those who pervert the words from their places, and say, 'We hear but we rebel, and do thou listen without hearing,' and (who say) 'râ'hinâ',[15] distorting it with their tongues and taunting about religion. But had they said, 'We hear and we obey, so listen and look upon us,' it would have been better for them and more upright;—but may Allah curse them in their misbelief, for they will not believe except a few.

[50] O ye who have been given the Book! believe in what we have revealed, confirming what ye had before; ere we deface your faces and turn them into hinder parts, or curse you as we cursed the fellows of the Sabbath[16] when Allah's command was done.

Verily, Allah pardons not associating aught with Him, but He pardons anything short of that to whomsoever He pleases; but he who associates aught with Allah, he hath devised a mighty sin.

Do ye not see those who purify themselves? Nay, Allah purifies whom He will, and they shall not be wronged a straw.[17]

Behold, how they devise against Allah a lie, and that is manifest sin enough.

Do ye not see those to whom a portion of the Book has been given? They believe in Jibt and Tâghût,[18] and they say of those who misbelieve, 'These are better guided in the way than those who believe.' [55] These are those whom Allah has cursed, and whom Allah has cursed no helper shall he find.

Shall they have a portion of the kingdom? Why even then they would not give to men a jot.[19]

Do they envy man for what Allah has given of His grace? We have given to Abraham's people the Book and wisdom, and we have given them a mighty kingdom. And of them are some who believe therein, and of them are some who turn from it, but Hell is flaming enough for them.

Verily, those who disbelieve in our signs, we will broil them with fire; whenever their skins are well done, then we will change them for other skins, that they may taste the torment. Verily, Allah is glorious and wise.

[60] But those who believe and do aright, we will make them enter gardens beneath which rivers flow, and they shall dwell therein for ever and aye, for them therein are pure wives, and we will make them enter into a shady shade. Verily, Allah bids you pay your trusts to their owners, and when ye judge between men to judge with justice. Verily, Allah, excellent is what He admonishes you with; verily, Allah both hears and sees.

O ye who believe! obey Allah, and obey the Apostle and those in authority amongst you; and if ye quarrel about anything, refer to Allah and the Apostle, if ye believe in Allah and the last day; that is better and fairer as a settlement.

Do ye not see those who pretend that they believe in what has been revealed to them, and what was revealed before thee; they wish to refer their judgement to Tâghût,[20] but they are bidden to disbelieve therein, and Satan wishes to lead them into a remote error. And when it is said to them, 'Come round to what Allah has sent down and unto the Apostle,' thou seest the hypocrites turning from thee, turning away.

[65] How then when there befalls them a mischance through what their hands have sent on before? Then will they come to you, and swear by Allah, 'We meant naught

but good and concord.' These, Allah knows what is in their hearts. Turn thou away from them and admonish them, and speak to them into their souls with a searching word.

We have never sent an apostle save that he should be obeyed by the permission of Allah; and if they, when they have wronged themselves, come to thee and ask pardon of Allah, and the Apostle asks pardon for them, then they will find Allah easy to be turned, compassionate.

But no! by thy Lord! they will not believe, until they have made thee judge of what they differ on; then they will not find in themselves aught to hinder what thou hast decreed, and they will submit with submission. But had we prescribed for them, 'Kill yourselves, or go ye forth out of your houses,' they would not have done it, save only a few of them; but had they done what they are admonished, then it would have been better for them, and a more firm assurance.

[70] And then we would surely have brought them from ourselves a mighty hire, and would have guided them into a right path.

Whoso obeys Allah and the Apostle, these are with those Allah has been pleased with, of prophets and confessors and martyrs and the righteous;—a fair company are they.

That is grace from Allah, and Allah knows well enough.

O ye who believe! take your precautions and sally in detachments or altogether. Verily, there is of you who tarries behind, and, if a mischance befalls you, says, 'Allah has been gracious to me, since I am not with them a martyr.'

[75] But if there befalls you grace from Allah, he would say—as though there were no friendship between you and him—'O would that I had been with thee to attain this mighty happiness!' Let those then fight in Allah's way who sell this life of the world for the next; and whoso fights in Allah's way, then, be he killed or be he victorious, we will give him a mighty hire.

What ails you that ye do not fight in Allah's way, and for the weak men and women and children, who say, 'Lord, bring us out of this town²¹ of oppressive folk, and make for us from Thee a patron, and make for us from Thee a help'?

Those who believe fight in the way of Allah; and those who disbelieve fight in the way of Tâghût; fight ye then against the friends of Satan, verily, Satan's tricks are weak.

Do ye not see those to whom it is said, 'Restrain your hands, and be steadfast in prayer and give alms'; and when it is prescribed for them to fight then a band of them fear men, as though it were the fear of Allah or a still stronger fear, and they say, 'O our Lord! why hast thou prescribed for us to fight, couldst thou not let us abide till our near appointed time?' Say, 'The enjoyment of this world is but slight, and the next is better for him who fears';—but they shall not be wronged a straw.

[80] Wheresoe'er ye be death will overtake you, though ye were in lofty towers. And if a good thing befall them, they say, 'This is from Allah,' but if a bad thing, they say, 'This is from thee.' Say, 'It is all from Allah.' What ails these people? They can hardly understand a tale.

What befalls thee of good it is from Allah; and what

befalls thee of bad it is from thyself. We have sent thee to mankind as an apostle, and Allah sufficeth for a witness.

Whoso obeys the prophet he has obeyed Allah; and he who turns back—we have not sent thee to watch over them.

They say, 'Obedience!' but when they sally forth from you, a company of them brood by night over something else than that which thou hast said; but Allah writes down that over which they brood. Turn then from them and rely on Allah, for Allah sufficeth for a guardian. Do they not meditate on the Qur'ân? if it were from other than Allah they would find in it many a discrepancy.

[85] And when there comes to them a matter of security or fear they publish it; but if they were to report it to the Apostle and to those in authority amongst them, then those of them who would elicit it from them would know it; but were it not for Allah's grace upon you and His mercy ye had followed Satan, save a few.

Fight, then, in the way of Allah; impose not aught on any but thyself, and urge on the believers; it may be that Allah will restrain the violence of those who misbelieve, for Allah is more violent and more severe to punish.

Whoso intercedes with a good intercession shall have a portion therefrom; but he who intercedes with a bad intercession shall have the like thereof, for Allah keeps watch over all things.

And when ye are saluted with a salutation, salute with a better than it, or return it;—verily, Allah of all things takes account.

Allah, there is no Allah but He! He will surely assemble

you on the resurrection day, there is no doubt therein; who is truer than Allah in his discourse?

[90] Why are ye two parties about the hypocrites, when Allah hath overturned them for what they earned? Do ye wish to guide those whom Allah hath led astray? Whoso Allah hath led astray ye shall not surely find for him a path. They would fain that ye misbelieve as they misbelieve, that ye might be alike; take ye not patrons from among them until they too flee in Allah's way; but if they turn their backs, then seize them and kill them wheresoever ye find them, and take from them neither patron nor help,—save those who reach a people betwixt whom and you is an alliance—or who come to you while their bosoms prevent them from fighting you or fighting their own people. But had Allah pleased He would have given you dominion over them, and they would surely have fought you. But if they retire from you and do not fight you, and offer you peace,—then Allah hath given you no way against them.

Ye will find others who seek for quarter from you, and quarter from their own people; whenever they return to sedition they shall be overturned therein: but if they retire not from you, nor offer you peace, nor restrain their hands, then seize them and kill them wheresoever ye find them;—over these we have made for you manifest power.

It is not for a believer to kill a believer save by mistake; and whosoever kills a believer by mistake then let him free a believing neck;[22] and the blood money must be paid to his people save what they shall remit as alms. But if he be from a tribe hostile to you and yet a believer, then let him free a believing neck. And if it be a tribe betwixt whom and you there is an alliance, then let the blood money be paid to his friends, and let him free a believing neck; but he who cannot find the means, then let him fast for two consecutive months—a penance this from Allah, for Allah is knowing, wise.

[95] And whoso kills a believer purposely, his reward is Hell, to dwell therein for aye; and Allah will be wrath with him, and curse him, and prepare for him a mighty woe.

O ye who believe! when ye are knocking about in the way of Allah be discerning, and do not say to him who offers you a salutation, 'Thou art no believer,' craving after the chances of this world's life,[23] for with Allah are many spoils! So were ye aforetime, but Allah was gracious to you, be ye then discerning; verily, Allah of what ye do is well aware.

Not alike are those of the believers who sit at home without harm, and those who are strenuous in Allah's way with their wealth and their persons. Allah hath preferred those who are strenuous with their wealth and their persons to those who sit still, by many degrees, and to each hath Allah promised good, but Allah hath preferred the strenuous for a mighty hire over those who sit still,—degrees from him, and pardon and mercy, for Allah is forgiving and merciful.

Verily, the angels when they took the souls of those who had wronged themselves,[24] said, 'What state were ye in?' they say, 'We were but weak in the earth'; they said, 'Was not Allah's earth wide enough for you to flee away therein?' These are those whose resort is Hell, and a bad journey shall it be!

[100] Save for the weak men, and women, and children, who could not compass any stratagem, and were not guided to a way; these it may be Allah will pardon, for Allah both pardons and forgives.

Whosoever flees in the way of Allah shall find in the earth many a spacious refuge; and he who goes forth from his house, fleeing unto Allah and His prophet, and then death catches him up,—his hire devolves on Allah, and Allah is forgiving and merciful.

And when ye knock about in the earth, it is no crime to you that ye come short in prayer, if ye fear that those who disbelieve will set upon you; verily, the misbelievers are your obvious foes.

When thou art amongst them, and standest up to pray with them, then let a party of them stand up with thee, and let them take their arms; and when they adore, let them go behind you, and let another party who have not yet prayed come forward and pray with thee; and let them take their precautions and their arms.

Fain would those who misbelieve that ye were careless of your arms and your baggage, that they might turn upon you with a single turning. And it is no crime to you if ye be annoyed with rain or be sick, that ye lay down your arms; but take your precautions,—verily, Allah has prepared for those who misbelieve a shameful woe.

But when ye have fulfilled your prayer, remember Allah standing and sitting and lying on your sides; and when ye are in safety then be steadfast in prayer; verily, prayer is for the believers prescribed and timed!

[105] And do not give way in pursuit of the people; if ye suffer they shall surely suffer too, even as ye suffer; and ye hope from Allah, but they hope not! and Allah is knowing, wise.

Verily, we have revealed to thee the Book in truth that thou mayest judge between men of what Allah has shown thee; so be not with the treacherous a disputant; but ask Allah's pardon: verily, Allah is forgiving, merciful.

And wrangle not for those who defraud themselves; for Allah loves not him who is a fraudulent sinner. They hide themselves from men; but they cannot hide themselves from Allah, for He is with them while they brood at night over speeches that please Him not;—but Allah doth compass what they do!

Here are ye, wrangling for them about this world's life;—but who shall wrangle with Allah for them on the day of judgement, or who shall be a guardian over them?

[110] Yet whoso does evil and wrongs himself, and then asks pardon of Allah, shall find Allah forgiving and merciful; and whoso commits a crime, he only commits it against himself, for Allah is knowing, wise.

And whoso commits a fault or a sin and throws it on the innocent, he hath to bear a calumny and a manifest sin.

Were it not for Allah's grace upon thee, and His mercy, a party of them would have tried to lead thee astray; but they only lead themselves astray; they shall not hurt you in aught: for Allah hath sent down upon thee the Book and the wisdom, and taught thee what thou didst not know, for Allah's grace was mighty on thee.

There is no good in most of what they talk in private; save in his who bids almsgiving, or kindness, or reconciliation between men; and whoso does this, craving the good pleasure of Allah, we will give to him a mighty hire.

[115] But he who severs himself from the prophet after that we have made manifest to him the guidance, and follows other than the way of the believers, we will turn our backs on him as he hath turned his back; and we will make him reach Hell, and a bad journey shall it be.

Verily, Allah forgives not associating aught with Him, but He pardons anything short of that, to whomsoever he will; but whoso associates aught with Allah, he hath erred a wide error.

Verily, they call not beside Him on aught save females; and they do not call on aught save a rebellious devil.

Allah curse him! for he said, 'I will take from thy servants a portion due to me; and I will lead them astray; and I will stir up vain desires within them; and I will order them and they shall surely crop the ears of cattle; and I will order them and they shall surely after Allah's creation';²⁵ but he who takes the devil for his patron instead of Allah, he loses with a manifest loss. He promises them, and stirs up vain desires within them, but the devil promises only to deceive.

[120] These, their resort is Hell; they shall not find an escape therefrom! But those who believe, and do what is right, we will make them enter into gardens beneath which rivers flow, to dwell therein for aye,—Allah's promise in truth; and who is truer than Allah in speech? Not for your vain desires, nor the vain desires of the

people of the Book. He who doeth evil shall be recompensed therewith, and shall not find for him beside Allah a patron, or a help. But he who doeth good works,—be it male or female,—and believes, they shall enter into Paradise, and they shall not be wronged a jot.

Who has a better religion than he who resigns his face to Allah, and does good, and follows the faith of Abraham, as a *hanîf*?—for Allah took Abraham as a friend.

[125] And Allah's is what is in the heavens and in the earth, and Allah encompasses all things!

They will ask thee a decision about women; say, 'Allah decides for you about them, and that which is rehearsed to you in the Book; about orphan women to whom ye do not give what is prescribed for them, and whom ye are averse from marrying; and about weak children; and that ye stand fairly by orphans;—and what ye do of good, verily, that Allah knows.'

And if a woman fears from her husband perverseness or aversion, it is no crime in them both that they should be reconciled to each other, for reconciliation is best. For souls are prone to avarice; but if ye act kindly and fear Allah, of what ye do He is aware.

Ye are not able, it may be, to act equitably to your wives, even though ye covet it; do not however be quite partial, and leave one as it were in suspense; but if ye be reconciled and fear, then Allah is forgiving and merciful; but if they separate, Allah can make both independent out of His abundance; for Allah is abundant, wise.

[130] Allah's is what is in the heavens and what is in the earth! We have ordained to those who have been given the

Book before you, and to you too that ye fear Allah;—but if ye misbelieve, verily, Allah's is what is in the heavens and what is in the earth, and Allah is rich and to be praised!

Allah's is what is in the heavens and what is in the earth! and Allah sufficeth for a guardian!

If He will He can make ye pass away, O men! and can bring others;—Allah is able to do all that.

He who wishes for a reward in this world,—with Allah is the reward of this world and of the next, and Allah both hears and sees.

O ye who believe! be ye steadfast in justice, witnessing before Allah though it be against yourselves, or your parents, or your kindred, be it rich or poor, for Allah is nearer akin than either.

Follow not, then, lusts, so as to act partially; but if ye swerve or turn aside, Allah of what ye do is well aware.

[135] O ye who believe! believe in Allah and His apostles, and the Book which He hath revealed to His Apostle, and the Book which He sent down before; for whoso disbelieves in Allah, and His angels, and His Apostle, and the last day, has erred a wide error.

Verily, those who believe and then misbelieve, and then believe and then misbelieve, and then increase in misbelief, Allah will never pardon them, nor will He guide them in the path.

Give to the hypocrites the glad tidings that for them is grievous woe!

Those who take the misbelievers for their patrons rather than believers,—do they crave honour from them? Verily, honour is altogether Allah's!

He hath revealed this to you in the Book,[26] that when ye hear the signs of Allah disbelieved in and mocked at, then sit ye not down with them until they plunge into another discourse, for verily, then ye would be like them. Verily, Allah will gather the hypocrites and misbelievers into Hell together.

[140] Those who lie in wait for you, and if the victory be yours from Allah, say, 'Were we not with you?' and if the misbelievers have a chance, they say, 'Did we not get the mastery over you, and defend you from the believers?' But Allah shall judge between you on the resurrection day; for Allah will not give the misbelievers a way against believers.

Verily, the hypocrites seek to deceive Allah, but He deceives them; and when they rise up to pray, they rise up lazily to be seen of men, and do not remember Allah, except a few; wavering between the two, neither to these nor yet to those! but whomsoever Allah doth lead astray thou shall not find for him a way.

O ye who believe! take not misbelievers for patrons rather than believers; do ye wish to make for Allah a power against you?

Verily, the hypocrites are in the lowest depths of hell-fire, and thou shalt not find for them a help.

[145] Save those who turn again, and do right, and take tight hold on Allah, and are sincere in religion to Allah; these are with the believers, and Allah will give to the believers mighty hire.

Why should Allah punish you, if ye are grateful and believe? for Allah is grateful and knowing.

Allah loves not publicity of evil speech, unless one has been wronged; for Allah both hears and knows.

If ye display good or hide it, or pardon evil, verily, Allah is pardoning and powerful!

Verily, those who disbelieve in Allah and His apostles desire to make a distinction between Allah and His apostles, and say, 'We believe in part and disbelieve in part, and desire to take a midway course between the two': [150] these are the misbelievers, and we have prepared for misbelievers shameful woe! But those who believe in Allah and His apostles, and who do not make a distinction between any one of them,—to these we will give their hire, for Allah is forgiving and merciful!

The people of the Book will ask thee to bring down for them a book from heaven; but they asked Moses a greater thing than that, for they said, 'Show us Allah openly'; but the thunderbolt caught them in their injustice. Then they took the calf, after what had come to them of manifest signs; but we pardoned that, and gave Moses obvious authority. And we held over them the mountain[27] at their compact, and said to them, 'Enter ye the door adoring'; and we said to them, 'Transgress not on the Sabbath day,' and we took from them a rigid compact.

But for that they broke their compact, and for their misbelief in Allah's signs, and for their killing the prophets undeservedly, and for their saying, 'Our hearts are uncircumcised,'—nay, Allah hath stamped on them their misbelief, so that they cannot believe except a few,— [155] and for their misbelief, and for their saying about Mary a mighty calumny, and for their saying, 'Verily, we have killed the Messiah, Jesus the son of Mary, the apostle of Allah,' . . . but they did not kill him, and they did not crucify him, but a similitude was made for them. And verily, those who differ about him are in doubt concerning him; they have no knowledge concerning him, but only follow an opinion. They did not kill him, for sure! nay, Allah raised him up unto Himself; for Allah is mighty and wise![28]

And there shall not be one of the people of the Book but shall believe in him before his death;[29] and on the day of judgement he shall be a witness against them.

And for the injustice of those who are Jews have we forbidden them good things which we had made lawful for them, and for their obstructing so much the way of Allah, and for their taking usury when we had forbidden it, and for their devouring the wealth of people in vain,—but we have prepared for those of them who misbelieve a grievous woe.

[160] But those amongst them who are firm in knowledge, and the believers who believe in what is revealed to thee, let what is revealed before thee, and the steadfast in prayer, and the givers of alms, and the believers in Allah and the last day,—unto these we will give a mighty hire.

Verily, we have inspired thee as we inspired Noah and the prophets after him, and as we inspired Abraham, and Ishmael, and Jacob, and the tribes, and Jesus, and Job, and Jonas, and Aaron, and Solomon; and to David did we give Psalms.

Of apostles we have already told thee of some before; and of apostles some we have not told thee of;—

But Moses did Allah speak to, speaking;—apostles giving glad tidings and warning, that men should have no argument against Allah, after the apostles, for Allah is mighty, wise!

But Allah bears witness to what He has revealed to thee: He revealed it in His knowledge, and the angels bear witness too; though Allah is witness enough.

[165] Verily, those who misbelieve and obstruct the way of Allah, have erred a wide error.

Verily, those who misbelieve and are unjust, Allah will not pardon them, nor will He guide them on the road—save the road to Hell, to dwell therein for aye;—that is easy enough to Allah!

O ye folk! the Apostle has come to you with truth from your Lord: believe then, for it is better for you. But if ye misbelieve, then Allah's is what is in the heavens and the earth, and Allah is knowing, wise.

O ye people of the Book! do not exceed in your religion, nor say against Allah aught save the truth. The Messiah, Jesus the son of Mary, is but the apostle of Allah and His Word, which He cast into Mary and a spirit from Him; believe then in Allah and His apostles, and say not 'Three'. Have done! it were better for you. Allah is only one Allah, celebrated be His praise that He should beget a Son! His is what is in the heavens and what is in the earth; and Allah sufficeth for a guardian.

[170] The Messiah doth surely not disdain to be a servant of Allah, nor do the angels who are nigh to Him; and whosoever disdains His service and is too proud, He will gather them altogether to Himself.

But as for those who believe and do what is right, He will pay their hire and will give increase to them of His grace. But as for those who disdain and are too proud, He will punish them with a grievous woe, and they shall not find for them other than Allah a patron or a help.

O ye folk! proof has come to you from your Lord, and we have sent down to you manifest light. As for those who believe in Allah, and take tight hold of Him, He will make them enter into mercy from Him and grace; and He will guide them to Himself by a right way.

[175] They will ask thee for a decision; say, 'Allah will give you a decision concerning remote kinship.'[30]

If a man perish and have no child, but have a sister, let her have half of what he leaves; and he shall be her heir, if she have no son. But if there be two sisters, let them both have two thirds of what he leaves; and if there be brethren, both men and women, let the male have like the portion of two females. Allah makes this manifest to you lest ye err; for Allah all things doth know.

THE CHAPTER OF THE TABLE

V (*Medina*)

In the name of the merciful and compassionate Allah.

O ye who believe! fulfil your compacts.—Lawful for you are brute beasts, save what is here recited to you, not allowing you the chase while ye are on pilgrimage; verily, Allah ordaineth what He will.

O ye who believe! do not deem the monuments of Allah to be lawful, nor the sacred month,[1] nor the offering, nor its neck garlands, nor those who sojourn at the sacred house, craving grace from their Lord and His pleasure.

But when ye are in lawful state again, then chase; and let not ill will against the people who turned you from the Sacred Mosque[2] make you transgress; but help one another in righteousness and piety, and do not help one another to sin and enmity; but fear Allah,—verily, Allah is keen to punish.

Forbidden to you is that which dies of itself, and blood, and the flesh of swine, and that which is devoted to other than Allah, and the strangled and the knocked down, and that which falls down, and the gored, and what wild beasts have eaten—except what ye slaughter in time—and what is sacrificed to idols,[3] and dividing carcasses by arrows.[4]

Today shall those who disbelieve in your religion despair; do ye not then fear them, but fear me— [5] Today is perfected for you your religion, and fulfilled upon you is my favour, and I am pleased for you to have Islam for a religion. But he who is forced by hunger, not inclined wilfully to sin, verily, Allah is forgiving, compassionate.

They will ask thee what is lawful for them? Say, 'Lawful for you are good things and what ye have taught beasts of prey (to catch), training them like dogs;—ye teach them as Allah taught you;—so eat of what they catch for you, and mention the name of Allah over it, and fear Allah, for verily, Allah is swift in reckoning up.'

Lawful for you today are good things, and the food of those to whom the Book has been given is lawful for you, and your food is lawful for them; and chaste women of those who believe, and chaste women of those to whom the Book has been given before you,—when you have given them their hire, living chastely and not fornicating, and not taking paramours. But whoso disbelieves in the faith, of a truth his work is vain, and he shall be in the next life of those who lose.

O ye who believe! when ye rise up to prayer wash your faces, and your hands as far as the elbows, and wipe your heads, and your feet down to the ankles. And if ye are polluted, then purify yourselves. But if ye are sick, or on a journey, or if one of you comes from the privy, or if ye have touched women and cannot find water, then take fine surface sand and wipe your faces and your hands therewith. Allah does not wish to make any hindrance for you; but he wishes to purify you and to fulfil his favour upon you; haply ye may give thanks.

[10] Remember the favour of Allah to you and His covenant which He covenanted with you, when ye said, 'We hear and we obey';[5] and fear Allah, verily, Allah knows the nature of men's breasts.

O ye who believe! stand steadfast to Allah as witnesses with justice; and let not ill will towards people make you sin by not acting with equity. Act with equity, that is nearer to piety, and fear Allah; for Allah is aware of what ye do.

Allah has promised to those who believe and work righteousness, that for them is pardon and a mighty hire.

But those who disbelieve and call our signs lies, these are the fellows of Hell.

O ye who believe! remember Allah's favour towards you, when a people intended to stretch their hands against you, but He withheld their hands from you;[6] and upon Allah let believers rely.

[15] Allah did take a compact from the children of Israel, and raised up of them twelve wardens; and Allah said, 'Verily, I am with you, if ye be steadfast in prayer, and give alms, and believe in my apostles, and assist them, and lend to Allah a goodly loan; then will I cover your offences and make you enter gardens beneath which rivers flow: and whoso disbelieves after that, he hath erred from the level way.'

And for that they broke their compact, we cursed them, and placed in their hearts hardness, so that they perverted the words from their places, and forgot a portion of what they were reminded of.[7]

But thou wilt not cease to light upon treachery amongst them, save a few of them; but pardon them and shun them; verily, Allah loves the kind.

And of those who say, 'Verily, we are Christians,' we have taken a compact; but they have forgotten a portion of what they were reminded of; wherefore have we excited amongst them enmity and hatred till the resurrection day; but Allah will tell them of what they have done.

O ye people of the Book! our Apostle has come to you to explain to you much of what ye had hidden of the Book, and to pardon much. There has come to you from Allah a light, and a perspicuous Book; Allah guides thereby those who follow His pleasure to the way of peace, and brings them into a right way.

They misbelieve who say, 'Verily, Allah is the Messiah the son of Mary'; say, 'Who has any hold on Allah, if he wished to destroy the Messiah the son of Mary, and his mother, and those who are on earth altogether?'

[20] Allah's is the kingdom of the heavens and the earth and what is between the two; He createth what He will, for Allah is mighty over all!

But the Jews and the Christians say, 'We are the sons of Allah and His beloved.' Say, 'Why then does He punish you for your sins? Nay, ye are mortals of those whom He has created! He pardons whom He pleases, and punishes whom He pleases; for Allah's is the kingdom of the heavens and the earth, and what is between the two, and unto Him the journey is.'

O people of the Book! our Apostle has come to you, explaining to you the interval of apostles; lest ye say, 'There came not to us a herald of glad tidings nor a warner.' But there has come to you now a herald of glad tidings and a warner, and Allah is mighty over all!

When Moses said to his people, 'O my people! remember the favour of Allah towards you when He made amongst you prophets, and made for you kings, and brought you what never was brought to anybody in the worlds. O my people! enter the Holy Land which Allah has prescribed for you; and be ye not thrust back upon your hinder parts and retreat losers': [25] They said, 'O Moses! verily, therein is a people, giants; and we will surely not enter therein until they go out from thence; but if they go out then we will enter in.' Then said two men of those who fear,—Allah had been gracious to them both,—'Enter ye upon them by the door, and when ye have entered it, verily, ye shall be victorious; and upon Allah do ye rely if ye be believers.' They said, 'O Moses! we shall never enter it so long as they are therein; so, go thou and thy Lord and fight ye twain; verily, we will sit down here.' Said he, 'My Lord, verily, I can control only myself and my brother; therefore part us from these sinful people.' He said, 'Then, verily, it is forbidden them; for forty years shall they wander about in the earth; so vex not thyself for the sinful people.'

[30] Recite to them the story of the two sons of Adam; truly when they offered an offering and it was accepted from one of them, and was not accepted from the other, that one said, 'I will surely kill thee'; he said, 'Allah only accepts from those who fear. If thou dost stretch forth to me thine hand to kill me, I will not stretch forth mine hand to kill thee; verily, I fear Allah the Lord of the worlds; verily, I wish that thou mayest draw upon thee my sin and thy sin, and be of the fellows of the Fire, for that is the reward of the unjust.' But his soul allowed him to slay his brother, and he slew him, and in the morning he was of those who lose. And Allah sent a crow to scratch in the earth and show him how he might hide his brother's shame, he said, 'Alas, for me! Am I too helpless to become like this crow and hide my brother's shame?' and in the morning he was of those who did repent.

[35] For this cause have we prescribed to the children of Israel that whoso kills a soul, unless it be for another soul or for violence in the land, it is as though he had

killed men altogether; but whoso saves one, it is as though he saved men altogether.

Our apostles came to them with manifest signs; then, verily, many of them did after that commit excesses in the earth.

The reward of those who make war against Allah and His Apostle, and strive after violence in the earth, is only that they shall be slaughtered or crucified, or their hands cut off and their feet on alternate sides, or that they shall be banished from the land;—that is a disgrace for them in this world, and for them in the next is mighty woe; save for those who repent before ye have them in your power, for know ye that Allah is forgiving, merciful.

O ye who believe! fear Allah and crave the means to approach Him, and be strenuous in His way, haply ye will prosper then.

[40] Verily, those who disbelieve, even though they had what is in the earth, all of it, and the like thereof with it, to offer as a ransom from the punishment of the resurrection day, it would not be accepted from them; but for them is grievous woe. They may wish to go forth from the Fire, but they shall not go forth therefrom, for them is lasting woe.

The man thief and the woman thief, cut off the hands of both as a punishment, for that they have erred;—an example from Allah, for Allah is mighty, wise.

But whoso turns again after his injustice and acts aright, verily, Allah will turn to him, for, verily, Allah is forgiving, merciful.

Do ye not know that Allah, His is the kingdom of the

heavens and the earth; He punishes whom He pleases, and forgives whom He pleases, for Allah is mighty over all?

[45] O thou Apostle! let not those grieve thee who vie in misbelief; or those who say with their mouths 'We believe', but their hearts do not believe; or of those who are Jews, listeners to a lie,—listeners to other people, but who come not to thee. They pervert the words from their places and say, 'If this is what ye are given, take it; but if ye are not given it, then beware!' But he whom Allah wishes to mislead, thou canst do nothing with Allah for him; these are those whose hearts Allah wishes not to purify, for them in this world is disgrace, and for them in the next is mighty woe,—listeners to a lie, eaters of unlawful things!

But if they come to thee, then judge between them or turn aside from them; but if thou turnest aside from them they shall not harm thee at all, but if thou judgest, then judge between them with justice, verily, Allah loves the just. But how should they make thee their judge, when they have the law wherein is Allah's judgement? Yet they turn back after that, for they do not believe.

Verily, we have revealed the law in which is guidance and light; the prophets who were resigned did judge thereby those who were Jews, as did the masters[8] and doctors by what they remembered of the Book of Allah and by what they were witnesses of. Fear not men, but fear me, and sell not my signs for a little price; for whoso will not judge by what Allah has revealed, these be the misbelievers.

We have prescribed for thee therein 'a life for a life, and

an eye for an eye, and a nose for a nose, and an ear for an ear, and a tooth for a tooth, and for wounds retaliation'; but whoso remits it, it is an expiation for him, but he whoso will not judge by what Allah has revealed, these be the unjust.

[50] And we followed up the footsteps of these (prophets) with Jesus the son of Mary, confirming that which was before him and the law, and we brought him the gospel, wherein is guidance and light, verifying what was before it of the law, and a guidance and an admonition unto those who fear.

Then let the people of the gospel judge by that which is revealed therein, for whoso will not judge by what Allah has revealed, these be the evil-doers.

We have revealed to thee the Book in truth verifying what was before it, and preserving it; judge then between them by what Allah has revealed, and follow not their lusts, turning away from what is given to thee of the truth.

For each one of you have we made a law and a pathway; and had Allah pleased He would have made you one nation, but He will surely try you concerning that which He has brought you. Be ye therefore emulous in good deeds; to Allah is your return altogether, and He will let you know concerning that wherein ye do dispute.

Wherefore judge thou between them by what Allah has revealed, and follow not their lusts; but beware lest they mislead thee from part of what Allah has revealed to thee; yet if they turn back, then know that Allah wishes to fall on them for some sins of theirs,—verily, many men are evil-doers.

[55] Is it the judgement of the Ignorance they crave?[9] But who is better than Allah to judge for people who are sure?

O ye who believe! take not the Jews and Christians for your patrons: they are patrons of each other; but whoso amongst you takes them for patrons, verily, he is of them, and, verily, Allah guides not an unjust people.

Thou wilt see those in whose hearts is a sickness vying with them; they say, 'We fear lest there befall us a reverse.' It may be Allah will give the victory, or an order from Himself, and they may awake repenting of what they thought in secret to themselves.

Those who believe say, 'Are these they who swore by Allah with their most strenuous oath that they were surely with you?'—their works are in vain and they shall wake the losers.

O ye who believe! whoso is turned away from his religion—Allah will bring (instead) a people[10] whom He loves and who love Him, lowly to believers, lofty to unbelievers, strenuous in the way of Allah, fearing not the blame of him who blames. That is Allah's grace! He gives it unto whom He pleases, for Allah both comprehends and knows.

[60] Allah only is your patron, and His Apostle and those who believe, who are steadfast in prayer and give alms, bowing down. Whoso taketh as patrons Allah and His apostles and those who believe;—verily, Allah's crew, they are victorious!

O ye who believe! take not for patrons those who take your religion for a jest or a sport, from amongst those who have been given the Book before and the misbelievers; but fear Allah if ye be believers. Nor those who, when ye call to prayer, take it for a jest and a sport; that is because they are a people who do not understand.

Say, 'O people of the Book! do ye disavow us, for aught but that we believe in Allah, and what was revealed to us before, and for that most of you are evil-doers?'

[65] Say, 'Can I declare unto you something worse than retribution from Allah?' Whomsoever Allah has cursed and been wroth with—and he has made of them apes and swine—and who worship Tâghût, they are in a worse plight and are more erring from the level path. When they come to you they say, 'We believe'; but they entered in with unbelief, and they went out therewith, and Allah knows best what they did hide.

Thou wilt see many of them vying in sin and enmity, and in eating unlawful things,—evil is it that they have done. The masters and their doctors prohibit them from speaking sin and eating unlawful things,—evil is what they have performed.

The Jews say, 'Allah's hand is fettered'; their hands are fettered and they are cursed for what they said; nay! His hands are outspread, He expends how He pleases! and that which has been sent down to thee from thy Lord will surely increase many of them in their rebellion and misbelief, for we have cast amongst them enmity and hatred till the resurrection day. Whenever they light a fire[11] for war, Allah puts it out; they strive for corruption in the earth, but Allah loves not the corrupt.

[70] But did the people of the Book believe and fear, we

would cover their offences, and we would make them enter into gardens of pleasure; and were they steadfast in the law and the gospel, and what has been sent down to them from their Lord, they should eat from above them and below them. Amongst them are a nation who are moderate, but many of them—bad is what they do.

O thou Apostle! preach what has been revealed to thee from they Lord; if thou do it not thou hast not preached His message, and Allah will not hold thee free from men; for Allah guides not people who misbelieve.

Say, 'O people of the Book! ye rest on naught until ye stand fast by the law and the gospel, and what is revealed to you from your Lord.' But what has been revealed to thee from thy Lord will of a surety increase many of them in rebellion and misbelief, vex not thyself then for a people who misbelieve.

Verily, those who believe and those who are Jews, and the Sabæans, and the Christians, whosoever believes in Allah and the last day, and does what is right, there is no fear for them, nor shall they grieve.

We took a compact of the children of Israel, and we sent to them apostles; every time there came to them an apostle with what their souls loved not, a part of them they did call liars and a part of them they slew.

[75] And they reckoned that there would be no disturbance; but they were blind and deaf! and then Allah turned again towards them: and then many amongst them were blind and deaf! but Allah saw what they did.

They misbelieve who say, 'Verily, Allah is the Messiah the son of Mary'; but the Messiah said, 'O children of

Israel! worship Allah, my Lord and your Lord'; verily, he who associates aught with Allah, Allah hath forbidden him Paradise, and his resort is the Fire, and the unjust shall have none to help them.

They misbelieve who say, 'Verily, Allah is the third of three'; for there is no Allah but one, and if they do not desist from what they say, there shall touch those who misbelieve amongst them grievous woe.

Will they not turn again towards Allah and ask pardon of Him? for Allah is forgiving and merciful.

The Messiah the son of Mary is only a prophet: prophets before him have passed away; and his mother was a confessor; they used both to eat food.—See how we explain to them the signs, yet see how they turn aside!

[80] Say, 'Will ye serve, other than Allah, what can neither hurt you nor profit you?' but Allah, He both hears and knows.

Say, 'O people of the Book! exceed not the truth in your religion, and follow not the lusts of a people who have erred before, and who lead many astray, and who go away from the level path.'

Those of the children of Israel who disbelieved were cursed by the tongue of David and Jesus the son of Mary; that is because they rebelled and did transgress; they would not desist from the wrong they did; evil is that which they did. Thou wilt see many of them taking those who disbelieve for their patrons; evil is that which their souls have sent before them, for Allah's wrath is on them, and in the torment shall they dwell for aye. But had they believed in Allah and the prophet, and what was revealed to him, they had not taken these for their patrons; but many of them are evil-doers.

[85] Thou wilt surely find that the strongest in enmity against those who believe are the Jews and the idolaters; and thou wilt find the nearest in love to those who believe to be those who say, 'We are Christians'; that is because there are amongst them priests and monks, and because they are not proud.

And when they hear what has been revealed to the prophet, you will see their eyes gush with tears at what they recognize as truth therein; and they will say, 'O our Lord! we believe, so write us down amongst the witnesses. Why should we not believe in Allah and the truth that is given to us, nor desire that our Lord should make us enter with the upright people?'

Therefore has Allah rewarded them, for what they said, with gardens beneath which rivers flow, to dwell therein for aye; that is the reward of those who do good; but those who disbelieve and say our signs are lies, they are the fellows of Hell.

O ye who believe! forbid not the good things which Allah has made lawful for you, nor transgress; verily, Allah loves not the transgressors.

[90] But eat of what Allah has provided you lawfully of good things; and fear Allah, in whom ye believe.

Allah will not catch you up for a casual word in your oaths, but He will catch you up for having what ye make deliberate oaths about; and the expiation thereof is to feed ten poor men with the middling food ye feed your families withal, or to clothe them, or to free a neck;[12] but he who has not the means, then let him fast three days. That is the expiation of your oaths, when ye have sworn to keep your oaths; thus does Allah explain to you His signs,—haply ye may be grateful.

O ye who believe! verily, wine, and *el mâisar*,[13] and statues,[14] and divining (arrows) are only an abomination of Satan's work; avoid them then that haply ye may prosper. Satan only desires to place enmity and hatred between you by wine and *mâisar*, and to turn you from the remembrance of Allah and from prayer; but will ye not desist, and obey Allah, and obey the apostles, and beware, for if ye turn back then know that our Apostle has only his message to preach?

There is no crime in those who believe and do right, for having tasted food, when they fear Allah, and believe, and do what is right, and then fear Him, and believe, and then fear, and do good, for Allah loves those who do good.

[95] O ye who believe! Allah will try you with something of the game that your hands and your lances take, that Allah may know who fears Him in secret; and whoso transgresses after that, for him is grievous woe.

O ye who believe! kill not game while ye are on pilgrimage. But he amongst you who kills it purposely, his compensation is the like of that which he has killed, in sheep—of which two equitable persons amongst you shall be judge—an offering brought to the Kaabah; or as an expiation, the food of poor persons, or an equivalent thereof in fasting, that he may taste the evil result of his deed. Allah pardons bygones; but whoso returns, Allah will take vengeance on him, for Allah is mighty and the avenger.

Lawful for you is the game of the sea, and to eat thereof; a provision for you and for travellers; but forbidden you is the game of the land while ye are on pilgrimage; so fear Allah to whom ye shall be gathered.

Allah has made the Kaabah, the sacred House, to be a station for men, and the sacred month, and the offering and its neck garland; this is that ye may know that Allah knows what is in the heavens and what is in the earth, and that Allah knows all things. Know that Allah is keen to punish, but that Allah is forgiving, merciful.

The Apostle has only to preach his message, but Allah knows what ye show and what ye hide.

[100] Say, 'The vile shall not be deemed equal with the good, although the abundance of the vile please thee.' Fear Allah then, O ye who have minds! haply ye may prosper.

O ye who believe! ask not about things which if they be shown to you will pain you; but if ye ask about them when the (whole) Qur'ân is revealed, they shall be shown to you. Allah pardons that, for Allah is forgiving and clement. People before you have asked about that, yet on the morrow did they disbelieve therein.

And Allah has not ordained any *ba'hîrah* or *sâibah*, nor *wazîlah* nor *'hâmî*,¹⁵ but those who misbelieve invent a lie against Allah, for most of them do not understand.

And when it is said to them, 'Come round to what Allah has revealed unto His Apostle,' they say, 'Enough for us is what we found our fathers agreed upon.' What! though their fathers knew nothing and were not guided.

O ye who believe! mind yourselves; he who errs can do you no hurt when ye are guided: unto Allah is your return altogether, and He will declare to you that which ye do not know.

[105] O ye who believe! let there be a testimony between you when any one of you is on the point of death—at the time he makes his will—two equitable persons from amongst you; or two others from some other folk, if ye be knocking about in the land, and the calamity of death befall you; ye shall shut them both up after prayer, and they shall both swear by Allah, if ye doubt them, (saying), 'We will not sell (our testimony) for a price, though it were to a relative, nor will we hide Allah's testimony, verily, then, we should be among sinners.' But if it shall be lit upon that they too have deserved the imputation of sin, then let two others stand up in their place with those who think them deserving of the imputation, the nearest two in kin, and they shall both swear by Allah, 'Indeed, our testimony is truer than the testimony of those two, and we have not transgressed, for then we should surely be of the unjust': thus is it easier for men to bear testimony according to the purport thereof, else must they fear lest an oath be given to rebut their own oath; but let them fear Allah and listen, for Allah guides not the people who do ill.

On the day when Allah shall assemble the apostles and shall say, 'How were ye answered?' they will say, 'We have no knowledge; verily, thou art He who knoweth the unseen.'

When Allah said, 'O Jesus, son of Mary! remember my favours towards thee and towards thy mother, when I aided thee with the Holy Ghost, till thou didst speak to men in the cradle and when grown up.

[110] 'And when I taught thee the Book and wisdom and the law and the gospel; when thou didst create of clay, as it were, the likeness of a bird, by my power, and didst blow thereon, it became a bird; and thou didst heal the blind from birth, and the leprous by my permission; and when thou didst bring forth the dead by my permission; and when I did ward off the children of Israel from thee, when thou didst come to them with manifest signs, and those who misbelieved amongst them said, "This is naught but obvious magic."

'And when I inspired the apostles that they should believe in him and in my Apostle, they said, "We believe; do thou bear witness that we are resigned." '

When the apostles said, 'O Jesus, son of Mary! is thy Lord able to send down to us a table from heaven?' he said, 'Fear Allah, if ye be believers'; and they said, 'We desire to eat therefrom that our hearts may be at rest, and that we may know that what thou hast told us is the truth, and that we may be thereby amongst the witnesses.' Said Jesus the son of Mary, 'O Allah, our Lord! send down to us a table from heaven to be to us a festival,—to the first of us and to the last, and a sign from Thee,—and grant us provision, for Thou art the best of providers.'

[115] Allah said, 'Verily, I am about to send it down to you; but whoso disbelieves amongst you after that, verily, I will torment him with the torment which I have not tormented any one with in all the worlds.'

And when Allah said, 'O Jesus, son of Mary! is it thou who didst say to men, take me and my mother for two gods, beside Allah?' He said, 'I celebrate Thy praise! what ails me that I should say what I have no right to? If I had said it, Thou wouldst have known it; Thou knowest what is in my soul, but I know not what is in Thy soul; verily, Thou art one who knoweth the unseen. I never told them save what Thou didst bid me,—"Worship Allah, my Lord and your Lord," and I was a witness against them so long as I was amongst them; but when Thou didst take me away to thyself Thou wert the watcher over them, for Thou art witness over all. If Thou shouldst punish them, verily, they are Thy servants; if Thou shouldst forgive them, verily, Thou art the mighty and the wise.' Allah said, 'This is the day when their confession shall profit the confessors, for them are gardens beneath which rivers flow, to dwell therein for ever and for aye.'

Allah is well pleased with them, and they well pleased with Him; that is the mighty happiness.

[120] Allah's is the kingdom of the heavens, and the earth, and all that is therein, and He is mighty over all.

THE CHAPTER OF CATTLE[1]

VI (Mecca)

In the name of the merciful and compassionate Allah!

Praise belongs to Allah who created the heavens and the earth, and brought into being the darkness and the light.[2] Yet do those who misbelieve hold Him to have peers.

He it is who created you from clay; then He decreed a

term,—a term³ ordained with Him. And yet ye doubt thereof.

He is Allah in the heavens and the earth. He knows your secret conduct and your plain, and He knows what ye earn.⁴

There came not to them any sign of the signs of their Lord, but they turned away; [5] and they have called the truth a lie now that it has come to them, but there shall come to them the message of that at which they mocked.

Do not they see how many a generation we have destroyed before them, whom we had settled in the earth as we have not settled for you, and sent the rain of heaven upon them in copious showers, and made the waters flow beneath them? Then we destroyed them in their sins, and raised up other generations after them.

Had we sent down to thee a book on paper, and they had touched it with their hands, still those who misbelieve would have said, 'This is naught but obvious magic.' They say, 'Why has not an angel been sent down to him?' but if we had sent down an angel, the affair would have been decided, and then they would have had no respite.

And had we made him⁵ an angel, we should have made him as a man too; and we would have made perplexing for them that which they deem perplexing now.

[10] There have been prophets before thee mocked at, but that encompassed them which the scoffers among them mocked at.

Say, 'Go about in the earth, then wilt thou see how has been the end of those who called them liars.'

Say, 'Whose is what is in the heavens and the earth?'

Say, 'Allah's, who has imposed mercy on himself.' He will surely gather you together for the resurrection day. There is no doubt in that, but those who waste their souls[6] will not believe.

His is whatsoever dwells in the night or in the day, He both hears and knows.

Say, 'Other than Allah shall I take for a patron, the Originator of the heavens and the earth? He feedeth men, but is not fed.' Say, 'I am bidden to be the first of those resigned'; and it was said to me, 'Be not thou of the idolaters.' [15] Say, 'I fear, if I rebel against my Lord, the torment of the mighty day.'

Whomsoever it is averted from on that day, Allah will have had mercy on; and that is obvious happiness.

And if Allah touch thee with harm, there is none to take it off but He; and if He touch thee with good, He is mighty over all. He is sovereign over His servants, He is the wise, the aware!

Say, 'What is the greatest witness?' Say, 'Allah is witness between you and me.' This Qur'ân was inspired to me to warn you and those it reaches. Do ye really bear witness that with Allah are other gods? Say, 'I bear not witness thereto': say, 'He is but one Allah, and I am clear of your associating (gods with him).'

[20] Those to whom we have brought the Book know him[7] as they know their sons;—those who lose their souls do not believe.

Who is more unjust than he who forges against Allah a lie, or says His signs are lies? Verily, the unjust shall not prosper.

On the day when we shall gather them all together, then shall we say to those who have associated others with ourself, 'Where are your associates whom ye did pretend?' Then they will have no excuse but to say, 'By Allah our Lord, we did not associate (others with thee)!' See how they lie against themselves, and how what they did forge deserts them! [25] And they are some who listen unto thee, but we have placed a veil upon their hearts lest they should understand it, and in their ears is dulness of hearing; and though they saw each sign they would not believe therein; until when they come to thee to wrangle with thee, the unbelievers say, 'These are but old folks' tales.'

They forbid it and they avoid it;—but they destroy none but themselves; yet they do not perceive.

But couldst thou see when they are set over the Fire and say, 'Would that we were sent back! We would not call our Lord's signs lies, but we would be of the believers.' Nay! now is shown to them what they did hide before; and could they be sent back, they would return to that they were forbidden, for they are very liars.

They say there is naught but this life of ours in the world and we shall not be raised. [30] But couldst thou see when they are set before their Lord; he says, 'Is not this the truth?' They say, 'Yea, by our Lord!' he says, 'Then taste the torment, for that ye did misbelieve!'

Losers are they who disbelieved in meeting Allah, until when the hour comes suddenly upon them they say, 'Woe is us for our neglect thereof!' for they shall bear their burdens on their backs, evil is what they bear.

The life of this world is nothing but a game and a sport,

and surely the next abode were better for those who fear. What! do they not understand?

Full well we know that verily that which they say grieves thee; but they do not call thee only a liar, for the unjust gainsay the signs of Allah. Called liars too were apostles before thee; but they were patient of being called liars and of being hurt until our help came to them; for there is none to change the words of Allah—now has there come to thee the story of those He sent.

[35] And if their turning from thee be hard for thee, and if thou canst seek for a shaft down into the earth, or a ladder up into the sky, to bring them a sign—but if Allah pleased He would bring them all to guidance, be thou not then of the ignorant.

He only answers the prayer of those who listen; but the dead will Allah raise up, then unto Him shall they return. They say, 'Unless there be sent down some sign from his Lord'—say, 'Verily, Allah is able to send down a sign, but most of them do not know.'

There is not a beast upon the earth nor a bird that flies with both its wings, but is a nation like to you; we have omitted nothing from the Book; then to their Lord shall they be gathered. Those who say our signs are lies— deafness, dumbness, in the dark! whom He pleases does Allah lead astray, and whom He pleases He places on the right way.

[40] Say, 'Look you now! if there should come Allah's torment, or there should come to you the hour, on other than Allah would ye call, if ye do tell the truth?' Nay, it is on Him that ye would call, and He will avert that which

ye call upon Him for if He but please; and ye shall forget that which ye did associate with Him.

Ere this we sent unto nations before thee, and we caught them in distress and trouble that haply they might humble themselves. And do they not, when our violence falls upon them, humble themselves?—but their hearts were hard, and Satan made seemly to them that which they had done.

And when they forgot what they were reminded of, we opened for them the gates of everything, until when they rejoiced at what they had, we caught them up suddenly, and lo! they were in despair.

[45] And the uttermost part of the people who did wrong were cut off; praise be to Allah, Lord of the worlds!

Say, 'Look you now! if Allah should catch your hearing and your sight, and should set a seal upon your hearts—who is god but Allah to bring you it again?'

Say, 'Look you now! if Allah's torment should come upon you suddenly or openly, would any perish save the people who do wrong?'

We do not send our messengers save as heralds of glad tidings and of warning, and whoso believes and acts aright, there is no fear for them, and they shall not be grieved, but those who say our signs are lies, torment shall touch them, for that they have done so wrong.

[50] Say, 'I do not say to you, mine are the treasuries of Allah, nor that I know the unseen; I do not say to you, I am an angel—if I follow aught but what I am inspired with—': say, 'Is the blind equal to him who sees—?' What! do ye not reflect?

Admonish therewith those who fear that they shall be gathered unto their Lord; there is no patron for them but Him, and no intercessor; haply they may fear.

Repulse not those who call upon their Lord in the morning and in the evening, desiring His face; they have no reckoning against thee at all, and thou hast no reckoning against them at all;—repulse them and thou wilt be of the unjust.

So have we tried some of them by others, that they may say, 'Are these those unto whom Allah has been gracious amongst ourselves?' Does not Allah know those who give thanks?

And when those who believe in our signs come to thee, say, 'Peace be on you! Allah hath prescribed for Himself mercy; verily, he of you who does evil in ignorance, and then turns again and does right,—verily, He is forgiving and merciful.'

[55] Thus do we detail our signs, that the way of the sinners may be made plain.

Say, 'I am forbidden to worship those ye call upon beside Allah'; say, 'I will not follow your lusts, for then should I err and not be of the guided.'

Say, 'I stand on a manifestation from my Lord, which ye call a lie. I have not with me what ye fain would hasten on, that the matter might be settled between me and you; but Allah knows best who are the unjust.'

With Him are the keys[8] of the unseen. None knows them save He; He knows what is in the land and in the sea; and there falls not a leaf save that He knows it; nor a grain in the darkness of the earth, nor aught that is moist, nor aught that is dry, save that is in His perspicuous Book.

[60] He it is who takes you to Himself at night,9 and knows what ye have gained in the day; then He raises you up again, that your appointed time may be fulfilled; then unto Him is your return, and then will He inform you of what ye have done.

He triumphs over His servants; He sends to them guardian angels, until, when death comes to any one of you, our messengers take him away; they pass not over any one, and then are they returned to Allah, their true sovereign.

Is not His the rule? but He is very quick at reckoning up.

Say, 'Who rescues you from the darkness of the land and of the sea?' ye call upon Him in humility and in secret, 'Indeed, if He would rescue us from this, we will surely be of those who give Him thanks.' Say, 'Allah rescues from the darkness thereof, and from every trouble, yet ye associate others with Him.'

[65] Say, 'He is able to send torment on you from above you and from beneath your feet, and to confuse you in sects, and to make some of you taste the violence of others.'

See how we turn about the signs, that haply they may discriminate. Thy people called it a lie, and yet it is the truth. Say, 'I have not charge over you; to every prophecy is a set time, and in the end ye shall know.'

When thou dost see those who plunge deeply into the discussion of our signs, turn from them until they plunge deeply into some other discourse; for it may be that Satan may make thee forget; but sit not, after thou hast remembered, with the unjust people.

Those who fear are not bound to take account of them at all, but mind!—haply they may fear.

Leave those who have taken their religion for a play and a sport, whom this world's life hath deceived, and remind them thereby that a soul shall be given up for what it has earned; nor has it, beside Allah, patron or intercessor; and though it should compensate with the fullest compensation, it would not be accepted. Those who are given up for what they have gained, for them is a drink of boiling water, and grievous woe for that they have mis-believed.

[70] Say, 'Shall we call on what neither profits us nor harms us, and be thrown back upon our heels after Allah has guided us, like him whom Satan hath led away bewildered in the earth, who has companions who call him to guidance, "Come to us"?' Say, 'Verily, Allah's guidance is the guidance, and we are bidden to resign ourselves unto the Lord of the worlds, and be ye steadfast in prayer and fear Him, for He it is to whom we shall be gathered.'

He it is who has created the heavens and the earth in truth; and on the day when He says, 'BE', then it is. His word is truth; to Him is the kingdom on the day when the trumpets shall be blown; the knower of the unseen and of the evident; He is wise and well aware.

When Abraham said to his father Âzar,[10] 'Dost thou take idols for gods? Verily, I see thee and thy people in obvious error.' [75] Thus did we show Abraham the kingdom of heaven and of the earth, that he should be of those who are sure. And when the night overshadowed him he saw a star and said, 'This is my Lord'; but when it set he said, 'I love not those that set.' And when he saw the moon beginning to rise he said, 'This is my Lord'; but when it set he said, 'If Allah my Lord guides me not I shall surely be of the people who err.' And when he saw the sun beginning to rise he said, 'This is my Lord, this is greatest of all'; but when it set he said, 'O my people! verily, I am clear of what ye associate with Allah; verily, I have turned my face to him who originated the heaven and the earth, as a *hanîf*, and I am not of the idolaters.' [80] And his people disputed with him;—he said, 'Do ye dispute with me concerning Allah, when He has guided me? but I fear not what ye associate with Him unless my Lord should wish for anything. My Lord doth comprehend all things in His knowledge, will ye not then remember? How should I fear what ye associate with Him, when ye yourselves fear not to associate with Allah what He has sent down to you no power to do? Which then of the two sects is worthier of belief, if indeed ye know?'

Those who believe and do not obscure their faith with wrong, they are those who shall have security, and they are guided.

These are our arguments which we gave to Abraham against his people;—we raise the rank of whom we will; verily, thy Lord is wise and knowing. And we gave to him Isaac and Jacob, each did we guide. And Noah we guided before and all his seed,—David and Solomon and Job and Joseph and Moses and Aaron,—for thus do we reward those who do good. [85] And Zachariah and John and Jesus and Elias, all righteous ones; and Ishmael and Elisha and Jonas and Lot, each one have we preferred above the worlds; and of their fathers and their seed and brethren; we have chosen them and guided them into a right way.

That is Allah's guidance; He guides those whom He will of His servants; and if they associate aught with Him,—vain is that which they have worked.

It is to these we give the Book and judgement and prophecy; and if these disbelieve therein we have given them in charge to a people who shall not disbelieve.

[90] It is these that Allah hath guided, and by their guidance be thou led.

Say, 'I will not ask you for it a hire: it is naught save a reminder to the worlds.'

They do not prize Allah at His true worth when they say, 'Allah has never revealed to mortal anything.' Say, 'Who revealed the Book wherewith Moses came, a light and a guidance unto men? Ye put it on papers which ye show, though ye hide much;[11] and ye are taught what ye knew not, neither you nor your fathers.' Say, 'Allah', then leave them in their discussion to play.

This is the Book which we have revealed, a blessing and a confirmation to those which were before it, and that the mother of cities[12] may be warned, with those who are round about her. Those who believe in the last day believe therein, and they unto their prayers will keep.

Who is more unjust than he who devises against Allah a lie, or says, 'I am inspired,'[13] when he was not inspired at all? and who says, 'I will bring down the like of what

Allah has sent down'; but didst thou see when the unjust are in the floods of death, and the angels stretch forth their hands, 'Give ye forth your souls; today shall ye be recompensed with the torment of disgrace, for that ye did say against Allah what was not true, and were too proud to hear His signs.¹⁴ And ye come now single-handed as we created you at first, and ye have left behind your backs that which we granted you; and we see not with you your intercessors whom ye pretended were partners¹⁵ amongst you; betwixt you have the ties been cut asunder; and strayed away from you is what ye did pretend.'

[95] Verily, Allah it is who cleaves out the grain and the date stone; He brings forth the living from the dead, and it is He who brings the dead from the living. There is Allah! how then can ye be beguiled?

He it is who cleaves out the morning, and makes night a repose, and the sun and the moon two reckonings—that is the decree of the mighty, the wise!

He it is who made for you stars that ye might be guided thereby in the darkness of the land and of the sea. Now have we detailed the signs unto a people who do know.

He it is who made you spring from one soul, and gave you a settlement and a depository.¹⁶ Now have we detailed the signs unto a people who discern.

He it is who sends down from the heavens water; and we bring forth therewith growths of everything; and we bring forth therefrom green things, wherefrom we bring forth grain in full ear; and the palm, from its spathe come clusters within reach; and gardens of grapes and olives and pomegranates, alike and unlike;—behold its fruit when it fruits and ripens! Verily, in that ye have a sign for the people who believe.

[100] Yet they made the jinn[17] partners with Allah, though He created them! and they ascribed to Him sons and daughters, though they have no knowledge; celebrated be His praise! and exalted be He above what they attribute to Him! The inventor of the heavens and the earth! how can He have a son, when He has no female companion, and when He has created everything, and everything He knows?

There is Allah for you,—your Lord! There is no god but He, the Creator of everything; then worship Him, for He o'er everything keeps guard!

Sight perceives Him not, but He perceives men's sights; for He is the subtle, the aware.

Now has an insight from your Lord come unto you, and he who looks therewith it is for himself; but he who is blind thereto, it is against his soul; and I am not your keeper.

[105] Thus do we turn about the signs, that they may say, 'Thou hast studied,' and that we may explain to those who know.

Follow what is revealed to thee from thy Lord; there is no god but He, and shun the idolaters.

But had Allah pleased, they would not have associated aught with Him; but we have not made thee a keeper over them, nor art thou for them a warder.

Do not abuse those who call on other than Allah, for then they may abuse Allah openly in their ignorance. So do we make seemly to every nation their work, then unto their Lord is their return, and He will inform them of what they have done.

They swore by Allah with their most strenuous oath, that if there come to them a sign they will indeed believe therein. Say, 'Signs are only in Allah's hands;—but what will make you understand that even when one has come, they will not believe?'

[110] We will overturn their hearts and their eyesights, even as they believed not at first; and we will leave them, in their rebellion, blindly wandering on.

And had we sent down unto them the angels, or the dead had spoken to them, or we had gathered everything unto them in hosts,[18] they would not have believed unless that Allah pleased—but most of them are ignorant.

So have we made for every prophet an enemy,—devils of men and jinns; some of them inspire others with specious speech to lead astray; but had thy Lord pleased they would not have done it; so leave them with what they do devise.

And let the hearts of those who believe not in the hereafter listen to it; and let them be well pleased with it; and let them gain what they may gain!

Of other than Allah shall I crave a decree, when it is He who has sent down to you the Book in detail, and those to whom we gave the Book know that it is sent down from thy Lord, in truth? Be thou not then of those who doubt.

[115] The words of thy Lord are fulfilled in truth and justice; there is none to change His words, for He both hears and knows.

But if thou followest most of those who are in the land, they will lead thee astray from the path of Allah; they only follow suspicion and they only (rest on) conjecture.

Thy Lord, He knows best who errs from His path, and He knows best the guided.

Eat then of what Allah's name has been pronounced over, if ye believe in His signs. What ails you that ye do not eat from what Allah's name is pronounced over, when He has detailed to you what is unlawful for you? Save what ye are forced to; but, verily, many will lead you astray by their fancies, without knowledge. Verily, thy Lord knows best the transgressors.

[120] Leave alone the outside of sin and the inside thereof; verily, those who earn sin shall be recompensed for what they have gained.

But eat not of what the name of Allah has not been pronounced over, for, verily, it is an abomination. Verily, the devils inspire their friends that they may wrangle with you; but if ye obey them, verily, ye are idolaters.

Is he who was dead and we have quickened him, and made for him a light, that he might walk therein amongst men, like him whose likeness is in the darkness whence he cannot come forth? Thus is made seemly to the misbelievers what they have done.

And thus have we placed in every town the great sinners thereof, that they may use craft therein; but they use not craft except against themselves, although they do not understand.

And when there comes to them a sign, they say, 'We will not believe until we are brought like what the apostles were brought'; Allah knows best where to put His message. There shall befall those who sin, meanness in Allah's eyes, and grievous torment for the craft they used.

[125] Whomsoever Allah wishes to guide, He expands his breast to Islam; but whomsoever He wishes to lead astray, He makes his breast tight and straight, as though he would mount up into heaven;[19] thus does Allah set His horror on those who do not believe.

This is the way of thy Lord—straight. We have detailed the signs unto a mindful people; for them is an abode of peace; and their Lord, He is their patron for what they have done.

And on the day when He shall gather them all together, 'O assembly of the jinns! ye have got much out of mankind.' And their clients from among mankind shall say, 'O our Lord! much advantage had we one from another'; but we reached our appointed time which thou hadst appointed for us. Says He, 'The Fire is your resort, to dwell therein for aye! save what Allah pleases; verily, thy Lord is wise and knowing.'

Thus do we make some of the unjust patrons of the others, for that which they have earned.

[130] O assembly of jinns and men! did there not come to you apostles from among yourselves, relating to you our signs, and warning you of the meeting of this very day of yours? They say, 'We bear witness against ourselves.' The life of this world deceived them, and they bear witness against themselves that they were unbelievers.

That is because thy Lord would never destroy towns unjustly while their people are careless; but for every one are degrees of what they have done; and thy Lord is not careless of that which they do.

Thy Lord is rich, merciful; if He pleases He will take you off, and will cause what He pleases to succeed you; even as He raised you up from the seed of other people.

Verily, what ye are promised will surely come, nor can ye frustrate it.

[135] Say, 'O my people! act according to your power, verily, I am acting too; and soon shall ye know whose is the future of the abode!' Verily, the unjust shall not prosper.

They set apart for Allah, from what He raises of tilth and of cattle, a portion, and they say, 'This is Allah's';—as they pretend—'and this is for our associates';[20] but that which is for their associates reaches not to Allah, and that which was for Allah does reach to their associates;—evil is it what they judge.[21]

Thus too have their associates made seemly to many of the idolaters the killing of their children,[22] to destroy them, and to obscure for them their religion;[23] but had Allah pleased they would not have done it, leave them alone and that which they have forged.

And they say, 'These cattle and tilth are inviolable; none shall taste thereof, save such as we please'—as they pretend—and there are cattle whose backs are prohibited, and cattle over whom Allah's name is not pronounced,—forging a lie against Him! He shall reward them for what they have forged.

[140] And they say, 'What is in the wombs of these cattle is unlawful for our wives, but if it be (born) dead,

then are they partners therein.' He will reward them for their attribution; verily, He is wise and knowing.

Losers are they who kill their children foolishly, without knowledge, and who prohibit what Allah has bestowed upon them, forging a lie against Allah; they have erred and are not guided.

He it is who brought forth gardens with trailed[24] and untrailed vines, and the palms and corn land, with various food, and olives, and pomegranates, alike and unlike. Eat from the fruit thereof whene'er it fruits, and bring the dues thereof on the day of harvest, and be not extravagant; verily, He loves not the extravagant.

Of cattle are there some to ride on and to spread.[25] Eat of what Allah has bestowed upon you, and follow not the footsteps of Satan; verily, he is to you an open foe.

Eight pairs,—of sheep two, and of goats two; say, 'Are the two males unlawful, or the two females, or what the wombs of the two females contain? Inform me with knowledge if ye tell the truth.' [145] And of camels two, and cows two; say, 'Are the two males unlawful, or the two females, or what the wombs of the two females contain? Were ye witnesses when Allah ordained for you these?— Then who is more unjust than he who devises a lie against Allah, to lead men astray without knowledge? Verily, Allah guides not the unjust people.'[26]

Say, 'I cannot find in what I am inspired with anything unlawful for the taster to taste; unless it be dead (of itself), or blood that has been shed, or the flesh of swine,—for that is a horror—or an abomination that is consecrated to other than Allah. But he who is forced, not wilfully nor transgressing,—then, verily, thy Lord is forgiving and merciful.'

To those who were Jews did we prohibit everything that hath a solid hoof; and of oxen and sheep did we prohibit to them the fat, save what the backs of both do bear, or the inwards, or what is mixed with bone; with that did we recompense them for their rebellion, for, verily, we are true.

And if they give thee the lie, say, 'Your Lord is of ample mercy, nor shall His violence be turned back from the sinful people.'

Those who associate others with Allah will say, 'Had Allah pleased, we had not so associated, nor our fathers; nor should we have forbidden aught.' Thus did they give the lie to those who came before them, until they tasted of our violence! Say, 'Have ye any knowledge? If so, bring it forth to us: ye only follow suspicion, and ye do but conjecture.'

[150] Say, 'Allah's is the searching argument; and had He pleased He would have guided you all.'

Say, 'Come on then with your witnesses, who bear witness that Allah has prohibited these!' but if they do bear witness, bear thou not witness with them; nor follow the lust of those who say our signs are lies, and those who do not believe in the last day, or those who for their Lord make peers.

Say, 'Come! I will recite what your Lord has forbidden you, that ye may not associate aught with Him, and (may show) kindness to your parents, and not kill your children through poverty;—we will provide for you and them;—

and draw not nigh to flagrant sins, either apparent or concealed, and kill not the soul, which Allah hath forbidden save by right;[27] that is what Allah ordains you, haply ye may understand.'

And draw not nigh unto the wealth of the orphan, save so as to better it, until he reaches full age; and give weight and measure with justice. We do not compel the soul save what it can compass; and when ye pronounce, then be just, though it be in the case of a relative.

And Allah's compact fulfil ye; that is what He ordained you, haply ye may be mindful. Verily, this is my right way; follow it then, and follow not various paths, to separate yourselves from His way; that is what He has ordained you, haply ye may fear!

[155] Then we gave Moses the Book, complete for him who acts aright, and a decision and a guidance and a mercy; haply in the meeting of their Lord they will believe.

This is the Book which we have sent down; it is a blessing; follow it then and fear; haply ye may obtain mercy. Lest ye say, 'The Book was only sent down to two sects before us; verily, we, for what they read, care naught.' Or, lest ye should say, 'Had we had a book revealed to us we should surely have been more guided than they'; but there is come to them a manifest sign from their Lord, and a guidance and a mercy; who then is more unjust than he who calls Allah's signs lies, and turns from them? We will reward those who turn from our signs with an evil punishment for that they turned away.

What do they expect but that the angels should come

for them, or that thy Lord should come, or that some signs[28] of thy Lord should come? On the day when some signs do come, its faith shall profit no soul which did not believe before, unless it has earned some good by its faith. Say, 'Wait ye expectant, then we wait expectant too.'

[160] Verily, those who divided their religion and became sects, thou hast not to do with them, their matter is in Allah's hands, He will yet inform them of that which they have done.

He who brings a good work shall have ten like it; but he who brings a bad work shall be recompensed only with the like thereof, for they shall not be wronged.

Say, 'As for me, my Lord has guided me to the right way, a right religion,—the faith of Abraham the Hanîf, for he was not of the idolaters.'

Say, 'Verily, my prayers and my devotion and my life and my death belong to Allah, the Lord of the worlds. He has no partner; that is what I am bidden; for I am first of those who are resigned.'

Say, 'Other than Allah shall I crave for a Lord when He is Lord of all?' but no soul shall earn aught save against itself;[29] nor shall one bearing a burden bear the burden of another; and then unto your Lord is your return, and He will inform you concerning that whereon ye do dispute.

[165] He it is who made you vicegerents, and raised some of you above others in degree, to try you by that which he has brought you;—verily, thy Lord is swift to punish, but, verily, He is forgiving and merciful.

THE CHAPTER OF AL AARÂF¹

VII (*Mecca*)

In the name of the merciful and compassionate Allah.

A. L. M. S. A book revealed to thee,—so let there be no straitness in thy breast, that thou mayest warn thereby,—and a reminder to the believers.

Follow what has been revealed to you from your Lord, and follow not beside Him patrons; little is it that ye mind.

Yet how many a town have we destroyed, and our violence came upon it by night, or while they slept at noon; and their cry, when our violence came upon them, was only to say, 'Verily, we were unjust!' [5] But we will of a surety question those to whom the prophets were sent, and we will narrate to them with knowledge, for we were not absent. The balance on that day is true, and whosesoever scales are heavy, they are prosperous; but whosesoever scales are light, they it is who lose themselves, for that they did act unjustly by our signs.

We have established you in the earth, and we have made for you therein livelihoods; little is it that ye thank; [10] and we created you, then we fashioned you, then we said unto the angels, 'Adore Adam', and they adored, save Iblîs, who was not of those who did adore.

Said He, 'What hinders thee from adoring when I order thee?' He said, 'I am better than he; Thou hast created me from fire, and him Thou hast created out of clay.'

Said He, 'Then go down therefrom; what ails thee that thou shouldst be big with pride therein? Go forth! verily, thou art of the little ones.'

He said, 'Respite me until the day when they shall be raised.' He said, 'Verily, thou art of the respited'; [15] said he, 'For that Thou hast led me into error, I will lie in wait for them in Thy straight path; then I will surely come to them, from before them and from behind them; and most of them Thou shalt not find thankful.' He said, 'Go forth therefrom, despised, expelled; whoso follows thee, I will surely fill Hell with you altogether. But, O Adam, dwell thou and thy wife in Paradise and eat from whence ye will, but draw not night unto this tree or ye will be of the unjust.'

But Satan whispered to them to display to them what was kept back from them of their shame, and he said, 'Your Lord has only forbidden you this tree lest ye should be twain angels, or should become of the immortals'; [20] and he swore to them both, 'Verily, I am unto you a sincere adviser'; and he beguiled them by deceit, and when they twain tasted of the tree, their shame was shown them, and they began to stitch upon themselves the leaves of the garden. And their Lord called unto them, 'Did I not forbid you from that tree there, and say to you, Verily, Satan is to you an open foe?' They said, 'O our Lord! we have wronged ourselves—and if Thou dost not forgive us and have mercy on us, we shall surely be of those who are lost!' He said, 'Go ye down, one of you to the other a foe; but for you in the earth there is an abode, and a provision for a season.' He said, 'Therein shall ye live and therein shall ye die, from it shall ye be brought forth.'

[25] O sons of Adam! we have sent down to you garments wherewith to cover your shame, and plumage;[2]

but the garment of piety, that is better. That is one of the signs of Allah, haply ye may remember.

O sons of Adam! let not Satan infatuate you as he drove your parents out of Paradise, stripping from them their garments, and showing them their shame; verily, he sees you—he and his tribe, from whence ye cannot see them. Verily, we have made the devils patrons of those who do not believe, and when they commit an abomination they say, 'We found our fathers at this, and Allah bade us do it.'

Say, 'Allah bids you not to do abomination; do ye say against Allah that which ye do not know?'

Say, 'My Lord bids only justice:—set steadfastly your faces at every mosque and pray to Him, being sincere in your religion. As He brought you forth in the beginning, shall ye return. A sect He guides, and for a sect of them was error due; verily, they did take the devils for their patrons instead of Allah, and they did count that they were guided.'

O sons of Adam! take your ornaments to every mosque;[3] and eat and drink, but do not be extravagant, for He loves not the extravagant.

[30] Say, 'Who has prohibited the ornaments of Allah which He brought forth for His servants, and the good things of His providing?' say, 'On the day of judgement they shall only be for those who believed when in the life of this world.'[4] Thus do we detail the signs unto a people that do know.

Say, 'My Lord has only prohibited abominable deeds, the apparent thereof and the concealed thereof, and sin, and greed for that which is not right, and associating with Allah what He has sent down no power for, and saying against Allah that which ye do not know.'

Every nation has its appointed time, and when their appointed time comes they cannot keep it back an hour, nor can they bring it on.

O sons of Adam! verily, there will come to you apostles from amongst you, narrating unto you my signs; then whoso fears Allah and does what is right, there is no fear for them, nor shall they grieve. But those who say my signs are lies, and who are too big with pride for them, these are the fellows of the Fire, they shall dwell therein for aye!

[35] Who is more unjust than he who devises against Allah a lie, or says His signs are lies? These, their portion of the Book shall reach them,[5] until when our messengers come to take their souls away, and say, 'Where is what ye used to call upon instead of Allah?' They say, 'They have strayed away from us'; and they shall bear witness against themselves that they have been misbelievers.

He will say, 'Enter ye—amongst the nations who have passed away before you, both of jinns[6] and men—into the fire'; whenever a nation enters therein, it curses its mate;[7] until, when they have all reached it, the last of them will say unto the first, 'O our Lord! these it was who led us astray, give them double torment of the Fire!' He will say, 'To each of you double! but ye do not know.' And the first of them will say unto the last, 'Ye have no preference over us, so taste ye the torment for that which ye have earned!'

Verily, those who say our signs are lies and are too big

with pride for them; for these the doors of heaven shall not be opened, and they shall not enter into Paradise until a camel shall pass into a needle's eye.

It is thus that we reward the sinners; for them is a couch of hellfire, with an awning above them! thus do we reward the unjust!

[40] But those who believe and do what is right—we will not oblige a soul more than its capacity—they are the fellows of Paradise, they shall dwell therein for aye.

We will strip away what ill feeling is in their breasts—there shall flow beneath them rivers, and they shall say, 'Praise belongs to Allah who guided us to this! for we should not have been guided had not Allah guided us!—the apostles of our Lord did come to us with truth!' And it shall be cried out to them, 'This is Paradise which ye have as an inheritance for that which ye have done!' And the fellows of Paradise will call out to the fellows of the Fire, 'We have now found that what our Lord promised us is true; have ye found that what your Lord promised you is true?' They will say, 'Yea!' And a crier from amongst them will cry out, 'The curse of Allah is on the unjust who turn from the way of Allah and crave to make it crooked, while in the hereafter they do disbelieve!'

And betwixt the two there is a veil, and on al Aarâf are men who know each by marks; and they shall cry out to the fellows of Paradise, 'Peace be upon you!' they cannot enter it although they so desire. [45] But when their sight is turned towards the fellows of the Fire, they say, 'O our Lord! place us not with the unjust people.' And the fellows on al Aarâf will cry out to the men whom they know by their marks, and say, 'Of no avail to you were your collections, and what ye were so big with pride about; are these those ye swore that Allah would not extend mercy to? Enter ye Paradise; there is no fear for you, nor shall ye be grieved.'

But the fellows of the Fire shall cry out to the fellows of Paradise, 'Pour out upon us water, or something of what Allah has provided you with.'[8] They will say, 'Allah has prohibited them both to those who misbelieve; who took their religion for a sport and a play; whom the life of the world beguiled.'—Today do we forget them as they forgot the meeting of this day, and for that they did deny our signs!

[50] Now we have brought them a book explaining it in knowledge, a guidance and a mercy to a people who believe.

Do they wait now for aught but its interpretation?—on the day when its interpretation shall come, those who forgot it before will say, 'There did come to us the apostles of our Lord in truth, have we intercessors to intercede for us? or, could we return, we would do otherwise than we did.' They have lost themselves, and that which they devised has strayed away from them.

Verily, your Lord is Allah who created the heavens and the earth in six days; then He made for the Throne.[9] He covers night with the day—it pursues it incessantly—and the sun and the moon and the stars are subject to His bidding. Aye!—His is the creation and the bidding,— blessed be Allah the Lord of the worlds!

Call on your Lord humbly and secretly, verily, He loves

not the transgressors. And do not evil in the earth after it has been righted; and call upon Him with fear and earnestness; verily, the mercy of Allah is nigh unto those who do well.

[55] He it is who sends forth the winds as heralds before His mercy; until when they lift the heavy cloud which we drive to a dead land, and send down thereon water, and bring forth therewith every kind of fruit;—thus do we bring forth the dead; haply ye may remember.

And the good land brings forth its vegetation by the permission of its Lord; and that which is vile brings forth naught but scarcity. Thus do we turn about our signs for a people who are grateful.

We did send Noah unto his people, and he said, 'O my people! serve Allah, ye have no god but Him; verily, I fear for you the torment of the mighty day.' Said the chiefs of his people, 'Verily, we do surely see you in obvious error.' Said he, 'O my people! there is no error in me; but I am an apostle from the Lord of the worlds. [60] I preach to you the messages of my Lord, and I give you sincere advice; and I know from Allah what ye know not. What! do ye wonder that there came to you a reminder from your Lord by a man from amongst yourselves, to warn you, and that ye may fear? but haply ye may receive mercy.'

But they called him a liar, and we rescued him and those who were with him in the ark; and we drowned those who said our signs were lies, verily, they were a blind people.

And unto 'Âd[10] (we sent) their brother Hûd,[11] who said,

'O my people! serve Allah, ye have no god save Him; what! will ye not then fear?' Said the chiefs of those who misbelieved amongst his people, 'Verily, we see thee in folly, and, verily, we certainly think thou art of the liars.' [65] He said, 'O my people! there is no folly in me; but I am an apostle from the Lord of the worlds; I preach to you the messages of your Lord; and, verily, I am to you a faithful adviser. What! do ye then wonder that there comes to you a reminder from your Lord by a man from amongst yourselves, to warn you? Remember when He made you vicegerents after Noah's people and increased you in length of stature; remember, then, the benefits of Allah,—haply ye may prosper!' They said, 'Hast thou come to us that we may worship Allah alone, and leave what our fathers used to worship? Then bring us what thou dost threaten us with, if thou art of those who tell the truth!' He said, 'There shall fall upon you from your Lord horror and wrath; do ye wrangle with me about names, which ye and your fathers have named yourselves, for which Allah sent down no power; wait then expectant, and I with you will wait expectant too!' [70] But we rescued him and those with him, by mercy from ourselves, and we cut off the hindermost parts of those who said our signs were lies and who were not believers.

Unto Thamûd (we sent) their brother Zâli'h, who said, 'O my people! worship Allah; we have no god but Him: there has come to you a manifest sign from your Lord. This she-camel of Allah's is a sign for you; leave her then to eat in the land of Allah, and touch her not with evil, or there will overtake you grievous woe. And remember how he made you vicegerents after 'Âd and stablished you in the earth, so that ye took for yourselves castles on its plains and hewed out mountains into houses;[12] and remember the benefits of Allah, and waste not the land, despoiling it.' Said the chiefs of those who were big with pride from amongst his people to those who were weak,— to those amongst them who believed, 'Do ye know that Zâli'h is sent from his Lord?' They said, 'We do believe in that with which he is sent.' Said those who were big with pride, 'Verily, in what ye do believe we disbelieve.' [75] Then they did hamstring the camel, and rebelled against the bidding of their Lord and said, 'O Zâli'h! bring us what thou didst threaten us with, if thou art of those who are sent.' Then the earthquake took them, and in the morning they lay prone in their dwellings; and he turned away from them and said, 'O my people! I did preach to you the message of my Lord, and I gave you good advice! but ye love not sincere advisers.'[13]

And Lot, when he said to his people, 'Do ye approach an abomination which no one in all the world ever anticipated you in? Verily, ye approach men with lust rather than women—nay, ye are a people who exceed.' [80] But his people's answer only was to say, 'Turn them out of your village, verily, they are a people who pretend to purity.' But we saved him and his people, except his wife, who was of those who lingered; and we rained down upon them a rain;—see then how was the end of the sinners!

And unto Midian did we send their brother Sho'hâib[14] who said, 'O my people! serve Allah, ye have no god save

Him. There has come to you a manifest sign from your
Lord; then give good weight and measure, and be not
niggardly of your gifts to men, and do not evil in the earth
after it has been righted. That is better for you if ye are
believers; and sit not down in every path, threatening and
turning from the path of Allah those who believe in Him,
and craving to make it crooked. Remember when ye were
few and He multiplied you; and see what was the end of
the evil-doers! [85] And if there be a party of you who
believe in what I am sent with, and a party who believe
not, then wait patiently until Allah judges between us, for
He is the best of judges.' Said the crowd of those who
were big with pride amongst His people, 'We will of a
surety turn thee out, O Sho'hâib! and those who believe
with thee, from our village; or else thou shalt return unto
our faith.' Said he, 'What even if we be averse therefrom?
We shall have devised a lie against Allah if we return unto
your faith, after Allah has saved us from it; and what
should ail us that we should return thereto, unless that
Allah our Lord should please? Our Lord embraces
everything in His knowledge;—on Allah do we rely. O
our Lord! open between us and between our people in
truth, for Thou art the best of those who open.'15 And the
chiefs of those who disbelieved amongst his people said,
'If ye follow Sho'hâib, verily, ye shall be the losers'; then
there took them the earthquake, and in the morning they
lay in their dwellings prone. [90] Those who called
Sho'hâib a liar, (were) as though they had not dwelt
therein!—Those who called Sho'hâib a liar, they were the
losers then! And he turned away from them and said, 'O

my people! I preached to you the messages of my Lord, and I gave you good advice; how should I be vexed for a people who do misbelieve?'

We have not sent unto a city any prophet except we overtook the people thereof with trouble and distress, that haply they might humble themselves; and then did we give them, in exchange for evil, good, until they increased and said, 'Distress and joy both touched our fathers'; then we overtook them suddenly ere they could perceive.— Had the people of the town but believed and feared, we would have opened up for them blessings from the heavens and from the earth; but they said it was a lie, so we overtook them for that which they had earned.

[95] Were the people of these cities then secure that our violence would not come on them by night, while they slept? Were the people of these cities secure that our violence would not come on them in the morning whilst they played? Were they secure from the craft of Allah? None feel secure from the craft of Allah except a people that shall lose.

Is it not shown to those who inherit the earth after its (former) people, that, did we please, we would smite[16] them in their sins, and would set a stamp upon their hearts, and then they should not hear?

These cities, we do relate to thee their stories. There came to them our apostles with manifest signs; but they did not at all believe in what they called a lie before.— Thus doth Allah set a stamp upon the hearts of those who misbelieve.

[100] Nor did we find in most of them a covenant; but

we did find most of them workers of abomination.

Then we raised up after them Moses with our signs to Pharaoh and his chiefs; but they dealt unjustly therewith, and see what was the end of the evil-doers!

Moses said, 'O Pharaoh! verily, I am an apostle from the Lord of the worlds; it is not right for me to speak against Allah aught but the truth. I have come to you with a manifest sign from my Lord; send then the children of Israel with me.' Said he, 'If thou hast come with a sign, then bring it, if thou art of those who speak the truth.' Then he threw his rod down, and lo! it was an obvious snake; [105] and he drew out his hand, and lo! it was white to the beholders. Said the chiefs of Pharaoh's people, 'Verily, this is surely a knowing magician; he desires to turn you out of your land;—what is it then ye bid?' They said, 'Give him and his brother some hope; and send into the cities to collect and bring you every knowing magician.' [110] And the magician came to Pharaoh and said, 'Is there indeed a reward for us if we are conquerors?' He said, 'Yea! and ye shall be of those who draw nigh unto me.' They said, 'O Moses! wilt thou cast down (thy rod) or shall we be (first) to throw?' Said he, 'Throw down'; and when they threw down, they did enchant the people's eyes, and made them dread, and brought a mighty magic. But we inspired Moses (saying), 'Throw down thy rod, and it will gulp down that which they devise'; [115] and the truth stood fast, and vain was that which they had done; and they were conquered there, and turned back feeling small! and the magicians threw themselves down adoring. Said they, 'We believe in the

Lord of the worlds, the Lord of Moses and Aaron!'
[120] Said Pharaoh, 'Do ye believe in him ere I give you
leave? This is craft which ye have devised in the land, to
turn its people out therefrom, but soon shall ye know! I
will cut off your hands and your feet from opposite sides,
then I will crucify you altogether!' They said, 'Verily, we
unto our Lord return! nor dost thou take vengeance on us,
save for that we believe in the signs of our Lord, when
they come to us.

'O our Lord! pour out upon us patience, and take us to
Thyself resigned.'[17] And the chiefs of Pharaoh's people
said, 'Will ye leave Moses and his people to do evil in the
land, and to leave thee and thy gods?' Said he, 'We will
have their sons slain and their women we will let live, for,
verily, we are triumphant over them.'

[125] Said Moses unto his people, 'Ask for aid from
Allah and be patient; verily, the earth is Allah's! He gives
it for an inheritance to whom He pleases of His servants,
and the future is for those who fear.' They said, 'We have
been hurt before thou didst come to us, and since thou
hast come to us.' Said he, 'It may be that your Lord will
destroy your foe, and will make you succeed him in the
earth; and He will see how ye act.'

We had overtaken Pharaoh's people with the years (of
death) and scarcity of fruits, that haply they might
remember; but when there came to them a good thing they
said, 'This is ours'; and if there befell them an evil, they
took the augury from Moses and those with him;—is not
their augury only in Allah's hands?—but most of them
know not.

And they said, 'Whatever thou dost bring us as a sign to enchant us therewith, yet will we not believe in thee.'

[130] Then we sent upon them the flood and the locusts and the lice and the frogs and the blood,—signs detailed; but they were big with pride and were a people who did sin.

And when there fell upon them the plague, they said, 'O Moses! call upon thy Lord for us, as He has covenanted with thee; verily, if thou dost remove the plague from us, we will believe in thee; and we will assuredly send with thee the children of Israel.' But when we removed from them the plague until the appointed time which they should reach, lo! then they broke their promise. But we took vengeance on them, and we drowned them in the sea, for that they said our signs were lies and were careless thereof. And we gave as an inheritance unto the people who had been weak, the eastern quarters of the earth and the western quarters thereof, which we had blest; and the good word of thy Lord was fulfilled on the children of Israel, for that they were patient; and we destroyed that which Pharaoh and his people had made and that which they had piled.[18] And with the children of Israel we passed across the sea; and they came unto a people devoted to their idols, and said, 'O Moses! make for us a god as they have gods.' Said he, 'Verily, ye are ignorant people.' [135] Verily, these—destroyed shall be that which they are given to; and vain is that which they have done.

He said, 'Other than Allah then do ye crave for a god, when He has preferred you above the worlds?'

And when we saved you from Pharaoh's people who

wrought you evil woe, killing your sons, and letting your women live; and in that was a mighty trial from your Lord.

And we appointed for Moses thirty nights, and completed them with ten (more), so that the time appointed by his Lord was completed to forty nights. And Moses said unto his brother Aaron, 'Be thou my vicegerent amongst my people, and do what is right, and follow not the path of the evil-doers.'

And when Moses came to our appointment, and his Lord spake unto him, he said, 'O my Lord! show me,—that I may look on thee!' He said, 'Thou canst not see me; but look upon the mountain, and if it remain steady in its place, thou shalt see me'; but when his Lord appeared unto the mountain He made it dust, and Moses fell down in a swoon!

[140] And when he came to himself, he said, 'Celebrated be thy praise! I turn repentant unto Thee, and I am the first of those who are resigned.'

He said, 'O Moses! verily, I have chosen thee over the people with my messages and my words, take then what I have brought thee, and be of those who thank.' And we wrote for him upon tablets an admonition concerning everything, and a detailing of everything: 'Take them then with firmness, and bid thy people take them for what is best thereof. I will show you the abode of those who work abominations; I will turn from my signs those who are big with pride in the earth without right; and if they see every sign they shall not believe therein, and if they see the path of rectitude they shall not take it for a path; but if they see the path of error they shall take it for a path;—

that is because they have said our signs are lies and have been careless of them.'

[145] But those who say our signs and the meeting of the last day are lies,—vain are their works: shall they be rewarded save for that which they have done?

And Moses' people after him took to themselves of their ornaments a corporeal calf that lowed;[19] did they not see that it could not speak with them, nor could it guide them in the path? They took it and they were unjust; but when they bit their hands with fruitless rage and saw that they had gone astray, they said, 'Verily, if our Lord have not compassion on us and forgive us we shall surely be of those who lose!'

And when Moses returned unto his people angry and grieved, he said, 'Evil is it that ye have done after me! Would ye hasten on the bidding of your Lord?' and he threw down the tablets and took his brother by the head to drag him towards him, but he said, 'O son of my mother! verily, the people weakened me and well-nigh killed me; make not then mine enemies glad about me, and put me not with the unjust people.' [150] He said, 'O Lord! pardon me and my brother, and let us enter into Thy mercy; for Thou art the most merciful of the merciful. Verily, these have taken to themselves a calf; there shall reach them wrath from their Lord, and abasement in the life of this world; for thus do we reward those who forge a lie. But those who have done bad works, and then turn again after them and believe,—verily, thy Lord, after that, is forgiving and merciful.'

And when Moses' wrath calmed down he took the

tables, in the inscription of which was guidance and mercy for those who dread their Lord.

And Moses chose from his people seventy men for our appointment; and when the earthquake took them he said, 'O my Lord! hadst Thou willed, Thou hadst destroyed them before and me. Wilt Thou destroy us for what the fools amongst us have done? This is naught but Thy trial, wherewith Thou dost lead astray whom Thou pleasest and guidest whom Thou pleasest; Thou art our patron! Forgive us and have mercy on us, for Thou art the best of those who do forgive!

[155] 'And write down for us in this world good, and in the future too; verily, we are guided unto Thee.' He said, 'My punishment—with it I fall on whom I will; and my mercy embraceth everything; and I will write it down for those who fear, and who give alms, and those who in our signs believe,—who follow the Apostle—the illiterate prophet,[20] whom they find written down with them in the law and the gospel, bidding them what is reasonable and forbidding them what is wrong, and making lawful for them what is good, and making unlawful evil things; and setting down for them their burdens and the yokes which were upon them;—to those who believe in him and aid him and help him and follow the law which has been sent down with him—they shall be the prosperous.'

Say, 'O ye folk! verily, I am the Apostle of Allah unto you all',—of Him whose is the kingdom of the heavens and the earth, there is no god but He! He quickens and He kills! Believe then in Allah and His Apostle, the illiterate prophet,—who believes in Allah and in His words—then follow him that haply ye may be guided.

Amongst Moses' people is a nation guided in truth, and thereby act they justly.

[160] And we cut them up into twelve tribes, each a nation; and we revealed unto Moses, when his people asked him for drink, 'Strike with thy staff the rock!' and there gushed forth from it twelve springs, each folk knew their drinking place. And we overshadowed them with the cloud; and sent down upon them the manna and the quails, 'Eat of the good things we have provided you with!'—Yet they did not wrong us, but it was themselves they wronged.

And when it was said unto them, 'Dwell in this city and eat therefrom as ye will, and say, '*hittatun*', and enter the gate adoring; so will we pardon you your sins;—we will increase those who do well.' But those amongst them who did wrong changed it for another word than which was said to them; and we sent upon them a plague from heaven for that they were unjust.

Ask them too about the city which stood by the sea, when they transgressed upon the Sabbath; when their fish came to them on the Sabbath day sailing straight up to them; but on the days when they kept not the Sabbath, they came not to them, thus did we try them for the abominations that they wrought.[21]

And when a nation from amongst them said, 'Why do ye warn a people whom Allah would destroy, or punish with severe torment?' they said, 'As an excuse to your Lord, that haply they may fear.' [165] But when they forgot what they had been reminded of, we saved those who forbade evil, but we overtook those who did wrong with punishment;—evil was the abomination that they did, but when they rebelled against what they were forbidden, we said to them, 'Become ye apes, despised and spurned!' and then thy Lord proclaimed that He would surely send against them till the resurrection day, those who should wreak them evil torment; verily, thy Lord is quick at following up, but, verily, He is forgiving, merciful.

We cut them up in the earth into nations. Of them are the righteous, and of them are the reverse of that; we have tried them with good things and with bad things; haply they may return.

But there succeeded them successors who inherited the Book! They take the goods of this lower world and say, 'It will be forgiven us.' But if the like goods came to them they would take them too! Was there not taken from them a covenant by the Book, that they should not say against Allah aught but the truth? Yet they study therein! But the abode of the future life is better for those who fear—do ye not then understand? But those who hold fast by the Book and are steadfast in prayer—verily, we will not waste the hire of those who do right.

[170] And when we shook the mountain over them, as though it were a shadow, and they thought it would fall upon them (saying), 'Take ye what we have given you with firmness, and remember what is therein; haply ye may fear.'

And when thy Lord took from the children of Adam out of their loins their seed, and made them bear witness against themselves, 'Am I not your Lord?' They said, 'Yea!

we do bear witness'—lest ye should say on the day of resurrection, 'Verily, for this we did not care'; or say, 'Verily, our fathers associated others with Allah before us, and we were but their seed after them: wilt Thou then destroy us for what vain doers did?'—Thus do we detail the signs; haply they may return.

Read to them the declaration of him to whom we brought our signs, and who stepped away therefrom, and Satan followed him, and he was of those who were beguiled.[22] [175] Had we pleased we would have exalted him thereby, but he crouched upon the earth and followed his lust, and his likeness was as the likeness of a dog, whom if thou shouldst attack he hangs out his tongue, or if thou should leave him, hangs out his tongue too. That is the likeness of the people who say our signs are lies. Tell them then these tales—haply they may reflect.

Evil is the likeness of a people who say our signs are lies; themselves it is they wrong!

We have created for Hell many of the jinn and of mankind; they have hearts and they discern not therewith; they have eyes and they see not therewith; they have ears and they hear not therewith; they are like cattle, nay, they go more astray! These it is who care not.

But Allah's are the good names; call on Him then thereby, and leave those who pervert His names;[23] they shall be rewarded for that which they have done.

[180] And of those whom we have created is a nation who are guided in truth and thereby act with equity; but they who say our signs are lies, we will bring them down by degrees from whence they know not. I will let them

range;—verily, my stratagem is efficacious!

Do they not then reflect that their companion[24] is not possessed?[25] He is but an obvious warner! Do they not behold the kingdoms of the heavens and of the earth, and what things Allah has created, and (see that), it may be, their time is already drawing nigh? In what relation then will they believe? [185] He whom Allah leads astray there is no guide for him! He leaves them in their rebellion, blindly wandering on.

They will ask you about the Hour, for what time it is fixed?—say, 'The knowledge thereof is only with my Lord; none shall manifest it at its time but He; it is heavy in the heavens and the earth, it will not come to you save on a sudden.'

They will ask as though thou wert privy to it, say, 'The knowledge thereof is only with Allah',—but most folk do not know.

Say, 'I canot control profit or harm for myself, save what Allah will. If I knew the unseen I should surely have much that is good, nor would evil touch me; I am but a warner and a herald of good tidings unto a people who believe.'

He it is who created you from one soul, and made therefrom its mate to dwell therewith; and when he covered her she bore a light burden and went about therewith; but when it grew heavy they called on Allah, Lord of them both, 'Surely if thou givest us a rightly-shaped child we shall of a surety be of those who thank.'[190] And when He gave them both a rightly-shaped child they joined partners with Him for that which

He had given them, but exalted be Allah above that which they associate with Him.[26] Will they associate with Him those who cannot create aught, but are themselves created, which have no power to help them, and cannot even help themselves?

But if ye call them unto guidance they will not follow you. It is the same to them if Thou dost call them or if Thou dost hold thy tongue.

Those whom ye call on other than Allah are servants like yourselves. Call on them then, and let them answer you, if so be ye tell the truth! Have they feet to walk with? or have they hands to hold with? or have they eyes to see with? or have they ears to hear with? Call upon your partners; then plot against me, and do not wait.

[195] Verily, my patron is Allah, who hath sent down the Book, and He is the patron of the righteous. But those whom ye call on beside Him cannot help you, nor can they even help themselves. But if ye call them unto the guidance they will not hear, thou mayest see them looking towards thee, yet they do not see. Take to pardon, and order what is kind, and shun the ignorant; and if an incitement from the devil incites you, then seek refuge in Allah: verily, He both hears and knows.

[200] Verily, those who fear Allah, if a wraith from the devil touch, mention Him, and lo! they see.[27]

And their brethren he shall increase in error, then they shall not desist.

Shouldst Thou not bring them a sign[28] they say, 'Hast Thou not yet made choice of one?' Say, 'I only follow what is inspired to me by my Lord. These are perceptions from my Lord, and a guidance and a mercy to a people who believe.'

And when the Qur'ân is read, then listen thereto and keep silence; haply ye may obtain mercy.

And remember thy Lord within thyself humbly and with fear, not openly in words, in the morning and in the evening; and be not of those who do not care. [205] Verily, they who are with my Lord are not too big with pride for His service, but they do celebrate His praise, and Him they do adore.

THE CHAPTER OF THE SPOILS

VIII (*Medina*)

In the name of the merciful and compassionate Allah.

They will ask thee about the spoils. Say, 'The spoils are Allah's and the Apostle's; fear Allah and settle it amongst yourselves; obey Allah and the Apostle if ye do believe.'

Verily, the believers are those who, when Allah's name is mentioned, their hearts sink with fear; and when His signs are rehearsed to them they increase them in faith; and on their Lord do they rely; who are steadfast in prayer, and of what we have bestowed upon them give in alms; these are in truth believers; to them are degrees with their Lord, and forgiveness, and a generous provision.

[5] As thy Lord caused thee to go forth from thy house¹ with the truth, although a sect of the believers were averse therefrom. They wrangled with thee about the truth after

it was made plain, as though they were being driven on to death and looked thereon; and when Allah promised you that one of the two troops should be yours, and ye would fain have had those who had no arms. Allah wished to prove the truth true by His words, and to cut off the hinder-most parts of those who misbelieve—to prove the truth true, and to make vain the vain, although the sinners are averse.[2]

When ye asked for succour from your Lord, and He answered you, 'I will assist you with a thousand angels, with others in reserve.'

[10] Allah made it only glad tidings to quiet your hearts therewith; for victory is only from Allah! Verily, Allah is mighty and wise.

When drowsiness covered you as a security from Him, and He sent down upon you from the heavens water to purify you withal, and to take away from you the plague of Satan, and to tie up your hearts and to make firm your footsteps.[3]

When your Lord inspired the angels—'Verily, I am with you; make ye firm then those who believe; I will cast dread into the hearts of those who misbelieve,—strike off their necks then, and strike off from them every fingertip.'

That is, because they went into opposition against Allah and His Apostle; for he who goes into opposition against Allah and His Apostle—verily, Allah is keen to punish.

There, taste it! since for the misbelievers is the torment of the Fire.

[15] O ye who believe! when ye meet those who misbelieve in swarms, turn not to them your hinder parts;

for he who turns to them that day his hinder parts save turning to fight or rallying to a troop, brings down upon himself wrath from Allah, and his resort is Hell, and an ill journey shall it be!

Ye did not slay them, but it was Allah who slew them; nor didst thou shoot when thou didst shoot, but Allah did shoot,[4] to try the believers from Himself with a goodly trial; verily, Allah both hears and knows. There! verily, Allah weakens the stratagem of the misbelievers.

If ye wish[5] the matter to be decided, a decision has now come to you; but if ye desist, it is better for you; and if ye turn back we will turn too, and your troop shall avail nothing, great in number though it be, since Allah is with the believers!

[20] O ye who believe! obey Allah and His Apostle, and turn not from Him while ye hear, and be not like those who say, 'We hear', and yet they hear not.

Verily, the worst of beasts in Allah's sight are the deaf, the dumb who do not understand. Had Allah known any good in them, He would have made them hear; but had He made them hear, they would have turned back and have swerved aside.

O ye who believe! answer Allah and His Apostle when He calls you to that which quickens you; and know that Allah steps in between man and his heart; and that to Him ye shall be gathered. [25] And fear temptation, which will not light especially on those of you who have done wrong; but know that Allah is keen to punish.

Remember when ye were few in number and weak in the land, fearing lest people should snatch you away; then

He sheltered you and aided you with victory, and provided you with good things; haply ye may give thanks.

O ye who believe! be not treacherous to Allah and His Apostle; nor be treacherous to your engagement while ye know!

Know that your wealth and your children are but a temptation, and that Allah—with Him is mighty hire!

O ye who believe! if ye fear Allah He will make for you a discrimination,[6] and will cover for you your offences, and will forgive you; for Allah is Lord of mighty grace.

[30] And when those who misbelieve were crafty with thee to detain thee a prisoner, or kill thee, or drive thee forth; they were crafty, but Allah was crafty too, for Allah is best of crafty ones!

But when our verses were rehearsed to them they said, 'We have already heard.—If we pleased we could speak like this; verily, this is nothing but tales of those of yore.'

When they said, 'O Allah! if this be truth, and from Thee, then rain upon us stones from heaven or bring us grievous woe!'

But Allah would not torment them while thou art amongst them; nor was Allah going to torment them while they asked Him to forgive. But what ails them that Allah should not torment them while they turn folk away from the Holy Mosque, though they are not the guardians thereof—its guardians are only the pious?—but most of them know not.

[35] Their prayer at the House was naught but whistling and clapping hands!—taste then the torment for that ye misbelieved!

Verily, those who misbelieve expend their wealth to turn folk from the path of Allah; but they shall spend it, and then it shall be for them sighing, and then they shall be overcome! Those who misbelieve, into Hell shall they be gathered!—that Allah may distinguish the vile from the good, and may put the vile, some on the top of the other, and heap up all together, and put it into Hell!—These are those who lose!

Say to those who misbelieve, if they desist they will be forgiven what is past; but if they return,—the course of those of former days has passed away.[7]

[40] Fight them then that there should be no sedition, and that the religion may be wholly Allah's; but if they desist, then Allah on what they do doth look. But if they turn their backs, then know that Allah is your Lord; a good Lord is He, and a good help; and know that whenever ye seize anything as a spoil, to Allah belongs a fifth thereof, and to His Apostle, and to kindred and orphans, and the poor and the wayfarer; if ye believe in Allah and what we have revealed unto our servants on the day of the discrimination,—the day when the two parties met; and Allah is mighty over all. When ye were on the near side of the valley, and they were on the far side, and the camels were below you; had ye made an appointment then[8] ye would have failed to keep your appointment— but it was that Allah might accomplish a thing that was as good as done! that he who was to perish might perish with a manifest sign; and that he who was to live might live with a manifest sign; for, verily, Allah hears and knows!

[45] When Allah showed thee them in thy dream as though they were but few; but had He shown thee them as though they were many, ye would have been timid, and ye would have quarrelled about the matter;—but Allah preserved you; verily, He knows the nature of men's breasts!

And when He showed them to you, as ye encountered them, as few in your eyes; and made you seem few in their eyes; that Allah might accomplish a thing that was as good as done; for unto Allah do things return!

O ye who believe! when ye encounter a troop, then stand firm and remember Allah; and haply ye may prosper! and fear Allah and His Apostle, and do not quarrel or be timid, so that your turn of luck go from you; but be ye patient, verily, Allah is with the patient. And be not like those who went forth from their homes with insolence, and for appearance sake before men, and to turn folks off Allah's way; for all they do Allah comprehends.

[50] And when Satan made their works appear seemly to them, and said, 'There is none amongst mankind to conquer you today, for, verily, I am your neighbour!' and when the two troops came in sight of each other, he turned upon his heels and said, 'Verily, I am clear of you! Verily, I see what you see not![9] Verily, I fear Allah, for Allah is keen to punish!'

And when the hypocrites and those in whose hearts was sickness said, 'Their religion hath beguiled these men,[10] but he who relies upon Allah, verily, Allah is mighty and wise.'

Couldst thou see when the angels take away the souls of those who misbelieve; they smite them on their faces and hinder parts.—'Taste ye the torment of burning! that is for what your hands have sent on before; and for that Allah is no unjust one towards his servants.'

As was the wont of Pharaoh's people and those before them! They disbelieved in the signs of Allah, and Allah overtook them in their sins; verily, Allah is strong and keen to punish.

[55] That is because Allah is not one to change a favour He has favoured a people with, until they change what they have in themselves, and for that Allah both hears and knows.

As was the wont of Pharaoh's people and those before them! they said our signs were lies, and we destroyed them in their sins, and drowned Pharaoh's people; and all of them were evil-doers.

Verily, the worst of beasts in Allah's eyes are those who misbelieve and will not believe; with whom if thou dost make a league, they break their league each time, for they fear not Allah; but shouldst thou ever catch them in war, then make those who come after them run by their example,¹¹ haply they may remember then.

[60] And shouldst thou ever fear from any people treachery, then throw it back to them in like manner; verily, Allah loves not the treacherous. Deem not that those who misbelieve can win; verily, they cannot make (Allah) powerless!

Prepare ye against them what force and companies of horse ye can, to make the enemies of Allah, and your enemies, and others beside them, in dread thereof. Ye do not know them, but Allah knows them! and whatever ye expend in Allah's way He will repay you; and ye shall not be wronged. But if they incline to peace, incline thou to it too, and rely upon Allah; verily, He both hears and knows.

But if they wish to betray thee, then Allah is enough for thee! He it is who supports thee with His help and with the believers; and reconciles their hearts! Didst thou expend all that is in the earth thou couldst not reconcile their hearts, but Allah reconciled them, verily, He is mighty and wise!

[65] O thou prophet! Allah is sufficient for thee, with those of the believers who follow thee! O thou prophet! urge on the believers to fight. If there be of you twenty patient men, they shall conquer two hundred; if there be of you a hundred, they shall conquer a thousand of those who misbelieve, because they are a people who did not discern.—Now has Allah made it light for you; He knows that there is a weakness amongst you: but if there be amongst you but a patient hundred, they will conquer two hundred; and if there be of you a thousand, they will conquer two thousand, by the permission of Allah,—for Allah is with the patient!

It has not been for any prophet to take captives until he hath slaughtered in the land! Ye wish to have the goods of this world, but Allah wishes for the next, for Allah is mighty, wise! Were it not for a book from Allah that had gone before, there would have touched you, for that which ye took, a mighty punishment.[12]

Eat of what spoils ye have taken, what is lawful and good; and fear Allah, verily, Allah is forgiving and merciful.

[70] O thou prophet! say to such of the captives as are in your hands, 'If Allah knows of any good in your hearts, he will give you better than that which is taken from you, and will forgive you; for Allah is forgiving and merciful.'

But if they desire to betray thee,—they have betrayed Allah before! but He hath given you power over them; for Allah is knowing, wise!

Verily, those who believe and have fled and fought strenuously with their wealth and persons in Allah's way, and those who have given refuge[13] and help, these shall be next of kin to each other.[14] But those who believe, but have not fled, ye have naught to do with their claims of kindred, until they flee as well. But if they ask you for aid for religion's sake, then help is due from you, except against a people between whom and you there is an alliance; for Allah on what ye do doth look.

And those who misbelieve, some of them are next of kin to others—unless ye act the same there will be sedition in the land, and great corruption.

[75] Those who believe and have fled and fought strenuously in Allah's cause, and those who have given a refuge and a help, those it is who believe; to them is forgiveness and generous provision due. And those who have believed afterwards and have fled and fought strenuously with you; these too are of you, but blood relations are nearer in kin by the Book of Allah. Verily, Allah all things doth know.

THE CHAPTER OF REPENTANCE OR IMMUNITY

IX (*Medina*)

An immunity from Allah and His Apostle to those idolaters with whom ye have made a league.[1]

Roam ye at large in the land for four months, but know that ye cannot make Allah helpless, and that Allah disgraces the misbelievers.

A proclamation from Allah and His Apostle to the people on the day of the greater pilgrimage, that Allah is clear of the idolaters as is His apostle! If then ye repent it is better for you; but if ye turn your backs, then know that ye cannot make Allah helpless. Give to those who misbelieve glad tidings of grievous woe!—Except to those of the idolaters with whom ye have made a league, and who then have not failed you at all, and have not backed up any one against you. Fulfil for them then your covenant until the time agreed upon with them; verily, Allah loves those who fear.

[5] But when the sacred months are passed away, kill the idolaters wherever ye may find them; and take them, and besiege them, and lie in wait for them in every place of observation; but if they repent, and are steadfast in prayer, and give alms, then let them go their way; verily, Allah is forgiving and merciful.

And if any one of the idolaters ask thee for aid, then aid him, in order that he may hear the word of Allah; then let him reach his place of safety,—that is, because they are a folk who do not know.

How can there be for the idolaters a treaty with Allah and with His Apostle, save those with whom ye have made a league at the Sacred Mosque! Then while they stand by you, stand ye by them; verily, Allah loves those who fear.

How!—if they prevail against you, they will not observe either ties of blood or ties of clientship; they please you with their mouths, but their hearts refuse; and most of them do work abomination. They barter Allah's signs for a little price, and they turn folk from His way; verily, they—evil is that which they have done.

[10] They will not observe in a believer ties of kindred nor ties of clientship; but they it is are the transgressors.

But if they repent and are steadfast in prayer and give alms, then they are your brethren in religion—we detail the signs unto a people that do know.

But if they break faith with you after their treaty, and taunt your religion, then fight the leaders of misbelief; verily, they have no faith, haply they may desist.

Will ye not fight a people who broke their oaths, and intended to expel the Apostle? They began with you at first, are ye afraid of them? Allah is more deserving that ye should fear Him! If ye be believers, kill them! Allah will torment them by your hands, and disgrace them, and aid you against them, and heal the breasts of a people who believe; [15] and will remove rage from their hearts; for Allah turns unto Him whomsoever He pleases, and Allah is knowing, wise!

Did ye reckon that ye would be left, when Allah knows not as yet those of you who fought strenuously, and who did not take other than Allah and His Apostle, and the believers for an intimate friend? for Allah is well aware of what ye do. It is not for idolaters to repair to the mosques of Allah, bearing witness against themselves to unbelief; they it is whose works are vain, and in the Fire shall they dwell for aye!

He only shall repair to the mosques of Allah who believes in Allah and the last day, and is steadfast in prayer, and gives the alms, and fears only Allah;—it may be that these will be of those who are guided.

Have ye made out the giving drink to the pilgrims and the repairing to the Sacred Mosque² to be like being one who believes in Allah and in the last day, and is strenuous in the way of Allah?—they are not equal in Allah's sight, and Allah guides not an unjust people.

[20] Those who believe and who have fled and been strenuous in the way of Allah, with their wealth and with their persons, are highest in rank with Allah, and these it is who are happy. Their Lord gives them glad tidings of mercy from Himself, and goodwill; and gardens shall they have therein and lasting pleasure, to dwell therein for aye! Verily, Allah, with Him is mighty here.

O ye who believe! take not your fathers and your brothers for patrons if they love misbelief rather than faith; for whosoever amongst you takes them for patrons these are the unjust.

Say, 'If your fathers, and your sons, and your brethren, and your wives, and your clansmen, and the wealth which ye have gained, and the merchandise which ye fear may be slack, and the dwellings which ye love are dearer to you than Allah and His Apostle, and than fighting strenuously in His way,—then wait awhile, until Allah brings His bidding, for Allah guides not a people who work abomination!'

[25] Allah has helped you in many a place, and on the day of Honein³ when ye were so pleased with your numbers; but it did not serve you at all, and the road grew too strait for you, where it had been broad; and then ye turned your backs retreating; then Allah sent down His *shechina*⁴ upon His Apostle and upon the believers; and sent down armies which ye could not see, and punished those who misbelieved; for that is the reward of the misbelievers, then Allah turns after that to whom He will, for Allah is forgiving and merciful!

O ye who believe! it is only the idolaters who are unclean; they shall not then approach the Sacred Mosque after this year. But if ye fear want⁵ then Allah will enrich you from His grace if He will; verily, Allah is knowing, wise!

Fight those who believe not in Allah and in the last day, and who forbid not what Allah and His Apostle have forbidden, and who do not practise the religion of truth from amongst those to whom the Book has been brought, until they pay the tribute by their hands and be as little ones.

[30] The Jews say Ezra is the son of Allah; and the Christians say that the Messiah is the son of Allah; that is what they say with their mouths, imitating the sayings of those who misbelieved before.—Allah fight them! How they lie!⁶

They take their doctors and their monks for lords⁷

rather than Allah, and the Messiah the son of Mary; but they are bidden to worship but one Allah, there is no god but He; celebrated be His praise, from what they join with Him!

They desire to put out the light of Allah with their mouths, but Allah will not have it but that we should perfect His light, averse although the misbelievers be!

He it is who sent His Apostle with guidance and the religion of truth, to make it prevail over every other religion, averse although idolaters may be!

O ye who believe! verily, many of the doctors and the monks devour the wealth of men openly, and turn folk from Allah's way; but those who store up gold and silver and expend it not in Allah's way,—give them glad tidings of grievous woe! [35] On the day when it shall be heated in the Fire of Hell, and their brows shall be branded therewith, and their sides and their backs!— 'This is what ye stored up for yourselves, taste then what ye stored up!'

Verily, the number of months with Allah is twelve months in Allah's Book, on the day when He created the heavens and the earth; of these are four that are sacred; that is the subsisting religion. Then do not wrong yourselves therein, but fight the idolaters one and all, as they fight you one and all, and know that Allah is with those who fear.

Verily, putting off is but an increase in misbelief[8] to lead astray therewith those who misbelieve. They make it lawful one year, but they make it unlawful another year, that they may come to an understanding as to the number which Allah has made sacred, and make lawful what Allah has prohibited. Seemly to them are their evil works, but Allah guides not a misbelieving people.

O ye who believe! what ailed you when ye were told to march forth in Allah's way, that ye sank down heavily upon the earth? Were ye content with the life of this world instead of the next? But the provision of this world's life is but a little to the next. Unless ye march forth He will punish you with grievous woe, and will put in your stead a people other than you! Ye cannot hurt Him at all, for Allah is mighty over all!

[40] Unless ye help him[9]—and Allah did help him, when those who misbelieved drove him forth the second of two.[10] When they twain were in the cave; when he said to his comrade, 'Grieve not, verily, Allah is with us'; and Allah sent down His *shechina* upon him, and aided him with hosts ye could not see, and made the word of those who misbelieved inferior, and the word of Allah superior; for Allah is mighty and wise. March ye then, light and heavy, and fight strenuously with your wealth and persons in Allah's way; that is better for you if ye did but know!

Were there goods nigh at hand, and a moderate journey, they would have followed you; but the distance was too far for them; they will swear by Allah, 'If we could, we would have gone forth with you.' They destroy themselves, but Allah knows that they lie!

Allah forgive thee; why didst thou give them leave (to stay) until it was made manifest to thee who spake the truth—until thou mightest know the liars?

Those who believe in Allah and in the last day will not beg off from fighting strenuously with their wealth and their persons; but Allah knows those who fear.

[45] It is only those who believe not in Allah and in the last day who beg off from thee, and those whose hearts are in doubt, and in their doubt do hesitate.

Had they wished to go forth, they would have prepared for it a preparation; but Allah was averse from their starting off, and made them halt, and they were told to sit with those who sit. Had they gone forth with you they would but have made you more trouble, and they would have hurried about amongst you craving a sedition; amongst you are some who would have listened to them; but Allah knows those who are unjust! They used to crave sedition before and upset thy affairs; until the truth came, and Allah's bidding was made manifest, averse although they were.

Of them are some who say, 'Permit me,'[11] and do not try me!' Have they not fallen into the trial already, but Hell shall encompass the misbelievers.

[50] If good befall thee it seems ill to them; but if a calamity befall thee they say, 'We had taken care for our affair before'; and they turn their backs and they are glad.

Say, 'Nought shall befall us save what Allah has written down for us; He is our Lord, and upon Allah believers do rely!'

Say, 'Do ye await for us aught but one of the two best things?'[12] we too await for you that Allah will inflict on you torment from Himself, or by our hands. Wait then; and we with you are waiting too!

Say, 'Expend ye in alms, whether ye will or no, it shall not be accepted from you; verily, ye are a people who do work abomination.'

But nought hinders their alms giving from being accepted save that they misbelieve in Allah and His Apostle, and perform not prayer save lazily, and expend not in alms save reluctantly.

[55] Let not their wealth please you nor their children, Allah only wishes to torment them therewith in the life of this world, and that their souls may pass away while still they misbelieve.

They swear by Allah that, verily, they are of you; but they are not of you, and they are a people who do stand aside in fear. Could they but have found a refuge, or some caves, or a place in which to creep, they would have turned round in haste thereto.

Of them are some who defame thee, with respect to alms; though if they are given a part thereof, they are content; and if they are not given a part thereof, then are they in a rage. Would that they were content with what Allah and His Apostle had brought them, and would say, 'Allah is enough for us! Allah will bring us of His grace, and so will His Apostle; verily, unto Allah is our desire!'

[60] Alms are only for the poor and needy, and those who work for them,[13] and those whose hearts are reconciled,[14] and those in captivity, and those in debt, and those who are on Allah's path, and for the wayfarer;—an ordinance this from Allah, for Allah is knowing, wise.

And of them are some who are by the ears[15] with the prophet, and say, 'He is all ear.' Say, 'An ear of good for you!' he believes in Allah, and believes in those who do believe, and is a mercy unto such of you as believe; but those who are by the ears with the Apostle of Allah, for them is grievous woe!

They swear by Allah to please you; but Allah and His Apostle are more worthy for them to please if they be believers. Do they not know that whoso setteth himself against Allah and His Apostle, for him is the Fire of Hell, to dwell therein for aye? and that is mighty shame!

[65] The hypocrites are cautious lest there be revealed against them a surah[16] to inform them of what is in their hearts; say, 'Mock ye! verily, Allah will bring forth that of which ye are so cautious!' But if thou shouldst ask them, they will say, 'We did but discuss and jest'; say, 'Was it at Allah and His signs, and His Apostle, that ye mocked?'

Make no excuse! Ye have misbelieved after your faith; if we forgive one sect of you, we will torment another sect, for that they sinned!

The hypocrites, men and women, some of them follow others, bidding what is wrong and forbidding what is right, and they clench their hands.[17] They forget Allah and He forgets them! Verily, the hypocrites, they are the doers of abomination!

Allah has promised unto the hypocrites, men and women, and unto the misbelievers, hellfire, to dwell therein for aye; it is enough for them! Allah shall curse them, and theirs shall be enduring woe.

[70] Ye are like those who were before you. They were stronger than you and more abundant in wealth and

children; they enjoyed their portion then, and ye enjoy your portion, as they enjoyed their portion before you; and ye discuss as they discussed. Their works are vain in this world and the next, and they it is who lose.

Did there not come to them the declaration of those who were before them? of the people of Noah and 'Ad and Thamûd, and of the people of Abraham, and the people of Midian? and of the overturned (cities)?[18] Their apostles came to them with manifest signs; for Allah would not wrong them, but it was themselves they wronged.

And the believers, men and women, are some the patrons of others; they bid what is reasonable, and forbid what is wrong, and are steadfast in prayer, and give alms, and obey Allah and His Apostle. On these will Allah have mercy; verily, Allah is mighty, wise!

Allah has promised to believers, men and women, gardens beneath which rivers flow, to dwell therein for aye; and goodly places in the garden of Eden. But good-will from Allah is the greatest of all! that is the mighty happiness!

O thou prophet! strive strenuously against the misbe-lievers and the hypocrites, and be stern against them; for their resort is Hell, and an ill journey shall it be.

[75] They swear by Allah they did not speak it, but they did speak the word of misbelief; and they disbe-lieved after they had embraced Islam, and they designed what they could not attain; and they only disapproved it because Allah and His Apostle had enriched them of His grace.[19] If they turn again 'tis better for them; but if they turn their backs, Allah will torment them with mighty

woe in this world and in the next, nor shall they have upon the earth a patron or protector.

And of them are some who make a treaty with Allah, that 'If He bring us of His grace, we will give alms and we will surely be among the righteous.' But when He gave them of His grace they were niggardly thereof, and turned their backs and swerved aside. So He caused hypocrisy to pursue them in their hearts unto the day when they shall meet Him,—for that they did fail Allah in what they promised Him, and for that they were liars!

Do they not know that Allah knows their secrets and their whisperings, and that Allah knows the unseen things?

[80] Those who defame such of the believers as willingly give their alms, and such as can find nothing to give but their exertions, and who mock at them,—Allah will mock at them, and for them is grievous woe!

Ask forgiveness for them or ask not forgiveness for them! if they shouldst ask forgiveness for them seventy times, yet would not Allah forgive them; that is because they disbelieved in Allah and His Apostle, for Allah guides not a people who work abomination.

Those who were left behind[20] rejoiced in staying behind the Apostle of Allah, and were averse from fighting strenuously with their wealth and their persons in Allah's way, and said, 'March not forth in the heat.' Say, 'The Fire of Hell is hotter still, if ye could but discern!' Let them then laugh little, and let them weep much, as a recompense for that which they have earned!

But if Allah bring thee back to a sect of them, and they

ask thee then for leave to sally forth; say, 'Ye shall by no means ever sally forth with me, nor shall ye ever fight a foe with me! Verily, ye were content to sit at home the first time, sit ye then now with those who stay behind.'

[85] Pray not for any one of them who dies, and stand not by his tomb; verily, they disbelieved in Allah and His Apostle and died workers of abomination!

Let not their wealth and their children please you, Allah only wishes to torment them therewith in this world, and that their souls may pass away the while they misbelieve.

Whenever a surah is sent down to them, 'Believe ye in Allah, and fight strenuously together with His Apostle', those of them who have the means will ask thee for leave to stay at home and say, 'Let us be amongst those who stay behind.' They are content to be with those who are left behind. A stamp is set upon their hearts that they should not discern.

But the Apostle and those who believe with him are strenuous with their wealth and with their persons; these shall have good things, and these it is shall prosper.

[90] Allah has prepared for them gardens beneath which rivers flow, to dwell therein for aye; that is the mighty happiness!

There came certain desert Arabs that they might be excused; and those stayed behind who had called Allah and His Apostle liars. There shall befall those of them who misbelieved, a mighty woe. For the weak, and the sick, and those who cannot find wherewith to expend in alms there is no hindrance, so they be only sincere towards

Allah and His Apostle. There is no way against those who do well; for Allah is forgiving and merciful. Nor against those to whom, when they came to thee that thou shouldst mount them, thou didst say, 'I cannot find wherewith to mount you', turned their backs while their eyes poured forth with tears, for grief that they could not find wherewith to expend. Only is there a way against those who ask thee for leave to stay at home while they are rich; content to be with those who are left behind; on whose hearts Allah has set a stamp, so that they should not know.

[95] They make excuses to you when ye return to them: say, 'Make no excuse, we believe you not; Allah has informed us concerning you. Allah sees your works and His Apostle too!' Then shall ye be brought back unto Him who knows the unseen and the seen; and He shall inform you of that which ye have done.

They will adjure you by Allah when ye have come back to them, to turn aside from them; turn ye aside then from them; verily, they are a plague, and their resort is Hell! A recompense for that which they have earned!

They will adjure you to be pleased with them; but if ye are pleased with them, Allah will not be pleased with a people who work abomination.

The Arabs of the desert are keener in misbelief and hypocrisy, and are more likely not to know the bounds which Allah has sent down to His Apostle; but Allah is knowing and wise.

And of the Arabs of the desert are some who take what they expend to be a forced loan, and they wait a turn of fortune against you; against them shall a turn of evil fortune be; for Allah both hears and knows.

[100] And of the Arabs of the desert are some who believe in Allah and the last day, and who take what they expend in alms to be a means of approach to Allah and to the Apostle's prayers,—is it not a means of approach for them? Allah will make them enter into His mercy; verily, Allah is forgiving and merciful.

As for the foremost in the race, the first of those who fled,[21] and the helpers,[22] and those who followed them in their kindness, Allah is well pleased with them, and they are well pleased with Him; He has prepared for them gardens beneath which rivers flow, to dwell therein for aye; that is the mighty happiness.

And of those who are round about you of the Arabs of the desert, some are hypocrites, and of the people of Medina, some are stubborn in hypocrisy; thou dost not know them—we know them; we will torment them twice over; then shall they be sent off into mighty woe.

And others have confessed their sins,—that they have mixed with a righteous action another evil action;—haply it may be Allah will turn again to them; verily, Allah is forgiving and merciful.

Take from their wealth alms to cleanse and purify them thereby; and pray for them; verily, thy prayer is a repose for them; for Allah both hears and knows.

[105] Do they not know that Allah accepts repentance from His servants, and takes alms; and that Allah is He who is easily turned and merciful.

And say, 'Act ye'; and Allah and His Apostle and the believers shall see your acts, and ye shall be brought back to Him who knows the seen and the unseen, and He shall inform you of that which ye have done.

And others are in hopes of Allah's bidding; whether He will torment them, or whether He turn again towards them; for Allah is knowing, wise.

And there are those who have taken to a mosque for mischief, and for misbelief, and to make a breach amongst the believers, and for an ambush for him who made war against Allah and His Apostle before; they surely swear, 'We only wished for what was good'; but Allah bears witness that they are liars.

Never stand up therein!—there is a mosque founded on piety from the first day;[23] it is more right that thou shouldst stand therein;—therein are men who love to be clean; for Allah doth love the clean.

[110] Is he who has laid his foundation upon the fear of Allah and of His goodwill better, or he who has laid his foundation upon a crumbling wall of sand, which crumbles away with him into the Fire of Hell?—but Allah guides not a people who do wrong.

The building which they[24] have built will not cease to be a source of doubt in their hearts until their hearts are cut asunder;[25] but Allah is knowing, wise.

Verily, Allah hath bought of the believers their persons and their wealth, for the paradise they are to have; they shall fight in the way of Allah, and they shall slay and be slain: promised in truth, in the law and the gospel and the Qur'ân;—and who is more faithful to His covenant than Allah?

Be ye glad then in the covenant which ye have made with

Him, for that is the mighty happiness! Those who repent, those who worship, those who praise, those who fast, those who bow down, those who adore, those who bid what is right and forbid what is wrong, and those who keep the bounds of Allah,—glad tidings to those who believe!

[115] It is not for the prophet and those who believe to ask forgiveness for the idolaters, even though they be their kindred, after it has been made manifest to them that they are the fellows of Hell.

Nor was Abraham's asking pardon for his father aught else but through a promise he had promised him; but when it was made manifest to him that he was an enemy to Allah, he cleansed himself of him; verily, Abraham was pitiful and clement.

Nor will Allah lead astray a people after He has guided them until that is made manifest to them which they have to fear; verily, Allah all things doth know.

Verily, Allah's is the kingdom of the heavens and the earth! He quickens and He kills! Nor have ye beside Allah a patron or protector.

Allah has now turned towards the prophet and those who fled with him, and towards the helpers who followed him in the hour of difficulty, after that the hearts of a part of them had well-nigh gone amiss.

Then He turned unto them; verily to them He is kind and merciful:—unto the three²⁶ who were left behind, so that the earth with all its ample space was too strait for them, and their souls were straitened for them, and they thought that there was no refuge for them from Allah save unto Him.

Then He turned again towards them that they might also turn; verily, Allah, He is easily turned and merciful!

[120] O ye who believe! fear Allah and be with those who speak the truth.

It was not for the people of Medina, and those around about them of the Arabs of the desert, to stay behind the Apostle of Allah and not to prefer their souls to his: that is because neither thirst, nor toil, nor heat, nor hunger befell them on Allah's way. Nor do they stop to anger the misbelievers, nor do they get any (harm) from the enemy without a good work being written down to them; verily, Allah wastes not the hire of those who do well.

Nor do they expend in alms a small or great expense, nor do they cross a wady[27] without it being written down to them; that Allah may reward them with better than that which they have done.

The believers should not march forth altogether; and if a troop of every division of them march not forth, it is only that they may study their religion and warn their people when they return to them, that haply they may beware.

O ye who believe! fight those who are near to you of the misbelievers, and let them find in you sternness; and know that Allah is with those who fear.

[125] And whenever a surah is sent down, there are some of them who say, 'Which of you has this increased in faith?' But as for those who believe, it does increase them in faith, and they shall rejoice: but as for those in whose hearts is sickness, it only adds a plague to their plague, and they die misbelievers.

Do they not see that they are tried in every year once or twice? Yet they do not turn again, nor do they mind!

And whenever a surah is sent down, some of them look at the others—'Does any one see you?'—Then they turn away! Allah has turned their hearts, for that they are a people who do not discern.

There has come to you an apostle from amongst yourselves; hard for him to bear is it that ye commit iniquity; he is anxious over you after the believers, pitiful, compassionate.

[130] But if they turn their backs, then say, 'Allah is enough for me! There is no god but He! Upon Him do I rely, for He is Lord of the mighty throne!'

THE CHAPTER OF JONAH
(PEACE BE ON HIM!)

X (*Mecca*)

In the name of the merciful and compassionate Allah.

A. L. R. Those are the signs of the wise Book! Was it a wonder to the folk[1] that we inspired a man from amongst themselves, 'Warn thou the folk; and give glad tidings to those who believe, that for them there is an advance of sincerity[2] gone before them with their Lord?' The misbelievers say, 'Verily, this is an obvious sorcerer!'

Verily, your Lord is Allah, who created the heavens and the earth in six days; then He made for the throne, to govern the affair; there is no intercessor, except after His permission. That is Allah for you—your Lord! Then worship Him—do ye not mind?

To Him is your return all of you—Allah's promise in truth; verily, He produces the creature, then He makes it return again, that He may recompense those who believe and do what is right with justice; but those who misbelieve, for them is a drink of boiling water, and grievous woe, for that they did misbelieve.

[5] He it is who made the sun for a brightness, and the moon for a light, and decreed for it mansions, that ye may know the number of the years and the reckoning.—Allah only created that in truth. He details the signs unto a people who do know.

Verily, in the alternation of night and day, and in what Allah has created of the heavens and the earth, are signs unto a people who do fear.

Verily, those who hope not for our meeting, and are content with the life of this world, and are comforted thereby, and those who are neglectful of our signs,—these, their resort is fire for that which they have earned!

Verily, those who believe and do what is right, their Lord guides them by their faith; beneath them shall rivers flow in the gardens of pleasure.

[10] Their cry therein shall be, 'Celebrated be Thy praises, O Allah!' and their salutation therein shall be, 'Peace!' and the end of their cry shall be, 'Praise (belongs) to Allah, the Lord of the worlds!'

And if Allah should hasten on the bad to men as they would hasten on the good, their appointed time would surely be fulfilled. But we will let those who hope not for our meeting go on in their rebellion, blindly wandering on.

When distress touches man, he calls us to his side, whether sitting or standing; but when we have removed from him his distress, he passes on as though he had not called on us in a distress that touched him. Thus unto the extravagant is made seemly that which they have done.

We have already destroyed generations before you when they did wrong, and there came to them their apostles with manifest signs, but they would not believe. Thus do we reward the sinful people.

[15] Then we made you their successors in the earth after them, that we may see how ye will act.

But when our evident signs are recited to them, those who hope not for our meeting say, 'Bring a Qur'ân other than this; or change it.' Say, 'It is not for me to change it of my own accord; I do not follow aught but what I am inspired with; verily, I fear, if I rebel against my Lord, the torment of a mighty day!'

Say, 'Had Allah pleased, I should not have recited it to you, nor taught you therewith. I have tarried a lifetime amongst you before it;—have ye not then any sense?'

Who is more unjust than he who forges against Allah a lie, or says His signs are lies? Verily, the sinners shall not prosper.

They worship beside Allah what can neither harm them nor profit them, and they say, 'These are our intercessors with Allah!' Say, 'Will ye inform Allah of aught in the heavens or the earth, that He knows not of?' Celebrated be His praise! and exalted be He, above what they associate with Him!

[20] People were but one nation once, then they disagreed; and had it not been for thy Lord's word already passed, there would have been decided between them that concerning which they disagreed.

They say, 'Why is not a sign sent down upon him from his Lord?' Say, 'The unseen is only Allah's; but wait ye for a while, verily, I with you am one of those who wait!'

When we have let men taste of mercy after distress which has touched them, lo! they use a stratagem against our signs! Say, 'Allah is quicker at stratagem.' Verily, our messengers[3] write down what stratagem ye use.

He it is who makes you travel in the land and sea, until when ye are in the ships—and these carry them[4] afloat with a favouring wind, and they rejoice therein, there comes to them a violent wind, and there comes to them the wave from every place, and they think that they are encompassed about; then they call on Allah, sincere in religion towards Him, 'If thou dost save from this we will surely be of those who thank.' But when He has saved them, lo! they are wilfulness in the earth unjustly;—O ye folk! your wilfulness against yourselves is but a provision of this world's life; then unto us is your return, and we will inform you of that which ye have done!

[25] Verily, the likeness of this world's life is like water which we send down from the sky, and the plants of the earth, from which men and cattle eat, are mingled therewith; until when the earth puts on its gilding and is adorned, the people thereof think that they have power over it. Our order comes to it by night or day, and we make it as it were mown down—as though it had not

yesterday been rich!—Thus do we detail the signs unto a people who reflect.

Allah calls unto the abode of peace, and guides whom He will into the right path.

To those who do what is good, goodness and increase! nor shall blackness or abasement cover their faces! These are the fellows of Paradise, they shall dwell therein for aye.

But, as for those who have earned ill, the reward of evil is the like thereof; abasement shall cover them! They shall have none to defend them against Allah;—as though their faces were veiled with the deep darkness of the night; these are the fellows of the Fire, and they shall dwell therein for aye.

And on the day we gather them all together then we will say to those who associated other gods (with us), 'To your places, ye and your associates!' and we will part them; and their associates will say, 'It was not us ye worshipped.—[30] But Allah is witness enough between us and you, that we were heedless of your worshipping us.' There shall every soul prove what it has sent on before; and they shall be returned unto Allah, their Allah, their true sovereign, and that which they devised shall stray away from them.

Say, 'Who provides you from the heaven and the earth? who has dominion over hearing and sight? and who brings forth the living from the dead, and brings forth the dead from the living? and who governs the affair?' And they will say, 'Allah.' Say, 'Do ye not then fear?'

That is Allah, your true Lord! and what is there after the truth but error? How then can ye turn away?

Thus is the word of thy Lord verified against those who commit abomination; verily, they will not believe. Say, 'Is there any of your associates who can produce a creature and then turn it back again?' Say, 'Allah produces a creature, then turns it back again; how then can ye lie?' [35] Say, 'Is there any of your associates who guides unto the truth?' Say, 'Allah guides unto the truth.' Is then He who guides unto the truth more worthy to be followed, or he that guides not except he be himself guided? What ails you then, how ye judge?

But most of them follow only suspicion; verily, suspicion does not avail against the truth at all; verily, Allah knows what they do.

This Qur'ân could not have been devised by any beside Allah; but it verifies that which was before it, and details the Book—there is no doubt therein—from the Lord of the worlds.

Do they say, 'He⁵ hath devised it'? Say then, 'Bring a surah like it,—and call, if ye can, on other than Allah, if ye do tell the truth!'

[40] Yet they call that a lie, the knowledge of which they cannot compass, while its interpretation has not yet come to them; so did those before them charge with lying, and see what was the end of the unjust!

Of them are some who believe therein; and of them are some who do not believe therein; but thy Lord knows best who are corrupters.

But if they call thee liar, say, 'I have my work, and ye have your work; ye are clear of what I work, and I am clear of what ye work.'

There are some of them who listen to thee—canst thou make the deaf to hear, although they have no sense? And of them are some who look at thee—canst thou guide the blind, although they cannot see?

[45] Verily, Allah wrongs not man at all, but men do wrong themselves.

And on the day when we will gather them together it will be as though they had not tarried save an hour of the day, they shall know each other. Lost are those who called the meeting with Allah a lie, and were not guided!

Either we will show thee something of that with which we threatened them, or we will take thee to ourself, for unto us is their return; then is Allah a witness to what they do.

Every nation has its apostle; and when their apostle comes to them, it is decided between them with justice, and they are not wronged.

But they say, 'When is this threat (to come), if ye tell the truth?'

[50] Say, 'I have no power over myself for harm or for profit, save what Allah will. Every nation has its appointed time; when their appointed time comes to them they cannot delay it for an hour or bring it on.'

Say, 'Let us see now when the torment comes to you, by night or day, what will the sinners fain bring on thereof? And when it has fallen—will ye believe in it now!—And yet ye wish to bring it on! Then shall it be said to those who have done wrong, "Taste ye the torment of eternity! Shall ye be recompensed except for that which ye have earned?"' They will ask thee to inform them whether it be true. Say, 'Aye, by my Lord! verily, it is the truth, nor can ye weaken him.'

[55] And if every soul that hath done wrong had whatever is in the earth, it would give it as a ransom. They will utter their repentance when they see the torment; and it shall be decided between them with justice, nor shall they be wronged.

Is not indeed what is in the heavens and what is in the earth Allah's? Is not indeed the promise of Allah true? Though most of them know not. He quickens and He kills, and unto Him are ye returned!

O ye folk! there has come to you a warning from your Lord, and a balm for what is in your breasts, and a guidance and a mercy to believers.

Say, 'By the grace of Allah and by His mercy,—and in that let them rejoice! It is better than that which they collect!'

[60] Let us see now what Allah has sent down to you of provision! and yet ye have made of it unlawful and lawful. Say, 'Does Allah permit you, or against Allah do ye forge lies?'

What will those who forge lies against Allah think on the resurrection day? Verily, Allah is Lord of grace towards men, but most of them do not give thanks!

Nor shalt thou be in any affair, nor shalt thou recite concerning it a Qur'ân[6]—nor shall ye do a work, without our being witness against you, when ye are engaged therein: nor does the weight of an atom escape thy Lord in earth or in heaven; nor is there less than that or greater, but it is in the perspicuous Book.

Are not, verily, the friends of Allah those on whom there is no fear, neither shall they be grieved?—They who believed and who did fear—[65] for them are good tidings in the life of this world, and in the future too; there is no changing the words of Allah! That is the mighty happiness!

Let not their speech grieve thee; verily, power is wholly Allah's! He both hears and knows.

Is not, verily, whoever is in the heavens and whoever is in the earth Allah's? What then do they follow who call on associates other than Allah?

Verily, they follow nothing but suspicion, and verily, they are telling naught but lies.

He it is who made for you the night, that ye might rest therein, and the day to see therein; verily, in that are signs unto a people who can hear.

They say, 'Allah has taken to Himself a son.' Celebrated be His praises! He is the rich one! His is whatever is in the heavens, and whatever is in the earth. Ye have no authority for this! will ye say against Allah, that which ye do not know?

[70] Say, 'Verily, those who forge against Allah a lie shall not prosper!'

A provision in this world—then unto us is their return! then we will make them taste keen torment for that they misbelieved.

Recite to them the story of Noah, when he said to his people, 'O my people! if my stay with you be grievous to you, and my reminding you of the signs of Allah, yet upon Allah do I rely! Collect then your affairs and your associates;⁷ nor let your affair (be ordered) for you in the dark; then decide respecting me, and do not wait; and if ye turn your backs, I ask you not for hire; my hire is only due from Allah, and I am bidden to be of those resigned.' But they called him a liar; and we saved him, and those with him, in the ark; and we made these[8] successors, and drowned those who had said our signs were lies; see then how was the end of those who had been warned!

[75] Then we raised up after him apostles unto their people, and they came to them with manifest signs; but they would not believe in what they had called a lie before. Thus do we set a stamp upon the hearts of the transgressors.

Then we raised up after them Moses and Aaron, unto Pharaoh and his chiefs with our signs; but they were too big with pride, and were a sinful people; and when the truth came to them from us they said, verily, 'This is obvious sorcery.'

Moses said, 'Will ye say of the truth when it comes to you, "Is this sorcery?" But sorcerers shall not prosper.'

They said, 'Hast thou come to turn us away from what we found our fathers at, that there may be for you twain grandeur in the earth? But we will not believe you.'

[80] And Pharaoh said, 'Bring me every knowing sorcerer'; and when the sorcerers came, Moses said to them, 'Throw down what ye have to throw!' and when they threw down, Moses said, 'What ye have brought is sorcery! Verily, Allah will make it vain; verily, Allah rights not the work of evil-doers!'

But Allah verifies the truth by His words, although the sinners are averse therefrom.

But none believed in Moses, save a race of his own people, through fear of Pharaoh and his chiefs; lest he should afflict them, for verily, Pharaoh was lofty in the earth, and verily, he was extravagant.

And Moses said, 'O my people! if ye did believe in Allah, then on Him rely, if ye be resigned.' [85] They said, 'Upon Allah do we rely. O our Lord! make us not a cause of trial for a people who do wrong, but save us by Thy mercy from the people who misbelieve!'

And we inspired Moses and his brother thus, 'Establish, ye twain, houses for your people in Egypt; and make ye your houses a qibla;⁹ and be ye steadfast in prayer, and give glad tidings to those who believe.'

Moses said, 'O our Lord! verily, Thou hast brought to Pharaoh and his chiefs ornaments and wealth in the life of this world; O our Lord! that they may err from Thy way! O our Lord! confound their wealth and harden their hearts that they may not believe until they see grievous woe!' He said, 'Your prayer is answered; be upright then, ye two, and follow not the path of those who do not know!'

[90] And we brought the children of Israel across the sea; and Pharaoh and his hosts followed them eager and hostile, until when drowning overtook him, he said, 'I believe that there is no god but He in whom the children of Israel believe, and I am of those who are resigned!'— 'Now!¹⁰ but thou didst rebel aforetime, and wert of those who do evil; but today we will save thee in thy body, that thou mayest be to those who come after thee a sign, for verily, many men are careless of our signs!'¹¹

And we established the people of Israel with a sure

establishment, and we provided them with good things; nor did they disagree until there came to them the knowledge. Verily, thy Lord shall decide between them on the resurrection day concerning that whereon they did dispute.

And if thou art in doubt of that which we have sent down unto thee, ask those who read the Book before thee; verily, the truth is come to thee from thy Lord, be not then of those who are in doubt. And be not of those who say the signs of Allah are lies, or thou wilt be of those who lose! [95] Verily, those against whom Allah's word is pronounced will not believe, even though there come to them every sign, until they see the grievous woe. Were it not so, a city would have believed and its faith would have profited it. But (none did) except the people of Jonas; when they believed we removed from them the torment of disgrace in this world, and we gave them provision for a while. But had thy Lord pleased, all who are in the earth would have believed altogether; as for thee, wilt thou force men to become believers?

[100] It is not for any person to believe save by the permission of Allah; He puts horror on those who have no sense.

Say, 'Behold what is in the heavens and in the earth! but signs and warners avail not a people who do not believe. Do they await aught but the like of the days of those who passed away before them?' Say, 'Wait ye then! Verily, I am with you one of those who wait.' Then we will save our apostles and those who believe; thus is it due from us to save believers.

Say, 'O ye folk! if ye are in doubt concerning my religion, I will not worship those ye worship other than Allah; but I worship Allah, 'who takes you to Himself, and I am bidden to be of the believers!' [105] And, 'Make steadfast thy face to the religion as a *hanîf*;[12] and be not of the idolaters; and call not besides Allah on what can neither profit thee nor harm thee; for if thou dost, verily, thou art then of the unjust!'

And should Allah touch thee with harm, there is none to remove it save He; and if He wish thee well, there is none to repel His grace; He makes it fall on whom He will of His servants; for He is pardoning and merciful!

Say, 'O ye people! there has come to you the truth from your Lord, and he who is guided, his guidance is only for his soul; and he who errs, errs only against it; and I am not a guardian over you.'

Follow what is revealed to thee, and be patient until Allah judges, for He is the best of judges.

THE CHAPTER OF HÛD

XI (*Mecca*)

A. L. R. A book whose signs are confirmed and then detailed, from the wise one, the aware: that ye worship not other than Allah,—verily, I am to you from Him a warner and a herald of glad tidings; and that ye seek pardon from your Lord, then turn again to Him! He will cause you to enjoy a good provision to a named and appointed time,

devise has strayed away from them. No doubt but that in the hereafter these are those who lose!

[25] Verily, those who believe and do what is right, and humble themselves to their Lord, they are the fellows of Paradise; they shall dwell therein for aye. The two parties' likeness is as the blind and the deaf, and the seeing and the hearing; shall they two be equal in likeness? will ye not mind?

We did send Noah unto his people, 'Verily, I am to you an obvious warner; that ye should not worship any save Allah. Verily, I fear for you the torment of the grievous day. But the chiefs of those who misbelieved amongst his people said, 'We only see in thee a mortal like ourselves; nor do we see that any follow thee except the reprobates amongst us by a rash judgement; nor do we see that you have any preference over us; nay more, we think you liars!' [30] He said, 'O my people! let us see! if I stand upon a manifest sign from my Lord, and there come to me mercy from Him, and ye are blinded to it; shall we force you to it while ye are averse therefrom?

'O my people! I do not ask you for wealth in return for it; my hire is only from Allah; nor do I repulse those who believe; verily, they shall meet their Lord. But I see you, a people who are ignorant. O my people! who will help me against Allah, were I to repulse you? do ye not then mind? I do not say that I have the treasures of Allah; nor do I know the unseen; nor do I say, "Verily, I am an angel"; nor do I say of those whom your eyes despise, "Allah will never give them any good!"—Allah knows best what is in their souls—verily, then should I be of the unjust.'

They said, 'O Noah! thou hast wrangled with us, and hast multiplied wranglings with us; bring us then what thou hast threatened us with, if thou art of those who tell the truth.' [35] Said he, 'Allah will only bring it on you if He pleases, nor can ye make Him helpless; nor will my advice profit you, should I wish to advise you, if Allah wish to lead you into error. He is your Lord, and unto Him shall ye be returned.'

Do they say, 'He has devised it'?³ Say, 'If I have devised it, then on me be my sin. But I am clear of that wherein ye sin.'

And Noah was inspired, 'None shall surely believe amongst thy people but those who have believed already; take not then ill that which they do. And make the ark under our eyes, and at our inspiration; and plead not with me for those who have done wrong; verily, they shall be drowned.'

[40] So he made the ark, and every time the chiefs of his people passed by him they jested at him. Said he, 'If ye jest at us, verily, we shall jest at you even as ye are jesting, and ye shall surely know.

'He to whom a torment comes, it shall shame him, and there shall light upon him lasting torment.'

Until at length when our order came, and the oven boiled,⁴ we said, 'Load therein of every kind two, and likewise thy family,—save those on whom the sentence has already been passed—likewise those who believe'; but there believed not with him save a few. And he said, 'Ride ye therein; in the name of Allah is its course, and its mooring. Verily, my Lord is forgiving and merciful.'

And it floated on with them mid waves like mountains;

and Noah cried to his son who had gone aside, 'O my boy! ride with us and be not with the misbelievers.' [45] Said he, 'I will betake me to a mountain that shall save me from the water.' Said he, 'There is none to save today from the command of Allah, except for him on whom He may have mercy.' And the wave came between them, and he was amongst the drowned.[5]

And it was said, 'O earth! swallow down thy water!' and, 'O heaven! hold!' and the water abated; and the affair was decided, and it[6] settled on Jûdî,[7] and it was said, 'Away with the people who are evil-doers!'

And Noah went unto his Lord and said, 'My Lord, verily, my son is of my people, and, verily, Thy promise is true, and Thou art the justest of judges.' He said, 'O Noah! he is not of thy people; verily, it is a work that is not right. Then, ask me not for that of which thou knowest naught. Verily, I admonish thee that thou shouldst not be of the ignorant.' He said, 'My Lord, verily, I seek refuge in Thee from asking Thee for aught of which I know nothing; and, unless Thou dost forgive me and have mercy on me, I shall be of those who lose.'

[50] It was said, 'O Noah! descend in safety from us, and blessings upon thee and upon (some) nations of those who are with thee;[8] but (some) nations we will allow to enjoy prosperity and then there shall touch them from us grievous woe.' These are stories of the unseen which we reveal to thee; thou didst not know them, thou nor thy people before this. Be patient, then; verily, the issue is for those who fear.

And unto 'Âd (we sent) their brother Hûd; he said, 'O

my people! serve Allah; ye have no god but Him. Ye do but devise a lie. O my people! I do not ask you for hire in return; my hire is only from Him who created me: have ye then no sense?

'O my people! ask pardon of your Lord; then turn to Him; He will send the skies down on you in torrents; [55] and He will add strength to your strength: do not then turn back sinners.'

They said, 'O Hûd! thou hast not come to us with a manifest sign; nor will we leave our gods at thy word; nor will we believe in thee. We can only say that some of our gods have attacked thee with evil.' Said he, 'Verily, I call Allah to witness, and do ye bear witness too, that I am free from that which ye associate beside Him.

'Plot then against me altogether, and give me no delay. Verily, I rely upon Allah, my Lord and your Lord. There is no beast that walks, but He taketh it by its forelock. Verily, my Lord is on the right way!

[60] 'But if ye turn your backs,—then I have conveyed to you what I was sent to you with; and my Lord will make another people your successors. Ye cannot harm Him at all; verily, my Lord is guardian over all!'

And when our order came we saved Hûd, and those who believed with him, by mercy from us; and we saved them from harsh torment. That (tribe of) 'Âd denied the signs of their Lord, and rebelled against His apostles, and followed the bidding of every headstrong tyrant. They were followed in this world by a curse, and on the resurrection day—'Did not 'Âd disbelieve their Lord? Aye! away with 'Âd the people of Hûd!'

And unto Thamûd (we sent) their brother Zâli'h; said he, 'O my people! worship Allah; ye have no god but Him. He it is that produced you from the earth, and made you live therein! Then ask pardon of Him; then turn again to Him: verily, my Lord is nigh and answers!'

[65] They said, 'O Zâli'h! thou wert amongst us one we hoped in before this: dost thou forbid us to worship what our fathers worshipped? Verily, we are in hesitating doubt as to that to which thou callest us.'

He said, 'O my people! let us see; if I stand upon a manifest sign from my Lord, and there come from Him mercy, who will help me against Allah if I rebel against Him? Ye will add only to my loss.

'O my people! this she-camel[9] of Allah is a sign for you; leave her, then, to feed in Allah's earth, and touch her not with evil, or there will catch you torment that is nigh.' But they did hamstring her, and he said, 'Enjoy yourselves in your houses for three days;—that is the promise that shall not be belied.'

And when our order came we saved Zâli'h, and those who believed with him, by our mercy, from disgrace upon that day. Verily, thy Lord He is powerful and mighty.

[70] And the noise caught those who had done wrong; and on the morrow they were lying corpses in their houses, as though they had never dwelt therein. Did not Thamûd indeed disbelieve in their Lord? Aye! away with Thamûd!

Our messengers did come to Abraham with glad tidings; they said, 'Peace!' He said, 'Peace be it!' nor did he delay to bring the roasted calf. But when he saw that their hands

reached not thereto, he could not understand them, and
harboured fear of them. They said, 'Fear not. Verily, we
are sent unto the people of Lot.' And his wife was standing
by, laughing; and we gave her the glad tidings of Isaac,
and of Jacob after Isaac. [75] Said she, 'Alas for me! shall
I bear a son when I am an old woman, and this husband
of mine an old man? Verily, this is a wonderful thing!'
They said, 'Dost thou wonder at the bidding of Allah?
Allah's mercy and blessings upon you, ye people of the
house! Verily, He is to be praised and glorified.'

And when his terror left Abraham, and the glad tidings
came to him, he wrangled with us about the people of
Lot; verily, Abraham was clement, pitiful, relenting.

'O Abraham! avoid this; verily, the bidding of thy Lord
has come; verily, there is coming to them torment that
cannot be put off.'

[80] And when our messengers came to Lot, he was
grieved for them; but his arm was straitened for them,[10]
and he said, 'This is a troublesome day!' And his people
came to him, rushing at him, for before that they used to
work evil. He said, 'O my people! here are my daughters,
they are purer for you; then, fear Allah, and do not
disgrace me through my guests;—is there not among you
one right-thinking man?'

They said, 'Thou knowest that we have no claim on thy
daughters; verily, thou knowest what we want!' He said,
'Had I but power over you; or could I but resort to some
strong column . . .!'[11] (The angels) said, 'O Lot! verily, we
are the messengers of thy Lord, they shall certainly not
reach thee; then travel with thy people in the darkness of

the night, and let none of you look round except thy wife: verily, there shall befall her what befalls them. Verily, their appointment is for the morning! and is not the morning nigh?'

And when our bidding came, we made their high parts their low parts.¹² And we rained down upon them stones and baked clay¹³ one after another, marked,¹⁴ from thy Lord, and these are not so far from the unjust!¹⁵

[85] And unto Midian (we sent) their brother Sho'hâib.¹⁶ He said, 'O my people! serve Allah; ye have no god but Him, and give not short measure and weight. Verily, I see you well off; but, verily, I fear for you the torments of an encompassing day. O my people! give measure and weight fairly, and defraud not men of their things; and wreak not wrong in the earth, corrupting it. Allah's residue¹⁷ is better for you if ye be believers. But I am not a guardian over you.'

They said, 'O Sho'hâib! Do thy prayers bid thee that we should forsake what our fathers served, or that we should not do as we please with our wealth? Thou art, forsooth, the clement and straightforward one!'

[90] He said, 'O my people! Do ye see? If I stand upon a manifest sign from my Lord, and He provides me from Himself with a goodly provision, and I consent not with you to that which I forbid you, I only wish to better you so far as I can,—nor comes my grace through any one but Allah; on Him do I rely, and unto Him I turn. O my people! let not a breach with me make you so sin that there befall you the like of that which befell the people of Noah, or the people of Hûd, or the people of Zâli'h—nor are the

people of Lot so far from you! Ask pardon, then, from your Lord, then turn to Him; verily, my Lord is merciful, loving!'

They said, 'O Sho'hâib! we do not understand much of what thou sayest, and we see that thou art weak amongst us; and were it not for thy family we would stone thee, nor couldst thou be powerful over us.'

He said, 'O my people! are my family more esteemed by you than Allah? or have you taken Him as something to cast behind your backs? Verily, my Lord, whate'er ye do, doth comprehend. [95] O my people! act according to your power; verily, I too will act, and ye at length shall know! To whomsoever torment comes it shall disgrace him, and him who is a liar. Watch then; verily, I with you am watching too!'

And when our bidding came we saved Sho'hâib, and those who believed with him, by our mercy; and the noise caught those who had done wrong, and on the morrow they were in their houses prone, as though they had not dwelt therein. Aye! 'Away with Midian!' as it was, 'Away with Thamûd!'

And we sent Moses with our signs and with obvious power unto Pharaoh and his chiefs; but they followed Pharaoh's bidding, and Pharaoh's bidding was not straightforward.

[100] He shall approach his people on the resurrection day, and take them down to water[18] at the Fire,—an evil watering place to water at!

In this (world) were they followed by a curse; and on the resurrection day evil shall be the aid they are aided with!

That is one of the stories of the cities which we recite to thee—some of them are standing now and some mown down!

We did not wrong them, but they wronged themselves. Their gods availed them naught, on which they called instead of Allah, when once the bidding of thy Lord had come; nor did they add save to their downfall!

Thus is thy Lord's overtaking when He overtakes the cities that have done wrong; verily, His overtaking is grievous, keen.

[105] Verily, in that is a sign to him who fears the torment of the last day;—that is a day unto which men shall be gathered;—that is a witnessed day!

We will not delay it, save unto a numbered and appointed time. The day when it shall come no soul shall speak save by His permission, and amongst them (shall be) the wretched and the glad.

And as for those who are wretched—why, in the Fire! there shall they groan and sob! to dwell therein for aye, so long as the heavens and the earth endure; save what thy Lord will. Verily, thy Lord is one who works His will.

[110] And as for those who are glad—why, in Paradise! to dwell therein for aye, so long as the heavens and the earth endure; save what thy Lord will,[19]—a ceaseless boon!

Be not then in doubt concerning what these men do serve;—they only serve as their fathers served before; and we will give them their portion undiminished.

We gave Moses the Book before, and then they disagreed concerning it, and, had it not been for a word that had been passed by thy Lord, it would have been decided between them; but, verily, they are (still) in hesitating doubt concerning it.

But, verily, every one thy Lord will surely repay for their works; verily, He of what they do is well aware!

Do thou then be upright, as thou art bidden, and whosoever turns repentantly with thee; and transgress ye not:—verily, He on what ye do doth look.

[115] Lean not unto those who do wrong, lest the Fire touch you, for ye have no patrons but Allah; and, moreover, ye shall not be helped!

And be thou steadfast in prayer at the two ends of the day, and the (former and latter) parts of the night. Verily, good works remove evil works;—that is a reminder to the mindful! And be thou patient, for Allah wastes not the hire of those who do good.

And were there among the generations before you any endowed with a remnant (of piety) forbidding evil-doing in the earth, save a few of those whom we saved; but the evil-doers followed what they enjoyed, and were sinners.

Thy Lord would not have destroyed the cities unjustly while the people of them were well doers.

[120] Had thy Lord pleased, He would have made men one nation; but they will not cease to differ, save those thy Lord has had mercy on. For this has He created them, and the word of thy Lord is fulfilled, 'I will surely fill Hell with jinns and mankind altogether.'

And all that we relate to thee of the stories of the apostles is what will stablish thy heart: and herein has the truth come to thee, and an admonition and a reminder to the believers.

Say to those who believe not, 'Act according to your power, verily, we are acting too! And wait ye, verily, we are waiting too!'

Allah's are the unseen things of the heavens and of the earth; and unto Him the affair doth all return. Then serve Him and rely on Him; for thy Lord is not heedless of that which ye do.

THE CHAPTER OF JOSEPH (PEACE BE ON HIM!)

XII (*Mecca*)

In the name of the merciful and compassionate Allah.

A. L. R. Those are the signs of the perspicuous Book. Verily, we have revealed it, an Arabic Qur'ân; haply ye may understand.

We tell thee the best of stories, in inspiring thee with this Qur'ân, though thou wert before it among the heedless.

When Joseph said to his father, 'O my sire! verily, I saw eleven stars, and the sun, and the moon,—I saw them adoring me!'

[5] He said, 'O my boy! tell not thy vision to thy brethren, for they will plot a plot against thee; verily, the devil is to man an open foe.'

Thus does thy Lord choose thee, and teach thee the interpretation of sayings, and fulfil His favour upon thee, and upon Jacob's people, as He fulfilled it upon they two forefathers before thee, Abraham and Isaac,—verily, thy Lord is knowing, wise!

In Joseph and his brethren were signs to those who enquire!

When they said, 'Surely, Joseph and his brother are dearer to our father than we, a band¹ although we be; verily, our father is in obvious error.

'Slay Joseph, or cast him in some land; that your father's face may be free for you, and ye may be, after he is gone, a people who do right.'

[10] A speaker from amongst them spake, 'Slay not Joseph, but throw him into the bottom of the pit; some of the travellers may pick him up, if so ye do.'

Said they, 'O our father! what ails thee that thou wilt not trust us with Joseph while we are unto him sincere? Send him with us tomorrow to revel and to play, and, verily, we over him will keep good guard.'

Said he, 'Verily, it grieves me that ye should go off with him, for I fear lest the wolf devour him while ye of him do take no heed.'

Said they, 'Why, if the wolf should devour him while we are (such) a band, verily, we then should deserve to lose!'

[15] And when they had gone off with him and agreed to put him in the depths of the pit, and we inspired him, 'Thou shalt surely inform them of this affair of theirs and they shall not perceive.'²

And they came to their father at eve and weeping said, 'O our father! verily, we went forth to race and left Joseph by our goods, and the wolf devoured him,—but thou wilt not believe us, truth tellers though we be.'

And they brought his shirt with lying blood upon it. Said he, 'Nay, but your souls have induced you to do this; but patience is fair! and Allah is He whom I ask for aid against that which ye describe.'

And travellers came and sent their water drawer; and he let down his bucket. Said he, 'O glad tidings! this is a youth.' And they kept him secret, as a chattel; but Allah knew what they were doing.

[20] And they sold him for a mean price,—drachmæ counted out,—and they parted with him cheaply.

And the man from Egypt who had bought him said to his wife, 'Honour his abiding here; it may be he will be of use to us, or we may adopt him as a son.'

Thus did we stablish Joseph in the land; and we did surely teach him the interpretation of sayings; for Allah can overcome His affairs, though most men do not know.

And when he had reached his strength[3] we brought him judgement and knowledge, for thus do we reward those who do good.

And she in whose house he was desired him for his person; and she locked the doors and said, 'Come along with thee!' Said he, 'Refuge in Allah! verily, my Lord has made good my abiding here; verily, the wrongdoers shall not prosper.'

And she was anxious for him, and he would have been anxious for her, had it not been that he saw the demonstration[4] of his Lord; thus did we turn evil and fornication from him; verily, he was of our sincere servants.

[25] And they raced to the door and she rent his shirt from behind; and they met her master at the door. Said

she, 'What is the recompense of him who wishes evil for thy family, but that imprisonment or a grievous torment?'

Said he, 'She desired me for my person.' And a witness from among her family bore witness: 'If his shirt be rent from in front, then she speaks the truth and he is of the liars; but if his shirt be rent from behind, then she lies and he is of the truth tellers.'

And when he saw his shirt rent from behind he said, 'This is one of your tricks; verily, your tricks are mighty! Joseph! turn aside from this. And do thou, woman, ask pardon for thy fault; verily, thou wert of the sinners.'

[30] And women in the city said, 'The wife of the prince desires her young man for his person; he has infatuated her with love: verily, we see her in obvious error.' And when she heard of their craftiness, she sent to them and prepared for them a banquet, and gave each of them a knife; and she said, 'Come forth to them!' And when they saw him they said, 'Great Allah!' and cut their hands[5] and said, 'Allah forbid! This is no mortal, this is nothing but an honourable angel.' Said she, 'This is he concerning whom ye blamed me. I did desire him for his person, but he was too continent. But if he do not what I bid him he shall surely be imprisoned and shall surely be among the small!' Said he, 'My Lord! Prison is dearer to me than what they call on me to do; and unless Thou turn from me their craftiness I shall feel a passion for them and shall be among the ignorant!' And his Lord answered him and turned from him their craftiness; verily, He both hears and knows!

[35] Then it appeared good to them, even after they had seen the signs,[6] to imprison him until a time.

And there entered the prison with him two young men. Said one of them, 'Verily, I see myself[7] pressing wine.' And the other said, 'Verily, I see myself bearing on my head loaves from which the birds do eat; inform us of the interpretation thereof; verily, we see that thou art of those who do good.'

He said, 'There shall not come to you any food with which ye are provided, but I will inform you both of its interpretation before it comes to you. That is (some) of what my Lord has taught me; verily, I have left the faith of a people who do not believe in Allah, while in the future too they disbelieve. And I have followed the faith of my fathers, Abraham and Isaac and Jacob; we could not associate aught with Allah; that is from Allah's grace upon us and upon men: but most men give not thanks. O ye twain fellow prisoners! Are manifold lords better, or Allah, the one, the dominant? [40] What ye worship beside Him are naught but names which ye have named, ye and your fathers, for which Allah has sent down no authority. Judgement is only Allah's; He bids you worship only Him. That is the standard of religion,—but most men do not know. O ye twain fellow prisoners! as for one of you, he shall pour out wine for his lord: and as for the other, he shall be crucified, and the birds shall eat of his head. The matter is decreed whereon ye asked me for a decision!'

And he said to him whom he thought would escape of those two, 'Remember me with thy lord!' But Satan made him[8] forget the remembrance of his lord, so he tarried in prison a few years.

Then said the king, 'Verily, I see seven fat kine which seven lean kine devoured; and seven green ears of corn and others dry. O ye chiefs! Explain to me my vision, if a vision ye can expound!'

Said they, 'Confused dreams, and naught of the exposition of such dreams know we!'

[45] Then he who had escaped of those twain said,—remembering after a while,—'Verily, I will inform you of the interpretation thereof, so send me.'

'Joseph! O thou truth teller! explain to us the seven fat kine which seven lean devoured; and the seven green ears of corn and others dry. Haply I may go back to the men, haply they then may know!'

He said, 'Ye shall sow for seven years, as is your wont; but what ye reap, let it remain in the ear, except a little whereof ye shall eat. Then there shall come after that seven severe (years) which shall devour what ye have put by before for them, save a little of what ye shall preserve. Then there will come after that a year in which men shall have rain and in which they shall press.'⁹

[50] Then said the king, 'Bring him to me.'

And when the messenger came to him, he said, 'Go back to thy lord, and ask him, "What meant the women who cut their hands? Verily, my lord knows their craftiness!" '

He said, 'What was your design when ye desired Joseph for his person?' They said, 'Allah forbid! we know no bad of him.' Said the wife of the prince, 'Now does the truth appear! I desired him for his person and, verily, he is of those who tell the truth.'

'That' (said Joseph) 'was that he might know that I did

not betray him in his absence, and that Allah guides not the craft of those who do betray! Yet I do not clear myself, for the soul is very urgent to evil, save what my Lord has had mercy on; verily, my Lord is forgiving and merciful!'

And the king said, 'Bring him to me. I will take him specially for myself.' And when he had spoken with him he said, 'Verily, today thou art with us in a permanent place of trust.'

[55] He said, 'Place me over the treasures of the land; verily, I will be a knowing keeper.'

Thus did we stablish Joseph in the land that he might settle in what part thereof he pleased—we overtake with our mercy whom we will, nor do we waste the hire of those who do good; and surely the hire of the future life is better for those who believe and who have feared.

And his brethren came to Joseph, and they entered in unto him and he knew them, but they recognized not him.

And when he had equipped them with their equipment he said, 'Bring me a brother that ye have from your father; do ye not see that I give good measure, and that I am the best of entertainers? [60] But if ye bring him not to me, no measure shall ye have with me, nor shall ye come nigh me.'

They said, 'We will desire him of our father, and we will surely do it.'

Then he said to his young men, 'Put their chattels[10] in their packs, haply they may know it when they are come back to their family; haply they may return.'

And when they returned to their father, they said, 'O our father! Measure is withheld from us; so send with us our brother that we may get measure, and, verily, him we will keep!'

He said, 'Shall I entrust you with him, save as I entrusted you with his brother before? But Allah is the best of keepers, and He is the most merciful of the merciful.'

[65] And when they opened their goods they found their chattels restored to them. Said they, 'O our father! What more can we crave? Here are our chattels restored to us, and we shall guard our brother, and shall have an additional measure beside that—a small measure.'¹¹

He said, 'I will by no means send him with you until you give me a compact from Allah that ye will surely bring him to me, unless ye be encompassed.'¹²

So when they had given him their compact he said, 'Allah over what ye say has charge.'

And he said, 'O my sons! enter not by one gate, but enter by several gates; but I cannot avail you aught against Allah. Judgement is only Allah's; upon Him do I rely, and on Him do the reliant rely.'

And when they had entered as their father bade them, it availed them nothing against Allah, save for a want in Jacob's soul which it fulfilled; for, verily, he was possessed of knowledge, for that we had taught him;—but most men do not know.

And when they entered in unto Joseph, he took his brother to stay with him, and said, 'Verily, I am thy brother—then take not ill that which they have been doing.'

[70] And when he had equipped them with their

equipment he placed the drinking cup in his brother's pack; then a crier cried out, 'O ye caravan! verily, ye are thieves!'

They said, approaching them, 'What is it that ye miss?'

Said they, 'We miss the goblet of the king, and whoso brings it shall have a camel load, and I am guarantee thereof.'

They said, 'By Allah! Ye knew we came not to do evil in the land, and that we were not thieves.'

They said, 'And what shall be the recompense thereof if ye be liars?'

[75] They said, 'The recompense thereof is he in whose pack it is found—he shall be the recompense thereof; thus do we recompense the unjust.'

And he began with their sacks before the sacks of his brother; then he drew it forth from his brother's sack. Thus did we devise a stratagem for Joseph. He could not take his brother by the king's religion[13] except Allah pleased;—we raise the degrees of whomsoever we please, and over every possessor of knowledge is one who knows.

They said, 'If he has stolen, a brother of his has stolen before him.'

But Joseph kept it secret in his soul and disclosed it not to them. Said he, 'Ye are in a bad case, and Allah knows best about what ye describe.'

They said, 'O prince! Verily, he has a father, a very old man; take then one of us instead of him; verily, we can see that thou art of those who do good.'

Said he, '(I seek) refuge in Allah from taking any save him with whom we found our property; verily, we should then be certainly unjust.'

[80] And when they despaired of him they retired to consult privately. Said the eldest of them, 'Do ye not know that your father has taken a compact from Allah against you? Aforetime ye exceeded in the matter of Joseph—I will surely not quit the land until my father give me leave, or Allah judge for me, for He is the best of judges.

'Return ye to your father and say, "O our father! verily, thy son has committed theft, and we bore testimony to naught but what we knew; for of the unforeseen we were not keepers!"

'Ask then in the city where we were, and of the caravan in which we approached it, for, verily, we tell the truth.'

Said he, 'Nay, your souls have induced you to do this thing. But patience is fair. It may be that Allah will give me them all together;—verily, He is knowing, wise.'

And he turned away from them and said, 'O my lament for Joseph!' and his eyes grew white with grief, for he repressed (his woe).

[85] They said, 'By Allah! thou wilt not cease to remember Joseph till thou art at the point of death, or art of those who perish!'

Said he, 'I only complain of my emotion and my grief to Allah, for I know that from Allah which ye know nothing of.

'O my sons! go and enquire concerning Joseph and his brother, and despair not of Allah's comfort; for, verily, none need despair of Allah's comfort save a misbelieving people!'

And when they entered in unto him they said, 'O prince! distress has touched both us and our families, and we have brought trifling chattels. So give us full measure and bestow upon us in charity; verily, Allah rewards the charitable.'

He said, 'Do ye know what ye did with Joseph and his brother, while ye were ignorant?'

[90] They said, 'Art thou then indeed Joseph?' He said, 'I am Joseph, and this is my brother; Allah has been gracious towards us. Verily, whoso fears Allah and is patient,—verily, Allah wastes not the hire of those who do good!'

They said, 'By Allah! Allah has chosen thee over us; and we indeed were sinners.'

He said, 'No reproach against you today! Allah will pardon you, for He is the most merciful of the merciful. Take this my shirt, and throw it over the face of my father, he will become able to see; and bring me your families all together.'

And when the caravan departed, their father said, 'Verily, I find the smell of Joseph, unless ye think I dote!'

[95] They said, 'By Allah! thou art in thy old error.' And when the herald of glad tidings came he threw it on his face, and he was restored to sight.

Said he, 'Did I not tell you that I know from Allah that of which ye know not?'

They said, 'O our father! ask pardon for us of our sins;—verily, we were sinners!'

He said, 'I will ask pardon for you from my Lord; verily, He is the pardoning and merciful.'

[100] And when they entered in unto Joseph, he took

his father to stay with him, and said, 'Enter ye into Egypt, if it please Allah, safe.' And he raised his father upon the throne, and they fell down before him adoring.

And he said, 'O my sire! This is the interpretation of my vision aforetime; my Lord has made it come true, and He has been good to me, in bringing me forth out of prison, and bringing you from the desert, after Satan had made a breach between me and my brethren;—verily, my Lord is kind to whomsoever He will;—verily, He is the knowing, the wise!

'O my Lord! thou hast given me dominion, and hast taught me the interpretation of sayings; O Originator of the heavens and the earth! Thou art my patron in this world and the next; take me to Thyself resigned, and let me reach the righteous!'

That is one of the stories of the unseen which we inspire thee with, though thou wert not with them when they agreed in their affair, when they were so crafty.—And yet most men, though thou shouldst be urgent, will not believe.

Thou dost not ask them for it a hire; it is naught but a reminder to the world.

[105] How many a sign in the heavens and the earth do they pass by and turn away therefrom!

Nor do most of them believe in Allah without associating (other gods) with Him.

Are they safe, then, from overwhelming vengeance coming on them from the torment of Allah? or from the Hour coming upon them suddenly while they do not perceive?

Say, 'This is my way; I call now unto Allah on clear proof, I and those who follow me; and celebrated be Allah's praises, for I am not of the idolaters.'

Nor did we ever send before thee any save men whom we inspired, of the people of the cities. Have they not journeyed on in the earth, and beheld how was the end of those before them? But the abode of the future is surely better for those who believe;—what! have they then no sense?

[110] Until when the apostles despaired and they thought that they were proved liars, our help came to them, and whosoever we pleased was saved; but our violence is not averted from the sinful people.

Their stories were a lesson to those endowed with minds. It was not a tale forged, but a verification of what was before it, and a detailing of everything, and a guide and a mercy to a people who believe.

THE CHAPTER OF THUNDER

XIII (*Mecca*)

In the name of the merciful and compassionate Allah.

A. L. M. R. Those are the signs of the Book, and that which is sent down to thee from thy Lord is the truth; but most people will not believe. Allah it is who has raised the heavens without columns that ye can see; then He made for the throne, and subjected the sun and the moon; each one runs on to a stated and appointed time; He governs the affair, details the signs;—haply of the meeting with your Lord ye will be sure.

And He it is who has stretched out the earth and placed therein firm mountains and rivers, and of every fruit has He placed therein two kinds. He makes the night cover the day;—verily, in that are signs unto a people who reflect.

And on the earth are neighbouring portions, and gardens of grapes and corn and palms growing together (from one root) and not growing together; they are watered with one water, yet we distinguish one over the other as food;—verily, in that are signs unto a people who have sense.

[5] And if thou shouldst wonder, wondrous is their speech: 'What! when we have become dust, shall we really then be created anew?'

These are they who disbelieve in their Lord, and these are they with fetters round their necks, and these are the fellows of the Fire; they shall dwell therein for aye!

They will wish thee to hasten on the evil rather than the good; examples have passed away before them: but thy Lord is possessor of forgiveness unto men, notwithstanding their injustice; but, verily, thy Lord is keen to punish.

Those who misbelieve say, 'Unless a sign be sent down upon him from his Lord. . . .'—Thou art only a warner, and every people has its guide.

Allah knows what each female bears, and what the wombs fall short of or add; for dimensions of everything are with Him.

[10] He who knows the unseen and the visible,—the great, the lofty one.

Alike among you is he who keeps secret his speech and he who displays it; and he who hides by night and he who stalks abroad by day. Each of them has pursuers[1] before him and behind him, to keep guard over him at the command of Allah; verily, Allah changes not what a people has until they change it for themselves. And when Allah wishes evil to a people there is no averting it, nor have they a protector beside Him.

He it is who shows you the lightning for fear and hope;[2] and He brings up the heavy clouds.

And the thunder celebrates His praise, and the angels too for fear of Him; and He sends the thunderclap and overtakes therewith whom He will;—yet they wrangle about Allah! But He is strong in might.

[15] On Him is the call of truth, and those who call on others than Him shall not be answered at all, save as one who stretches out his hand to the water that it may reach his mouth, but it reaches it not! The call of the misbelievers is only in error.

And Allah do those who are in the heavens and the earth adore, whether they will or no! as do their shadows also morn and eve.

Say, 'Who is Lord of the heavens and the earth?' say, 'Allah'; say, 'Do ye take beside Allah patrons who cannot control profit or harm for themselves?' say, 'Shall the blind and the seeing be held equal? or shall the darkness and the light be held equal? or have they made associates with Allah who can create as He creates, so that the creation seem familiar to them?' say, 'Allah is the creator of everything, and He is the one, the dominant.'

He sends down from the sky water, and the water-courses flow according to their bulk, and the torrent bears along the floating scum: and from what they set fire to, craving ornaments or utensils, comes a scum like that;—thus does Allah hit the truth and the falsehood;—and as for the scum it is thrown off, and as for what profits man it stays on the earth. Thus does Allah strike out parables!

For those who respond to their Lord is good; but those who respond not to Him, had they all that is in the earth and the like thereof as well, they would give it for a ransom; these shall have an evil reckoning up! and their resort is Hell,—an evil couch shall it be!

Is he who knows that naught but the truth is sent down upon thee from thy Lord like him who is blind? Only those possessed of minds will remember!

[20] Those who fulfil Allah's covenant and break not the compact, and those who attain what Allah has bidden to be attained, and dread their Lord and fear the evil reckoning up; and those who are patient, craving their Lord's face, and are steadfast in prayer, and expend in alms of what we have bestowed upon them secretly and openly, and ward off evil with good,—these shall have the recompense of the abode, gardens of Eden, into which they shall enter with the righteous amongst their fathers and their wives and their seed; and the angels shall enter in unto them from every gate:—'Peace be upon you! for that ye were patient; and goodly is the recompense of the abode.'

[25] And those who break Allah's covenant after compacting for it, and who cut asunder what Allah hath

bidden to be joined, and who do evil in the earth, these—upon them is the curse of Allah, and for them is an evil abode.

Allah extends his bounty freely to whomsoever He will, or He metes it out; and they rejoice in the life of this world, but the life of this world is naught but a (temporary) provision compared with the next.

Those who misbelieve say, 'Unless a sign is sent down upon him from his Lord. . . .' Say, 'Allah leads whom He will astray, but guides unto Him those who turn again.

'Those who believe and whose hearts are comforted by the mention of Allah,—aye! by the mention of Allah shall their hearts be comforted, who believe and do what is right. Good cheer for them and an excellent resort.'

Thus have we sent thee to a nation before which other nations have passed away, to recite to them that which we have inspired thee with; yet they misbelieve in the merciful! Say, 'He is my Lord; there is no god but He; upon Him do I rely, and unto Him is my repentance.'

[30] And though it were a Qur'ân by which the mountains were moved, or by which the earth were cut up, or the dead made to speak³—nay, Allah's is the command altogether! Did not those who believed know⁴ that if Allah had pleased He would have guided men altogether?

And a striking calamity shall not cease to overtake those who misbelieve for what they have wrought, or to alight close by their dwellings; until Allah's promise comes—verily, Allah fails not in His promise.

Before thee have apostles been mocked at; and those

who misbelieved have I allowed to range at large; and then it caught them up! How then was my punishment?

Shall He who is standing over every soul (to note) what it has earned——? And they join partners with Allah! Say, 'Name them; can ye inform Him of what He does not know in the earth? or is it for name's sake only (that ye call upon them)?

'Nay, then, stratagem is made seemly to those who misbelieve, and they turn folks from the path of Allah! But whomsoever Allah doth lead astray, no guide has he.'

For them is torment in this world's life; but surely the torment of the next is more wretched still—nor have they against Allah a keeper.

[35] The likeness of the Paradise which those who fear Allah are promised, beneath it rivers flow, its food is enduring, and likewise its shade! That is the recompense of those who fear; but the recompense of misbelievers is the Fire!

And those to whom we brought the Book rejoice in that which we have sent down to thee; but of the confederates are some who deny a part thereof.

Say, 'I am only bidden to serve Allah and not to associate any with Him; on Him I call and to Him is my recourse.'

Thus have we sent it down, an Arabic judgement, but hadst thou followed their lusts, after the knowledge that has come to thee, thou hadst not had against Allah a patron or a keeper.

And we sent apostles before thee, and we made for them wives and seed; and no apostle could bring a sign by

Allah's permission;—for every period there is a book.

Allah blots out what He will, or He confirms; and with Him is the Mother of the Book.[5]

[40] Either we will let thee see a part of what we threaten them with, or we will take thee to ourself; but thy duty is only to deliver thy message, and ours to reckon up.

Did they not see that we come to the land and diminish the borders thereof?[6] Allah judges, and there is none to reverse His judgement, and He is swift at reckoning up!

And those who were before them were crafty too; but Allah's is the craft altogether! He knows what every soul earns; and the misbelievers shall know whose is the recompense of the abode.

And those who misbelieve say, 'Thou art not sent!' Say, 'Allah is witness enough between me and you; and so is he who has the knowledge of the Book!'

THE CHAPTER OF ABRAHAM
(PEACE BE ON HIM!)

XIV (*Mecca*)

In the name of the merciful and compassionate Allah.

A. L. M. A book which we have sent down to thee, to bring men forth from darkness into light, by permission of their Lord, unto the way of the mighty and praiseworthy one.

Allah is He whose is whatsoever is in the heavens and whatsoever is in the earth. Alas for the misbelievers, for their torment is keen! Who love this world's life better than the next, and turn folks from the path of Allah, and crave to make it crooked; these are in remote error.

We have not sent any apostle save with the language of his people, that he might explain to them. But Allah leads whom He will astray, and guides whom He will; and He is the mighty, the wise.

[5] We did send Moses with our signs, 'Bring forth thy people from the darkness into the light, and remind them of the days¹ of Allah!' Verily, in that are signs to every patient, grateful one.

When Moses said to his people, 'Remember the favours of Allah towards you, when He saved you from Pharaoh's people, who sought to wreak you evil woe, slaughtering your sons and letting your women live'; in that was a great trial for you from your Lord. When your Lord proclaimed, 'If ye give thanks I will surely give you increase; but if ye misbelieve, verily, my torment is severe!' And Moses said, 'If ye misbelieve, ye and those who are on the earth altogether—then, verily, Allah is rich, and to be praised!'

Has not the story come to you of those who were before you, of the people of Noah, and 'Âd, and Thamûd, [10] and those who came after them? None knows them save Allah. Apostles came unto them with manifest signs; but they thrust their hands into their mouths² and said, 'Verily, we disbelieve in that which ye are sent with, and we are in hesitating doubt concerning that to which ye call us!' Their apostles said, 'Is there doubt about Allah, the originator of the heavens and the earth? He calls you to pardon you for your sins, and to respite you until an appointed time.'

They said, 'Ye are but mortals like ourselves; ye wish to turn us from what our fathers used to serve. Bring us, then, obvious authority!'

Their apostles said unto them, 'We are only mortals like yourselves; but Allah is gracious unto whomsoever He will of His servants, and it is not for us to bring you an authority, save by His permission; but upon Allah do the believers rely!' [15] What ails us that we should not rely on Allah when He has guided us in our paths? We will be surely patient in your hurting us; for upon Allah rely those who do rely.

And those who misbelieved said to their apostles, 'We will drive you forth from our land; or else ye shall return to our faith!' And their Lord inspired them, 'We will surely destroy the unjust; and we will make you to dwell in the land after them. That is for him who fears my place and fears my threat!'

Then they asked for an issue; and disappointed was every rebel tyrant! Behind such a one is Hell, and he shall be given to drink liquid pus![3] [20] He shall try to swallow it, but cannot gulp it down; and death shall come upon him from every place, and yet he shall not die; and behind him shall be rigorous woe!

The likeness of those who disbelieve on their Lord,— their works are as ashes whereon the wind blows fiercely on a stormy day. They have no power at all over that which they have earned.—That is the remote error!

Dost not thou see that Allah created the heavens and the earth in truth? If He please He can take you off and bring a new creation; nor is that hard for Allah!

They all come out to Allah; and the weak say to those who were big with pride, 'We were followers of yours, can ye now avail us aught against Allah's torment?'

[25] They say, 'If Allah had guided us we would have guided you. It is the same to us if we are agonized or if we are penitent, we have no escape.'

And Satan says, when the affair is decided, 'Verily, Allah promised you a promise of truth; but I promised you and failed you; for I had no authority over you. I only called you, and ye did answer me; then blame me not, but blame yourselves; I cannot help you, nor can you help me. I disbelieved in your associating me (with Allah) before; verily, the wrongdoers, for them is grievous woe!'

But I will cause those who believe and do aright to enter gardens beneath which rivers flow, to dwell therein for aye by the permission of their Lord; their salutation therein is 'Peace!'

Dost thou not see how Allah strikes out a parable? A good word is like a good tree whose root is firm, and whose branches are in the sky; [30] it gives its fruit at every season by the permission of its Lord—but Allah strikes out parables for men that haply they may be mindful.

And the likeness of a bad word is as a bad tree, which is felled from above the earth, and has no staying place.

Allah answers those who believe with the sure word in this world's life and in the next; but Allah leads the wrongdoers astray; for Allah does what He will.

Dost not thou see those who have changed Allah's favours for misbelief, and have made their people to alight at the abode of perdition?—in Hell they shall broil, and an ill resting place shall it be!

[35] And they made peers for Allah, to lead men astray from His path. Say, 'Enjoy yourselves, for, verily, your journey is to the Fire.'

Say to my servants who believe, that they be steadfast in prayer and expend in alms of what we have bestowed upon them in secret and in public, before there comes the day when there shall be no buying and no friendship.

Allah it is who created the heavens and the earth; and sent down from the sky water, and brought forth therewith fruits as a provision for you; and subjected to you the ships, to float therein upon the sea at His bidding; and subjected for you the rivers; and subjected for you the sun and the moon, constant both; and subjected for you the night and the day; and brought you of everything ye asked Him: but if ye try to number Allah's favours, ye cannot count them;—verily, man is very unjust and ungrateful.

And when Abraham said, 'My Lord, make this land⁴ safe, and turn me and my sons away from serving idols!

'My Lord, verily, they have led many men astray; but he who follows me, verily, he is of me; but he who rebels against me,—verily, thou art pardoning, merciful!

[40] 'O our Lord! verily, I have made some of my seed dwell in a valley without corn, by thy Sacred House.⁵ O our Lord! let them be steadfast in prayer and make the

hearts of men yearn towards them, and provide them with fruits, haply they may give thanks.

'O our Lord! verily, Thou knowest what we hide and what we publish; for naught is hid from Allah in the earth or in the sky. Praise to Allah who hath bestowed on me, notwithstanding my old age, Ishmael and Isaac!—verily, my Lord surely hears prayer.

'O my Lord! make me steadfast in prayer, and of my seed likewise! O our Lord! and accept my prayer! O our Lord! pardon me and my parents and the believers on the reckoning day!'

So think not Allah careless of what the unjust do; He only respites them until the day on which all eyes shall stare!

Hurrying on, raising up their heads, with their looks not turned back to them,[6] and their hearts void; and warn men of the day when the torment shall come!

[45] And those who have done wrong shall say, 'O our Lord! respite us until an appointed time nigh at hand, and we will respond to Thy call, and follow the apostles!'— 'What! did ye not swear before, ye should have no decline?'

And ye dwelt in the dwellings of those who had wronged themselves; and it was made plain to you how we did with them; and we struck out parables for you: but they plotted their stratagems, but with Allah is a stratagem for them, although at their stratagem the mountains should give way.

Think then not indeed that Allah fails in his promise to his apostles;—verily, Allah is mighty, the Lord of vengeance; on the day when the earth shall be changed for another earth, and the heavens too; and (all) shall go forth unto Allah, the one, the dominant.

[50] Thou shalt see the sinners on that day bound together in fetters; with shirts of pitch, and fire covering their faces;—that Allah may reward each soul according to what it has earned; verily, Allah is swift at reckoning up!

This is a message to be delivered to men that they may be warned thereby, and know that only He is Allah,—one,—and that those who have minds may remember.

THE CHAPTER OF EL 'HAJR[1]

XV (*Mecca*)

In the name of the merciful and compassionate Allah!

A. L. R. Those are the signs[2] of the Book and of a perspicuous Qur'ân.

Many a time will those who disbelieve fain they had been resigned.[3]

Leave them to eat and enjoy themselves and let hope beguile them, but they at length shall know!

We never destroyed a city without it had its noted doom.

[5] No nation can hasten on its appointed time, nor put it off.

But they say, 'O thou to whom the Reminder has been sent down! Verily, thou art possessed. Why dost thou not bring us the angels if thou dost tell the truth?'

We sent not down the angels save by right; nor even then would these be respited.

Verily, we have sent down the Reminder, and, verily, we will guard it.

[10] And we sent before thee among the sects of those of yore. But there never came an apostle to them but they mocked at him. Such conduct also will we put into the hearts of the sinners. They will not believe therein, but the course of those of yore is run. But had we opened to them a door of the sky and they had mounted up into it all the while; [15] then also had they said, 'Our eyesight is only intoxicated; nay, we are an enchanted people!'

And we have placed in the sky the signs of the zodiac, and have made them seemly to the beholders; and we have guarded them from every pelted devil;[4] save from such as steal a hearing, and there follows him an obvious shooting star.

And the earth we have stretched out and have thrown on it firm mountains, and have caused to grow upon it of everything a measured quantity. [20] And we have made for you means of livelihood therein, and for those for whom ye have not to provide.

Nor is there aught but the treasuries of it are with us, and we do not send it down save in a noted quantity.

And we send forth the impregnating winds,[5] and we send down water from the sky, and we give it to you to drink, nor is it ye who store it up.

And we, verily, we quicken and kill; and we are of (all things) heirs.

And we already know the foremost of you, and we know the laggards too!

[25] And, verily, it is your Lord who will gather you; verily, He is wise and knowing.

And we did create man from crackling clay of black mud wrought in form.

And the jinn had we created before of smokeless fire.

And when thy Lord said to the angels, 'Verily, I am creating a mortal from crackling clay of black mud wrought into shape;

[30] 'And when I have fashioned it, and breathed into it of my spirit, then fall ye down before it adoring.'

And the angels adored all of them together, save Iblîs, who refused to be among those who adored.

He said, 'O Iblîs! what ails thee that thou art not among those who adore?'

Said he, 'I would not adore a mortal whom Thou hast created from crackling clay of black mud wrought into form.'

He said, 'Then get thee forth therefrom, and, verily, thou art to be pelted! [35] And, verily, the curse is upon thee until the day of judgement.'

Said he, 'O my Lord! respite me until the day when they shall be raised.' He said, 'Then, verily, thou art of the respited until the day of the noted time.'

He said, 'O my Lord! for that Thou hast seduced me I will surely make it seem seemly for them on earth, and I will surely seduce them all together; [40] save such of Thy servants amongst them as are sincere.' Said He, 'This is a right way against me. Verily, my servants thou hast no authority over, save over those who follow thee of such as are seduced: and, verily, Hell is promised to them all together. It has seven doors; at every door is there a separate party of them.'

[45] Verily, those who fear Allah shall dwell amidst gardens and springs: 'Enter ye therein with peace in safety!' And we will strip off whatever ill feeling is in their breasts; as brethren on couches face to face.[6]

No toil shall touch them therein, nor shall they be brought forth therefrom.

Inform my servants that I am the pardoning, the merciful; [50] and that my woe is the grievous woe.

And inform them concerning Abraham's guests when they entered in unto him and said, 'Peace!' he said, 'Verily, we are afraid of you.' They said, 'Be not afraid! Verily, we give thee glad tidings of a knowing boy.' He said, 'Do ye give me this glad tidings although old age has touched me? Give me the glad tidings then!' [55] They said, 'We give the glad tidings of the truth, then be not of those who despair!' He said, 'Who would despair of the mercy of his Lord save those who err?' He said, 'What is your business, O ye messengers?' They said, 'Verily, we are sent unto a sinful people; save only Lot's family, them will we save all together, [60] except his wife; we have decreed, verily, she shall be of those who linger.'

And when the messengers came unto Lot's family, he said, 'Verily, ye are a people whom I recognize not.' They said, 'Nay, but we have come to thee with that whereof they[7] did doubt. And we have brought thee the truth, and, verily, we speak the truth! [65] Travel then with thy family in the deep darkness of the night, and follow thou their rear; and let not any one of you turn round to look; but go on to where ye are bidden.'

And we decided for him this affair because the uttermost one of these people should be cut off on the morrow.

Then the people of the city came, glad at the tidings. Said he, 'Verily, these are my guests, therefore disgrace me not; but fear Allah, and put me not to shame.'

[70] They said, 'Have we not forbidden thee[8] everybody in the world?' He said, 'Here are my daughters, if do it ye must.'—By thy life![9] verily, they were surely in their intoxication blindly wandering on!—

And the noise caught them at the dawn. And we made the higher parts (of the cities) their lower parts, and rained down on them stones of baked clay. [75] Verily, in that is a sign to those who mark. And, verily, the (cities) are on a path that still remains.[10] Verily, in that is a sign to the believers.

And the fellows of the Grove[11] too were unjust; and we took vengeance on them, and, verily, they both[12] are for an obvious example.

[80] And the fellows of El 'Hajr[13] called the messengers liars, and we brought them our signs, but they therefrom did turn away. And they did hew them in the mountain houses to dwell in in safety.

But the noise caught them in the morn; and that which they had earned availed them naught.

[85] We did not create the heavens and the earth and all that is between them both, save in truth. And, verily, the Hour is surely coming; then do thou pardon with a fair pardon.

Verily, thy Lord He is the creator, the knowing! We

have already brought thee Seven of the Repetition,[14] and the mighty Qur'ân.

Let not thine eyes strain after what we have allowed a few pairs of them[15] to enjoy, nor grieve for them; but lower thy wing[16] to the believers, and say, 'Verily, I am an obvious warner.'

[90] As we sent down (punishment) on the separatists[17] who dismember the Qur'ân.

But, by thy Lord! we will question them, one and all, about what they have done.

Therefore, publish what thou art bidden, and turn aside from the idolaters.

[95] Verily, we are enough for thee against the scoffers.

Who place with Allah other gods; but they at length shall know! And we knew that thy breast was straitened at what they say.

Then celebrate the praises of thy Lord, and be thou of those who adore.

And serve thy Lord until the certainty shall come to thee.

THE CHAPTER OF THE BEE

XVI (*Mecca*)

In the name of the merciful and compassionate Allah.

Allah's bidding will come; seek not then to hasten it on. Celebrated be His praises from what they join with Him!

He sends down the angels with the Spirit at His bidding upon whom He will of His servants (to say), 'Give warning that there is no god but Me; Me therefore do ye fear.' He created the heavens and the earth in truth! Exalted be He above that which they join with Him!

He created man from a clot; and yet, behold, he is an open opponent!

[5] The cattle too have we created for you; in them is warmth and profit, and from them do ye eat.

In them is there beauty for you when ye drive them home to rest, and when ye drive them forth to graze. And they bear your heavy burdens to towns which ye could not otherwise reach, except with great wretchedness of soul;—verily, your Lord is kind and merciful.

And horses too, and mules, and asses, for you to ride upon and for an ornament.—He creates also what ye know not of. Allah's it is to show the path; from it some turn aside: but had He pleased He would have guided you one and all.

[10] He it is who sends down water from the sky, whence ye have drink, and whence the trees grow whereby ye feed your flocks.

He makes the corn to grow, and the olives, and the palms, and the grapes, and some of every fruit;—verily, in that is a sign unto a people who reflect.

And He subjected to you the night and the day, and the sun, and the moon, and the stars are subjected to His bidding. Verily, in that are signs to a people who have sense.

And what He has produced for you in the earth varying in hue, verily, in that is a sign for a people who are mindful.

He it is who has subjected the sea, that ye may eat fresh

flesh therefrom; and ye bring forth from it ornaments which ye wear,—and thou mayest see the ships cleaving through it,—and that ye may search after His grace,—and haply ye may give thanks.

[15] And He has cast firm mountains on the earth lest it move with you; and rivers and roads; haply ye may be guided.

And landmarks; and by the stars too are they guided.

Is He who creates like him who creates not?—are they then unmindful?

But if ye would number the favours of Allah, ye cannot count them. Verily, Allah is forgiving, merciful.

Allah knows what ye keep secret, and what ye disclose.

[20] And those on whom ye call beside Allah cannot create anything, for they are themselves created. Dead, not living, nor can they perceive!

When shall they be raised?

Your Allah is one Allah, and those who believe not in the hereafter their hearts are given to denial, and they are big with pride!

Without a doubt Allah knows what ye keep secret and what ye disclose!

[25] Verily, He does not love those big with pride!

And when it is said to them, 'What is it that your Lord has sent down?' they say, 'Old folks' tales!'

Let them bear the burden of their sins entirely on the resurrection day, and some of the burdens of those whom they led astray without knowledge.—Aye! an ill burden shall they bear.

Those who were before them devised a stratagem, but

Allah brought their building off its foundations, and the roof fell over them, and the torment came to them, from whence they could not perceive.[1]

Then on the resurrection day He will put them to shame, and say, 'Where are your associates whom ye divided into parties about?' Those to whom knowledge is brought will say, 'Verily, disgrace today, and evil are upon the misbelievers!'

[30] Those whom the angels took away were wronging themselves; then they offered peace: 'We have done no evil.'—'Yea! verily, Allah knows what ye did. Wherefore enter ye the doors of Hell, to dwell therein for aye; for ill is the resort of the proud.'

And it will be said to those who fear Allah, 'What is it that your Lord has sent down?' They will say, 'The best,' for those who do good, good in this world; but certainly the abode of the next is best, and surely pleasant is the abode of those who fear.

Gardens of Eden which they shall enter, beneath them rivers flow; therein shall they have what they please;—thus does Allah reward those who fear Him.

To those whom the angels take off in a goodly state they shall say, 'Peace be upon you! Enter ye into Paradise for that which ye have done.'

[35] Do they expect other than that the angels should come to take them off, or that thy Lord's bidding should come?—thus did those before them; Allah did not wrong them; but it was themselves they wronged.

And the evil which they had done befell them, and that environed them at which they used to mock!

And those who associated (others with Allah) said, 'Had Allah pleased we had not served aught beside Him, neither we nor our fathers; nor had we prohibited aught without Him';—thus did those before them: but have messengers aught to do but to deliver their message plainly?

We have sent in every nation an apostle (to say), 'Serve ye Allah, and avoid Tâghût!' and amongst them are some whom Allah has guided, and amongst them are some for whom error is due;—go ye about then on the earth, and behold how was the end of those who called (the apostles) liars!

If thou art ever so eager for their guidance, verily, Allah guides not those who go astray, nor have they any helpers.

[40] They swear by their most strenuous oath, 'Allah will not raise up him who dies.'—Yea! a promise binding on him true!—but most men do not know. To explain to them that which they disputed about, and that those who misbelieved may know that they are liars.

We only say unto a thing we wish, 'BE', and it is.

But those who fled for Allah's sake, after they were wronged, we will surely establish them in this world with good things; but the hire of the future life is greater, if ye did but know.

Those who are patient, and upon their Lord rely!

[45] And we have not sent before thee any but men whom we inspire,—ask ye those who have the Reminder,[2] if ye know not yourselves,—with manifest signs and with scriptures; and we have sent down the Reminder to thee too, that thou mayest explain to men what has been sent

down to them, and haply they may reflect.

Are those who were so crafty in evil sure that Allah will not cleave open the earth with them, or bring them torment from whence they cannot perceive, or seize them in their going to and fro? for they cannot make Him helpless.

Or that He should seize them with a gradual destruction? for, verily, your Lord is kind, merciful.

[50] Do they not regard whatever thing Allah has created; its shadow falls on the right or the left, adoring Allah and shrinking up?

Whatever is in the heavens and in the earth, beast or angel, adores Allah; nor are they big with pride!

They fear their Lord above them, and they do what they are bidden.

And Allah says, 'Take not to two gods; Allah is only one; me then do ye fear!'

His is what is in the heavens and in the earth; to Him is obedience due unceasingly; other than Allah then will ye fear?

[55] And whatever favours ye have, they are from Allah; then, whenever distress touches you, unto Him ye turn for succour. Yet, when He removes the distress from you, lo! a party of you join partners with their Lord.

That they may disbelieve in what we have brought them and may enjoy,—but at length they shall know!

And they set aside for what they know not a portion of what we have bestowed upon them.³—By Allah! ye shall be questioned concerning that which ye have devised.

They make for Allah daughters;—celebrated be His

praise!—and for themselves they like them not.⁴

[60] When any one of them has tidings of a female child, his face is overclouded and black, and he has to keep back his wrath.

He skulks away from the people, for the evil tidings he has heard;—is he to keep it with its disgrace, or to bury it in the dust?—aye! evil is it that they judge!

For those who disbelieve in the future life is a similitude of evil: but for Allah is the loftiest similitude; for He is the mighty, the wise!

If Allah were to punish men for their wrongdoing He would not leave upon the earth a single beast; but He respites them until a stated time; and when their time comes they cannot put it off an hour, nor can they bring it on.

They set down to Allah what they abhor themselves; and their tongues describe the lie that 'good is to be theirs'. Without a doubt theirs is the Fire, for, verily, they shall be sent on there!

[65] By Allah! we sent (messengers) to nations before thee, but Satan made their works seemly to them, for he is their patron today, and for them is grievous woe!

We have only sent down to thee the Book, that thou mayest explain to them that which they did dispute about, and as a guidance and a mercy to a people who believe.

And Allah sends down water from the sky, and quickens therewith the earth after its death; verily, in that is a sign to a people who can hear.

Verily, ye have in cattle a lesson; we give you to drink from that which is in their bellies, betwixt chyme and blood,—pure milk,—easy to swallow for those who drink.

And of the fruit of the palms and the grapes ye take therefrom an intoxicant and a goodly provision; verily, in that is a sign to a people who have sense!

[70] And thy Lord inspired the bee, 'Take to houses in the mountains, and in the trees, and in the hives they build.

'Then eat from every fruit, and walk in the beaten paths of thy Lord'; there cometh forth from her body a draught varying in hue,[5] in which is a cure for men; verily, in that are signs unto a people who reflect.

Allah created you; then He will take you to Himself; but amongst you are some whom He will thrust into the most decrepit age; so that he may not know aught that once he knew. Verily, Allah is knowing, powerful.

And Allah has preferred some of you over others in providing for you; but those who have been preferred will not restore their provision to those whom their right hands possess[6] that they may share equally therein:—is it Allah's favours they gainsay?

And Allah has made for you from amongst yourselves wives, and has made for you from your wives sons and grandchildren; and has provided you with good things;— is it in vanity that they believe, while for Allah's favour they are ungrateful?

[75] And they serve beside Allah what cannot control for them any provision from the heavens or the earth, and have no power at all.

Do not then strike out parables for Allah! Verily, Allah knows, but ye do not know.

Allah has struck out a parable; an owned slave, able to do nothing; and one whom we have provided with a good provision, and who expends therefrom in alms secretly and openly:—shall they be held equal?—Praise be to Allah, most of them do not know!

And Allah has struck out a parable: two men, one of them dumb, able to do nothing, a burden to his lord; wherever he directs him he comes not with success; is he to be held equal with him who bids what is just and who is on the right way?

Allah's are the unseen things of the heavens and the earth; nor is the matter of the hour aught but as the twinkling of an eye, or nigher still! Verily, Allah is mighty over all!

[80] Allah brings you forth out of the wombs of your mothers knowing naught; and He makes for you hearing, and sight, and hearts,—haply ye may give thanks!

Do they not see the birds subjected in the vault of the sky?—none holds them in but Allah: verily, in that is a sign unto a people who believe.

Allah made for you in your houses a repose; and made for you, of the skins of cattle, houses,⁷ that ye may find them light, on the day ye move your quarters and the day when ye abide; and from their wool, and from their fur, and from their hair come furniture and chattels for a season.

And Allah has made for you, of what He has created, shades; and has made for you shelters in the mountains; and He has made for you shirts to keep you from the heat, and shirts⁸ to keep you from each other's violence:—thus does He fulfil His favours towards you,—haply ye yet may be resigned.

But if they turn their backs,—thine is only to preach thy plain message.

[85] They recognize the favours of Allah, and yet they deny them, for most men are ungrateful.

And on the day when we shall send from every nation a witness; then shall those who misbelieve not be allowed (to excuse themselves), and they shall not be taken back into favour.

And when those who join their partners with Allah say, 'Our Lord! these be our partners on whom we used to call beside Thee.' And they shall proffer them the speech, 'Verily, ye are liars!' And they shall proffer on that day peace unto Allah; and that which they had devised shall stray away from them.

[90] Those who misbelieve and turn folks off Allah's path, we will add torment to their torment, for that they were evil-doers.

And on the day when we will raise up in every nation a witness against them from among themselves, and we will bring thee as a witness against these;[9] for we have sent down to thee a book explaining clearly everything, and a guidance, and a mercy, and glad tidings to the believers.

Verily, Allah bids you do justice and good, and give to kindred (their due), and He forbids you to sin, and do wrong, and oppress; He admonishes you, haply ye may be mindful!

Fulfil Allah's covenant when ye have covenanted, and break not your oaths after asseverating them, for ye thereby make Allah your surety; verily, Allah knows what ye do.

And be not like her who unravels her yarn, fraying it out after she hath spun it close, by taking your oaths for mutual intrigue, because one nation is more numerous than another; Allah only tries you therewith, but He will make manifest to you on the resurrection day that whereon ye did dispute.[10]

[95] But had Allah pleased He would have made you one nation; but He leads astray whom He will, and guides whom He will;—but ye shall be questioned as to that which ye have done.

Take not therefore your oaths for mutual intrigue, lest a foot slip after being planted firmly, and ye taste of evil for that ye turned folks off the path of Allah, and for you there be mighty woe!

And sell not Allah's covenant for a little price; with Allah only is what is better for you, if ye did but know.

What ye have is spent, but what Allah has endures; and we will recompense the patient with their hire for the best deeds they have done.

Whoso acts aright, male or female, and is a believer, we will quicken with a goodly life; and we will recompense them with their hire for the best deeds they have done.

[100] When thou dost read the Qur'ân, ask refuge with Allah from Satan the pelted one.[11]

Verily, he has no power over those who believe and who upon their Lord rely. His power is only over those who take him for a patron, and over the idolaters.

And whenever we change one verse for another,—Allah

knows best what He sends down. They say, 'Thou art but a forger!'—Nay, most of them do not know. Say, 'The Holy Spirit[12] brought it down from thy Lord in truth, to stablish those who believe, and for a guidance and glad tidings to those who are resigned.'[13]

[105] We knew that they said, 'It is only some mortal who teaches him.'—The tongue of him they lean towards is barbarous, and this is plain Arabic.

Verily, those who believe not in Allah's signs, Allah will not guide them, and for them is grievous woe.

Only they are the forgers of a lie who believe not in Allah's signs; and these, they are the liars.

Whoso disbelieves in Allah after having believed, unless it be one who is forced and whose heart is quiet in the faith,—but whoso expands his breast to misbelieve,— on them is wrath from Allah, and for them is mighty woe!

That is because they preferred the love of this world's life to the next;—but, verily, Allah guides not the unbelieving people. [110] These are they on whose hearts, and hearing, and eyesight, Allah has set a stamp, and these, they are the careless. Without a doubt that in the next life they will be the losers.

Then, verily, thy Lord, to those who fled[14] after they had been tried, and then fought strenuously and were patient,—verily, thy Lord after that will be forgiving and merciful.

On the day every soul will come to wrangle for itself, and every soul shall be paid what it has earned, and they shall not be wronged.

Allah has struck out a parable: a city[15] which was safe

and quiet, its provision came to it in plenty from every place, and then it denied Allah's favours, and Allah made it feel[16] the clothing of hunger and fear, for that which they had wrought.

And there came to them an apostle from amongst themselves, but they called him a liar, and the torment seized them, while yet they were unjust.

[115] Eat, then, from what Allah has provided you with, things lawful and good, and give thanks for the favours of Allah, if it be Him ye serve.

He has only forbidden you that which dies of itself, and blood, and the flesh of swine, and that which is devoted to other than Allah; but he who is forced, neither revolting nor transgressing, it is no sin for him: verily, Allah is forgiving and merciful.

And say not of the lie your tongues pronounce, 'This is lawful, and this is unlawful,' forging against Allah a lie; verily, those who forge against Allah a lie shall not prosper. A little enjoyment—then for them is grievous woe!

For those who are Jews we have forbidden what we have narrated to thee before;[17] we did not wrong them, but it was themselves they wronged.

[120] Then, verily, thy Lord to those who have done evil in ignorance and then repented after that and done aright,— verily, thy Lord afterwards is forgiving and merciful.

Verily, Abraham was a high priest,[18] a *haníf*, and was not of the idolaters: thankful for His favours; He chose him and He guided him unto the right way.

And we gave him in this world good things; and, verily, in the next he will be among the righteous.

Then we inspired thee, 'Follow the faith of Abraham, a *hanîf*, for he was not of the idolaters.'

[125] The Sabbath was only made for those who dispute thereon; but, verily, thy Lord will judge between them on the resurrection day concerning that whereon they do dispute.

Call unto the way of thy Lord with wisdom and goodly warning; and wrangle with them in the kindest way; verily, thy Lord He knows best who has erred from His way, for He knows best the guided ones.

But if ye punish, punish (only) as ye were punished; but if ye are patient, it is best for those who are patient.[19]

Be thou patient then; but thy patience is only in Allah's hands. Do not grieve about them; and be not in a strait at their craftiness;—verily, Allah is with those who fear Him, and with those who do well.

THE CHAPTER OF
THE NIGHT JOURNEY[1]

XVII (*Mecca*)

In the name of the merciful and compassionate Allah.

Celebrated be the praises of Him who took His servant a journey by night from the Sacred Mosque[2] to the Remote Mosque,[3] the precinct of which we have blessed, to show him of our signs! Verily, He both hears and looks.

And we gave Moses the Book and made it a guidance

to the children of Israel: 'Take ye to no guardian but me.'

Seed of those we bore with Noah (in the ark)! verily, he was a thankful servant!

And we decreed to the children of Israel in the Book, 'Ye shall verily do evil in the earth twice,[4] and ye shall rise to a great height (of pride).'

[5] And when the threat for the first (sin) of the two came, we sent over them servants of ours, endued with violence, and they searched inside your houses; and it was an accomplished threat.

Then we rallied you once more against them, and aided you with wealth and sons, and made you a numerous band.

'If ye do well, ye will do well to your own souls; and if ye do ill, it is against them!

'And when the threat for the last came[5]—to harm your faces and to enter the mosque as they entered it the first time, and to destroy what they had got the upper hand over with utter destruction.'

It may be that thy Lord will have mercy on you;—but if ye return we will return, and we have made Hell a prison for the misbelievers.

Verily, this Qur'ân guides to the straightest path, and gives the glad tidings to the believers [10] who do aright that for them is a great hire; and that for those who believe not in the hereafter, we have prepared a mighty woe.

Man prays for evil as he prays for good; and man was ever hasty.

We made the night and the day two signs; and we blot out the sign of the night and make the sign of the day visible, that ye may seek after plenty from your Lord, and that ye may number the years and the reckoning; and we have detailed everything in detail.

And every man's augury[6] have we fastened on his neck; and we will bring forth for him on the resurrection day a book offered to him wide open. [15] 'Read thy book, thou art accountant enough against thyself today!'

He who accepts guidance, accepts it only for his own soul: and he who errs, errs only against it; nor shall one burdened soul bear the burden of another.

Nor would we punish until we had sent an apostle. And when we desired to destroy a city we bade[7] the opulent ones thereof; and they wrought abomination therein; and its due sentence was pronounced; and we destroyed it with utter destruction.

How many generations have we destroyed after Noah! but thy Lord of the sins of his servant is well aware, and sees enough.

Whoso is desirous of this life that hastens away, we will hasten on for him therein what we please,—for whom we please. Then we will make Hell for him to broil in— despised and outcast.

[20] But whoso desires the next life, and strives for it and is a believer—these, their striving shall be gratefully received.

To all—these and those—will we extend the gifts of thy Lord; for the gifts of thy Lord are not restricted.

See how we have preferred some of them over others, but in the next life are greater degrees and greater preference.

Put not with Allah other gods, or thou wilt sit despised and forsaken.

Thy Lord has decreed that ye shall not serve other than Him; and kindness to one's parents, whether one or both of them reach old age with thee; and say not to them, 'Fie!' and do not grumble at them, but speak to them a generous speech. [25] And lower to them the wing of humility out of compassion, and say, 'O Lord! have compassion on them as they brought me up when I was little!' Your Lord knows best what is in your souls if ye be righteous, and, verily, He is forgiving unto those who come back penitent.

And give thy kinsman his due and the poor and the son of the road; and waste not wastefully, for the wasteful were ever the devil's brothers; and the devil is ever ungrateful to his Lord.

[30] But if thou dost turn away from them to seek after mercy from thy Lord,[8] which thou hopest for, then speak to them an easy speech.

Make not thy hand fettered to thy neck, nor yet spread it out quite open, lest thou shouldst have to sit down blamed and straitened in means. Verily, thy Lord spreads out provision to whomsoever He will or He doles it out. Verily, He is ever well aware of and sees His servants.

And slay not your children[9] for fear of poverty; we will provide for them; beware! for to slay them is ever a great sin!

And draw not near to fornication; verily, it is ever an abomination, and evil is the way thereof.

[35] And slay not the soul that Allah has forbidden you, except for just cause; for he who is slain unjustly we have given his next of kin authority; yet let him not exceed in slaying; verily, he is ever helped.

And draw not near to the wealth of the orphan, save to improve it, until he reaches the age of puberty, and fulfil your compacts; verily, a compact is ever enquired of.

And give full measure when ye measure out, and weigh with a right balance; that is better and a fairer determination.

And do not pursue that of which thou hast no knowledge; verily, the hearing, the sight, and the heart, all of these shall be enquired of.

And walk not on the earth proudly; verily, thou canst not cleave the earth, and thou shalt not reach the mountains in height.

[40] All this is ever evil in the sight of your Lord and abhorred.

That is something of what thy Lord has inspired thee with of wisdom; do not then put with Allah other gods, or thou wilt be thrown into Hell reproached and outcast. What! has your Lord chosen to give you sons, and shall He take for Himself females from among the angels? Verily, ye are speaking a mighty speech.

Now have we turned it in various ways in this Qur'ân, so let them bear in mind; but it will only increase them in aversion.

Say, 'Were there with Him other gods, as ye say, then would they seek a way against the Lord of the throne.'

[45] Celebrated be His praises, and exalted be He

above what they say with a great exaltation!

The seven heavens and the earth celebrate His praises, and all who therein are; nor is there aught but what celebrates His praise: but ye cannot understand their celebration;—verily, He is clement and forgiving.

And when thou readest the Qur'ân we place between thee and those who believe not in the hereafter a covering veil. And we place covers upon their hearts, lest they should understand, and dulness in their ears.

And when thou dost mention in the Qur'ân thy Lord by Himself they turn their backs in aversion.

[50] We know best for what they listen when they listen to thee; and when they whisper apart—when the wrongdoers say, 'Ye only follow a man enchanted.'

Behold, how they strike out for you parables, and err, and cannot find the way!

They say, 'What! when we have become bones and rubbish are we to be raised up a new creature?' Say, 'Be ye stones, or iron, or a creature, the greatest your breasts can conceive—!' Then they shall say, 'Who is to restore us?' Say, 'He who originated you at first'; and they will wag their heads and say, 'When will that be?' Say, 'It may, perhaps, be nigh.'

The day when He shall call on you and ye shall answer with praise to Him, and they will think that they have tarried but a little.

[55] And say to my servants that they speak in a kind way;[10] verily, Satan makes ill will between them; verily, Satan was ever unto man an open foe.

Your Lord knows you best; if He please He will have

mercy upon you, or if He please He will torment you: but we have not sent thee to take charge of them.

And thy Lord best knows who is in the heavens and the earth; we did prefer some of the prophets over the others, and to David did we give the Psalms.

Say, 'Call on those whom ye pretend other than Allah'; but they shall not have the power to remove distress from you, nor to turn it off.

Those on whom they call,[11] seek themselves for a means of approaching their Lord, (to see) which of them is nearest: and they hope for His mercy and they fear His torment; verily, the torment of thy Lord is a thing to beware of.

[60] There is no city but we will destroy it before the day of judgement, or torment it with keen torment;—that is in the Book inscribed.

Naught hindered us from sending thee with signs, save that those of yore said they were lies; so we gave Thamûd the visible she-camel, but they treated her unjustly! for we do not send (any one) with signs save to make men fear.

And when we said to thee, 'Verily, thy Lord encompasses men!' and we made the vision which we showed thee only a cause of sedition unto men, and the cursed tree[12] as well; for we will frighten them, but it will only increase them in great rebellion.

And when we said to the angels, 'Adore Adam'; and they adored, save Iblîs, who said, 'Am I to adore one whom Thou hast created out of clay?'

Said he, 'Dost thou see now? this one whom Thou hast honoured above me, verily, if Thou shouldst respite me until the resurrection day, I will of a surety utterly destroy his seed except a few.'

[65] Said He, 'Begone! and whoso of them follows thee—verily, Hell is your recompense, an ample recompense. Entice away whomsoever of them thou canst with thy voice; and bear down upon them with thy horse and with thy foot; and share with them in their wealth and their children; and promise them,—but Satan promises them naught but deceit. Verily, my servants, thou hast no authority over them; thy Lord is guardian enough over them!'

It is your Lord who drives the ships for you in the sea that ye may seek after plenty from Him; verily, He is ever merciful to you. And when distress touches you in the sea, those whom ye call on, except Him, stray away from you; but when He has brought you safe to shore, ye turn away; for man is ever ungrateful.

[70] Are ye sure that He will not cleave with you the side of the shore, or send against you a heavy sandstorm? Then ye will find no guardian for yourselves.

Or are ye sure that He will not send you back therein another time, and send against you a violent wind, and drown you for your misbelief? then ye will find for yourselves no protector against us.

But we have been gracious to the children of Adam, and we have borne them by land and sea, and have provided them with good things, and have preferred them over many that we have created.

The day when we will call all men by their high priest; and he whose book is given in his right hand—these shall read their book, nor shall they be wronged a straw. But he who in this life is blind shall be blind in the next too, and err farther from the way.

[75] They had well-nigh beguiled thee from what we inspired thee with, that thou shouldst forge against us something else, and then they would have taken thee for a friend; and had it not been that we stablished thee, thou wouldst have well-nigh leant towards them a little: then would we have made thee taste of torment both of life and death, then thou wouldst not have found against us any helper.¹³

And they well-nigh enticed thee away from the land, to turn thee out therefrom; but then—they should not have tarried after thee except a little.

[This is] the course of those of our prophets whom we have sent before thee; and thou shalt find no change in our course.

[80] Be thou steadfast in prayer from the declining of the sun until the dusk of the night, and the reading of the dawn; verily, the reading of the dawn is ever testified to.

And for the night, watch thou therein as an extra service. It may be that thy Lord will raise thee to a laudable station.

And say, 'O my Lord! make me enter with a just entry; and make me come forth with a just coming forth; and grant me from Thee authority to aid.'

And say, 'Truth has come, and falsehood has vanished! Verily, falsehood is transient.'

And we will send down of the Qur'ân that which is a healing and a mercy to the believers, but it will only increase the wrongdoers in loss.

[85] And when we favour man he turns away and retires aside, but when evil touches him he is ever in despair. Say, 'Every one acts after his own manner, but your Lord knows best who is most guided in the way.'

They will ask thee of the spirit.[14] Say, 'The spirit comes at the bidding of my Lord, and ye are given but a little knowledge thereof.'

If we had wished we would have taken away that with which we have inspired thee; then thou wouldst have found no guardian against us, unless by a mercy from thy Lord; verily, His grace towards thee is great!

[90] Say, 'If mankind and jinns united together to bring the like of this Qur'ân, they could not bring the like, though they should back each other up!'

We have turned about for men in this Qur'ân every parable; but most men refuse to accept it, save ungratefully.

And they say, 'We will by no means believe in thee, until there gush forth for thee a fountain from the earth; or there be made for thee a garden of palms and grapes, and rivers come gushing out amidst them; or thou make the sky to fall down upon us in pieces; or thou bring us Allah and the angels before us; [95] or there be made for thee a house of gold; or thou climb up into the heaven; and even then we will not believe in thy climbing there, until thou send down on us a book that we may read!'

Say, 'Celebrated be the praises of my Lord! was I aught but a mortal apostle?'

Naught prohibited men from believing when the guidance came to them, save their saying, 'Allah has sent a mortal for an apostle.'

Say, 'Were there angels on the earth walking in quiet, we had surely sent them an angel as an apostle.'

Say, 'Allah is witness enough between me and you; verily, He is ever of His servants well aware, and sees.'

He whom Allah guides, he is guided indeed; and he whom Allah leads astray, thou shalt never find patrons for them beside Him; and we will gather them upon the resurrection day upon their faces, blind, and dumb, and deaf; their resort is Hell; whenever it grows dull we will give them another blaze!

[100] That is their reward for that they disbelieved in our signs, and said, 'What! When we are bones and rubbish, shall we then be raised up a new creation?'

Could they not see that Allah who created the heavens and the earth is able to create the like of them, and to set for them an appointed time; there is no doubt therein, yet the wrongdoers refuse to accept it, save ungratefully!

Say, 'Did ye control the treasuries of the mercy of my Lord, then ye would hold them through fear of expending; for man is ever niggardly!'

And we did bring Moses nine manifest signs; then ask the children of Israel (about) when he came to them, and Pharaoh said to him, 'Verily, I think thee, O Moses! enchanted.'

He said, 'Well didst thou know that none sent down these save the Lord of the heavens and the earth as visible signs; and, verily, I think thee, O Pharaoh! ruined.'

[105] And he desired to drive them out of the land; but we drowned him and those with him, one and all.

And after him we said to the children of Israel, 'Dwell ye in the land; and when the promise of the hereafter comes to pass, we will bring you in a mixed crowd (to judgement).

'In truth have we sent it down, and in truth has it come down; and we have not sent thee as aught but a herald of glad tidings and a warner.

'And a Qur'ân which we have divided, that thou mayst read it to mankind leisurely, and we sent it down, sending it down.'[15]

Say, 'Believe ye therein, or believe not; verily, those who were given the knowledge before it, when it is read to them fall down upon their beards adoring! and they say, "Celebrated be the praises of our Lord! Verily, the promise of our Lord is ever fulfilled"—they fall down upon their beards weeping, and it increases their humility.'

[110] Say, 'Call on Allah, or call on the Merciful One, whichever ye may call on Him by; for His are the best of names.'[16]

And do not say thy prayers openly, nor yet murmur them, but seek a way between these.

And say, 'Praise belongs to Allah, who has not taken to Himself a son, and has not had a partner in His kingdom, nor had a patron against (such) abasement.' And magnify Him greatly![17]

THE CHAPTER OF THE CAVE

XVIII (*Mecca*)

In the name of the merciful and compassionate Allah. Praise belongs to Allah, who sent down to His servant the Book, and put no crookedness therein,—straight, to give warning of keen violence from Him; and to give the glad tidings to the believers, who do what is right, that for them is a goodly reward wherein they shall abide for ever and for aye; and to give warning to those who say, 'Allah hath taken to Himself a son.'

They have no knowledge thereof, nor their fathers; a serious word it is that comes forth from their mouths! Verily, they only speak a lie!

[5] Haply thou wilt grieve thyself to death for sorrow after them, if they believe not in this new revelation. Verily, we have made what is on the earth an ornament thereof, to try them, which of them is best in works, but, verily, we are going to make what is thereon bare soil.

Hast thou reckoned that the Fellows of the Cave and Er-raqîm were a wonder amongst our signs?'[1]

When the youths resorted to the cave and said, 'O our Lord! bring us mercy from Thee, and dispose for us our affair aright!'

[10] And we struck their ears (with deafness) in the cave for a number of years. Then we raised them up again, that we might know which of the two crews[2] could best calculate the time of their tarrying. We will narrate to thee their story in truth. Verily, they were youths who

believed in their Lord, and we added to their guidance, and we braced up their hearts, when they stood up and said, 'Our Lord is the Lord of the heavens and the earth, we will not call upon any god beside Him, for then we should have said an extravagant thing. These people of ours have taken to other gods beside Him. Though they do not bring any manifest authority for them. And who is more unjust than he who forges against Allah a lie?

[15] 'So when ye have gone apart from them and what they serve other than Allah, then resort ye to the cave. Our Lord will unfold His mercy to you, and will dispose for you your affair advantageously.'

And thou mightst have seen the sun when it rose decline from their cave towards the right hand, and when it set leave them on the left hand, while they were in the spacious part thereof. That is one of the signs of Allah. Whom Allah guides he is guided indeed, and whom He leads astray thou shalt surely find for him no patron to guide aright. Thou mightst have reckoned them waking though they were sleeping, as we turned them towards the right and towards the left; and their dog spreading out his forepaws on the threshold. Hadst thou come suddenly upon them thou wouldst surely have turned and fled away from them, and wouldst surely have been filled by them with dread.

Thus did we raise them up that they might question each other. Spake a speaker amongst them, 'How long have ye tarried?' They said, 'We have tarried a day or part of a day.' They said, 'Your Lord knows best your tarrying; so send one of you with this coin of yours to the city, and let him look which of them has purest food, and let him bring you provision thereof; and let him be subtle and not let any one perceive you. Verily, they—should they perceive you—would stone you, or would force you back again unto their faith, and ye would never prosper then.'

[20] Thus did we make their people acquainted with their story, that they might know that Allah's promise is true; and that the hour, there is no doubt concerning it. When they disputed amongst themselves concerning their affair, and said, 'Build a building over them, their Lord knows best about them'; and those who prevailed in their affair said, 'We will surely make a mosque over them.'

They will say, 'Three, and the fourth of them was their dog': and they will say, 'Five, and the sixth of them was their dog': guessing at the unseen: and they will say, 'Seven, and the eighth of them was their dog.' Say, 'My Lord knows best the number of them; none knows them but a few.'

Dispute not therefore concerning them save with a plain disputation, and ask not any one of them[3] concerning them.

And never say of anything, 'Verily, I am going to do that tomorrow,' except 'if Allah please'; and remember thy Lord when thou hast forgotten, and say, 'It may be that my Lord will guide me to what is nearer to the right than this.'[4]

They tarried in their cave three hundred years and nine more. [25] Say, 'Allah knows best of their tarrying. His are the unseen things of the heavens and the earth—He can see! and hear!'[5]

They have no patron beside Him, nor does He let any one share in His judgement. So, recite what thou art inspired with of the Book of thy Lord; there is no changing His words; nor shalt thou ever find a refuge beside Him; and keep thyself patient, with those who call upon their Lord morning and evening, desiring His face; nor let thine eyes be turned from them, desiring the adornment of the life of this world; and obey not him[6] whose heart we have made heedless of remembrance of us, and who follows his lusts, for his affair is ever in advance (of the truth).

But say, 'The truth is from your Lord, so let him who will, believe; and let him who will, disbelieve.' Verily, we have prepared for the evil-doers a fire, sheets of which shall encompass them; and if they cry for help, they shall be helped with water like molten brass, which shall roast their faces:—an ill drink and an evil couch!

Verily, those who believe and act aright,—verily, we will not waste the hire of him who does good works.

[30] These, for them are gardens of Eden; beneath them rivers flow; they shall be adorned therein with bracelets of gold, and shall wear green robes of silk, and of brocade; reclining therein on thrones;—pleasant is the reward, and goodly the couch!

Strike out for them a parable: two men, for one of whom we made two gardens of grapes, and surrounded them with palms, and put corn between the two. Each of the two gardens brought forth its food and did not fail in aught. And we caused a river to gush forth amidst them; and he had fruit, and said unto his fellow, who was his next-door neighbour, 'I am more wealthy than thee, and mightier of household.'

And he went in unto his garden, having wronged himself: said he, 'I do not think that this will ever disappear; and I do not think that the hour is imminent; and if even I be sent back unto my Lord, I shall find a better one than it in exchange.'

[35] Said unto him his fellow, who was his next-door neighbour, 'Thou hast disbelieved in Him who created thee from earth, and then from a clot, then fashioned thee a man; but Allah, He is my Lord; nor will I associate any one with my Lord. Why couldst thou not have said, when thou didst go into thy garden, "What Allah pleases![7] there is no power save in Allah,"—to look at, I am less than thee in wealth and children; but haply my Lord will give me something better than thy garden, and will send upon it thunderclaps from the sky, and it shall be on the morrow bare slippery soil; or on the morrow its water may be deeply sunk, so that thou canst not get thereat!'

[40] And his fruits were encompassed, and on the morrow he turned down the palms of his hands[8] for what he had spent thereon, for it was fallen down upon its trellises. And he said, 'Would that I had never associated any one with my Lord!' And he had not any party to help him beside Allah, nor was he helped. In such a case the patronage is Allah's, the true; He is best at rewarding and best at bringing to an issue.

Strike out for them, too, a parable of the life of this world; like water which we send down from the sky, the vegetation of the earth is mingled therewith;—and on the morrow it is dried up, and the winds scatter it; for Allah is powerful over all.

Wealth and children are an adornment of the life of this world; but enduring good works are better with thy Lord, as a recompense, and better as a hope.

[45] And the day when we will move the mountains, and thou shalt see the (whole) earth stalking forth; and we will gather them, and will not leave one of them behind. Then shall they be presented to thy Lord in ranks.—Now have ye come to us as we created you at first! Nay, but ye thought that we would never make our promise good!

And the Book shall be placed,[9] and thou shalt see the sinners in fear of what is in it; and they will say, 'Alas, for us! what ails this Book, it leaves neither small nor great things alone, without numbering them?' and they shall find present what they have done; and thy Lord will not wrong any one.

And when we said to the angels, 'Adore Adam', they adored him, save only Iblîs, who was of the jinn, who revolted from the bidding of his Lord. 'What! will ye then take him and his seed as patrons, rather than me, when they are foes of yours? Bad for the wrongdoers is the exchange!'

I did not make them witnesses of the creation of the heavens and the earth, nor of the creation of themselves, nor did I take those who lead astray for my supporters.

[50] On the day when He shall say, 'Call ye my partners whom ye pretend': and they shall call on them, but they shall not answer them; and we will set the vale of perdition between them; and the sinners shall see the Fire,

and shall think that they are going to fall therein, and shall find no escape therefrom. We have turned about in this Qur'ân for men every parable; but man is ever at most things a caviller.

Naught prevented men from believing when the guidance came to them, or from asking pardon of their Lord, except the coming on them of the course of those of yore, or the coming of the torment before their eyes.[10]

We sent not prophets save as heralds of glad tidings and as warners; but those who misbelieve wrangle with vain speech to make void the truth therewith; and they take my signs and the warnings given them as a jest.

[55] Who is more unjust than he who, being reminded of the signs of his Lord, turns away therefrom, and forgets what his hands have done before? Verily, we will place veils upon their hearts lest they should understand, and dulness in their ears!

And if thou shouldst call them to the guidance, they will not be guided then for ever.

But thy Lord is forgiving, endowed with mercy; were He to punish them for what they have earned He would have hastened for them the torment. Nay rather, they have their appointed time, and shall never find a refuge beside Him.

These cities, we destroy them when they were unjust; and for their destruction we set an appointed time.

And when Moses said to his servant, 'I will not cease until I reach the confluence of the two seas, or else I will go on for years.'[11]

[60] But when they reached the confluence of the two[12]

they forgot their fish, and it took its way in the sea with a free course.

And when they had passed by, he said to his servant, 'Bring us our dinners, for we have met with toil from this journey of ours.' Said he, 'What thinkest thou? when we resorted to the rock, then, verily, I forgot the fish, but it was only Satan who made me forget it, lest I should remember it; and it took its way in the sea wondrously!'

Said he, 'This is what we were searching for.'[13] So they turned back upon their footsteps, following them up.

Then they found a servant of our servants, to whom we had given mercy from ourselves, and had taught him knowledge from before us. [65] Said Moses to him, 'Shall I follow thee, so that thou mayest teach me, from what thou hast been taught, the right way?' Said he, 'Verily, thou canst never have patience with me. How canst thou be patient in what thou comprehendest no knowledge of?' He said, 'Thou wilt find me, if Allah will, patient; nor will I rebel against thy bidding.' He said, 'Then, if thou followest me, ask me not about anything until I begin for thee the mention of it.'

[70] So they set out until when they rode[14] in the bark, he scuttled it.

Said he, 'Hast thou scuttled it to drown its crew? Thou hast produced a strange thing.'

Said he, 'Did I not tell thee, verily, thou canst never have patience with me?'

Said he, 'Rebuke me not for forgetting, and impose not on me a difficult command.' So they set out until they met a boy, and he killed him. And he (Moses) said, 'Hast thou killed a pure person without (his killing) a person? Thou hast produced an unheard of thing.'

Said he, 'Did I not tell thee, verily, thou canst not have patience with me?'

[75] Said he, 'If I ask thee about anything after it, then do not accompany me. Now hast thou arrived at my excuse.' So they set out until when they came to the people of a city; and they asked the people thereof for food; but they refused to entertain them. And they found therein a wall which wanted[15] to fall to pieces, and he set it upright. Said (Moses), 'Hadst thou pleased thou mightst certainly have had a hire for this.'

Said he, 'This is the parting between me and thee. I will give thee the interpretation of that with which thou couldst not have patience. As for the bark it belonged to poor people, who toiled on the sea, and I wished to damage it, for behind it was a king who seized on every bark[16] by force. And as for the youth, his parents were believers, and we feared lest he should impose upon them rebellion and misbelief. [80] So we desired that their Lord would give them in exchange a better one than him in purity, and nearer in filial affection. And as for the wall, it belonged to two orphan youths in the city, and beneath it was a treasure belonging to them both, and their father was a righteous man, and their Lord desired that they should reach puberty, and then take out their treasure as a mercy from thy Lord; and I did it not on my own bidding. That is the interpretation of what thou couldst not have patience with.'[17]

And they will ask thee about Dhu 'l Qarnâin,[18] say, 'I

will recite to you a mention of him; verily, we stablished for him in the earth, and we gave him a way to everything; and he followed a way until when he reached the setting of the sun, he found it setting in a black muddy spring,[19] and he found thereat a people.'

[85] We said, 'O Dhu l' Qarnâin! thou mayest either torment these people, or treat them well.' Said he, 'As for him who does wrong, I will torment him, then shall he be sent back to his Lord, and He will torment him with an unheard of torment; but as for him who believes and acts aright, for him is an excellent reward, and we will tell him our easy bidding.'

Then he followed a way until when he reached the rising of the sun, he found it rise upon a people to whom we had given no shelter therefrom.

[90] So! And we comprehended the knowledge of what (forces) he had with him.

Then he followed a way until when he reached the point between the two mountains, he found below them both a people who could scarcely understand speech. They said, 'O Dhu 'l Qarnâin! verily, Yâjûj and Mâjûj[20] are doing evil in the land. Shall we then pay thee tribute, on condition that thou set between us and them a rampart?' He said, 'What my Lord hath established me in is better; so help me with strength, and I will set between you and them a barrier.

[95] 'Bring me pigs of iron until they fill up the space between the two mountain sides.' Said he, 'Blow until it makes it a fire.' Said he, 'Bring me, that I may pour over it, molten brass.'[21]

So they[22] could not scale it, and they could not tunnel it.

Said he, 'This is a mercy from my Lord; but when the promise of my Lord comes to pass, He will make it as dust, for the promise of my Lord is true.'

And we left some of them to surge on that day[23] over others, and the trumpet will be blown, and we will gather them together.

[100] And we will set forth Hell on that day before the misbelievers, whose eyes were veiled from my Reminder, and who were unable to hear. What! Did those who misbelieve reckon that they could take my servants for patrons beside me? Verily, we have prepared Hell for the misbelievers to alight in!

Say, 'Shall we inform you of those who lose most by their works? those who erred in their endeavours after the life of this world, and who think they are doing good deeds.'

[105] Those who misbelieve in the signs of their Lord and in meeting Him, vain are their works; and we will not give them right weight on the resurrection day. That is their reward,—Hell! for that they misbelieved and took my signs and my apostles as a mockery.

Verily, those who believe and act aright, for them are gardens of Paradise[24] to alight in, to dwell therein for aye, and they shall crave no change therefrom.

Say, 'Were the sea ink for the words of my Lord, the sea would surely fail before the words of my Lord fail; aye, though we brought as much ink again!'

[110] Say, 'I am only a mortal like yourselves; I am

inspired that your Allah is only one Allah. Then let him who hopes to meet his Lord act righteous acts, and join none in the service of his Lord.'

THE CHAPTER OF MARY

XIX (*Mecca*)

In the name of the merciful and compassionate Allah.

K. H. Y. 'H. Z. The mention of thy Lord's mercy to His servant Zachariah, when he called on his Lord with a secret calling. Said he, 'My Lord! verily, my bones are weak, and my head flares with hoariness;—and I never was unfortunate in my prayers to Thee, my Lord! [5] But I fear my heirs after me, and my wife is barren; then grant me from Thee a successor, to be my heir and the heir of the family of Jacob, and make him, my Lord! acceptable.'

'O Zachariah! verily, we give thee glad tidings of a son, whose name shall be John. We never made a namesake of his before.'[1]

Said he, 'My Lord! how can I have a son, when my wife is barren, and I have reached through old age to decrepitude?'

[10] He said, 'Thus says thy Lord, "It is easy for Me, for I created thee at first when yet thou wast nothing."'

Said he, 'O my Lord! make for me a sign.' He said, 'Thy sign is that thou shalt not speak to men for three nights (though) sound.'

Then he went forth unto his people from the chamber,

and he made signs to them: 'Celebrate (Allah's) praises morning and evening!'

'O John! take the Book with strength'; and we gave him judgement when a boy, and grace from us, and purity; and he was pious and righteous to his parents, and was not a rebellious tyrant.

[15] So peace upon him the day he was born, and the day he died, and the day he shall be raised up alive.

And mention, in the Book, Mary; when she retired from her family into an eastern place; and she took a veil (to screen herself) from them; and we sent unto her our spirit; and he took for her the semblance of a well-made man. Said she, 'Verily, I take refuge in the Merciful One from thee, if thou art pious.' Said he, 'I am only a messenger of thy Lord to bestow on thee a pure boy.'

[20] Said she, 'How can I have a boy when no man has touched me, and when I am no harlot?' He said, 'Thus says thy Lord, "It is easy for Me!" and we will make Him a sign unto man, and a mercy from us; for it is a decided matter.'

So she conceived him, and she retired with him into a remote place. And the labour pains came upon her at the trunk of a palm tree, and she said, 'O that I had died before this, and been forgotten out of mind!' and he called[2] to her from beneath her, 'Grieve not, for thy Lord has placed a stream beneath thy feet; [25] and shake towards thee the trunk of the palm tree, it will drop upon thee fresh dates fit to gather; so eat, and drink, and cheer thine eye; and if thou shouldst see any mortal say, "Verily, I have vowed to the Merciful One a fast, and I will not speak today with a human being."'

Then she brought it to her people, carrying it; said they, 'O Mary! thou hast done an extraordinary thing! O sister of Aaron!³ thy father was not a bad man, nor was thy mother a harlot!'

[30] And she pointed to him, and they said, 'How are we to speak with one who is in the cradle a child?' He said, 'Verily, I am a servant of Allah; He has brought me the Book, and He has made me a prophet, and He has made me blessed wherever I be; and He has required of me prayer and almsgiving so long as I live, and piety towards my mother, and has not made me a miserable tyrant; and peace upon me the day I was born, and the day I die, and the day I shall be raised up alive.'

[35] That is, Jesus the son of Mary,—by the word of truth whereon ye do dispute!

Allah could not take to himself any son! Celebrated be His praise! When He decrees a matter He only says to it, 'BE', and it is; and, verily, Allah is my Lord and your Lord, so worship Him; this is the right way.

And the parties have disagreed amongst themselves, but woe to those who disbelieve, from the witnessing of the mighty day! they can hear and they can see,⁴ on the day when they shall come to us; but the evil-doers are to-day in obvious error!

[40] And warn them of the day of sighing, when the matter is decreed while they are heedless, and while they do not believe.

Verily, we will inherit the earth and all who are upon it, and unto us shall they return!

And mention, in the Book, Abraham; verily, he was a

confessor,—a prophet. When he said to his father, 'O my sire! why dost thou worship what can neither hear nor see nor avail thee aught? O my sire! verily, to me has come knowledge which has not come to thee; then follow me, and I will guide thee to a level way.

[45] 'O my sire! serve not Satan; verily, Satan is ever a rebel against the Merciful. O my sire! verily, I fear that there may touch thee torment from the Merciful, and that thou mayest be a client of Satan.'

Said he, 'What! art thou averse from my gods, O Abraham? Verily, if thou dost not desist I will certainly stone thee; but get thee gone from me for a time!'

Said he, 'Peace be upon thee! I will ask forgiveness for thee from my Lord; verily, He is very gracious to me: but I will part from you and what ye call on beside Allah, and will pray my Lord that I be not unfortunate in my prayer to my Lord.'

[50] And when he had parted from them and what they served beside Allah, we granted him Isaac and Jacob, and each of them we made a prophet; and we granted them of our mercy, and we made the tongue of truth lofty for them.[5]

And mention, in the Book, Moses; verily, he was sincere, and was an apostle,—a prophet. We called him from the right side of the mountain; and we made him draw nigh unto us to commune with him, and we granted him, of our mercy, his brother Aaron as a prophet.

[55] And mention, in the Book, Ishmael; verily, he was true to his promise, and was an apostle,—a prophet; and

he used to bid his people prayers and alms giving, and was acceptable in the sight of his Lord.

And mention, in the Book, Idrîs;[6] verily, he was a confessor,—a prophet; and we raised him to a lofty place.

These are those to whom Allah has been gracious, of the prophets of the seed of Adam, and of those whom we bore with Noah, and of the seed of Abraham and Israel, and of those we guided and elected; when the signs of the Merciful are read to them, they fall down adoring and weeping.

[60] And successors succeeded them, who lost sight of prayer and followed lusts, but they shall at length find themselves going wrong, except such as repent and believe and act aright; for these shall enter Paradise, and shall not be wronged at all,—gardens of Eden, which the Merciful has promised to His servants in the unseen; verily, His promise ever comes to pass!

They shall hear no empty talk therein, but only 'peace'; and they shall have their provision therein, morning and evening; that is Paradise which we will give for an inheritance to those of our servants who are pious!

[65] We do not descend[7] save at the bidding of thy Lord; His is what is before us, and what is behind us, and what is between those; for thy Lord is never forgetful,—the Lord of the heavens and the earth, and of what is between the two; then serve Him and persevere in His service. Dost thou know a namesake of His?

Man will say, 'What! when I have died shall I then come forth alive?' Does not man then remember that we created him before when he was naught?

And by thy Lord! we will surely gather them together, and the devils too; then we will surely bring them forward around Hell, on their knees!

[70] Then we will drag off from every sect whichever of them has been most bold against the Merciful.

Then we know best which of them deserves most to be broiled therein.

There is not one of you who will not go down to it,— that is settled and decided by thy Lord.[8]

Then we will save those who fear us; but we will leave the evil-doers therein on their knees.

And when our signs are recited to them manifest, those who misbelieve say to those who believe, 'Which of the two parties is best placed and in the best company?'

[75] And how many generations before them have we destroyed who were better off in property and appearance?

Say, 'Whosoever is in error, let the Merciful extend to him length of days!—until they see what they are threatened with, whether it be the torment or whether it be the Hour, then they shall know who is worse placed and weakest in forces!'

And those who are guided Allah will increase in guidance.

And enduring good works are best with thy Lord for a reward, and best for restoration.

[80] Hast thou seen him who disbelieves in our signs, and says, 'I shall surely be given wealth and children?'[9]

Has he become acquainted with the unseen, or has he taken a compact with the Merciful? Not so! We will write down what he says, and we will extend to him a length of torment, and we will make him inherit what he says, and he shall come to us alone. They take other gods besides Allah to be their glory. [85] Not so! They¹⁰ shall deny their worship and shall be opponents of theirs!

Dost thou not see that we have sent the devils against the misbelievers, to drive them on to sin? but, be not thou hasty with them. Verily, we will number them a number (of days),—the day when we will gather the pious to the Merciful as ambassadors, and we will drive the sinners to Hell like (herds) to water! [90] They shall not possess intercession, save he who has taken a compact with the Merciful.

They say, 'The Merciful has taken to Himself a son';— ye have brought a monstrous thing! The heavens well-nigh burst asunder thereat, and the earth is riven, and the mountains fall down broken, that they attribute to the Merciful a son! but it becomes not the Merciful to take to Himself a son! There is none in the heavens or the earth but comes to the Merciful as a servant; He counts them and numbers them by number, [95] and they are all coming to Him on the resurrection day singly.

Verily, those who believe and act aright, to them the Merciful will give love.

We have only made it easy for thy tongue that thou mayest thereby give glad tidings to the pious, and warn thereby a contentious people.

How many a generation before them have we destroyed? Canst thou find any one of them, or hear a whisper of them?

THE CHAPTER OF T. H.

XX (*Mecca*)

In the name of the merciful and compassionate Allah.

T. H. We have not sent down this Qur'ân to thee that thou shouldst be wretched; only as a reminder to him who fears—descending from Him who created the earth and the high heavens, the Merciful settled on the throne! [5] His are what is in the heavens, and what is in the earth, and what is between the two, and what is beneath the ground! And if thou art public in thy speech—yet, verily, he knows the secret, and more hidden still.

Allah, there is no god but He! His are the excellent names.

Has the story of Moses come to thee? When he saw the fire and said to his family, 'Tarry ye; verily, I perceive a fire! [10] Haply I may bring you therefrom a brand, or may find guidance by the Fire.'[1] And when he came to it he was called to, 'O Moses! verily, I am thy Lord, so take off thy sandals; verily, thou art in the holy valley Tuvâ, and I have chosen thee. So listen to what is inspired thee; verily, I am Allah, there is no god but Me! then serve Me, and be steadfast in prayer to remember Me.

[15] 'Verily, the hour is coming, I almost make it appear,[2] that every soul may be recompensed for its efforts.

'Let not then him who believes not therein and follows his lusts ever turn thee away therefrom, and thou be ruined.

'What is that in thy right hand, O Moses?'

Said he, 'It is my staff on which I lean, and wherewith I beat down leaves for my flocks, and for which I have other uses.'

[20] Said He, 'Throw it down, O Moses!' and he threw it down, and behold! it was a snake that moved about.

Said He, 'Take hold of it and fear not; we will restore it to its first state.

'But press thy hand to thy side, it shall come forth white without harm,—another sign! to show thee of our great signs!

[25] 'Go unto Pharaoh, verily, he is outrageous!'

Said he, 'My Lord! expand for me my breast; and make what I am bidden easy to me; and loose the knot from my tongue,[3] that they may understand my speech; [30] and make for me a minister[4] from my people,—Aaron my brother; gird up my loins through him,[5] and join him with me in the affair; that we may celebrate Thy praises much and remember Thee much.

[35] 'Verily, Thou dost ever behold us!'

He said, 'Thou art granted thy request, O Moses! and we have already shown favours unto thee at another time. When we inspired thy mother with what we inspired her, "Hurl him into the ark, and hurl him into the sea; and the sea shall cast him on the shore, and an enemy of mine and of his shall take him";—for on thee have I cast my love, [40] that thou mayest be formed under my eye. When thy sister walked on and said, "Shall I guide you to one who will take charge of him?" And we restored thee to thy mother, that her eye might be cheered and that she should not grieve. And thou didst slay a person and we saved thee from the trouble, and we tried thee with various trials. And thou didst tarry for years amongst the people of Midian; then thou didst come (hither) at (our) decree, O Moses! And I have chosen thee for myself. Go, thou and thy brother, with my signs, and be not remiss in remembering me. [45] Go ye both to Pharaoh; verily, he is outrageous! and speak to him a gentle speech, haply he may be mindful or may fear.'

They two said, 'Our Lord! verily, we fear that he may trespass against us, or that he may be outrageous.'

He said, 'Fear not; verily, I am with you twain. I hear and see!

'So come ye to him and say, "Verily, we are the apostles of thy Lord; send then the children of Israel with us; and do not torment them. We have brought thee a sign from thy Lord, and peace be upon him who follows the guidance!

[50] ' "Verily, we are inspired that the torment will surely come upon him who calls us liars and turns his back." '

Said he, 'And who is your Lord, O Moses?'

He said, 'Our Lord is He who gave everything its creation, then guided it.'

Said he, 'And what of the former generations?'

He said, 'The knowledge of them is with my Lord in a book; my Lord misleads not, nor forgets! [55] Who made for you the earth a bed; and has traced for you paths therein; and has sent down from the sky water,—and we have brought forth thereby divers sorts of different vegetables. Eat and pasture your cattle therefrom; verily, in that are signs to those endued with intelligence. From it have we created you and into it will we send you back, and from it will we bring you forth another time.'

We did show him our signs, all of them, but he called them lies and did refuse.

Said he, 'Hast thou come to us, to turn us out of our land with thy magic, O Moses? [60] Then we will bring you magic like it; and we will make between us and thee an appointment; we will not break it, nor do thou either;—a fair place.'

Said he, 'Let your appointment be for the day of adornment,⁶ and let the people assemble in the forenoon.'⁷

But Pharaoh turned his back, and collected his tricks, and then he came.

Said Moses to them, 'Woe to you! do not forge against Allah a lie; lest He destroy you by torment; for disappointed has ever been he who has forged.'

[65] And they argued their matter among themselves; and secretly talked it over.

Said they, 'These twain are certainly two magicians, who wish to turn you out of your land by their magic, and to remove your most exemplary doctrine.⁸ Collect therefore your tricks, and then form a row; for he is prosperous today who has the upper hand.'

Said they, 'O Moses! either thou must throw, or we must be the first to throw.'

He said, 'Nay, throw ye!' and lo! their ropes and their staves appeared to move along. [70] And Moses felt a secret fear within his soul.

Said we, 'Fear not! thou shalt have the upper hand.

Throw down what is in thy right hand; and it shall devour what they have made. Verily, what they have made is but a magician's trick; and no magician shall prosper wherever he comes.'

And the magicians were cast down in adoration; said they, 'We believe in the Lord of Aaron and of Moses!'

Said he,[9] 'Do ye believe in Him before I give you leave? Verily, he is your master who taught you magic! Therefore will I surely cut off your hands and feet on alternate sides, and I will surely crucify you on the trunks of palm trees; and ye shall surely know which of us is keenest at torment and more lasting.'

[75] Said they, 'We will never prefer thee to what has come to us of manifest signs, and to Him who originated us. Decide then what thou canst decide; thou canst only decide in the life of this world! Verily, we believe in our Lord, that He may pardon us our sins, and the magic thou hast forced us to use; and Allah is better and more lasting!'

Verily, he who comes to his Lord a sinner,—verily, for him is Hell; he shall not die therein, and shall not live.

But he who comes to Him a believer who has done aright—these, for them are the highest ranks,—gardens of Eden beneath which rivers flow, to dwell therein for aye; for that is the reward of him who keeps pure.

And we inspired Moses, 'Journey by night with my servants, and strike out for them a dry road in the sea. [80] Fear not pursuit, nor be afraid!' Then Pharaoh followed them with his armies, and there overwhelmed them of the sea that which overwhelmed them. And Pharaoh and his people went astray and were not guided.

O children of Israel! We have saved you from your enemy; and we made an appointment with you on the right side of the mount; and we sent down upon you the manna and the quails. 'Eat of the good things we have provided you with, and do not exceed therein, lest my wrath light upon you; for whomsoever my wrath lights upon he falls!

'Yet am I forgiving unto him who repents and believes and does right, and then is guided.

[85] 'But what has hastened thee on away from thy people, O Moses?'

He said, 'They were here upon my track and I hastened on to Thee, my Lord! that thou mightest be pleased.'

Said He, 'Verily, we have tried thy people, since thou didst leave, and es Sâmarîy¹⁰ has led them astray.'

And Moses returned to his people, wrathful, grieving!

Said he, 'O my people! did not your Lord promise you a good promise? Has the time seemed too long for you, or do you desire that wrath should light on you from your Lord, that ye have broken your promise to me?'

[90] They said, 'We have not broken our promise to thee of our own accord. But we were made to carry loads of the ornaments of the people, and we hurled them down, and so did es Sâmarîy cast; and he brought forth for the people a corporeal calf which lowed.' And they said, 'This is your god and the god of Moses, but he has forgotten!' What! do they not see that it does not return them any speech, and cannot control for them harm or profit? Aaron too told them before, 'O my people! ye are only being tried thereby; and, verily, your Lord is

the Merciful, so follow me and obey my bidding.'

They said, 'We will not cease to pay devotion to it until Moses come back to us.'

Said he, 'O Aaron! what prevented thee, when thou didst see them go astray, from following me? Hast thou then rebelled against my bidding?'

[95] Said he, 'O son of my mother! seize me not by my beard, or my head! Verily, I feared lest thou shouldst say, "Thou hast made a division amongst the children of Israel, and hast not observed my word." '

Said he, 'What was thy design, O Sâmarîy?' Said he, 'I beheld what they beheld not, and I grasped a handful from the footprint of the messenger[11] and cast it; for thus my soul induced me.'

Said he, 'Then get thee gone; verily, it shall be thine in life to say, "Touch me not!"[12] and, verily, for thee there is a threat which thou shalt surely never alter. But look at thy god to which thou wert just now devout; we will surely burn it, and then we will scatter it in scattered pieces in the sea.

'Your Allah is only Allah who,—there is no god but He,—He embraceth everything in His knowledge.'

Thus do we narrate to thee the history of what has gone before, and we have brought thee a reminder from us.

[100] Whoso turns therefrom, verily, he shall bear on the resurrection day a burden:—for them to bear for aye, and evil for them on the resurrection day will it be to bear.

On the day when the trumpet shall be blown, and we will gather the sinners in that day blue-eyed.[13]

They shall whisper to each other, 'Ye have only tarried ten days.' We know best what they say, when the most exemplary of them in his way shall say, 'Ye have only tarried a day.'

[105] They will ask thee about the mountains; say, 'My Lord will scatter them in scattered pieces, and He will leave them a level plain, thou wilt see therein no crookedness of inequality.'

On that day they shall follow the caller in whom is no crookedness;[14] and the voices shall be hushed before the Merciful, and thou shalt hear naught but a shuffling.

On that day shall no intercession be of any avail, save from such as the Merciful permits, and who is acceptable to Him in speech.

He knows what is before them and what is behind them, but they do not comprehend knowledge of Him.

[110] Faces shall be humbled before the Living, the Self-subsistent; and he who bears injustice is ever lost.

But he who does righteous acts and is a believer, he shall fear neither wrong nor diminution.

Thus have we sent it down an Arabic Qur'ân; and we have turned about in it the threat,—haply they may fear, or it may cause them to remember.

Exalted then be Allah, the king, the truth! Hasten not the Qur'ân before its inspiration is decided for thee; but say, 'O Lord! increase me in knowledge.'[15]

We did make a covenant with Adam of yore, but he forgot it, and we found no firm purpose in him.

[115] And when we said to the angels, 'Adore Adam',

they adored, save Iblîs, who refused, And we said, 'O Adam! verily, this is a foe to thee and to the wife; never then let him drive you twain forth from the garden or thou wilt be wretched. Verily, thou hast not to be hungry there, nor naked! and, verily, thou shalt not thirst therein, nor feel the noonday heat!'

But the devil whispered to him. Said he, 'O Adam! shall I guide thee to the tree of immortality, and a kingdom that shall not wane?'

And they eat therefrom, and their shame became apparent to them; and they began to stitch upon themselves some leaves of the garden; and Adam rebelled against his Lord, and went astray.

[120] Then his Lord chose him, and relented towards him, and guided him. Said he, 'Go down, ye twain, therefrom altogether, some of you foes to the other. And if there should come to you from me a guidance; then whoso follows my guidance shall neither err nor be wretched. But he who turns away from my reminder, verily, for him shall be a straitened livelihood; and we will gather him on the resurrection day blind!'

[125] He shall say, 'My Lord! wherefore hast Thou gathered me blind when I used to see?' He shall say, 'Our signs came to thee, and thou didst forget them; thus to-day art thou forgotten!'

Thus do we recompense him who is extravagant and believes not in the signs of his Lord; and the torment of the hereafter is keener and more lasting!

Does it not occur to them[16] how many generations we have destroyed before them?—they walk in their very dwelling places; verily, in that are signs to those endued with intelligence.

And had it not been for thy Lord's word already passed (the punishment) would have been inevitable and (at) an appointed time.

[130] Bear patiently then what they say, and celebrate the praises of thy Lord before the rising of the sun, and before its setting, and at times in the night celebrate them; and at the ends of the day; haply thou mayest please (Him).

And do not strain after what we have provided a few[17] of them with—the flourish of the life of this world, to try them by; but the provision of thy Lord is better and more lasting.

Bid thy people prayer, and persevere in it; we do not ask thee to provide. We will provide, and the issue shall be to piety.

They say, 'Unless he bring us a sign from his Lord— What! has there not come to them the manifest sign of what was in the pages of yore?'

But had we destroyed them with torment before it, they would have said, 'Unless Thou hadst sent to us an apostle, that we might follow Thy signs before we were abased and put to shame.'

[135] Say, 'Each one has to wait, so wait ye! But in the end ye shall know who are the fellows of the level way, and who are guided!'

THE CHAPTER OF THE PROPHETS

XXI (*Mecca*)

In the name of the merciful and compassionate Allah.

Their reckoning draws nigh to men, yet in heedlessness they turn aside.

No reminder comes to them from their Lord of late, but they listen while they mock, and their hearts make sport thereof! And those who do wrong discourse secretly (saying), 'Is this man aught but a mortal like yourselves? will ye accede to magic, while ye can see?'

Say, 'My Lord knows what is said in the heavens and the earth, He hears and knows!'

[5] 'Nay!' they say, '—a jumble of dreams; nay! he has forged it; nay! he is a poet; but let him bring us a sign as those of yore were sent.'

No city before them which we destroyed believed—how will they believe? Nor did we send before them any but men whom we inspired? Ask ye the people of the Scriptures if ye do not know. Nor did we make them bodies not to eat food, nor were they immortal. Yet we made our promise to them good, and we saved them and whom we pleased; but we destroyed those who committed excesses.

[10] We have sent down to you a book in which is a reminder for you; have ye then no sense?

How many a city which had done wrong have we broken up, and raised up after it another people! And when they perceived our violence they ran away from it.

'Run not away, but return to what ye delighted in, and to your dwellings! haply ye will be questioned.' Said they, 'O woe is us! Verily, we were wrongdoers.'

[15] And that ceased not to be their cry until we made them mown down,—smouldering out!

We did not create the heaven and the earth and what is between the two in play. Had we wished to take to a sport, we would have taken to one from before ourselves; had we been bent on doing so. Nay, we hurl the truth against falsehood and it crashes into it, and lo! it vanishes, but woe to you for what ye attribute (to Allah)!

His are whosoever are in the heavens and the earth, and those who are with Him are not too big with pride for His service, nor do they weary. [20] They celebrate His praises by night and day without intermission. Or have they taken gods from the earth who can raise up (the dead)?

Were there in both (heaven and earth) gods beside Allah, both would surely have been corrupted. Celebrated then be the praise of Allah, the Lord of the throne, above what they ascribe!

He shall not be questioned concerning what He does, but they shall be questioned.

Have they taken gods beside Him? Say, 'Bring your proofs. This is the reminder of those who are with me, and of those who were before me.' Nay, most of them know not the truth, and they do turn aside.

[25] We have not sent any prophet before thee, but we inspired him that, 'There is no god but Me, so serve ye Me.'

And they say, 'The Merciful has taken a son;[1] celebrated be His praise!'—Nay, honoured servants; they do not speak until He speaks; but at His bidding do they act. He knows what is before them, and what is behind them, and they shall not intercede except for him whom He is pleased with; and they shrink through fear.

[30] And whoso of them should say, 'Verily, I am god instead of Him', such a one we recompense with Hell; thus do we recompense the wrongdoers.

Do not those who misbelieve see that the heavens and the earth were both solid, and we burst them asunder; and we made from water every living thing —will they then not believe?

And we placed on the earth firm mountains lest it should move with them, and He made therein open roads for paths, haply they may be guided! and we made the heaven a guarded roof; yet from our signs they turn aside!

He it is who created the night and the day, and the sun and the moon, each floating in a sky.

[35] We never made for any mortal before thee immortality; what, if thou shouldst die, will they live on for aye?

Every soul shall taste of death! We will test them with evil and with good, as a trial; and unto us shall they return!

And when those who misbelieve see thee,[2] they only take thee for a jest, 'Is this he who mentions your gods?' Yet they at the mention of the Merciful do disbelieve.

Man is created out of haste. I will show you my signs; but do not hurry Me.

And they say, 'When will this threat (come to pass), if ye tell the truth?'

[40] Did those who misbelieve but know when the fire

shall not be warded off from their faces nor from their backs, and they shall not be helped! Nay, it shall come on them suddenly, and shall dumbfound them, and they shall not be able to repel it, nor shall they be respited.

Prophets before thee have been mocked at, but that whereat they jested encompassed those who mocked.

Say, 'Who shall guard you by night and by day from the Merciful?' Nay, but they from the mention of their Lord do turn aside.

Have they gods to defend them against us? These cannot help themselves, nor shall they be abetted against us.

[45] Nay, but we have granted enjoyment to these men and to their fathers whilst life was prolonged. Do they not see that we come to the land and shorten its borders? Shall they then prevail?

Say, 'I only warn you by inspiration'; but the deaf hear not the call when they are warned. But if a blast of the torment of thy Lord touches them, they will surely say, 'O, woe is us! Verily, we were wrongdoers!'

We will place just balances upon the resurrection day, and no soul shall be wronged at all, even though it be the weight of a grain of mustard seed, we will bring it; for we are good enough at reckoning up.

We did give to Moses and Aaron the Discrimination, and a light and a reminder to those who fear; [50] who are afraid of their Lord in secret; and who at the Hour do shrink.

This is a blessed reminder which we have sent down, will ye then deny it?

And we gave Abraham a right direction before; for about him we knew. When he said to his father and to his people, 'What are these images to which ye pay devotion?' Said they, 'We found our fathers serving them.' [55] Said he, 'Both you and your fathers have been in obvious error.' They said, 'Dost thou come to us with the truth, or art thou but of those who play?'

He said, 'Nay, but your Lord is Lord of the heavens and the earth, which He originated; and I am of those who testify to this; and, by Allah! I will plot against your idols after ye have turned and shown me your backs!'

So he brake them all in pieces, except a large one they had; that haply they might refer it to that.

[60] Said they, 'Who has done this with our gods? Verily, he is of the wrongdoers!' They said, 'We heard a youth mention them who is called Abraham.'

Said they, 'Then bring him before the eyes of men; haply they will bear witness.'

Said they, 'Was it thou who did this to our gods, O Abraham?' Said he, 'Nay, it was this largest of them; but ask them, if they can speak.'

[65] Then they came to themselves and said, 'Verily, ye are the wrongdoers.' Then they turned upside down again:³ 'Thou knewest that these cannot speak.'

Said he, 'Will ye then serve, beside Allah, what cannot profit you at all, nor harm you? Fie upon you, and what ye serve beside Allah! have ye then no sense?'

Said they, 'Burn him, and help your gods, if ye are going to do so!'

We said, 'O fire! be thou cool and a safety for Abraham!'

[70] They desired to plot against him, but we made them the losers.

And we brought him and Lot safely to the land which we have blessed for the world, and we bestowed upon him Isaac and Jacob as a fresh gift, and each of them we made righteous persons; and we made them high priests⁴ to guide (men) by our bidding, and we inspired them to do good works, and to be steadfast in prayer, and to give alms; and they did serve us.

And Lot, to him we gave judgement and knowledge, and we brought him safely out of the city which had done vile acts; verily, they were a people who wrought abominations! [75] And we made him enter into our mercy; verily, he was of the righteous!

And Noah, when he cried aforetime, and we answered him and saved him and his people from the mighty trouble, and we helped him against the people who said our signs were lies; verily, they were a bad people, so we drowned them all together.

And David and Solomon, when they gave judgement concerning the field, when some people's sheep had strayed therein at night; and we testified to their judgement;⁵ and this we gave Solomon to understand. To each of them we gave judgement and knowledge; and to David we subjected the mountains to celebrate our praises, and the birds too,—it was we who did it.⁶

[80] And we taught him the art of making coats of mail for you, to shield you from each other's violence; are ye then grateful?

And to Solomon (we subjected) the wind blowing stormily, to run on at his bidding to the land⁷ which we have blessed,—for all things did we know,—and some devils to dive for him, and to do other works beside that; and we kept guard over them.

And Job, when he cried to his Lord, 'As for me, harm has touched me, but Thou art the most merciful of the merciful ones.' And we answered him, and removed from him the distress that was upon him; and we gave his family, and the like of them with them, as a mercy from us, and a remembrance to those who serve us.

[85] And Ishmael, and Idrîs, and Dhu 'l Kifl,[8] all of these were of the patient: and we made them enter into our mercy; verily, they were among the righteous.

And Dhu 'nnûn,[9] when he went away in wrath and thought that we had no power over him; and he cried out in the darkness, 'There is no god but Thou, celebrated be Thy praise! Verily, I was of the evil-doers!' And we answered him, and saved him from the trouble. Thus do we save believers!

And Zachariah, when he cried unto his Lord, 'O Lord! leave me not alone; for thou art the best of heirs.'[10] [90] And we answered him, and bestowed upon him John; and we made his wife right for him; verily, these vied in good works, and called on us with longing and dread, and were humble before us.

And she who guarded her private parts, and we breathed into her of our Spirit, and we made her and her son a sign unto the worlds. Verily, this your nation[11] is one nation; and I am your Lord, so serve me.

But they cut up their affair amongst themselves; they all shall return to us; and he who acts aright, and he who is a believer, there is no denial of his efforts, for, verily, we will write them down for him.

[95] There is a ban upon a city which we have destroyed that they shall not return, until Yâjûj and Mâjûj are let out,[12] and they from every hummock[13] shall glide forth.

And the true promise draws nigh, and lo! they are staring—the eyes of those who misbelieve! O, woe is us! we were heedless of this, nay, we were wrongdoers!

Verily, ye, and what ye serve beside Allah, shall be the pebbles of Hell,[14] to it shall ye go down!

Had these been Allah's they would not have gone down thereto: but all shall dwell therein for aye; [100] for them therein is groaning, but they therein shall not be heard.

Verily, those for whom the good (reward) from us was foreordained, they from it shall be kept far away; they shall not hear the slightest sound thereof, and they in what their souls desire shall dwell for aye. The greatest terror shall not grieve them; and the angels shall meet them (saying), 'This is your day which ye were promised!'

The day when we will roll up the heavens as es-Sijill rolls up the books;[15] as we produced it at its first creation will we bring it back again—a promise binding upon us; verily, we are going to do it. And already have we written in the Psalms [105] after the reminder that 'the earth shall my righteous servants inherit.'[16]

Verily, in this is preaching for a people who serve me!

We have only sent thee as a mercy to the worlds.

Say, 'I am only inspired that your Allah is one Allah; are ye then resigned?' But if they turn their backs say, 'I have proclaimed (war) against all alike, but I know not if what ye are threatened with be near or far!'

[110] Verily, He knows what is spoken openly, and He knows what ye hide.

I know not, haply it is a trial for you and a provision for a season.

Say, 'My Lord! judge thou with truth! and our Lord is the Merciful whom we ask for aid against what they ascribe!'

THE CHAPTER OF THE PILGRIMAGE

XXII (*Mecca*)

In the name of the merciful and compassionate Allah.

O ye folk! fear your Lord. Verily, the earthquake of the Hour is a mighty thing.

On the day ye shall see it, every suckling woman shall be scared away from that to which she gave suck; and every pregnant woman shall lay down her load; and thou shalt see men drunken, though they be not drunken: but the torment of Allah is severe.

And amongst men is one who wrangles about Allah without knowledge, and follows every rebellious devil; against whom it is written down that whoso takes him for a patron, verily, he will lead him astray, and will guide him towards the torment of the blaze!

[5] O ye folk! if ye are in doubt about the raising (of the dead),—verily, we created you from earth, then from a clot, then from congealed blood, then from a morsel, shaped or shapeless, that we may explain to you. And we make what we please rest in the womb until an appointed

time; then we bring you forth babes; then let you reach your full age; and of you are some who die; and of you are some who are kept back till the most decrepit age, till he knows no longer aught of knowledge. And ye see the earth parched, and when we send down water on it, it stirs and swells, and brings forth herbs of every beauteous kind.

That is because Allah, He is the truth, and because He quickens the dead, and because He is mighty over all; and because the Hour is coming, there is no doubt therein, and because Allah raises up those who are in the tombs.

And amongst men is one who wrangles about Allah without knowledge or guidance or an illuminating book; twisting his neck from the way of Allah; for him is disgrace in this world, and we will make him taste, upon the resurrection day, the torment of burning.

[10] That is for what thy hands have done before, and for that Allah is not unjust unto His servants.

And amongst men is one who serves Allah (wavering) on a brink; and if there befall him good, he is comforted; but if there befall him a trial, he turns round again, and loses this world and the next – that is an obvious loss. He calls, besides Allah, on what can neither harm him nor profit him;—that is a wide error.

He calls on him whose harm is nigher than his profit,— a bad lord and a bad comrade.

Verily, Allah makes those who believe and do aright enter into gardens beneath which rivers flow; verily, Allah does what He will.

[15] He who thinks that Allah will never help him in this world or the next – let him stretch a cord to the roof[1]

and put an end to himself; and let him cut it and see if his stratagem will remove what he is enraged at.

Thus have we sent down manifest signs; for, verily, Allah guides whom He will.

Verily, those who believe, and those who are Jews, and the Sabæans, and the Christians, and the Magians, and those who join other gods with Allah, verily, Allah will decide between them on the resurrection day; verily, Allah is witness over all.

Do they not see that Allah, whosoever is in the heavens adores Him, and whosoever is in the earth, and the sun, and the moon, and the stars, and the mountains, and the beasts, and many among men, though many a one deserves the torments?

Whomsoever Allah abases there is none to honour him; verily, Allah does what He pleases.

[20] These are two disputants[2] who dispute about their Lord, but those who misbelieve, for them are cut out garments of fire, there shall be poured over their heads boiling water, wherewith what is in their bellies shall be dissolved and their skins too, and for them are maces of iron. Whenever they desire to come forth therefrom through pain, they are sent back into it: 'And taste ye the torment of the burning!'

Verily, Allah will make those who believe and do right enter into gardens beneath which rivers flow; they shall be bedecked therein with bracelets of gold and with pearls, and their garments therein shall be of silk, and they shall be guided to the goodly speech, and they shall be guided to the laudable way.

[25] Verily, those who misbelieve and who turn men away from Allah's path and the Sacred Mosque, which we have made for all men alike, the dweller therein, and the stranger, and he who desires therein profanation with injustice, we will make him taste grievous woe.

And when we established for Abraham the place of the House, (saying), 'Associate naught with me, but cleanse my House for those who make the circuits, for those who stand to pray, for those who bow, and for those too who adore.

'And proclaim amongst men the Pilgrimage; let them come to you on foot and on every slim camel, from every deep pass, that they may witness advantages for them, and may mention the name of Allah for the stated days[3] over what Allah has provided them with of brute beasts, then eat thereof and feed the badly off, the poor.

[30] 'Then let them finish the neglect of their persons,[4] and let them pay their vows and make the circuit round the old House.

'That do. And whoso magnifies the sacred things of Allah it is better for him with his Lord.

'Cattle are lawful for you, except what is recited to you; and avoid the abomination of idols, and avoid speaking falsely, being *hanifs* to Allah, not associating aught with Him; for he who associates aught with Allah, it is as though he had fallen from heaven, and the birds snatch him up, or the wind blows him away into a far distant place.

'That—and he who makes grand the symbols[5] of Allah, they come from piety of heart.

'Therein have ye advantages for an appointed time, then the place for sacrificing them is at the old House.'

[35] To every nation have we appointed rites, to mention the name of Allah over what He has provided them with of brute beasts; and your Allah is one Allah, to Him then be resigned, and give glad tidings to the lowly, whose hearts when Allah is mentioned are afraid, and to those who are patient of what befalls them, and to those who are steadfast in prayer and of what we have given them expend in alms.

The bulky (camels) we have made for you one of the symbols of Allah, therein have ye good; so mention the name of Allah over them as they stand in a row,[6] and when they fall down (dead) eat of them, and feed the easily contented and him who begs.

Thus have we subjected them to you; haply, ye may give thanks!

Their meat will never reach to Allah, nor yet their blood, but the piety from you will reach to Him.

Thus hath He subjected them to you that ye may magnify Allah for guiding you: and give thou glad tidings to those who do good.

Verily, Allah will defend those who believe; verily, Allah loves not any misbelieving traitor.

[40] Permission is given to those who fight because they have been wronged,—and, verily, Allah to help them has the might,—who have been driven forth from their homes undeservedly, only for that they said, 'Our Lord is Allah'; and were it not for Allah's repelling some men with others, cloisters and churches and synagogues and mosques,

wherein Allah's name is mentioned much, would be destroyed. But Allah will surely help him who helps Him; verily, Allah is powerful, mighty.

Who, if we stablish them in the earth, are steadfast in prayer, and give alms, and bid what is right, and forbid what is wrong; and Allah's is the future of affairs.

But if they call thee liar, the people of Noah called him liar before them, as did 'Ad and Thamûd, and the people of Abraham, and the people of Lot, and the fellows of Midian; and Moses was called a liar too: but I let the misbelievers range at large, and then I seized on them, and how great was the change!

And how many a city have we destroyed while it yet did wrong, and it was turned over on its roofs, and (how many) a deserted well and lofty palace!

[45] Have they not travelled on through the land? and have they not hearts to understand with, or ears to hear with? for it is not their eyes which are blind, but blind are the hearts which are within their breasts.

They will bid thee hasten on the torment, but Allah will never fail in his promise; for, verily, a day with thy Lord is as a thousand years of what ye number.

And to how many a city have I given full range while it yet did wrong! then I seized on it, and unto me was the return.

Say, 'O ye folk! I am naught but a plain warner to you, but those who believe and do right, for them is forgiveness and a generous provision; [50] but those who strive to discredit our signs, they are the fellows of Hell!'

We have not sent before thee any apostle or prophet,

but that when he wished, Satan threw not something into his wish;[7] but Allah annuls what Satan throws; then does Allah confirm his signs, and Allah is knowing, wise—to make what Satan throws a trial unto those in whose hearts is sickness, and those whose hearts are hard; and, verily, the wrongdoers are in a wide schism—and that those who have been given 'the knowledge' may know that it is the truth from thy Lord, and may believe therein, and that their hearts may be lowly; for, verily, Allah surely will guide those who believe into a right way.

But those who misbelieve will not cease to be in doubt thereof until the Hour comes on them suddenly, or there comes on them the torment of the barren day.[8]

[55] The kingdom on that day shall be Allah's, He shall judge between them; and those who believe and do aright shall be in gardens of pleasure, but those who misbelieve and say our signs are lies, these—for them is shameful woe.

And those who flee in Allah's way, and then are slain or die, Allah will provide them with a goodly provision; for, verily, Allah is the best of providers.

He shall surely make them enter by an entrance that they like; for, verily, Allah is knowing, clement.

That (is so). Whoever punishes with the like of what he has been injured with, and shall then be outraged again, Allah shall surely help him; verily, Allah pardons, forgives.

[60] That for that Allah joins on the night to the day, and joins on the day to the night, and that Allah is hearing, seeing; that is for that Allah is the truth, and for

that what ye call on beside Him is falsehood, and that Allah is the high, the great.

Hast thou not seen that Allah sends down from the sky water, and on the morrow the earth is green? Verily, Allah is kind and well aware.

His is what is in the heavens and what is in the earth; and, verily, Allah is rich and to be praised.

Hast thou not seen that Allah has subjected for you what is in the earth, and the ship that runs on in the sea at His bidding, and He holds back the sky from falling on the earth save at His bidding?9 Verily, Allah to men is gracious, merciful.

[65] He it is who quickens you, then makes you die, then will He quicken you again—Verily, man is indeed ungrateful.

For every nation have we made rites which they observe; let them not then dispute about the matter, but call upon thy Lord; verily, thou art surely in a right guidance!

But if they wrangle with thee, say, 'Allah best knows what ye do.'

Allah shall judge between them on the resurrection day concerning that whereon they disagreed.

Didst thou not know that Allah knows what is in the heavens and the earth? Verily, that is in a book; verily, that for Allah is easy.

[70] And they serve beside Allah what He has sent down no power for, and what they have no knowledge of; but the wrongdoers shall have none to help them.

When our signs are read to them manifest, thou mayest

recognize in the faces of those who misbelieve disdain; they well-nigh rush at those who recite to them our signs. Say, 'Shall I inform you of something worse than that for you, the Fire which Allah has promised to those who misbelieve? An evil journey shall it be!'

O ye folk! a parable is struck out for you, so listen to it. Verily, those on whom ye call beside Allah could never create a fly if they all united together to do it, and if the fly should despoil them of aught they could not snatch it away from it—weak is both the seeker and the sought.

They do not value Allah at His true value; verily, Allah is powerful, mighty.

Allah chooses apostles of the angels and of men; verily, Allah hears and sees. [75] He knows what is before them and what is behind them; and unto Allah affairs return.

O ye who believe! bow down and adore, and serve your Lord, and do well, haply ye may prosper; and fight strenuously for Allah, as is His due. He has elected you, and has not put upon you any hindrance by your religion,—the faith of your father Abraham. He has named you Muslims before and in this (book), that the Apostle may be a witness against you, and that ye may be witnesses against men.

Be ye then steadfast in prayer, and give alms, and hold fast by Allah; He is your sovereign, and an excellent sovereign, and an excellent help!

THE CHAPTER OF BELIEVERS

XXIII (*Mecca*)

In the name of the merciful and compassionate Allah.

Prosperous are the believers who in their prayers are humble, and who from vain talk turn aside, and who in alms giving are active. [5] And who guard their private parts—except for their wives or what their right hands possess for then, verily, they are not to be blamed;—but whoso craves aught beyond that, they are the transgressors—and who observe their trusts and covenants, and who guard well their prayers: [10] these are the heirs who shall inherit Paradise; they shall dwell therein for aye!

We have created man from an extract of clay; then we made him a clot in a sure depository; then we created the clot congealed blood, and we created the congealed blood a morsel; then we created the morsel bone, and we clothed the bone with flesh; then we produced it another creation; and blessed be Allah, the best of creators![1]

[15] Then shall ye after that surely die; then shall ye on the day of resurrection be raised.

And we have created above you seven roads;[2] nor are we heedless of the creation.

And we send down from the heaven water by measure, and we make it rest in the earth; but, verily, we are able to take it away; and we produce for you thereby gardens of palms and grapes wherein ye have many fruits, and whence ye eat.

[20] And a tree growing out of Mount Sinai which

produces oil, and a condiment for those who eat.

And, verily, ye have a lesson in the cattle; we give you to drink of what is in their bellies; and ye have therein many advantages, and of them ye eat, and on them and on ships ye are borne!

We sent Noah unto his people, and he said, 'O my people! worship Allah, ye have no god but Him; do ye then not fear?'

Said the chiefs of those who misbelieved among his people, 'This is nothing but a mortal like yourselves who wishes to have preference over you, and had Allah pleased He would have sent angels; we have not heard of this amongst our fathers of yore: [25] he is nothing but a man possessed; let him bide then for a season.'

Said he, 'Help me, for they call me liar!'

And we inspired him, 'Make the ark under our eyes and inspiration; and when the oven boils over, conduct into it of every kind two, with thy family, except him of them against whom the word has passed; and do not address me for those who do wrong, verily, they are to be drowned!

'But when thou art settled, thou and those with thee in the ark, say, "Praise belongs to Allah, who saved us from the unjust people!"

[30] 'And say, "My Lord! make me to alight in a blessed alighting place, for Thou art the best of those who cause men to alight!" ' Verily, in that is a sign, and, verily, we were trying them.

Then we raised up after them another generation; and we sent amongst them a prophet of themselves (saying), 'Serve Allah, ye have no god but He; will ye then not fear?'

Said the chiefs of his people who misbelieved, and called the meeting of the last day a lie, and to whom we gave enjoyment in the life of this world, 'This is only a mortal like yourselves, who eats of what ye eat, [35] and drinks of what ye drink; and if ye obey a mortal like yourselves, verily, ye will then be surely losers! Does he promise you that when ye are dead, and have become dust and bones, that then ye will be brought forth?

'Away, away with what ye are threatened,—there is only our life in the world! We die and we live, and we shall not be raised! [40] He is only a man who forges against Allah a lie. And we believe not in him!'

Said he, 'My Lord! help me, for they call me liar!' He said, 'Within a little they will surely awake repenting!'

And the noise seized them deservedly; and we made them as rubbish borne by a torrent; so, away with the unjust people!

Then we raised up after them other generations.

[45] No nation can anticipate its appointed time, nor keep it back.

Then we sent our apostles one after another. Whenever its apostle came to any nation they called him a liar; and we made some to follow others; and we made them legends; away then with a people who do not believe!

Then we sent Moses and his brother Aaron with our signs, and with plain authority to Pharaoh and his chiefs, but they were too big with pride, and were a haughty people.

And they said, 'Shall we believe two mortals like ourselves, when their people are servants of ours?'

[50] So they called them liars, and were of those who perished.

And we gave Moses the Book, that haply they might be guided.

And we made the son of Mary and his mother a sign; and we lodged them both on a high place, furnished with security and a spring.

O ye apostles! eat of the good things and do right; verily, what ye do I know!

And, verily, this nation³ of yours is one nation, and I am your Lord; so fear me.

[55] And they have become divided as to their affair amongst themselves into sects,⁴ each party rejoicing in what they have themselves. So leave them in their flood (of error) for a time.

Do they reckon that that of which we grant them such an extent, of wealth and children, we hasten to them as good things—nay, but they do not perceive!

Verily, those who shrink with terror at their Lord, [60] and those who in the signs of their Lord believe, and those who with their Lord join none, and those who give what they do give while their hearts are afraid that they unto their Lord will return,—these hasten to good things and are first to gain the same. But we will not oblige a soul beyond its capacity; for with us is a book that utters the truth, and they shall not be wronged.

[65] Nay, their hearts are in a flood (of error) at this, and they have works beside this which they do.⁵ Until we catch the affluent ones amongst them with the torment; then lo! they cry for aid.

Cry not for aid today! Verily, against us ye will not be helped. My signs were recited to you, but upon your heels did ye turn back, big with pride at it,[6] in vain discourse by night.

[70] Is it that they did not ponder over the words, whether that has come to them which came not to their fathers of yore? Or did they not know their apostle, that they thus deny him? Or do they say, 'He is possessed by a jinn'? Nay, he came to them with the truth, and most of them are averse from the truth.

But if the truth were to follow their lusts, the heavens and the earth would be corrupted with all who in them are!—Nay, we brought them their reminder, but they from their reminder turn aside.

Or dost thou ask them for a tribute? But the tribute of thy Lord is better, for He is the best of those who provide.

[75] And, verily, thou dost call them to a right way; but, verily, those who believe not in the hereafter from the way do veer.

But if we had mercy on them, and removed the distress[7] they have, they would persist in their rebellion, blindly wandering on!

And we caught them with the torment,[8] but they did not abase themselves before their Lord, nor did they humble themselves; until we opened for them a door with grievous torment, then lo! they are in despair.

[80] He is who produced for you hearing, and sight, and minds,—little is it that ye thank. And He it is who created you in the earth, and unto Him shall ye be gathered. And He it is who gives you life and death; and His is the alter-

nation of the night and the day; have ye then no sense?

Nay, but they said like that which those of yore did say.

They said, 'What! when we have become earth and bones, are we then going to be raised? [85] We have been promised this, and our fathers too, before;—this is naught but old folks' tales!'

Say, 'Whose is the earth and those who are therein, if ye but know?'

They will say, 'Allah's'. Say, 'Do ye not then mind?'

Say, 'Who is Lord of the seven heavens, and Lord of the mighty throne?'

They will say, 'Allah.' Say, 'Do ye not then fear?'

[90] Say, 'In whose hand is the dominion of everything; He succours but is not succoured,—if ye did but know?'

They will say, 'Allah's.' Say, 'Then how can ye be so infatuated?'

Nay, we have brought them the truth, but, verily, they are liars!

Allah never took a son, nor was there ever any god with Him;—then each god would have gone off with what he had created, and some would have exalted themselves over others,—celebrated be His praises above what they attribute (to Him)!

He who knows the unseen and the visible, exalted be He above what they join with Him!

[95] Say, 'My Lord! if Thou shouldst show me what they are threatened,—my Lord! then place me not amongst the unjust people.'

Repel evil by what is better.⁹ We know best what they

attribute (to thee). And say, 'My Lord! I seek refuge in Thee from the incitings of the devils; [100] and I seek refuge in Thee from their presence!'

Until when death comes to any one of them he says, 'My Lord! send ye me back,[10] haply I may do right in that which I have left!'

Not so!—a mere word he speaks!—but behind them is a bar until the day they shall be raised.

And when the trumpet shall be blown, and there shall be no relation between them on that day, nor shall they beg of each other then!

[105] And he whose scales are heavy,—they are the prosperous. But he whose scales are light,—these are they who lose themselves, in Hell to dwell for aye! The Fire shall scorch their faces, and they shall curl their lips therein! 'Were not my signs recited to you? and ye said that they were lies!' They say, 'Our Lord! our misery overcame us, and we were a people who did err! Our Lord! take us out therefrom, and if we return,[11] then shall we be unjust.'

[110] He will say, 'Go ye away into it and speak not to me!'

Verily, there was a sect of my servants who said, 'Our Lord! we believe, so pardon us, and have mercy upon us, for Thou art the best of the merciful ones.'

And ye took them for a jest until ye forgot my reminder and did laugh thereat. Verily, I have recompensed them this day for their patience; verily, they are happy now.

He will say, 'How long a number of years did ye tarry on earth?' [115] They will say, 'We tarried a day or part of a day, but ask the Numberers.'[12]

He will say, 'Ye have only tarried a little, were ye but

to know it. Did ye then reckon that we created you for sport, and that to us ye would not return?' But exalted be Allah, the true; there is no god but He, the Lord of the noble throne! and whoso calls upon another god with Allah has no proof of it, but, verily, his account is with his Lord; verily, the misbelievers shall not prosper. And say, 'Lord, pardon and be merciful, for Thou art the best of the merciful ones!'

THE CHAPTER OF LIGHT

XXIV (*Medina*)

In the name of the merciful and compassionate Allah.

A chapter which we have sent down and determined, and have sent down therein manifest signs; haply ye may be mindful.

The whore and the whoremonger. Scourge each of them with a hundred stripes, and do not let pity for them take hold of you in Allah's religion, if ye believe in Allah and the last day; and let a party of the believers witness their torment. And the whoremonger shall marry none but a whore or an idolatress; and the whore shall none marry but an adulterer or an idolater; Allah has prohibited this to the believers; but those who cast (imputations) on chaste women and then do not bring four witnesses, scourge them with eighty stripes, and do not receive any testimony of theirs ever, for these are the workers of abomination.

[5] Except such as repent after that and act aright, for, verily, Allah is forgiving and compassionate.

And those who cast (imputation) on their wives and have no witnesses except themselves, then the testimony of one of them shall be to testify four times that, by Allah, he is of those who speak the truth; and the fifth testimony shall be that the curse of Allah shall be on him if he be of those who lie. And it shall avert the punishment from her if she bears testimony four times that, by Allah, he is of those who lie; and the fifth that the wrath of Allah shall be on her if he be of those who speak the truth.

[10] And were it not for Allah's grace upon you and His mercy, and that Allah is relenting, wise . . .¹

Verily, those who bring forward the lie, a band of you,—reckon it not as an evil for you, nay, it is good for you; every man of them shall have what he has earned of sin; and he of them who managed to aggravate it, for him is mighty woe.²

Why did not, when ye heard it, the believing men and believing women think good in themselves, and say, 'This is an obvious lie'? Why did they not bring four witnesses to it? But since they did not bring the witnesses, then they in Allah's eyes are the liars. And but for Allah's grace upon you, and His mercy in this world and the next, there would have touched you, for that which ye spread abroad, mighty woe. When ye reported it with your tongues, and spake with your mouths what ye had no knowledge of, and reckoned it a light thing, while in Allah's eyes it was grave.

[15] And why did ye not say when ye heard it, 'It is not

for us to speak of this! Celebrated be His praises, this is a mighty calumny!'

Allah admonishes you that ye return not to the like of it ever, if ye be believers; and Allah manifests to you the signs, for Allah is knowing, wise.

Verily, those who love scandal should go abroad amongst those who believe, for them is grievous woe in this world and the next; for Allah knows, but ye do not know.

[20] And but for Allah's grace upon you, and His mercy, and that Allah is kind and compassionate . . .!

O ye who believe! follow not the footsteps of Satan, for he who follows the footsteps of Satan, verily, he bids you sin and do wrong; and but for Allah's grace upon you and His mercy, not one of you would be ever pure; but Allah purifies whom He will, for Allah both hears and knows. And let not those amongst you who have plenty and ample means swear that they will not give aught to their kinsman and the poor[3] and those who have fled their homes in Allah's way, but let them pardon and pass it over. Do ye not like Allah to forgive you? and Allah is forgiving, compassionate.

Verily, those who cast imputations on chaste women who are negligent but believing shall be cursed in this world and the next; and for them is mighty woe. The day when their tongues and hands and feet shall bear witness against them of what they did, on [25] that day Allah will pay them their just due; and they shall know that Allah, He is the plain truth.

The vile women to the vile men, and the vile men to

the vile women; and the good women to the good men, and the good men to the good women: these are clear of what they say to them—forgiveness and a noble provision!

O ye who believe! enter not into houses which are not your own houses, until ye have asked leave and saluted the people thereof, that is better for you; haply ye may be mindful. And if ye find no one therein, then do not enter them until permission is given you, and if it be said to you, 'Go back!' then go back, it is purer for you; for Allah of what ye do doth know. It is no crime against you that ye enter uninhabited houses,—a convenience for you;—and Allah knows what ye show and what ye hide.

[30] Say to the believers that they cast down their looks and guard their private parts; that is purer for them; verily, Allah is well aware of what they do.

And say to the believing women that they cast down their looks and guard their private parts, and display not their ornaments, except those which are outside; and let them pull their kerchiefs over their bosoms and not display their ornaments save to their husbands and fathers, or the fathers of their husbands, or their sons, or the sons of their husbands, or their brothers, or their brothers' sons, or their sisters' sons, or their women, or what their right hands possess, or their male attendants who are incapable,⁴ or to children who do not note women's nakedness; and that they beat not with their feet that their hidden ornaments may be known;⁵—but turn ye all repentant to Allah, O ye believers! haply ye may prosper.

And marry the single amongst you, and the righteous

among your servants and your handmaidens. If they be poor, Allah will enrich them of His grace, for Allah both comprehends and knows. And let those who cannot find a match, until Allah enriches them of His grace, keep chaste.

And such of those whom your right hands possess as crave a writing,[6] write it for them, if ye know any good in them, and give them of the wealth of Allah which He has given you. And do not compel your slave girls to prostitution, if they desire to keep continent, in order to crave the goods of the life of this world; but he who does compel them, then, verily, Allah after they are compelled is forgiving, compassionate.[7]

Now have we sent down to you manifest signs, and the like of those who have passed away before you,[8] and as an admonition to those who fear.

[35] Allah is the light of the heavens and the earth; His light is as a niche in which is a lamp, and the lamp is in a glass, the glass is as though it were a glittering star; it is lit from a blessed tree, an olive neither of the east nor of the west, the oil of which would well-nigh give light though no fire touched it,—light upon light!—Allah guides to His light whom He pleases; and Allah strikes out parables for men, and Allah all things doth know.

In the houses Allah has permitted to be reared and His name to be mentioned therein—His praises are celebrated therein mornings and evenings.

Men whom neither merchandize nor selling divert from the remembrance of Allah and steadfastness in prayer and giving alms, who fear a day when hearts and eyes shall be upset;—that Allah may recompense them for the best that they have done, and give them increase of His grace; for Allah provides whom He pleases without count.

But those who misbelieve, their works are like the mirage in a plain, the thirsty counts it water till when he comes to it he finds nothing, but he finds that Allah is with him; and He will pay him his account, for Allah is quick to take account.

[40] Or like darkness on a deep sea, there covers it a wave above which is a wave, above which is a cloud,—darknesses one above the other,—when one puts out his hand he can scarcely see it; for he to whom Allah has given no light, he has no light.

Hast thou not seen that Allah,—all who are in the heavens and the earth celebrate His praises, and the birds too spreading out their wings; each one knows its prayer and its praise, and Allah knows what they do?

Hast thou not seen that Allah drives the clouds, and then reunites them, and then accumulates them, and thou mayest see the rain coming forth from their midst; and He sends down from the sky mountains[9] with hail therein, and He makes it fall on whom He pleases, and He turns it from whom He pleases; the flashing of His lightning well-nigh goes off with their sight?

Allah interchanges the night and the day; verily, in that is a lesson to those endowed with sight.

And Allah created every beast from water, and of them is one that walks upon its belly, and of them one that walks upon two feet, and of them one that walks upon four. Allah creates what He pleases; verily, Allah is mighty over all!

[45] Now have we sent down manifest signs, and Allah guides whom He pleases unto the right way.

They will say, 'We believe in Allah and in the Apostle, and we obey.' Then a sect of them turned their backs after that, and they are not believers.

And when they are called to Allah and His Apostle to judge between them, lo! a sect of them do turn aside. But had the right been on their side they would have come to him submissively enough.

Is there a sickness in their hearts, or do they doubt, or do they fear lest Allah and His Apostle should deal unfairly by them?—Nay, it is they who are unjust.

[50] The speech of the believers, when they are called to Allah and His Apostle to judge between them, is only to say, 'We hear and we obey'; and these it is who are the prosperous, for whoso obeys Allah and His Apostle and dreads Allah and fears Him, these it is who are the happy.

They swear by Allah with their most strenuous oath that hadst Thou ordered them they would surely go forth. Say, 'Do not swear—reasonable obedience;[10] verily, Allah knows what ye do.'

Say, 'Obey Allah and obey the Apostle; but if ye turn your backs he has only his burden to bear, and ye have only your burden to bear. But if ye obey him, ye are guided; but the Apostle has only his plain message to deliver.'

Allah promises those of you who believe and do right that He will give them the succession in the earth as He gave the succession to those before them, and He will establish for them their religion which He has chosen for them, and to give them, after their fear, safety in exchange;—they shall worship me, they shall not associate aught with me: but whoso disbelieves after that, those it is who are the sinners.

[55] And be steadfast in prayer and give alms and obey the Apostle, haply ye may obtain mercy.

Do not reckon that those who misbelieve can frustrate (Allah) in the earth, for their resort is the Fire, and an ill journey shall it be.

O ye who believe! let those whom your right hands possess, and those amongst you who have not reached puberty, ask leave of you three times: before the prayer of dawn, and when ye put off your clothes at noon, and after the evening prayer;—three times of privacy for you:[11] there is no crime on either you or them after these while ye are continually going one about the other. Thus does Allah explain to you His signs, for Allah is knowing, wise.

And when your children reach puberty let them ask leave as those before them asked leave. Thus does Allah explain to you His signs, for Allah is knowing, wise.

And those women who have stopped (childbearing), who do not hope for a match, it is no crime on them that they put off their clothes so as not to display their ornaments; but that they abstain is better for them, for Allah both hears and knows.

[60] There is no hindrance to the blind, and no hindrance to the lame, and no hindrance to the sick, and none upon yourselves that you eat from your houses, or

the houses of your fathers, or the houses of your mothers, or the houses of your brothers, or the houses of your sisters, or the houses of your paternal uncles, or the houses of your paternal aunts, or the houses of your maternal uncles, or the houses or your maternal aunts, or what ye possess the keys of, or of your friend, there is no crime on you that ye eat all together or separately.[12]

And when ye enter houses then greet each other with a salutation from Allah, blessed and good. Thus does Allah explain to you His signs, haply ye may understand.

Only those are believers who believe in Allah and His Apostle, and when they are with Him upon public business go not away until they have asked his leave; verily, those who ask thy leave they it is who believe in Allah and His Apostle.

But when they ask thy leave for any of their own concerns, then give leave to whomsoever thou wilt of them, and ask pardon for them of Allah; verily, Allah is forgiving and merciful.

Make not the calling of the Apostle amongst yourselves like your calling one to the other;[13] Allah knows those of you who withdraw themselves covertly. And let those who disobey his order beware lest there befall them some trial or there befall them grievous woe. Ay, Allah's is what is in the heavens and the earth, He knows what ye are at; and the day ye shall be sent back to Him then He will inform you of what ye have done, for Allah all things doth know.

THE CHAPTER OF
THE DISCRIMINATION[1]

XXV (*Mecca*)

In the name of the merciful and compassionate Allah.

Blessed be He who sent down the Discrimination to His servant that he might be unto the world a warner; whose is the kingdom of the heavens and the earth, and who has no partner in His kingdom, and created everything, and then decreed it determinately! And they take beside Him gods who create not aught, but are themselves created, and cannot control for themselves harm or profit, and cannot control death, or life, or resurrection.

[5] And those who misbelieve say, 'This is nothing but a lie which he has forged, and another people hath helped him at it'; but they have wrought an injustice and a falsehood.

And they say, 'Old folks' tales, which he has got written down while they are dictated to him morning and evening.'

Say, 'He sent it down who knows the secret in the heavens and the earth; verily, He is ever forgiving, merciful!'

And they say, 'What ails this prophet that he eats food and walks in the markets?—unless there be sent down to him an angel and be a warner with him. . . . Or there be thrown to him a treasury, or he have a garden to eat therefrom. . . .!' and the unjust say, 'Ye only follow an infatuated man.'

[10] See how they strike out for thee parables, and err, and cannot find a way.

Blessed be He who, if He please, can make for thee better than that, gardens beneath which rivers flow, and can make for thee castles!

Nay, but they call the Hour a lie; but we have prepared for those who call the Hour a lie a blaze: when it seizes them from a far-off place they shall hear its raging and roaring; and when they are thrown into a narrow place thereof, fastened together, they shall call there for destruction.

[15] Call not today for one destruction, but call for many destructions!

Say, 'Is that better or the garden of eternity which was promised to those who fear—which is ever for them a recompense and a retreat?' They shall have therein what they please, to dwell therein for aye: that is of thy Lord a promise to be demanded.

And the day He shall gather them and what they served beside Allah, and He shall say, 'Was it ye who led my servants here astray, or did they err from the way?'

They shall say, 'Celebrated be Thy praise, it was not befitting for us to take any patrons but Thee; but Thou didst give them and their fathers enjoyment until they forgot the Reminder and were a lost people!'

[20] And now have they proved you liars for what ye say, and they² cannot ward off or help. And he of you who does wrong we will make him taste great torment.

We have not sent before thee any messengers but that they ate food and walked in the markets; but we have made some of you a trial to others: will ye be patient? Thy Lord doth ever look.

And those who do not hope to meet us say, 'Unless the angels be sent down to us, or we see our Lord. . . !' They are too big with pride in their souls and they have exceeded with a great excess!

The day they shall see the angels,—no glad tidings on that day for the sinners, and they shall say, 'It is rigorously forbidden!'³

[25] And we will go on to the works which they have done, and make them like motes in a sunbeam scattered! The fellows of Paradise on that day shall be in a better abiding place and a better noonday rest.

The day the heavens shall be cleft asunder with the clouds, and the angels shall be sent down descending.

The true kingdom on that day shall belong to the Merciful, and it shall be a hard day for the misbelievers.

And the day when the unjust shall bite his hands⁴ and say, 'O, would that I had taken a way with the Apostle!⁵ [30] O, woe is me! would that I had not taken such a one for a friend now, for he did lead me astray from the Reminder after it had come to me, for Satan leaves man in the lurch!'

The Apostle said, 'O my Lord! verily, my people have taken this Qur'ân to be obsolete!'

Thus have we made for every prophet an enemy from among the sinners; but thy Lord is good guide and helper enough.

Those who misbelieve said, 'Unless the Qur'ân be sent down to him all at once . . .!⁶—thus—that we may stablish thy heart therewith, did we reveal it piecemeal.[7] [35] Nor shall they come to thee with a parable without our bringing thee the truth and the best interpretation.

They who shall be gathered upon their faces to hell,— these are in the worst place, and err most from the path.

And we did give to Moses the Book, and place with him his brother Aaron as a minister; and we said, 'Go ye to the people who say our signs are lies, for we will destroy them with utter destruction.'

And the people of Noah, when they said the apostles were liars, we drowned them, and we made them a sign for men; and we prepared for the unjust a grievous woe.

[40] And 'Âd and Thamûd and the people of ar Rass,[8] and many generations between them.

For each one have we struck out parables, and each one have we ruined with utter ruin.

Why, they[9] have come past the cities which were rained on with an evil rain; have they not seen them?—nay, they do not hope to be raised up again.

And when they saw thee they only took thee for a jest, 'Is this he whom Allah has sent as an apostle? He well-nigh leads us astray from our gods, had we not been patient about them.' But they shall know, when they see the torment, who errs most from the path. [45] Dost thou consider him who takes his lusts for his god? wilt thou then be in charge over him? or dost thou reckon that most of them will hear or understand? They are only like the cattle, nay, they err more from the way.

Hast thou not looked to thy Lord how He prolongs the shadow? but had He willed He would have made it stationary; then we make the sun a guide thereto, then we contract it towards us with an easy contraction.

And He it is who made the night for a garment; and sleep for repose, and made the day for men to rise up again. [50] And He it is who sent the winds with glad tidings before His mercy; and we sent down from the heavens pure water, to quicken therewith the dead country, and to give it for drink to what we have created,—the cattle and many folk.

We have turned it[10] in various ways amongst them that they may remember; though most men refuse aught but to misbelieve. But, had we pleased, we would have sent in every city a warner. So obey not the unbelievers and fight strenuously with them in many a strenuous fight.

[55] He it is who has let loose the two seas, this one sweet and fresh, that one bitter and pungent, and has made between them a rigorous prohibition.

And He it is who has created man from water, and has made for him blood relationship and marriage relationship; for thy Lord is mighty.

Yet they worship beside Allah what can neither profit them nor harm them; but he who misbelieves in his Lord backs up (the devil).

We have only sent thee to give glad tidings and to warn. Say, 'I ask you not for it a hire unless one please to take unto his Lord a way.'[11] [60] And rely thou upon the Living One who dies not; and celebrate His praise, for He knows well enough about the thoughts of His servants. He who created the heavens and the earth, and what is between them, in six days, and then made for the throne; the

Merciful One, ask concerning Him of One who is aware.

And when it is said, 'Adore ye the Merciful!' they say, 'What is the Merciful? Shall we adore what thou dost order us?' and it only increases their aversion.

Blessed be He who placed in the heavens zodiacal signs, and placed therein the lamp and an illuminating moon!

And He it is who made the night and the day alternating for him who desires to remember or who wishes to be thankful.

And the servants of the Merciful are those who walk upon the earth lowly, and when the ignorant address them, say, 'Peace!' [65] And those who pass the night adoring their Lord and standing;[12] and those who say, 'O our Lord! turn from us the torment of Hell; verily, its torments are persistent; verily, they are evil as an abode and a station.'

And those who when they spend are neither extravagant nor miserly, but who ever take their stand between the two; and who call not upon another god with Allah; and kill not the soul which Allah has prohibited save deservedly;[13] and do not commit fornication: for he who does that shall meet with a penalty; doubled for him shall be the torment on the resurrection day, and he shall be therein for aye despised. [70] Save he who turns again and believes and does a righteous work; for, as to those, Allah will change their evil deeds to good, for Allah is ever forgiving, merciful.

And he who turns again and does right, verily, he turns again to Allah repentant.

And those who do not testify falsely; and when they

pass by frivolous discourse, pass by it honourably; and those who when they are reminded of the signs of their Lord do not fall down thereat deaf and blind; and those who say, 'Our Lord! grant us from our wives and seed that which may cheer our eyes, and make us models to the pious!'

[75] These shall be rewarded with a high place[14] for that they were patient: and they shall meet therein with salutation and peace,—to dwell therein for aye; a good abode and station shall it be!

Say, 'My Lord cares not for you though you should not call (on Him); and ye have called (the Apostle) a liar, but it shall be (a punishment) which ye cannot shake off.'

THE CHAPTER OF THE POETS

XXVI (*Mecca*)

In the name of the merciful and compassionate Allah.

T. S. M. Those are the signs of the perspicuous Book; haply thou art vexing thyself to death that they will not be believers!

If we please we will send down upon them from the heaven a sign, and their necks shall be humbled thereto. But there comes not to them any recent Reminder from the Merciful One that they do not turn away from. [5] They have called (thee) liar! but there shall come to them a message of that at which they mocked.

Have they not looked to the earth, how we caused to

grow therein of every noble kind? Verily, in that is a sign; but most of them will never be believers! but, verily, thy Lord He is mighty and merciful.

And when thy Lord called Moses (saying), 'Come to the unjust people, [10] to the people of Pharaoh, will they not fear?' Said he, 'My Lord! verily, I fear that they will call me liar; and my breast is straitened, and my tongue is not fluent; send then unto Aaron,[1] for they have a crime against me, and I fear that they may kill me.'[2] Said He, 'Not so; but go with our signs, verily, we are with you listening.

[15] 'And go to Pharaoh and say, "Verily, we are the apostles of the Lord of the worlds (to tell thee to) send with us the children of Israel." '

And he said, 'Did we not bring thee up amongst us as a child? and thou didst dwell amongst us for years of thy life; and thou didst do thy deed which thou hast done, and thou art of the ungrateful!'

Said he, 'I did commit this, and I was of those who erred.

[20] 'And I fled from you when I feared you, and my Lord granted me judgement, and made me one of His messengers; and this is the favour thou hast obliged me with, that thou hast enslaved the children of Israel!'

Said Pharaoh, 'Who is the Lord of the worlds?' Said he, 'The Lord of the heavens and the earth and what is between the two, if ye are but sure.'

Said he to those about him, 'Do ye not listen?' [25] Said he, 'Your Lord and the Lord of your fathers of yore!'

Said he, 'Verily, your apostle who is sent to you is surely mad!'

Said he, 'The Lord of the east and of the west, and of what is between the two, if ye had but sense!'

Said he, 'If thou dost take a god besides Me I will surely make thee one of the imprisoned!'

Said he, 'What, if I come to thee with something obvious?'

[30] Said he, 'Bring it, if thou art of those who tell the truth!'

And he threw down his rod, and, behold, it was an obvious serpent! and he plucked out his hand, and, behold, it was white to the spectators!

He³ said to the chiefs around him, 'Verily, this is a knowing sorcerer, he desires to turn you out of your land! What is it then ye bid?'

[35] They said, 'Give him and his brother some hope, and send into the cities to collect and bring to thee every knowing sorcerer.'

And the sorcerers assembled at the appointed time on a stated day, and it was said to the people, 'Are ye assembled? Haply we may follow the sorcerers if we gain the upper hand.'

[40] And when the sorcerers came they said to Pharaoh, 'Shall we, verily, have a hire if we gain the upper hand?' Said he, 'Yes; and, verily, ye shall then be of those who are nigh (my throne).' And Moses said to them, 'Throw down what ye have to throw down.' So they threw down their ropes and their rods and said, 'By Pharaoh's might, verily, we it is who shall gain the upper hand!'

And Moses threw down his rod, and, lo, it swallowed up what they falsely devised!

[45] And the sorcerers threw themselves down, adoring. Said they, 'We believe in the Lord of the worlds, the Lord of Moses and Aaron!' Said he, 'Do ye believe in Him ere I give you leave? Verily, he is your chief who has taught you sorcery, but soon ye shall know. I will surely cut off your hands and your feet from opposite sides, and I will crucify you all together!'

[50] They said, 'No harm; verily, unto our Lord do we return! Verily, we hope that our Lord will forgive us our sins, for we are the first of believers!'

And we inspired Moses, 'Journey by night with my servants; verily, ye are pursued.'

And Pharaoh sent into the cities to collect; 'Verily, these are a small company. [55] And, verily, they are enraged with us; but we are a multitude, wary!

'Turn them out of gardens and springs, and treasuries, and a noble station!'—thus,—and we made the children of Israel to inherit them.

[60] And they followed them at dawn; and when the two hosts saw each other, Moses' companions said, 'Verily, we are overtaken!' Said he, 'Not so; verily, with me is my Lord, He will guide me.'

And we inspired Moses, 'Strike with thy rod the sea'; and it was cleft asunder, and each part was like a mighty mountain. And then we brought the others.

[65] And we saved Moses and those with him all together; then we drowned the others; and that is a sign: but most of them will never be believers! And, verily, thy Lord He is mighty, merciful.

And recite to them the story of Abraham; [70] when he said

to his father and his people, 'What do ye serve?' They said, 'We serve idols, and we are still devoted to them.' He said, 'Can they hear you when ye call, or profit you, or harm?'

They said, 'No; but we found our fathers doing thus.' [75] He said, 'Have ye considered what ye have been serving, ye and your fathers before you? Verily, they are foes to me, save only the Lord of the worlds, who created me and guides me, and who gives me food and drink. [80] And when I am sick He heals me; He who will kill me, and then bring me to life; and who I hope will forgive me my sins on the day of judgement! Lord, grant me judgement, and let me reach the righteous; and give me a tongue of good report amongst posterity; [85] and make me of the heirs of the paradise of pleasure; and pardon my father, verily, he is of those who err; and disgrace me not on the day when they are raised up again; the day when wealth shall profit not, nor sons, but only he who comes to Allah with a sound heart. [90] And Paradise shall be brought near to the pious; and Hell shall be brought forth to those who go astray, and it shall be said to them, "Where is what ye used to worship beside Allah? Can they help you, or get help themselves?" And they shall fall headlong into it, they and those who have gone astray, [95] and the hosts of Iblîs all together!

'They shall say, while they quarrel therein, "By Allah! we were surely in an obvious error, when we made you equal to the Lord of the worlds! but it was only sinners who led us astray. [100] But we have no intercessors and no warm friend; but had we a turn we would be of the believers." '—Verily, in that is a sign, but most of them will never be believers; and, verily, thy Lord He is mighty and merciful.

[105] The people of Noah said the apostles were liars, when their brother Noah said to them, 'Will ye not fear? Verily, I am a faithful apostle to you; then fear Allah and obey me. I do not ask you for it any hire; my hire is only with the Lord of the worlds. [110] So fear Allah and obey me.' They said, 'Shall we believe in thee, when the reprobates follow thee?' He said, 'I did not know what they were doing; their account is only with my Lord, if ye but perceive. And I am not one to drive away the believers, [115] I am only a plain warner.'

They said, 'Verily, if thou desist not, O Noah! thou shalt surely be of those who are stoned!' Said he, 'My Lord! Verily, my people call me a liar; open between me and between them an opening, and save me and those of the believers who are with me!'

So we saved him and those with him in the laden ark, [120] then we drowned the rest; verily, in that is a sign, but most of them will never be believers; and, verily, thy Lord He is mighty and merciful.

And 'Âd called the apostles liars; when their brother Hûd said to them, 'Will ye not fear? [125] Verily, I am to you a faithful apostle; then fear Allah and obey me. I do not ask you for it any hire; my hire is only with the Lord of the worlds. Do ye build on every height a landmark in sport, and take to works that haply ye may be immortal?

[130] 'And when ye assault ye assault like tyrants; but fear Allah and obey me; and fear Him who hath given you an extent of cattle and sons, and gardens and springs.

[135] Verily, I fear for you the torment of a mighty day!'

They said, 'It is the same to us if thou admonish or art not of those who do admonish; this is nothing but old folks' fictions, for we shall not be tormented!'

And they called him liar! but we destroyed them. Verily, in that is a sign, but most of them will never be believers. [140] And, verily, thy Lord is mighty, merciful.

Thamûd called the apostles liars; when their brother Zâli'h said to them, 'Do ye not fear? Verily, I am to you a faithful apostle; so fear Allah and obey me. [145] I do not ask you for it any hire; my hire is only with the Lord of the worlds. Shall ye be left here in safety with gardens and springs, and corn fields and palms, the spathes whereof are fine? and ye hew out of the mountains houses skilfully. [150] But fear Allah and obey me; and obey not the bidding of the extravagant, who do evil in the earth and do not act aright!'

They said, 'Thou art only of the infatuated; thou art but mortal like ourselves; so bring us a sign, if thou be of those who speak the truth!'

[155] He said, 'This she-camel shall have her drink and you your drink on a certain day; but touch her not with evil, or there will seize you the torment of a mighty day!'

But they hamstrung her, and on the morrow they repented; and the torment seized them; verily, in that is a sign; but most of them will never be believers: but verily, thy Lord He is mighty, merciful.

[160] The people of Lot called the apostles liars; when their brother Lot said to them, 'Do ye not fear? Verily, I am to you a faithful apostle; then fear Allah and obey me.

I do not ask you for it any hire; my hire is only with the Lord of the worlds. [165] Do ye approach males of all the world and leave what Allah your Lord has created for you of your wives? Nay, but ye are people who transgress!'

They said, 'Surely, if thou dost not desist, O Lot! thou shalt be of those who are expelled!'

Said he, 'Verily, I am of those who hate your deed; my Lord! save me and my people from what they do.'

[170] And we saved him and his people all together, except an old woman amongst those who lingered. Then we destroyed the others; and we rained down upon them a rain; and evil was the rain of those who were warned. Verily, in that is a sign; but most of them will never be believers. [175] And, verily, thy Lord He is mighty, merciful, compassionate.

The fellows of the Grove⁴ called the apostles liars; Sho'hâib said to them, 'Will ye not fear? Verily, I am to you a faithful apostle, then fear Allah and obey me. [180] I do not ask you for it any hire; my hire is only with the Lord of the worlds. Give good measure, and be not of those who diminish; and weigh with a fair balance, and do not cheat men of their goods; and waste not the land, despoiling it; and fear Him who created you and the races of yore!' [185] Said they, 'Thou art only of the infatuated; and thou art only a mortal like ourselves; and, verily, we think that thou art surely of the liars; so make a portion of the heaven to fall down upon us, if thou art of those who tell the truth!'

Said he, 'My Lord knows best what ye do!' but they called him liar, and the torment of the day of the shadow seized them; for it was the torment of a mighty day: [190] verily, in that is a sign; but most of them will never be believers; but, verily, thy Lord He is mighty, merciful!

And, verily, it⁵ is a revelation from the Lord of the worlds; the Faithful Spirit came down with it⁶ upon thy heart, that thou shouldst be of those who warn;— [195] in plain Arabic language, and, verily, it is (foretold) in the scriptures of yore! Have they not a sign, that the learned men of the children of Israel recognize it?⁷ Had we sent it down to any barbarian, and he had read it to them, they would not have believed therein. [200] Thus have we made for it⁸ a way into the hearts of the sinners; they will not believe therein until they see the grievous woe! and it shall come to them suddenly while they do not perceive! They will say, 'Shall we be respited?—What! do they wish to hasten on our torment?'

[205] What thinkest thou? if we let them enjoy themselves for years, and then there come to them what they are threatened, that will not avail them which they had to enjoy! But we do not destroy any city without its having warners as a reminder, for we are never unjust.

[210] The devils did not descend therewith; it is not fit work for them; nor are they able to do it. Verily, they are deposed from listening;⁹ call not then with Allah upon other gods, or thou wilt be of the tormented; but warn thy clansmen who are near of kin. [215] And lower¹⁰ thy wing to those of the believers who follow thee; but if they rebel against thee, say, 'Verily, I am clear of what ye do', and rely thou upon the mighty, merciful One, who sees thee when thou dost stand up, and thy posturing amongst

those who adore.¹¹ [220] Verily, He both hears and knows!

Shall I inform you upon whom the devils descend? They descend upon every sinful liar, and impart what they have heard;¹² but most of them are liars.

And the poets do those follow who go astray! [225] Dost thou not see that they wander distraught in every vale? and that they say that which they do not do? save those who believe, and do right, and remember Allah much, and defend themselves after they are wronged; but those who do wrong shall know with what a turn they shall be turned.¹³

THE CHAPTER OF THE ANT

XXVII (*Mecca*)

In the name of the merciful and compassionate Allah.

T. S. Those are the signs of the Qur'ân and the perspicuous Book; a guidance and glad tidings to the believers, who are steadfast at prayer, and give alms, and of the hereafter are sure; verily, those who believe not in the hereafter we have made seemly for them their works, and they shall wander blindly on! [5] These are they who shall have an evil torment, and they in the hereafter shall be those who most lose! Verily, thou dost meet with this Qur'ân from the wise, the knowing One!

When Moses said to his people, 'Verily, I perceive a fire, I will bring you therefrom news; or I will bring you a burning brand; haply ye may be warmed.' But when he came to it he was called to, 'Blessed be He who is in the fire, and he who is about it! and celebrated be the praises of Allah, the Lord of the worlds! O Moses! verily, I am Allah, the mighty, wise; [10] throw down thy staff!' and when he saw it quivering, as though it were a snake, he turned back fleeing, and did not return. 'O Moses! fear not; verily, as for me—apostles fear not with me; save only those who have done wrong and then substitute good for evil; for, verily, I am forgiving, merciful! but put thy hand in thy bosom, it shall come forth white without hurt;— one of nine signs to Pharaoh and his people; verily, they are a people who act abominably.'

And when our signs came to them visibly, they said, 'This is obvious sorcery!' and they gainsaid them—though their souls made sure of them—unjustly, haughtily; but, behold what was the end of the evil-doers!

[15] And we gave David and Solomon knowledge; and they both said, 'Praise belongs to Allah, who hath preferred us over many of His servants who believe!'

And Solomon was David's heir; and said, 'O ye folk! we have been taught the speech of birds, and we have been given everything; verily, this is an obvious grace!'

And assembled for Solomon were his hosts of the jinns, and men, and birds, and they were marshalled; until they came upon the valley of the ants. Said an ant, 'O ye ants! go into your dwellings, that Solomon and his hosts crush you not while they do not perceive.'

And he smiled, laughing at her speech, and said, 'O Lord! excite me to be thankful for Thy favour, wherewith Thou hast favoured me and my parents, and to do righteousness which may please Thee; and make me enter into Thy mercy amongst Thy righteous servants!'

[20] And he reviewed the birds, and said, 'How is it I see not the hoopoe? Is he then amongst the absent? I will surely torment him with a severe torment; or I will surely slaughter him; or he shall bring me obvious authority.'

And he tarried not long, and said, 'I have compassed what ye compassed not; for I bring you from Sebâ¹ a sure information: verily, I found a woman ruling over them, and she was given all things, and she had a mighty throne; and I found her and her people adoring the sun instead of Allah, for Satan had made seemly to them their works, and turned them from the path, so that they are not guided. [25] Will they not adore Allah who brings forth the secrets in the heavens, and knows what they hide and what they manifest?—Allah, there is no god but He, the Lord of the mighty throne!'

Said he, 'We will see whether thou hast told the truth, or whether thou art of those who lie. Go with this my letter and throw it before them, then turn back away from them, and see what they return.'

Said she, 'O ye chiefs! verily, a noble letter has been thrown before me. [30] It is from Solomon, and, verily, it is, "In the name of the merciful and compassionate Allah. Do not rise up against me, but come to me resigned!"' She said, 'O ye chiefs! pronounce sentence for me in my affair. I never decide an affair until ye testify for me.'

They said, 'We are endowed with strength, and endowed with keen violence; but the bidding is thine, see then what it is that thou wilt bid.'

She said, 'Verily, kings when they enter a city despoil it, and make the mighty ones of its people the meanest; thus it is they do! [35] So, verily, I am going to send to them a gift, and will wait to see with what the messengers return.'

And when he came to Solomon, he said, 'Do ye proffer me wealth, when what Allah has given me is better than what He has given you? Nay, ye in your gifts rejoice! Return to them, for we will surely come to them with hosts which they cannot confront; and we will surely drive them out therefrom mean and made small!'

Said he, 'O ye chiefs! which of you will bring me her throne before they come to me resigned?'

Said a demon of the jinns, 'I will bring thee it before thou canst rise up from thy place, for I therein am strong and faithful.'

[40] He who had the knowledge of the Book² said, 'I will bring it to thee before thy glance can turn.' And when he saw it settled down beside him, he said, 'This is of my Lord's grace, that He may try me whether I am grateful or ungrateful, and he who is grateful is only grateful for his own soul, and he who is ungrateful,—verily, my Lord is rich and generous.'

Said he, 'Disguise for her her throne; let us see whether she is guided, or whether she is of those who are not guided.' And when she came it was said, 'Was thy throne like this?' She said, 'It might be it'; and we were given knowledge before her, but we were resigned.³

But that which she served beside Allah turned her away; verily, she was of the unbelieving people. And it was said to her, 'Enter the court'; and when she saw it, she reckoned it to be an abyss of water, and she uncovered her legs. Said he, 'Verily, it is a court paved with glass!' [45] Said she, 'My Lord! verily, I have wronged myself, but I am resigned with Solomon to Allah the Lord of the worlds!'

And we sent unto Thamûd their brother Zâli'h, 'Serve Allah'; but behold, they were two parties who contended!

Said he, 'O my people! Why do ye hasten on evil acts before good deeds? Why do ye not ask forgiveness of Allah? haply ye may obtain mercy.' They said, 'We have taken an augury concerning thee and those who are with thee.' Said he, 'Your augury is in Allah's hands; nay, but ye are a people who are tried!'

And there were in the city nine persons who despoiled the land and did not right. [50] Said they, 'Swear to each other by Allah, we will surely fall on him by night and on his people; then we will surely say unto his next of kin, "We witnessed not the destruction of his people, and we do surely tell the truth!" ' And they plotted a plot, and we plotted a plot, but they did not perceive. Behold, how was the end of their plot, that we destroyed them and their people all together!

Thus are their houses overturned, for that they were unjust; verily, in that is a sign to people who do know!

But we saved those who believed and who did fear.

[55] And Lot when he said to his people, 'Do ye approach an abominable sin while ye can see? Do ye indeed approach men lustfully rather than women? Nay! ye are a people who are ignorant.' But the answer of his

people was only to say, 'Drive out Lot's family from your city! Verily, they are a folk who would keep pure.'

But we saved him and his family except his wife, her we destined to be of those who lingered; and we rained down upon them rain, and evil was the rain of those who were warned.

[60] Say, 'Praise belongs to Allah; and peace be upon His servants whom He has chosen! Is Allah best, or what they associate with Him?' He who created the heavens and the earth; and sends down upon you from the heaven water; and we cause to grow there with gardens fraught with beauty; ye could not cause the trees thereof to grow! Is there a god with Allah? Nay, but they are a people who make peers with Him! He who made the earth, settled, and placed amongst it rivers; and placed upon it firm mountains; and placed between the two seas a barrier; is there a god with Allah? Nay, but most of them know not! He who answers the distressed when he calls upon Him and removes the evil; and makes you successors in the earth; is there a god with Allah? Little is it that ye are mindful. He who guides you in the darkness, of the land and of the sea; and who sends winds as glad tidings before His mercy; is there a god with Allah? Exalted be Allah above what they associate with Him! [65] He who began the creation and then will make it return again; and who provides you from the heaven and the earth; is there a god with Allah? So bring your proofs if ye do speak the truth!

Say, 'None in the heavens or the earth know the unseen save only Allah; but they perceive not when they shall be raised!'—nay, but their knowledge attains to somewhat

of the hereafter; nay, but they are in doubt concerning it!
Nay, but they are blind!

And those who disbelieved said, 'What! when we have
become dust and our fathers too, shall we indeed be
brought forth? [70] We were promised this, we and our
fathers before us, this is nothing but old folks' tales!'

Say, 'Journey on through the land and see how was the
end of the sinners! and grieve not for them, and be not
straitened at what they plot.'

They say, 'When shall this threat be if ye do tell the
truth?' Say, 'It may be that there is pressing close behind
you a part of what ye would hasten on!' [75] But, verily,
thy Lord is full of grace to men, but most of them will not
be thankful; and, verily, thy Lord knows what their
breasts conceal and what they manifest; and there is no
secret thing in the heaven or the earth, save that it is in
the perspicuous Book!

Verily, this Qur'ân relates to the people of Israel most of
that whereon they do dispute; and, verily, it is a guidance
and mercy to the believers. [80] Verily, thy Lord decides
between them by His judgement, for He is mighty, knowing.
Rely thou then upon Allah, verily, thou art standing on
obvious truth. Verily, thou canst not make the dead to hear,
and thou canst not make the deaf to hear the call when they
turn their backs on thee; nor art thou a guide to the blind,
out of their error: thou canst only make to hear such as
believe in our signs, and such as are resigned.

And when the sentence falls upon them we will bring
forth a beast out of the earth that shall speak to them, (and
say) that, 'Men of our signs would not be sure.'

[85] And the day when we will gather from every nation a troop of those who said our signs were lies; and they shall be marshalled; until they come, and He will say, 'Did ye say my signs were lies, when ye had compassed no knowledge thereof? or what is it that ye were doing?' and the sentence shall fall upon them for that they did wrong, and they shall not have speech.

Did they not see that we have made the night for them to rest in, and the day to see by? Verily, in that are signs to people who believe.

And the day when the trumpet shall be blown and all who are in the heavens and the earth shall be startled, save whom Allah pleases! and all shall come abjectly to Him. [90] And thou shalt see the mountains, which thou dost deem solid, pass away like the passing of the clouds;—the work of Allah who orders all things; verily, He is well aware of what ye do!

He who brings a good deed shall have better than it; and from the alarm of that day they shall be safe: but those who bring an evil deed shall be thrown down upon their faces in the Fire. Shall ye be rewarded save for what ye have done?

I am bidden to serve the Lord of this country who has made it sacred, and whose are all things; and I am bidden to be of those who are resigned, and to recite the Qur'ân; and he who is guided he is only guided for himself; and he who errs,—say, 'I am only of those who warn!'

[95] And say, 'Praise be to Allah, He will show you His signs, and ye shall recognize them; for thy Lord is not heedless of what ye do!'

THE CHAPTER OF THE STORY

XXVIII (*Mecca*)

In the name of the merciful and compassionate Allah.

T. S. M. Those are the signs of the perspicuous Book; we recite to thee from the history of Moses and Pharaoh in truth unto a people who believe.

Verily, Pharaoh was lofty in the land and made the people thereof sects; one party of them he weakened, slaughtering their sons and letting their women live. Verily, he was of the despoilers.

And we wished to be gracious to those who were weakened in the earth, and to make them models, and to make them the heirs; [5] and to establish for them in the earth; and to show Pharaoh and Hâmân[1] and their hosts what they had to beware of from them.

And we inspired the mother of Moses, 'Suckle him; and when thou art afraid for him then throw him into the river, and fear not and grieve not; verily, we are going to restore him to thee, and to make him of the apostles!'

And Pharaoh's family picked him up that he might be for them a foe and a grief; verily, Pharaoh and Hâmân and their hosts were sinners.

And Pharaoh's wife said, 'He is a cheering of the eye to me, and to thee. Kill him not; it may be that he will profit us, or that we may take him for a son'; for they did not perceive.

And the heart of Moses' mother was void on the morrow;[2] she well-nigh disclosed him, had it not been that we bound up her heart that she might be of the believers.

[10] And she said to his sister, 'Follow him up.' And she looked after him from afar, and they did not perceive. And we made unlawful for him the wet nurses.³ And she said, 'Shall I guide you to the people of a house who will take care of him for you, and who will be sincere respecting him?'

So we restored him to his mother that her eye might be cheered, and that she might not grieve, and that she might know that the promise of Allah is true, though most of them know not.

And when he reached puberty, and was settled, we gave him judgement and knowledge; for thus do we reward those who do well. And he entered into the city at the time the people thereof were heedless, and he found therein two men fighting; the one of his sect and the other of his foes. And he who was of his sect asked his aid against him who was of his foes; and Moses smote him with his fist and finished him. Said he, 'This is of the work of Satan, verily, he is a misleading obvious foe.'

[15] Said he, 'My Lord! verily, I have wronged my soul, but forgive me.' So He forgave him; for He is forgiving and merciful.

Said he, 'My Lord! for that Thou hast been gracious to me, I will surely not back up the sinners.'

And on the morrow he was afraid in the city, expectant. And behold, he whom he had helped the day before cried (again) to him for aid. Said Moses to him, 'Verily, thou art obviously quarrelsome.' And when he wished to assault him who was the enemy to them both, he said, 'O Moses! dost thou desire to kill me as thou didst kill a person yesterday? Thou dost only desire to be a tyrant in the earth; and thou dost not desire to be of those who do right!' And a man came from the remote parts of the city running, said he, 'O Moses! verily, the chiefs are deliberating concerning thee to kill thee; go then forth; verily, I am to you a sincere adviser!'

[20] So he went forth therefrom, afraid and expectant. Said he, 'Lord, save me from the unjust people!'

And when he turned his face in the direction of Midian, he said, 'It may be that my Lord will guide me to a level path!' And when he went down to the water of Midian he found thereat a nation of people watering their flocks.

And he found beside them two women keeping back their flocks. Said he, 'What is your design?' They said, 'We cannot water our flocks until the herdsmen have finished; for our father is a very old man.' So he watered for them; then he turned back towards the shade and said, 'My Lord! verily, I stand in need of what Thou sendest down to me of good.'

[25] And one of the two came to him walking modestly; said she, 'Verily, my father calls thee, to reward thee with hire for having watered our flocks for us.' And when he came to him and related to him the story, said he, 'Fear not, thou art safe from the unjust people.' Said one of them, 'O my sire! hire him; verily, the best of those whom thou canst hire is the strong and faithful.'

Said he, 'Verily, I desire to marry thee to one of these daughters of mine, on condition that thou dost serve me for hire eight years; and if thou shalt fulfil ten it is of thyself; for I do not wish to make it wretched for thee; thou wilt find me, if it please Allah, of the righteous!'

Said he, 'That is between you and me; whichever of the two terms I fulfil, let there be no enmity against me, for Allah over what we say keeps guard.'

And when Moses had fulfilled the appointed time, and was journeying with his people, he perceived from the side of the mountain a fire; said he to his people, 'Tarry ye here; verily, I have perceived a fire, haply I may bring you good news therefrom, or a brand of fire that haply ye may be warmed.'[4]

[30] And when he came to it he was called to, from the right side of the wady, in the blessed valley, out of the tree, 'O Moses! verily, I am Allah the Lord of the worlds; so throw down thy rod'; and when he saw it quivering as though it were a snake, he turned away and fled and did not return. 'O Moses! approach and fear not, verily, thou art amongst the safe. Thrust thy hand into thy bosom, it shall come out white, without hurt; and then fold again thy wing, that thou dost now stretch out through dread; for those are two signs from thy Lord to Pharaoh and his chiefs; verily, they are a people who work abomination!'

Said he, 'My Lord! verily, I have killed a person amongst them, and I fear that they will kill me: and my brother Aaron, he is more eloquent of tongue than I; send him then with me as a support, to verify me; verily, I fear that they will call me liar!'

[35] Said He, 'We will strengthen thine arm with thy brother; and we will make for you both authority, and

they shall not reach you in our signs; ye two and those who follow you shall gain the upper hand.'

And when Moses came to them with our manifest signs, they said, 'This is only sorcery devised; and we have not heard of this amongst our fathers of yore.'

Moses said, 'My Lord knows best who comes with guidance from Him, and whose shall be the issue of the abode. Verily, the unjust shall not prosper!'

And Pharaoh said, 'O ye chiefs! I do not know any god for you except me; then set fire, O Hâmân! to some clay and make for me a tower, haply I may mount up to the Allah of Moses; for, verily, I think he is of those who lie!'

And he grew big with pride, he and his armies in the land, without right; and they thought that they to us should not return. [40] And we overtook him and his army, and we flung them into the sea; behold, then, how was the end of the unjust.

But we made them models calling to the Fire; and on the resurrection day they shall not be helped; and we followed them up in this world with a curse; and on the resurrection day they shall be abhorred!

And we gave Moses the Book, after that we had destroyed the former generations, as an insight to men and a guidance and a mercy; haply they may be mindful!

Thou wast not upon the western side when we decided for Moses, but afar off; nor wast thou of the witnesses. [45] But we raised up (other) generations, and life was prolonged for them; and thou wast not staying amidst the people of Midian, reciting to them our signs; but we were sending our apostles.

Nor wast thou by the side of the mountain when we called; but it is a mercy from thy Lord, that thou mayest warn a people to whom no warner has come before thee; haply they may be mindful! And lest there should befall them a mishap for what their hands have sent before, and they should say, 'Our Lord! why didst thou not send to us an apostle? for we would have followed thy signs and been of the believers.'

And when the truth comes to them from us they say, 'We are given the like of what Moses was given.' Did they not disbelieve in what Moses was given before?—they say, 'Two works of sorcery⁵ back up each other'; and they say, 'Verily, we do disbelieve in all.'

Say, 'Bring, then, a book from Allah which shall be a better guide than both, and I will follow it, if ye do tell the truth!'

[50] And if they cannot answer thee, then know that they follow their own lusts; and who is more in error than he who follows his own lust without guidance from Allah? Verily, Allah guides not an unjust people!

And we caused the word to reach them, haply they may be mindful!

Those to whom we gave the Book before it, they believe therein; and when it is recited to them they say, 'We believe in it as truth from our Lord; verily, we were resigned before it came!' These shall be given their hire twice over, for that they were patient, and repelled evil with good, and of what we have bestowed upon them give alms.

[55] And when they hear vain talk, they turn away from

it and say, 'We have our works, and ye have your works. Peace be upon you! we do not seek the ignorant!'

Verily, thou canst not guide whom thou dost like, but Allah guides whom He pleases; for He knows best who are to be guided.

And they say, 'If we follow the guidance we shall be snatched away from the land.' Have we not established for them a safe sanctuary, to which are imported the fruits of everything as a provision from us? But most of them do not know.

How many a city have we destroyed that exulted in its means of subsistence? These are their dwellings, never dwelt in after them, except a little; for we were the heirs.

But thy Lord would never destroy cities until He sent to the metropolis thereof an apostle, to recite to them our signs; nor would we destroy cities unless their people were unjust. [60] Whatever thing ye may be given, it is a provision for this world's life and the adornment thereof; but what is with Allah is better and more enduring; have ye then no sense?

Is He to whom we have promised a goodly promise, which he shall meet with, like him to whom we have given the enjoyment of the life of this world, and who upon the resurrection day shall be of the arraigned?

And on the day when He will call them and will say, 'Where are those associates which ye did pretend?' And those against whom the sentence is due shall say, 'Our Lord! these are those whom we have seduced; we seduced them as we were seduced ourselves: but we clear ourselves to thee;—they did not worship us!'

And it will be said, 'Call upon your partners'; and they will call upon them, but they will not answer them, and they shall see the torment; would that they had been guided.

[65] And the day when He shall call them and shall say, 'What was it ye answered the apostles?' and the history shall be blindly confusing to them on that day, and they shall not ask each other.

But, as for him who turns again and believes and does right, it may be that he will be among the prosperous. For thy Lord creates what He pleases and chooses; they have not the choice! Celebrated be the praise of Allah! and exalted be He above what they associate with Him!

Thy Lord knows what they conceal in their breasts and what they manifest.

[70] He is Allah, there is no god but He; to Him belongs praise, in the first and the last; and His is the judgement; and unto Him shall ye return!

Have ye considered, if Allah were to make for you the night endless until the resurrection day, who is the god, but Allah, to bring you light? Can ye not then hear?

Say, 'Have ye considered, if Allah were to make for you the day endless until the day of judgement, who is the god, except Allah, to bring you the night to rest therein? Can ye not then see?' But of His mercy He has made for you the night and the day, that ye may rest therein, and crave of His grace, haply ye may give thanks.

And the day when he shall call them and shall say, 'Where are my partners whom ye did pretend?' [75] And we will pluck from every nation a witness; and we will say, 'Bring your proof and know that the truth is Allah's'; and that which they had devised shall stray away from them.

Verily, Korah[6] was of the people of Moses, and he was outrageous against them; and we gave him treasuries of which the keys would bear down a band of men endowed with strength. When his people said to him, 'Exult not; verily, Allah loves not those who exult! but crave, through what Allah has given thee, the future abode; and forget not thy portion in this world, and do good, as Allah has done good to thee; and seek not evil doing in the earth; verily, Allah loves not the evil-doers!'

Said he, 'I have only been given it for knowledge which I have!' Did he not know that Allah had destroyed before him many generations of those who were stronger than he, and had amassed more? But the sinners need not to be asked concerning their crimes.

And he went out amongst the people in his ornaments; those who desired the life of this world said, 'O would that we had the like of what Korah has been given! Verily, he is endowed with mighty fortune!'

[80] But those who had been given knowledge said, 'Woe to you! the reward of Allah is better for him who believes and does right; but none shall meet with it except the patient. And we clave the earth with him and with his house; and he had no troop to help him against Allah, nor was he of those who were helped!'

And on the morrow those who had yearned for his place the day before said, 'Ah, ah! Allah extends provision to whom He pleases of His servants, or He doles it out; had not Allah been gracious to us, the earth would have cleft open with us! Ah, ah! the unbelievers shall not prosper!'

That is the future abode; we make it for those who do not wish to be haughty in the earth, nor to do evil, and the end is for the pious.

He who brings a good deed shall have better than it; and he who brings an evil deed—those who do evil deeds shall only be rewarded for that which they have done. [85] Verily, He who hath ordained the Qur'ân for thee will restore thee to thy returning place. Say, 'My Lord knows best who brings guidance, and who is in obvious error; nor couldst thou hope that the Book would be thrown to thee, save as a mercy from thy Lord! Be not then a backer up of those who misbelieve; and let them not turn thee from the signs of Allah, after they have been sent down to thee; but call unto thy Lord and be not of the idolaters; and call not with Allah upon any other god; there is no god but He! Everything is perishable, except His face; His is the judgement, and unto Him shall ye return!

THE CHAPTER OF THE SPIDER

XXIX (*Mecca*)

In the name of the merciful and compassionate Allah.

A. L. M. Do men then reckon that they will be left alone to say, 'We believe', and not be tried? We did try those who were before them, and Allah will surely know those who are truthful, and He will surely know the liars. Do those who do evil reckon that they can outstrip us? Evil is it that they judge.

He who hopes for the meeting of Allah,—verily, Allah's appointed time will come; and He both hears and knows! [5] And he who fights strenuously, fights strenuously only for his own soul; verily, Allah is independent of the worlds.

Those who believe and do right, we will surely cover for them their offences; and we will surely reward them with better than that which they have done.

And we have enjoined on man kindness to his parents; and if they strive with thee that thou mayest join with me, what thou hast no knowledge of, then obey them not; to me is your return, and I will inform you of that which ye have done.

But those who believe and do right, we will make them enter amongst the righteous.

And there are those among men who say, 'We believe in Allah!' but when they are hurt in Allah's cause, they deem the trials of men like the torment of Allah; but if help come from thy Lord they will say, 'Verily, we were with you!' does not Allah know best what is in the breasts of the worlds? [10] Allah will surely know those who believe, and will surely know the hypocrites.

And those who misbelieved said to those who believed, 'Follow our path, we will bear your sins'; but they could not bear their sins at all; verily, they are liars! But they shall surely bear their own burdens, and burdens with their burdens; and they shall surely be asked upon the resurrection day concerning what they did devise.

And we sent Noah to his people, and he dwelt among them for a thousand years save fifty years; and the deluge overtook them while they were unjust: but we saved him and the fellows of the ark, and we made it a sign unto the worlds.

And Abraham when he said to his people, 'Serve Allah and fear Him, that is better for you if ye did but know. [15] Ye only serve beside Allah idols and do create a lie; verily, those whom ye serve beside Allah cannot control for themselves provision; then crave provision with Allah, and serve Him, and give thanks to Him; unto Him shall ye return! And if ye say it is a lie, nations before you called (the apostles) liars too; but an apostle has only his plain message to preach!'

Have they not seen how Allah produces the creation, and then turns it back? Verily, that to Allah is easy.

Say, 'Journey ye on in the land, and behold how the creation appeared; then Allah produces another production: verily, Allah is mighty over all!'

[20] He torments whom He will, and has mercy on whom He will; and unto Him shall ye be returned.

Nor can ye make Him helpless in the earth, nor in the heavens; nor have ye beside Allah a patron or a helper.

And those who disbelieve in Allah's signs and in meeting with Him, these shall despair of my mercy; and these, for them is grievous woe.

But the answer of his people was only to say, 'Kill him or burn him!' But Allah saved him from the Fire; verily, in that are signs unto a people who believe.

He said, 'Verily, ye take beside Allah idols, through

mutual friendship in the life of this world; then on the day of judgement ye shall deny each other, and shall curse each other, and your resort shall be the Fire, and ye shall have none to help.'

[25] And Lot believed him. And (Abraham) said, 'Verily, I flee unto my Lord! Verily, He is mighty, wise! and we granted him Isaac and Jacob; and we placed in his seed prophecy and the Book; and we gave him his hire in this world; and, verily, he in the next shall be among the righteous.'

And Lot when he said to his people, 'Verily, ye approach an abomination which no one in all the world ever anticipated you in! What! do ye approach men? and stop folks on the highway? and approach in your assembly sin?' but the answer of his people was only to say, 'Bring us Allah's torment, if thou art of those who speak the truth!'

Said he, 'My Lord! help me against a people who do evil!'

[30] And when our messengers came to Abraham with the glad tidings, they said, 'We are about to destroy the people of this city. Verily, the people thereof are wrong-doers.'

Said he, 'Verily, in it is Lot'; they said, 'We know best who is therein; we shall of a surety save him and his people, except his wife, who is of those who linger.' And when our messengers came to Lot, he was vexed for them, and his arm was straitened for them; and they said, 'Fear not, neither grieve; we are about to save thee and thy people, except thy wife, who is of those who linger. Verily, we are about to send down upon the people of this city a horror from heaven, for that they have sinned; and we have left therefrom a manifest sign unto a people who have sense.'

[35] And unto Midian we sent their brother Sho'hâib, and he said, 'My people, serve Allah, and hope for the last day; and waste not the land, despoiling it.'

But they called him liar; and the convulsion seized them, and on the morrow they lay in their dwellings prone.

And Âd and Thamûd—but it is plain to you from their habitations; for Satan made seemly to them their works, and turned them from the way, sagacious though they were!

And Korah and Pharaoh and Hâmân—Moses did come to them with manifest signs, but they were too big with pride in the earth, although they could not outstrip us!

And each of them we seized in his sin; and of them were some against whom we sent a sandstorm; and of them were some whom the noise seized; and of them were some with whom we cleaved the earth open; and of them were some we drowned: Allah would not have wronged them, but it was themselves they wronged.

[40] The likeness of those who take, beside Allah, patrons is as the likeness of a spider, that takes to himself a house; and, verily, the weakest of houses is a spider's house, if they did but know!

Verily, Allah knows whatever thing they call upon beside Him; for He is the mighty, wise.

These are parables which we have struck out for men;

but none will understand them, save those who know.

Allah created the heavens and the earth in truth; verily, in this is a sign unto believers.

Recite what has been revealed to thee of the Book; and be steadfast in prayer; verily, prayer forbids sin and wrong; and surely the mention of Allah is greater; for Allah knows what ye do. [45] And do not wrangle with the people of the Book, except for what is better; save with those who have been unjust amongst them and who say, 'We believe in what is sent down to us, and what has been sent down to you; our Allah and your Allah is one, and we are unto Him resigned.'

Thus did we send down to thee the Book; and every one to whom we have given the Book believes therein. But these will not believe therein; though none gainsay our signs except the misbelievers.

Thou couldst not recite before this any book, nor write it with thy right hand, for in that case those who deem it vain would have doubted. Nay, but it is evident signs in the breasts of those who are endued with knowledge, and none but the unjust would gainsay our signs!

They say, 'Unless there be sent down upon him signs from his Lord—'; say, 'Verily, signs are with Allah, and, verily, I am an obvious warner!'

[50] Is it not enough for them that we have sent down to thee the Book which thou dost recite to them? Verily, in that is a mercy and a reminder to a people who believe.

Say, 'Allah is witness enough between me and you; He knows what is in the heavens and what is in the earth; and those who believe in falsehood and misbelieve in Allah, they shall be the losers.' They will wish thee to hasten on the torment; but were it not for a stated and appointed time, the torment would have come upon them suddenly, while yet they did not perceive.

They will wish thee to hurry on the torment, but, verily, Hell encompasses the misbelievers!

[55] On the day when the torment shall cover them from above them and from beneath their feet, and He shall say, 'Taste that which ye have done!'

O my servants who believe! verily, my land is spacious enough;¹ me therefore do ye worship.

Every soul must taste of death, then unto us shall ye return; and those who believe and act aright, we will surely inform them of upper chambers in Paradise, beneath which rivers flow; to dwell therein for aye—pleasant is the hire of those who work! those who are patient and rely upon their Lord!

[60] How many a beast cannot carry its own provision! Allah provides for it and for you; He both hears and knows!

And if thou shouldst ask them, 'Who created the heavens and the earth, and subjected the sun and the moon?' they will surely say, 'Allah!' how then can they lie?

Allah extends provision to whomsoever He will of His servants, or doles it out to him; verily, Allah all things doth know.

And if thou shouldst ask them, 'Who sends down from the heavens water and quickens therewith the earth in its death?' they will surely say, 'Allah!' say, 'And praise be to Allah!' Nay, most of them have no sense.

This life of the world is nothing but a sport and a play;

but, verily, the abode of the next world, that is life,—if they did but know!

[65] And when they ride in the ship they call upon Allah, making their religion seem sincere to Him; but when He saves them to the shore, behold, they associate others with Him; that they may disbelieve in our signs; and that they may have some enjoyment: but soon they shall know.

Have they not seen that we have made a safe sanctuary whilst people are being snatched away around them? Is it then in falsehood that they will believe, and for the favours of Allah be ungrateful?

But who is more unjust than he who devises against Allah a lie, or calls the truth a lie when it comes to him? Is there not in Hell a resort for the misbelievers? but those who fight strenuously for us we will surely guide them into our way, for, verily, Allah is with those who do well.

THE CHAPTER OF THE GREEKS[1]

XXX (*Mecca*)

In the name of the merciful and compassionate Allah.

The Greeks are overcome in the nighest parts of the land; but after being overcome they shall overcome[2] in a few years; to Allah belongs the order before and after; and on that day the believers shall rejoice in the help of Allah;—Allah helps whom He will, and He is mighty, merciful. [5]—Allah's promise!—Allah breaks not

His promise, but most men do not know!

They know the outside of this world's life, but of the hereafter they are heedless. Have they not reflected in themselves, that Allah created not the heavens and the earth, and what is between the two except in truth, and for a stated and appointed time? But, verily, many men in the meeting of their Lord do disbelieve.

Have they not journeyed on in the land and seen how was the end of those before them who were stronger than they, and who turned up the ground and cultivated it more than they do cultivate it? And there came to them their apostles with manifest signs; for Allah would never wrong them: it was themselves they wronged!

Then evil was the end of those who did evil, in that they said the signs of Allah were lies and mocked thereat.

[10] Allah produces a creation, then He makes it go back again, then unto Him shall ye return.

And on the day when the Hour shall rise, the sinners shall be confused; and they shall not have amongst their partners intercessors; and their partners shall they deny.

And on the day when the Hour shall rise, on that day shall they be scattered apart; and as for those who believe and do right, they in the garden shall be joyful; [15] and as for those who misbelieved and said our signs and the meeting of the hereafter were lies, they shall be in the torment arraigned.

Celebrated be the praises of Allah, when ye are in the evening and when ye are in the morning! for to Him belongs praise in the heavens and the earth! and at the evening, and when ye are at noon.

He brings forth the living from the dead, and brings forth the dead from the living; and He quickens the earth after its death, and thus shall ye too be brought forth.

And of His signs is this, that He hath created you from dust; then, behold, ye are mortals who are spread abroad.

[20] And of His signs is this, that He hath created for you of yourselves wives with whom ye may cohabit; He has made between you affection and pity. Verily, in that are signs unto a people who reflect.

And of His signs is the creation of the heavens and the earth, and the diversity of your tongues and colours; verily, in that are signs unto the worlds.[3]

And of His signs is your sleep by night and by day; and your craving after His grace. Verily, in that are signs unto a people who do hear.

And of His signs is this, that He shows you lightning for fear and hope; and sends down from the sky water, and quickens therewith the earth after its death; verily, in that are signs unto a people who have sense.

And of His signs is this, that the heavens and the earth stand by His order; then when He calls you from the earth, lo! ye shall come forth. [25] His are those who are in the heavens and the earth, and all to Him are devoted. And He it is who produces a creation and then makes it to go back again; for it is very easy to Him; and His are the loftiest similitudes in the heavens and the earth; and He is the mighty, wise!

He has struck out for you a parable from yourselves; have ye of what your right hand possess partners in what we have bestowed upon you, so that ye share alike therein? Do ye fear them as ye fear each other?—Thus do we detail the signs unto a people who have sense.[4]

Nay, when those who are unjust follow their lusts without knowledge,—and who shall guide him whom Allah has led astray? and they shall have none to help.

Set thy face steadfast towards the religion as a *hanîf*, according to the constitution whereon Allah has constituted men; there is no altering the creation of Allah, that is the standard religion, though most men do not know.

[30] Turn repentant towards Him; and fear Him, and be steadfast in prayer; and be not of the idolaters.

Of those who have divided their religion and become sects, every party in what they have, rejoice.

And when distress touches men they call upon their Lord, repentant towards Him; then when He has made them taste mercy from Himself, behold! a party of them associate others with their Lord, that they may disbelieve in what we have brought them;—but enjoy yourselves; for hereafter ye shall know!

Or have we sent down to them authority which speaks of what they do associate with Him?

[35] And when we have made men taste of mercy, they rejoice therein; and if there befall them evil for what their hands have sent before, behold! they are in despair.

Have they not seen that Allah extends provision to whom He pleases, or doles it out? Verily, in that are signs unto a people who believe.

Then give to the kinsman his due, and to the poor and to the wayfarer; that is better for those who desire the face of Allah, and these it is who are prosperous.

And what ye put out to usury that it may increase with the wealth of men, it shall not increase with Allah; but what ye put out in alms, desiring the face of Allah—these it is who shall gain double.

It is Allah who created you and then provided for you; and then will make you die, and then will quicken you again; is there any of your partners who can do aught of that? Celebrated be His praises, and exalted be He above what they associate with Him!

[40] Trouble hath appeared in the land and the sea, for what men's hands have gained! to make them taste a part of that which they have done,—haply they may return!

Say, 'Journey on in the land, and behold what was the end of those before you,—most of them were idolaters!'

Set thy face steadfast to the standard religion, before there come a day from Allah which there is no averting; on that day shall they be parted into two bands.

He who misbelieves, upon him is his misbelief; but whoso does right, for themselves they are spreading couches:5

That He may reward those who believe and do right of His grace; verily, He loves not the misbelievers!

[45] And of His signs is this, that He sends forth the winds with glad tidings, to make you taste of His mercy, and to make the ships go on at His bidding, and that ye may crave of His grace, and haply ye may give thanks.

We have sent before thee apostles unto their people, and they came to them with manifest signs: and we took vengeance upon those who sinned, but due from us it was to help the believers.

Allah it is who sends forth the winds to stir up clouds;

then He spreads them forth over the sky as he pleases; and He breaks them up and ye see the rain come forth from amongst them; and when He causes it to fall upon whom He pleases of His servants, behold they hail it with joy, although before it was sent down upon them they were before then confused!

Look then to the vestiges of Allah's mercy, how He quickens the earth after its death; verily, that is the quickener of the dead, and He is mighty over all!

[50] But if we should send a wind and they should see it yellow,[6] they would after that become misbelievers.

But, verily, thou canst not make the dead to hear, nor canst thou make the deaf to hear the call, when they turn their backs and flee; nor hast thou to guide the blind out of their error; thou canst only make those to hear who believe in our signs and who are resigned.

Allah it is who created you of weakness, then made for you after weakness strength; then made for you after strength, weakness and grey hairs: He creates what He pleases, for He is the knowing, the powerful!

And on the day when the Hour shall rise, the sinners shall swear [55] that they have not tarried save an hour; thus were they wont to lie!

But those who are given knowledge and faith will say, 'We have tarried according to the Book of Allah, until the day of resurrection'; and this is the day of resurrection, but ye—ye do not know.

And on that day their excuse shall profit not those who did wrong; nor shall they be asked to please Allah again.

We have struck out to men in this Qur'ân every kind

of parable; but if thou shouldst bring them a sign⁷ then those who misbelieve will surely say, 'Ye are but followers of vanity; thus does Allah set a stamp upon the hearts of those who do not know.'

[60] Be thou patient then; verily, Allah's promise is true! and let them not flurry thee who are not sure.

THE CHAPTER OF LOQMÂN¹

XXXI (*Mecca*)

In the name of the merciful and compassionate Allah.

A. L. M. These are the signs of the wise Book, a guidance and a mercy to those who do well, who are steadfast in prayer and give alms and who of the hereafter are sure; these are in guidance from their Lord, and these are the prosperous.

[5] And amongst men is one² who buys sportive legends, to lead astray from Allah's path, without knowledge, and to make a jest of it; these, for them is shameful woe! And when our signs are recited to him, he turns his back, too big with pride, as though he heard them not,—as if in his two ears were dulness. But give to him glad tidings of grievous woe!

Verily, those who believe and do right, for them are gardens of pleasure, to dwell therein for aye;—Allah's promise in truth, and He is mighty, wise.

He created the heavens without pillars that ye can see, and He threw upon the earth firm mountains lest it should move with you; and He dispersed thereon every sort of beast; and we send down from the heavens water, and we caused to grow therein of every noble kind.

[10] This is Allah's creation; show me what others beside Him have created;—nay, the unjust are in obvious error!

We did give unto Loqmân wisdom, saying, 'Thank Allah; for he who thanks Allah is only thankful for his own soul; and he who is ungrateful—verily, Allah is independent, worthy of praise!'

And when Loqmân said to his son while admonishing him, 'O my boy! associate none with Allah, for, verily, such association is a mighty wrong.'—

For we have commended his parents to man; his mother bore him with weakness upon weakness; and his weaning is in two years;—'Be thankful to me and to thy parents; for unto me shall your journey be. But if they strive with thee that thou shouldst associate with me that which thou hast no knowledge of, then obey them not. But associate with them in the world with kindness, and follow the way of him who turns repentant unto me; then unto me is your return, and I will inform you of that which ye have done!'—

[15] 'O my son! verily, if there were the weight of a grain of mustard seed and it were (hidden) in the rock, or in the heaven, or in the earth, Allah would bring it (to light). Verily, Allah is subtle, well aware!

'O my son! be steadfast in prayer, and bid what is reasonable and forbid what is wrong; be patient of what befalls thee, verily, that is one of the determined affairs.

'And twist not thy cheek proudly, nor walk in the land

haughtily; verily, Allah loves not every arrogant boaster: but be moderate in thy walk, and lower thy voice; verily, the most disagreeable of voices is the voice of asses!'

Have ye not seen that Allah has subjected to you what is in the heavens and what is in the earth, and has poured down upon you His favours, outwardly and inwardly? But amongst men are those who wrangle about Allah, without knowledge, and without guidance, and without an illuminating book!

[20] And when it is said to them, 'Follow what Allah has sent down'; they say, 'Nay! we will follow what we found our fathers agreed upon';—what! though Satan calls them to the torment of the blaze?

But he who resigns his face unto Allah, and does good, he has grasped the firm handle; unto Allah is the issue of affairs. But he who misbelieves, let not his misbelief grieve thee; to us is their return, and we will inform them of what they do;—for, verily, Allah knows the nature of men's breasts!

We will let them enjoy themselves a little; then we will force them to rigorous woe!

And if thou shouldst ask them who created the heavens and the earth, they will surely say, 'Allah.' Say, 'Praise be to Allah!' but most of them do not know.

[25] Allah's is what is in the heavens and what is in the earth; verily, Allah, He is the independent, worthy of praise.

And were the trees that are in the earth pens, and the sea (ink) with seven more seas to swell its tide, the words of Allah would not be spent; verily, Allah is mighty, wise!

Your creation and your rising again are but as that of one soul; verily, Allah both hears and sees!

Dost thou not see that Allah joins on the night to the day, and joins on the day to the night, and has subjected the sun and the moon,—each of them runs on unto an appointed time? and that Allah of what ye do is well aware?

That is because Allah, He is true, and because what ye call on beside Him is falsehood, and because Allah, He is the high, the great!

[30] Dost thou not see that the ship rides on in the sea by the favour of Allah, that He may show you of His signs? Verily, in that are signs to every grateful person.

And when a wave like shadows covers them, they call on Allah, being sincere in their religion; and when He saves them to the shore, then amongst them are some who halt between two opinions. But none gainsays our signs save every perfidious misbeliever.

O ye folk! fear your Lord and dread the day when the father shall not atone for his son, nor shall the child atone aught for its parent.

Verily, the promise of Allah is true! Say, 'Let not the life of this world beguile you; and let not the beguiler beguile you concerning Allah.'

Verily, Allah, with Him is the knowledge of the Hour; and He sends down the rain; and He knows what is in the wombs; and no soul knows what it is that it shall earn to-morrow; and no soul knows in what land it shall die; verily, Allah is knowing, well aware!

THE CHAPTER OF ADORATION

XXXII (*Mecca*)

In the name of the merciful and compassionate Allah.

A. L. M. The revelation of the Book, there is no doubt therein, from the Lord of the worlds.

Do they say, 'He has forged it'? Nay! it is the truth from thy Lord, that thou mayest warn a people, to whom no warner has come before thee, haply they may be guided.

Allah it is who created the heavens and the earth and what is between the two in six days; then He made for the throne! Ye have no patron beside Him and no intercessor; are ye not then mindful?

He governs the affair from the heaven unto the earth; then shall it ascend to him in a day, the measure of which is as a thousand years of what ye number.

[5] That is He who knows the unseen and the visible; the mighty, the merciful, who has made the best of the creation of everything, and produced the creation of man from clay; then He made his stock from an extract of despicable water; then He fashioned him and breathed into him of His spirit, and made for you hearing and eyesight and hearts;—little is it that ye give thanks!

And they say, 'When we are lost in the earth, shall we then become a new creation?' [10] Nay! in the meeting of their Lord they disbelieve.

Say, 'The angel of death shall take you away, he who is given charge of you; then unto your Lord shall ye be returned.'

And couldst thou see when the sinners hang down their

heads before their Lord, 'O Lord! we have seen and we have heard; send us back then and we will do right. Verily, we are sure!'

Had we pleased we would have given to everything its guidance; but the sentence was due from me;—I will surely fill Hell with the jinns and with men all together: 'So taste ye, for that ye forgot the meeting of this day of yours,—verily, we have forgotten you! and taste ye the torment of eternity for that which ye have done!'

[15] They only believe in our signs who when they are reminded of them fall down adoring and celebrate the praises of their Lord, and are not too big with pride. As their sides forsake their beds, they call upon their Lord with fear and hope; and of what we have bestowed upon them do they give alms. No soul knows what is reserved for them of cheerfulness for eye, as a reward for that which they have done! Is he who is a believer like him who is a sinner? They shall not be held equal.

As for those who believe and do right, for them are the gardens of resort, an entertainment for that which they have done!

[20] But as for those who commit abomination their resort is the Fire. Every time that they desire to go forth therefrom, we will send them back therein, and it will be said to them, 'Taste ye the torment of the Fire which ye did call a lie!' and we will surely make them taste of the torment of the nearer torment beside the greater torment,'—haply they may yet return.

Who is more unjust than he who is reminded of the signs of his Lord, and then turns away from them?

Verily, we will take vengeance on the sinners!

And we did give Moses the Book; be not then in doubt concerning the meeting with him;[2] and we made it a guidance to the children of Israel.

And we made amongst them high priests who guided by our bidding, since they were patient and were sure of our signs.

[25] Verily, thy Lord, he shall decide between them on the resurrection day concerning that whereon they do dispute.

Is it not conspicuous to them how many generations we have destroyed before them? They walk over their dwellings! Verily, in that are signs: do they not then hear?

Have they not seen that we drive the water to the sterile land, and bring forth thereby corn from which their cattle and themselves do eat? Do they not then see?

And they say, 'When shall this decision come if ye do tell the truth?' Say, 'On the day of the decision their faith shall not profit those who misbelieved, nor shall they be respited'; [30] turn then from them and wait; verily, they are waiting too!

THE CHAPTER OF
THE CONFEDERATES[1]
XXXIII (*Medina*)

In the name of the merciful and compassionate Allah.

O thou prophet! fear Allah and obey not the misbelievers and hypocrites; verily, Allah is ever knowing, wise!

But follow what thou art inspired with from thy Lord; verily, Allah of what you do is ever well aware. And rely upon Allah, for Allah is guardian enough.

Allah has not made for any man two hearts in his inside; nor has He made your wives,—whom you back away from,—your real mothers;[2] nor has He made your adopted sons your real sons. That is what ye speak with your mouths; but Allah speaks the truth and He guides to the path!

[5] Call them by their fathers' names; that is more just in Allah's sight; but if ye know not their fathers, then they are your brothers in religion and your clients. There is no crime against you for what mistakes ye make therein; but what your hearts do purposely—but Allah is ever forgiving and merciful.

The prophet is nearer of kin to the believers than themselves, and his wives are their mothers. And blood relations are nearer in kin to each other by the Book of Allah than the believers and those who fled;[3] only your doing kindness to your kindred, that is traced in the Book.

And when we took of the prophets their compact,[4] from thee and from Noah, and Abraham, and Moses, and Jesus the son of Mary, and took of them a rigid compact, that He might ask the truth tellers of their truth. But He has prepared for those who misbelieve a grievous woe.

O ye who believe! remember Allah's favours towards you when hosts came to you and we sent against them a wind and hosts[5] that ye could not see;—and Allah knew what ye were doing.

[10] When they came upon you from above you and from below[6] you, and when your eyesights were distracted

and your hearts came up into your throats, and ye suspected Allah with certain suspicions.

There were the believers tried and were made to quake with a severe quaking.

And when the hypocrites and those in whose hearts was sickness said, 'Allah and His Apostle have only promised us deceitfully.' And when a party of them said, 'O people of Yathreb,[7] there is no place for you (here),[8] return then (to the city).' And a part of them asked leave of the prophet (to return), saying, 'Verily, our houses are defenceless'; but they were not defenceless, they only wished for flight.

But had they been entered upon from its environs and then been asked to show treason they would have done so; but they would only have tarried there a little while.[9]

[15] They had covenanted with Allah before, that they would not turn their backs; and Allah's covenant shall be enquired of.

Say, 'Flight shall avail you naught; if ye fly from death or slaughter, even then ye shall be granted enjoyment only for a little!'

Say, 'Who is it that can save you from Allah, if He wish you evil, or wish you mercy?' But they will not find beside Allah a patron or a helper.

Say, 'Allah knows the hinderers amongst you, and those who say to their brethren, "Come along unto us", and show but little valour;—covetous towards you.'[10] When fear comes thou wilt see them looking towards thee, their eyes rolling like one fainting with death; but when the fear has passed away they will assail you with sharp tongues, covetous of the best.[11] These have never believed, and Allah will make vain their works, for that is easy with Allah.

[20] They reckoned that the confederates would never go away; and if the confederates should come they would fain be in the desert with the Arabs, asking for news of you! and if they were amongst you they would fight but little.

Ye had in the Apostle of Allah a good example for him who hopes for Allah and the last day, and who remembers Allah much.

And when the believers saw the confederates they said, 'This is what Allah and His Apostle promised us; Allah and His Apostle are true!' and it only increased them in faith and resignation.

Amongst the believers are men who have been true to their covenant with Allah, and there are some who have fulfilled their vow,[12] and some who wait and have not changed[13] with fickleness.

That Allah might reward the truthful for their truth, and punish the hypocrites if He please, or turn again towards them;—verily, Allah is forgiving, merciful!

[25] And Allah drove back the misbelievers in their rage; they got no advantage;—Allah was enough for the believers in the fight, for Allah is strong, mighty!

And He drove down those of the people of the Book who had helped them[14] from their fortresses[15] and hurled dread into their hearts; a part ye slew and ye took captive a part: and He gave you their land, and their dwellings, and their property for an inheritance, and a land ye had not trodden, for Allah is ever mighty over all.

O thou prophet! say to thy wives, 'If ye be desirous of the life of this world and its adornments, come, I will give you them to enjoy and I will let you range handsomely at large! But if ye be desirous of Allah and His Apostle and of the abode of the hereafter, verily, Allah has prepared for those of you who do good a mighty hire!'[16]

[30] O ye women of the prophet! whosoever of you commits manifest fornication, doubled shall be her torment twice; and that is easy unto Allah!

But that one of you who is devoted to Allah and His Apostle and does right we will give her her hire twice over, and we have prepared for her a noble provision.

O ye women of the prophet! ye are not like any other women; if ye fear Allah then be not too complaisant in speech, or he in whose heart is sickness will lust after you; but speak a reasonable speech.

And stay still in your houses and show not yourselves with the ostentation of the ignorance of yore; and be steadfast in prayer, and give alms, and obey Allah and His Apostle;—Allah only wishes to take away from you[17] the horror as people of His House and to purify you thoroughly.

And remember what is recited in your houses of the signs of Allah and of wisdom; verily, Allah is subtle and aware!

[35] Verily, men resigned and women resigned,[18] and believing men and believing women, and devout men and devout women, and truthful men and truthful women, and patient men and patient women, and humble men and

humble women, and alms giving men and alms giving women, and fasting men and fasting women, and men who guard their private parts and women who guard their private parts, and men who remember Allah much and women who remember Him,—Allah has prepared for them forgiveness and a mighty hire.

It is not for a believing man or for a believing woman, when Allah and His Apostle have decided an affair, to have the choice in that affair; and whoso rebels against Allah and His Apostle has erred with an obvious error.

And when thou didst say to him Allah had shown favour to and thou hadst shown favour to, 'Keep thy wife to thyself and fear Allah'; and thou didst conceal in thy soul what Allah was about to display; and didst fear men, though Allah is more deserving that thou shouldst fear Him; and when Zâid had fulfilled his desire of her[19] we did wed thee to her that there should be no hindrance to the believers in the matter of the wives of their adopted sons when they have fulfilled their desire of them: and so Allah's bidding to be done.[20]

There is no hindrance to the prophet about what Allah has ordained for him;—(such was) the course of Allah with those who have passed away before,—and Allah's bidding is a decreed decree! Those who preach Allah's messages and fear Him and fear not any one except Allah,—but Allah is good enough at reckoning up.

[40] Mohammed is not the father of any of your men, but the Apostle of Allah, and the Seal of the Prophets; for Allah all things doth know!

O ye who believe! remember Allah with frequent

remembrance, and celebrate His praises morning and evening.

He it is who prays[21] for you and His angels too, to bring you forth out of the darkness into the light, for He is merciful to the believers.

Their salutation on the day they meet Him shall be 'Peace!' and he has prepared for them a noble hire.

O thou prophet! verily, we have sent thee as a witness and a herald of glad tidings and a warner, [45] and to call (men) unto Allah by His permission, and as an illuminating lamp.

Give glad tidings then to the believers, that for them is great grace from Allah. And follow not the unbelievers and the hypocrites; but let alone their ill-treatment,[22] is literally, 'may Allah pray for him and salute him!' and rely upon Allah, for Allah is guardian enough.

O ye who believe! when ye wed believing women, and then divorce them before ye have touched them, ye have no term that ye need observe; so make them some provision, and let them go handsomely at large.

O thou prophet! verily, we make lawful for thee thy wives to whom thou hast given their hire,[23] and what thy right hand possesses[24] out of the booty that Allah has granted thee, and the daughters of thy paternal uncle and the daughters of thy paternal aunts, and the daughters of thy maternal uncle and the daughters of thy maternal aunts, provided they have fled with thee, and any believing woman if she give herself to the prophet, if the prophet desire to marry her;—a special privilege this for thee, above the other believers.

[50] We knew what we ordained for them concerning their wives and what their right hands possess, that there should be no hindrance to thee; and Allah is forgiving, merciful.

Put off[25] whomsoever thou wilt of them and take to thyself whomsoever thou wilt, or whomsoever thou cravest of those whom thou hast deposed,[26] and it shall be no crime against thee. That is nigher to cheering their eyes and that they should not grieve, and should be satisfied with what thou dost bring them all; but Allah knows best what is in their hearts; and Allah is knowing, clement.

It is not lawful to thee to take women after (this), nor to change them for (other) wives, even though their beauty please thee; except what thy right hand possesses, for Allah is ever watchful over all.

O ye who believe! do not enter the houses of the prophet, unless leave be given you, for a meal,—not watching till it is cooked! But when ye are invited, then enter; and when ye have fed, disperse, not engaging in familiar discourse. Verily, that would annoy the prophet, and he would be ashamed for your sake,[27] but Allah is not ashamed of the truth.[28]

And when ye ask them[29] for an article, ask them from behind a curtain;[30] that is purer for your hearts and for theirs. It is not right for you to annoy the prophet of Allah, nor to wed his wives after him ever; verily, that is with Allah a serious thing. If ye display a thing or conceal it, verily, Allah all things doth know.

[55] There is no crime against them[31] (if they speak unveiled) to their fathers, or their sons, or their brothers,

or their brothers' sons, or their sisters' sons, or their women, or what their right hands possess; but let them fear Allah,—verily, Allah is witness over all.

Verily, Allah and His angels pray for the prophet. O ye who believe! pray for him and salute him with a salutation![32]

Verily, those who annoy Allah and His Apostle, Allah will curse them in this world and the next, and prepare for them shameful woe!

And those who annoy the believers for what they have not earned, such have to bear (the guilt of) calumny and obvious sin.

O thou prophet! tell thy wives and thy daughters, and the women of the believers, to let down over them their outer wrappers; that is nearer for them to be known and that they should not be annoyed; but Allah is forgiving, merciful.

[60] Surely if the hypocrites and those in whose hearts is a sickness and the insurrectionists in Medina do not desist, we will surely incite thee against them. Then they shall not dwell near thee therein save for a little while. Cursed wherever they are found,—taken and slain with slaughter!

Allah's course with those who have passed away before: and thou shalt never find in Allah's course any alteration.

The folk will ask thee about the Hour; say, 'The knowledge thereof is only with Allah, and what is to make thee perceive that the Hour is haply nigh?'

Verily, Allah has cursed the misbelievers and has prepared for them a blaze!

[65] To dwell therein for ever and for aye; they shall not find a patron or a helper!

On the day when their faces shall writhe in the Fire they shall say, 'O, would that we had obeyed Allah and obeyed the Apostle!'

And they shall say, 'Our Lord! verily, we obeyed our chiefs and our great men and they led us astray from the path! Our Lord! give them double torment and curse them with a great curse!'

O ye who believe! be not like those who annoyed Moses; but Allah cleared him of what they said, and he was regarded in the sight of Allah.[33]

[70] O ye who believe! fear Allah and speak a straight-forward speech. He will correct for you your works, and pardon you your sins; for he who obeys Allah and His Apostle has attained a mighty happiness.

Verily, we offered the trust[34] to the heavens and the earth and the mountains, but they refused to bear it, and shrank from it; but man bore it: verily, he is ever unjust and ignorant. That Allah may torment the hypocritical men and hypocritical women, and the idolaters and idol-atresses; and that Allah may turn relenting towards the believing men and believing women; verily, Allah is ever forgiving, merciful.

THE CHAPTER OF SEBÂ[1]

XXXIV (*Mecca*)

In the name of the merciful and compassionate Allah.

Praise belongs to Allah, whose is whatsoever is in the heavens and whatsoever is in the earth; His is the praise in the next world, and He is the wise and well aware!

He knows what goes into the earth, and what comes forth therefrom, and what comes down from the sky, and what ascends thereto; for He is the merciful, forgiving.

Those who misbelieve say, 'The Hour shall not come to us'; say, 'Yea, by my Lord it shall surely come to you! by Him who knows the unseen! nor shall there escape from it the weight of an atom, in the heavens or in the earth, or even less than that, or greater, save in the perspicuous Book'; and that He may reward those who believe and do right; these,—for them is forgiveness and a noble provision.

[5] But those who strive concerning our signs to frustrate them; these,—for them is the torment of a grievous plague.

And those to whom knowledge has been given see that what is sent down to thee from thy Lord is the truth, and guides unto the way of the mighty, the praiseworthy.

And those who misbelieve say, 'Shall we guide you to a man who will inform you that when ye are torn all to pieces, then ye shall be a new creation? He has forged against Allah a lie, or there is a jinn in him';—nay, those who believe not in the hereafter are in the torment and in the remote error!

Have they not looked at what is before them and what

is behind them of the heaven and the earth? If we pleased we would cleave the earth open with them, or we would make to fall upon them a portion of the heaven; verily, in that is a sign to every repentant servant.

[10] And we did give David grace from us, 'O ye mountains! echo (Allah's praises) with him, and ye birds!' and we softened for him iron: 'Make thou coats of mail and adapt the rings thereof, and do right; verily, I at what ye do do look.' And to Solomon the wind; its morning journey was a month, and its evening journey was a month; and we made to flow for him a fountain of molten brass; and of the jinns some to work before him by the permission of his Lord; and whoso swerves amongst them from our bidding we will give him to taste the torment and the blaze; and they made for him what he pleased of chambers, and images, and dishes like troughs, and firm pots;—work, O ye family of David! thankfully; few is it of my servants who are thankful.

And when we decreed for him death, naught guided them to his death save a reptile of the earth that ate his staff; and when he fell down it was made manifest to the jinns that, had they but known the unseen, they need not have tarried in the shameful torment.[2]

Sebâ had in their dwellings a sign; two gardens, on the right hand and on the left, 'Eat from the provision of your Lord; and give thanks to Him! a good country and a forgiving Lord!' [15] but they turned away, and we sent against them the flood of the dyke; and we changed for them their two gardens into two gardens that grew bitter fruit and tamarisk, and some few lote trees.[3]

This did we reward them with, for that they misbelieved; and do we so reward any but misbelievers?

And we made between them and the cities which we had blessed (other) cities which were evident; and we measured out the journey: 'Journey ye thereto nights and days in safety!' And they said, 'Our Lord! make a greater distance between our journeys'; and they wronged themselves, and we made them legends; and we tore them all to pieces; verily, in that are signs to every patient, grateful person. And Iblîs verified his suspicion concerning them, and they followed him, save a party of the believers.⁴

[20] Yet had he no authority over them, save that we might know who it was that believed in the hereafter from him who amongst them was in doubt; for thy Lord guards everything.

Say, 'Call on those whom ye pretend beside Allah'; they cannot control the weight of an atom in the heavens or in the earth; nor have they any partnership in either; nor has He amongst them any supporter; nor is intercession of any avail with Him, except for him whom He permits; so that when fright is removed from their hearts they say, 'What is it that your Lord says?' they say, 'The truth; for He is the high, the great.'

Say, 'Who provides from the heavens and the earth?' Say, 'Allah.' And, verily, we or ye are surely in guidance or in an obvious error.

Say, 'Ye shall not be asked about what we have sent, nor shall we be asked about what ye do.

[25] 'Our Lord shall assemble us together; then He shall

open between us in truth, for He is the opener who knows.'

Say, 'Show me those whom ye have added to Him as partners; not so! nay, but He is Allah, the mighty, the wise!'

We have only sent thee to men generally as a herald of glad tidings and a warner; but most men do not know.

And they say, 'When shall this promise be, if ye do speak the truth?' Say, 'For you is the appointment of a day of which ye shall not keep back an hour, nor shall ye bring it on!'

[30] And those who misbelieve say, 'We will never believe in this Qur'ân or in what is before it'; but couldst thou see when the unjust are set before their Lord, they shall rebut each other in speech.

Those who were thought weak shall say to those who were big with pride, 'Had it not been for you we should have been believers.' Those who were big with pride shall say to those who were thought weak, 'Was it we who turned you away from the guidance after it came to you? Nay, ye were sinners.'

And those who were thought weak shall say to those who were big with pride, 'Nay, but it was the plotting by night and day, when ye did bid us to disbelieve in Allah, and to make peers for Him!' and they shall display repentance when they see the torment; and we will put fetters on the necks of those who misbelieved. Shall they be rewarded except for that which they have done?

We have not sent to any city a warner but the opulent thereof said, 'We, in what ye are sent with, disbelieve.'

And they say, 'We have more wealth and children, and we shall not be tormented.'

[35] Say, 'Verily, my Lord extends provision to whom He pleases or doles it out, but most men do not know; but neither your wealth nor your children is that which will bring you to a near approach to us, save him who believes and does right; these, for them is a double reward for what they have done, and they in upper rooms⁵ shall be secure.'

And those who strive concerning our signs to frustrate them, these in the torment shall be arraigned. Verily, my Lord extends provision to whomsoever He will of His servants, or doles it out to him. And what ye expend in alms at all, He will repay it; for He is the best of providers.

And on the day He will gather them all together, then He will say to the angels, 'Are these those who used to worship you?'

[40] They shall say, 'Celebrated be thy praises! thou art our patron instead of them. Nay, they used to worship the jinns, most of them believe in them.⁶ But today they cannot control for each other, either profit or harm'; and we will say to those who have done wrong, 'Taste ye the torment of the Fire wherein ye did disbelieve!'

And when our signs are recited to them they say, 'This is only a man who wishes to turn you from what your fathers served'; and they say, 'This is only a lie forged', and those who misbelieve will say of the truth when it comes to them, 'It is only obvious sorcery!'

But we have not brought them any book which they may study, and we have not sent to them before thee a warner.

Those before them said it was a lie, and these⁷ have not reached a tithe of what we had given them. And they said my apostles were liars, and how great a change was then!

[45] Say, 'I only admonish you of one thing, that ye should stand up before Allah in twos or singly, and then that ye reflect that there is no jinn in your companion.⁸ He is only a warner to you before the keen torment.'

Say, 'I do not ask you for it a hire; that is for yourselves; my hire is only from Allah, and He is witness over all.'

Say, 'Verily, my Lord hurls forth the truth; and He well knows the unseen.'

Say, 'The truth has come, and falsehood shall vanish and shall not come back.'

Say, 'If I err I only err against myself; and if I am guided it is all what my Lord inspires me; verily, He is the hearing, the nigh!'

[50] And couldst thou see when they are scared, and there shall be no escape, and they shall be taken from a place that is nigh. And they say, 'We believe in it.' But how can they partake of it from a distant place? They mis-believed before, and conjectured about the unseen from a distant place. And there shall be a barrier between them and that which they lust after; as we did with their fellow sectaries before; verily, they were in hesitating doubt.

THE CHAPTER OF THE ANGELS¹
XXXV (*Mecca*)

In the name of the merciful and compassionate Allah.

Praise belongs to Allah, the originator of the heavens and the earth; who makes the angels His messengers, endued with wings in pairs, or threes or fours; He adds to creation what He pleases; verily, Allah is mighty over all!

What Allah opens to men of His mercy there is none to withhold; and what He withholds, there is none can send it forth after Him; for He is the mighty, the wise.

O ye folk! remember the favours of Allah towards you; is there a creator beside Allah, who provides you from the heavens and from the earth? There is no god but He; how then can ye lie?

And if they call thee liar, apostles were called liars before thee, and unto Allah affairs return.

[5] O ye folk! verily, Allah's promise is true; then let not the life of this world beguile you, and let not the beguiler beguile you concerning Allah. Verily, the devil is to you a foe, so take him as a foe; he only calls his crew to be the fellows of the blaze.

Those who misbelieve, for them is keen torment.

But those who believe and do right, for them is for-giveness and a great hire.

What! is he whose evil act is made seemly for him, so that he looks upon it as good,——? Verily, Allah leads astray whom He pleases and guides whom He pleases; let not thy soul then be wasted in sighing for them; verily, Allah knows what they do!

[10] It is Allah who sends the winds, and they stir up a cloud, and we irrigate therewith a dead country, and we quicken therewith the earth after its death; so shall the resurrection be!

Whosoever desires honour—honour belongs wholly to Allah; to Him good words ascend, and a righteous deed

He takes up; and those who plot evil deeds, for them is keen torment, and their plotting is in vain.

Allah created you from earth, then from a clot; then He made you pairs; and no female bears or is delivered, except by His knowledge; nor does he who is aged reach old age, or is aught diminished from his life, without it is in the Book; verily, that is easy unto Allah.

The two seas are not equal: one is sweet and fresh and pleasant to drink, and the other is salt and pungent; but from each do ye eat fresh flesh, and bring forth ornaments which ye wear; and thou mayest see the ships cleave through it, that ye may search after His grace, and haply ye may give thanks.

He turns the night into day, and He turns the day into night; and He subjects the sun and the moon, each of them runs on to an appointed goal; that is Allah, your Lord! His is the kingdom; but those ye call on beside Him possess not a straw.[2]

[15] If you call upon them they cannot hear your call, and if they hear they cannot answer you; and on the resurrection day they will deny your associating them with Allah; but none can inform thee like the One who is aware.

O ye folk! ye are in need of Allah; but Allah, He is independent, praiseworthy.

If He please He will take you off, and will bring a fresh creation; for that is no hard matter unto Allah.

And no burdened soul shall bear the burden of another; and if a heavily laden one shall call for its load (to be carried) it shall not be carried for it at all, even though it be a kinsman!—thou canst only warn those who fear their

Lord in the unseen and who are steadfast in prayer; and he who is pure is only pure for himself; and unto Allah the journey is.

[20] The blind is not equal with him who sees, nor the darkness with the night, nor the shade with the hot blast; nor are the living equal with the dead; verily, Allah causes whom he pleases to hear, and thou canst not make those who are in their graves hear; thou art but a warner!

Verily, we have sent thee in truth a herald of glad tidings and a warner; and there is no nation but its warner has passed away with it.

And if they called thee liar, those before thee called their apostles liars too, who came to them with manifest signs, and the Scriptures, and the illuminating Book.

Then I seized those who misbelieved, and what a change it was!

[25] Dost thou not see that Allah has sent down from the heaven water, and has brought forth therewith fruits varied in hue, and on the mountains dykes,³ white and red, various in hue, and some intensely black, and men and beasts and cattle, various in hue? Thus! none fear Allah but the wise among His servants; but, verily, Allah is mighty, forgiving.

Verily, those who recite the Book of Allah, and are steadfast in prayer, and give alms of what we have bestowed in secret and in public, hope for the merchandise that shall not come to naught; that He may pay them their hire, and give them increase of His grace; verily, He is forgiving, grateful.

What we have inspired thee with of the Book is true,

verifying what was before it; verily, Allah of His servants is well aware and sees.

Then we gave the Book for an inheritance to those whom we chose of our servants, and of them are some who wrong themselves, and of them are some who take a middle course, and of them are some who vie in good works by the permission of their Lord; that is great grace.

[30] Gardens of Eden shall they enter, adorned therein with bracelets of gold and pearls; and their garments therein shall be silk; and they shall say, 'Praise belongs to Allah, who has removed from us our grief; verily, our Lord is forgiving, grateful! who has made us alight in an enduring abode of His grace, wherein no toil shall touch us, and there shall touch us no fatigue.'

But those who misbelieve, for them is the Fire of Hell; it shall not be decreed for them to die, nor shall aught of the torment be lightened from them; thus do we reward every misbeliever; and they shall shriek therein, 'O our Lord! bring us forth, and we will do right, not what we used to do!'—'Did we not let you grow old enough for every one who would be mindful to be mindful? and there came to you a warner!—

[35] So taste it, for the unjust shall have none to help!' Verily, Allah knows the unseen things of the heavens and of the earth; verily, He knows the nature of men's breasts, He it is who made you vicegerents in the earth, and he who misbelieves, his misbelief is against himself; but their misbelief shall only increase the misbelievers in hatred with their Lord; and their misbelief shall only increase the misbelievers in loss.

Say, 'Have ye considered your associates whom ye call on beside Allah?' Show me what they created of the earth; have they a share in the heavens, or have we given them a book that they rest on a manifest sign? Nay, the unjust promise each other naught but guile.

Verily, Allah holds back the heavens and the earth lest they should decline; and if they should decline there is none to hold them back after Him; verily, He is clement, forgiving.

[40] They swore by Allah with their most strenuous oath, verily, if there come to them a warner they would be more guided than any one of the nations; but when a warner comes to them, it only increases them in aversion, and in being big with pride in the earth, and in plotting evil; but the plotting of evil only entangles those who practise it; can they then expect aught but the course of those of yore? But thou shalt not find any alteration in the course of Allah; and they shall not find any change in the course of Allah.

Have they not journeyed on in the land and seen what was the end of those before them who were stronger than they? But Allah, nothing can ever make Him helpless in the heavens or in the earth; verily, He is knowing, powerful.

Were Allah to catch men up for what they earn, He would not leave upon the back of it[4] a beast; but He respites them until an appointed time. [45] When their appointed time comes, verily, Allah looks upon His servants.

THE CHAPTER OF Y. S.

XXXVI (*Mecca*)

In the name of the merciful and compassionate Allah.

Y. S. By the wise Qur'ân, verily, thou art of the apostles upon a right way. The revelation of the mighty, the merciful! [5] That thou mayest warn a people whose fathers were not warned, and who themselves are heedless.

Now is the sentence due against most of them, for they will not believe. Verily, we will place upon their necks fetters, and they shall reach up to their chins, and they shall have their heads forced back; and we will place before them a barrier, and behind them a barrier; and we will cover them and they shall not see; and it is all the same to them if thou dost warn them or dost warn them not, they will not believe. [10] Thou canst only warn him who follows the reminder, and fears the Merciful in the unseen; but give him glad tidings of forgiveness and a noble hire.

Verily, we quicken the dead, and write down what they have done before, and what vestiges they leave behind; and everything have we counted in a plain model.¹

Strike out for them a parable: the fellows of the city when there came to it the apostles; when we sent those two and they called them both liars, and we strengthened them with a third; and they said, 'Verily, we are sent to you.'

They said, 'Ye are only mortals like ourselves, nor has the Merciful sent down aught; ye are naught but liars.'

[15] They said, 'Our Lord knows that we are sent to you, and we have only our plain message to preach.'

They said, 'Verily, we have augured concerning you, and if ye do not desist we will surely stone you, and there shall touch you from us a grievous woe.'

Said they, 'Your augury is with you; what! if ye are reminded—? Nay, ye are an extravagant people!'

And there came from the remote part of the city a man hastening up. Said he, 'O my people! follow the apostles; [20] follow those who do not ask you a hire, and who are guided. What ails me that I should not worship Him who originated me, and unto whom I must return? Shall I take gods beside Him? If the Merciful One desires harm for me, their intercession cannot avail me at all, nor can they rescue me. Verily, I should then be in obvious error; verily, I believe in your Lord, then listen ye to me!'

[25] It was said, 'Enter thou into Paradise!' said he, 'O, would that my people did but know! for that my Lord has forgiven me, and has made me of the honoured.'

And we did send down upon his people no hosts from heaven, nor yet what we were wont to send down; it was but a single noise, and lo! they were extinct.²

Alas for the servants! there comes to them no apostle but they mock at him!

[30] Have they not seen how many generations we have destroyed before them? Verily, they shall not return to them; but all of them shall surely altogether be arraigned.

And a sign for them is the dead earth which we have quickened and brought forth therefrom seed, and from it do they eat; and we made therein gardens and palms and grapes, and we have caused fountains to gush forth therein, [35] that they may eat from the fruit thereof, and of what their hands have made; will they not then give thanks?

Celebrated be the praises of Him who created all kinds, of what the earth brings forth, and of themselves, and what they know not of!

And a sign to them is the night, from which we strip off the day, and lo! they are in the dark; and the sun runs on to a place of rest for it;³ that is the ordinance of the mighty, the wise.

And the moon, we have ordered for it stations, until it comes again to be like an old dry palm branch.

[40] Neither is it proper for it to catch up the moon, nor for the night to outstrip the day, but each one floats on in its sky.

And a sign for them is that we bear their seed in a laden ship,⁴ and we have created for them the like thereof whereon to ride; and if we please, we drown them, and there is none for them to appeal to; nor are they rescued, save by mercy from us, as a provision for a season.

[45] And when it is said to them, 'Fear what is before you and what is behind you, haply ye may obtain mercy;'⁵ and thou bringest them not any one of the signs of their Lord, but they turn away therefrom; and when it is said to them, 'Expend in alms of what Allah has bestowed upon you', those who misbelieve say to those who believe, 'Shall we feed him whom, if Allah pleased, He would feed? Ye are only in an obvious error.'

They say, 'When shall this promise come to pass, if ye

do tell the truth?' They await but a single noise, that shall seize them as they are contending. [50] And they shall not be able to make a bequest; nor to their people shall they return; but the trumpet shall be blown, and, behold, from their graves unto their Lord shall they slip out!

They shall say, 'O, woe is us! who has raised us up from our sleeping place? This is what the Merciful promised, and the apostles told the truth!' It shall be but a single noise, and lo! they are all arraigned before us.

And on that day no soul shall be wronged at all, nor shall ye be rewarded for aught but that which ye have done.

[55] Verily, the fellows of Paradise upon that day shall be employed in enjoyment; they and their wives, in shade upon thrones, reclining; therein shall they have fruits, and they shall have what they may call for. 'Peace!'—a speech from the merciful Lord!

'Separate yourselves today, O ye sinners! [60] Did I not covenant with you, O children of Adam! that ye should not serve Satan? Verily, he is to you an open foe; but serve ye me, this is the right way. But he led astray a numerous race of you; what! had ye then no sense? this is Hell, which ye were threatened; broil therein today, for that ye misbelieved!'

[65] On that day we will seal their mouths, and their hands shall speak to us, and their feet shall bear witness of what they earned. And if we please we could put out their eyes, and they would race along the road; and then how could they see? And if we pleased we would transform them in their places, and they should not be able to go on, nor yet to return. And him to whom we

grant old age, we bow him down in his form; have they then no sense?

We have not taught him[6] poetry, nor was it proper for him; it is but a reminder and a plain Qur'ân, [70] to warn him who is living; but the sentence is due against the misbelievers.

Have they not seen that we have created for them of what our hands have made for them, cattle, and they are owners thereof? and we have tamed them for them, and of them are some to ride, and of them are what they eat, and therein have they advantages and beverages; will they not then give thanks?

But they take, beside Allah, gods that haply they may be helped. [75] They cannot help them; yet are they a host ready for them.[7]

But let not their speech grieve thee: verily, we know what they conceal and what they display.

Has not man seen that we have created him from a clot? and lo! he is an open opponent; and he strikes out for us a likeness; and forgets his creation; and says, 'Who shall quicken bones when they are rotten?' Say, 'He shall quicken them who produced them at first; for every creation does He know; [80] who has made for you fire out of a green tree, and lo! ye kindle therewith.'

Is not He who created the heavens and the earth able to create the like thereof? Yea! He is the knowing Creator; His bidding is only, when He desires anything to say to it, 'BE', and it is. Then celebrated be the praises of Him in whose hands is the kingdom of everything! and unto Him shall ye return.

THE CHAPTER OF THE 'RANGED'

XXXVII (*Mecca*)

In the name of the merciful and compassionate Allah.

By the (angels) ranged in ranks, and the drivers driving,[1] and the reciters of the reminder, 'Verily, your Allah is one, [5] the Lord of the heavens and the earth and what is between the two, and the Lord of the sunrises!'

Verily, we have adorned the lower heaven with the adornment of the stars, and to preserve it from every rebellious devil, that they may not listen to the exalted chiefs; for they are hurled at from every side,[2] driven off, and for them is lasting woe; [10] save such as snatches off a word, and there follows him a darting flame!

Ask them[3] whether they are stronger by nature or (the angels) whom we have created? We have created them of sticky clay.

Nay, thou dost wonder and they jest! and when they are reminded they will not remember; and when they see a sign they make a jest thereof, [15] and say, 'This is naught but obvious sorcery. What! when we are dead, and have become earth and bones, shall we then be raised? What! and our fathers of yore?'

Say, 'Yes, and ye shall shrink up', and it shall only be one scare, and, behold, they shall look on, [20] and they shall say, 'O, woe is us! this is the day of judgement, this is the day of decision, which ye did call a lie!' Gather ye together, ye who were unjust, with their mates and what they used to serve beside Allah, and guide them to the way of Hell, and stop them; verily, they shall be questioned. [25] 'Why do ye not help each other?' Nay, on that day they shall resign themselves, and some shall draw near to others, to question each other, and they shall say, 'Verily, ye came to us from the right.'⁴ They shall say, 'Nay, ye not believers, nor had we any authority over you; nay, ye were an outrageous people. [30] And the sentence of our Lord shall be due for us; verily, we shall surely taste thereof; we did seduce you—verily, we were erring too!' Therefore, verily, on that day they shall share the torment: thus it is that we will do with the sinners.

Verily, when it is said to them, 'There is no god but Allah', they get too big with pride, and say, [35] 'What! shall we leave our gods for an infatuated poet?' Nay, he came with the truth, and verified the apostles; verily, ye are going to taste of grievous woe, nor shall ye be rewarded save for that which ye have done!

Except Allah's sincere servants, [40] these shall have a stated provision of fruits, and they shall be honoured in the gardens of pleasure, upon couches facing each other;⁵ they shall be served all round with a cup from a spring, [45] white and delicious to those who drink, wherein is no insidious spirit, nor shall they be drunk therewith; and with them damsels, restraining their looks, large eyed; as though they were a sheltered egg; and some shall come forward to ask others; and a speaker amongst them shall say, 'Verily, I had a mate, [50] who used to say, "Art thou verily of those who credit? What! when we are dead, and have become earth and bones, shall we be surely judged?" ' He will say, 'Are ye looking down?' and he shall look down and see him in the midst of Hell. He shall say, 'By Allah, thou didst nearly ruin me! [55] And had it not been for the favour of my Lord, I should have been among the arraigned.'—'What! shall we not die save our first death? and shall we not be tormented?—Verily, this is mighty bliss! for the like of this then let the workers work.'

[60] Is that better as an entertainment, or the tree of Ez Zaqqûm?⁶ Verily, we have made it a trial to the unjust.⁷ Verily, it is a tree that comes forth from the bottom of Hell; its spathe is as it were the heads of devils; verily, they shall eat therefrom, and fill their bellies therefrom. [65] Then shall they have upon it a mixture of boiling water; then, verily, their return shall be to Hell.

Verily, they found their fathers erring, and they hurried on in their tracks; but there had erred before them most of those of yore, [70] and we had sent warners amongst them. Behold, then, what was the end of those who were warned, save Allah's sincere servants!

Noah did call upon us, and a gracious answer did we give; and we saved him and his people from a mighty trouble; [75] and we made his seed to be the survivors; and we left for him amongst posterity, 'Peace upon Noah in the worlds; verily, thus do we reward those who do well; verily, he was of our believing servants.' [80] Then we drowned the others.

And, verily, of his sect was Abraham; when he came to his Lord with a sound heart; when he said to his father and his people, 'What is it that ye serve? with a lie do ye desire gods beside Allah? [85] What then is your thought respecting the Lord of the worlds?'

And he looked a look at the stars and said, 'Verily, I am sick!' and they turned their backs upon him fleeing.[8] And he went aside unto their gods and said, 'Will ye not eat? [90] What ails you that ye will not speak?' And he went aside to them smiting with the right hand.

And they[9] rushed towards him. Said he, 'Do ye serve what ye hew out, when Allah has created you, and what ye make?'

[95] Said they, 'Build for him a pyre, and throw him into the flaming Hell!' They desired to plot against him, but we made them inferior. Said he, 'Verily, I am going to my Lord, He will guide me. My Lord! grant me (a son), one of the righteous'; and we gave him glad tidings of a clement boy.

[100] And when he reached the age to work with him, he said, 'O my boy! verily, I have seen in a dream that I should sacrifice thee,[10] look then what thou seest right.'

Said he, 'O my sire! do what thou art bidden; thou wilt find me, if it please Allah, one of the patient!'

And when they were resigned, and Abraham had thrown him down upon his forehead, we called to him, 'O Abraham! [105] thou hast verified the vision; verily, thus do we reward those who do well. This is surely an obvious trial.' And we ransomed him with a mighty victim; and we left for him amongst posterity, 'Peace upon Abraham; [110] thus do we reward those who do well; verily, he was of our servants who believe!' And we gave him glad tidings of Isaac, a prophet among the righteous; and we blessed him and Isaac;—of their seed is one who does well, and one who obviously wrongs himself.

And we were gracious unto Moses and Aaron. [115] We saved them and their people from mighty trouble, and we helped them and they had the upper hand; and we gave them both the perspicuous Book; and we guided them to the right way; and we left for them amongst posterity, [120] 'Peace upon Moses and Aaron; verily, thus do we reward those who do well; verily, they were both of our servants who believe!'

And verily Elyâs[11] was of the apostles; when he said to his people, 'Will ye not fear? [125] Do ye call upon Baal and leave the best of Creators, Allah your Lord and the Lord of your fathers of yore?'

But they called him liar; verily, they shall surely be arraigned, save Allah's sincere servants. And we left for him amongst posterity, [130] 'Peace upon Elyâsîn;[12] verily, thus do we reward those who do well; verily, he was of our servants who believe!'

And, verily, Lot was surely among the apostles; when we saved him and his people altogether, [135] except an old woman amongst those who lingered; then we destroyed the others; verily, ye pass by them in the morning and at night; have ye then no sense?

And, verily, Jonah was amongst the apostles; [140] when he ran away[13] into the laden ship; and he cast lots and was of those who lost; and a fish swallowed him, for he was to be blamed; and had it not been that he was of those who celebrated Allah's praises he would surely have tarried in the belly thereof to the day when men shall be raised.

[145] But we cast him on to the barren shore; and he was

sick; and we made to grow over him a gourd tree; and we sent him to a hundred thousand or more, and they believed; and we gave them enjoyment for a season.

Ask them,[14] 'Has thy Lord daughters while they have sons?'[15] [150] or have we created the angels females while they were witnesses?' Is it not of their lie that they say, 'Allah has begotten?' Verily, they are liars.

Has he preferred daughters to sons? What ails you? How ye judge! [155] Will ye not be mindful, or have ye obvious authority? Then bring your Book if ye do speak the truth.

And they made him to be related to the jinns, while the jinns know that they shall be arraigned; celebrated be Allah's praises from what they attribute!—[160] save Allah's sincere servants.

'Verily, ye and what ye worship shall not try any one concerning him, save him who shall broil in Hell; there is none amongst us but has his appointed place, and, [165] verily, we are ranged, and, verily, we celebrate His praises.'[16]

And yet they say, 'Had we a reminder from those of yore we should surely have been of Allah's sincere servants.'

[170] But they misbelieved in it;[17] but soon shall they know.

But our word has been passed to our servants who were sent that they should be helped; that, verily, our hosts should gain mastery for them.

Then turn thou thy back upon them for a time, [175] and look upon them, for soon they too shall look.

Would they hasten on our torment? but when it

descends in their court, ill will the morning be of those who have been warned!

But turn thy back upon them for a time; and look, for soon they too shall look.

[180] Celebrated be the praises of thy Lord, the Lord of glory, above what they attribute! and peace be upon the apostles and praise be to Allah, the Lord of the worlds!

THE CHAPTER OF S.[1]

XXXVIII (*Mecca*)

In the name of the merciful and compassionate Allah.

S. By the Qur'ân with its reminder! Nay, but those who misbelieve are in pride, schism!

How many a generation have we destroyed before them, and they cried out, but it was no time to escape!

And they wonder that a warner has come from amongst themselves, and the misbelievers say, 'This is a magician, a liar!' What! does he make the gods to be one Allah? Verily, this is a wondrous thing.

[5] And the chiefs of them went away: 'Go on and persevere in your gods; this is a thing designed; we never heard this in any other sect; this is nothing but a fiction! Has a reminder come down upon him from amongst us?' Nay, they are in doubt concerning my reminder; nay, they have not yet tasted of my torment!

Have they the treasures of the mercy of thy mighty Lord, the giver? or have they the kingdom of the heavens and of the earth, and what is between the two?—then let them climb up the ropes thereof.

[10] Any host whatever of the confederates shall there be routed.

Before them did Noah's people, and 'Âd, and Pharaoh of the stakes² call the apostles liars; and Thamûd and the people of Lot, and the fellows of the Grove, they were the confederates too.

They all did naught but call the apostles liars, and just was the punishment! Do these³ await aught else but one noise for which there shall be no pause?

[15] But they say, 'O our Lord, hasten for us our share before the day of reckoning!'

Be patient of what they say, and remember our servant David endowed with might; verily, he turned frequently to us. Verily, we subjected the mountains to celebrate with him our praises at the evening and the dawn; and the birds too gathered together, each one would oft return to him; and we strengthened his kingdom, and we gave him wisdom and decisive address.

[20] Has there come to thee the story of the antagonists when they scaled the chamber wall? When they entered in unto David, and he was startled at them, they said, 'Fear not, we are two antagonists; one of us has injured the other; judge then between us with the truth and be not partial, but guide us to a level way. Verily, this is my brother: he had ninety-nine ewes and I had one ewe; and he said, "Give her over to my charge"; and he overcame me in the discourse.' Said he, 'He wronged thee in asking for thy ewe in addition to his own ewes. Verily, many

associates do injure one another, except those who believe and do what is right, and very few are they!'

And he thought that we were trying him; and he asked pardon of his Lord and fell down bowing, and did turn; and we pardoned him; for, verily, he has a near approach to us and an excellent resort.

[25] O David! verily, we have made thee a vicegerent, judge then between men with truth and follow not lust, for it will lead thee astray from the path of Allah. Verily, those who go astray from the path of Allah, for them is keen torment, for that they did forget the day of reckoning!

And we have not created the heavens and the earth, and what is between the two, in vain. That is what those who misbelieved did think, but woe from the Fire to those who misbelieve!

Shall we make those who believe and do right like those who do evil in the earth? or shall we make the pious like the sinners?

A blessed Book which we have sent down to thee that they may consider its verses, and that those endowed with minds may be mindful.

And we gave to David, Solomon, an excellent servant; verily, he turned frequently to us. [30] When there were set before him in the evening the steeds that paw the ground,[4] and he said, 'Verily, I have loved the love of good things better than the remembrance of my Lord, until (the sun) was hidden behind the veil; bring them back to me'; and he began to sever their legs and necks.

And we did try Solomon, and we threw upon his throne

a form; then he turned repentant.[5] Said he, 'My Lord, pardon me and grant me a kingdom that is not seemly for any one after me; verily, thou art He who grants!'

[35] And we subjected to him the wind to run on at his bidding gently wherever he directed it; and the devils— every builder and diver, and others bound in fetters—'this is our gift, so be thou lavish or withhold without account!'

And, verily, he had with us a near approach, and a good resort.

[40] And remember our servant Job when he called upon his Lord that 'the devil has touched me with toil and torment!'

'Stamp with thy foot, this is a cool washing place and a drink.' And we granted him his family, and the like of them with them, as a mercy from us and a reminder to those endowed with minds,—'and take in thy hand a bundle, and strike therewith, and break not thy oath!' Verily, we found him patient,[6] an excellent servant; verily, he turned frequently to us.

[45] And remember our servants Abraham and Isaac and Jacob, endowed with might and sight; verily, we made them sincere by a sincere quality—the remembrance of the abode; and, verily, they were with us of the elect, the best.

And remember Ishmael and Elisha and Dhu-l-kifl, for each was of the righteous.[7] This is a reminder! Verily, for the pious is there an excellent resort,—[50] gardens of Eden with the doors open to them;—reclining therein; calling therein for much fruit and drink; and beside them maids of modest glance, of their own age,—'This is what ye were promised for the day of reckoning!'—'This is surely our provision, it is never spent!'

[55] Thus!—and, verily, for the rebellious is there an evil resort,—Hell; they shall broil therein, and an ill couch shall it be! This,—so let them taste it!—hot water, and pus, and other kinds of the same sort! 'This is an army plunged in with you! There is no welcome for them! Verily, they are going to broil in the Fire!'

[60] They shall say, 'Nay, for you too is there no welcome! It was ye who prepared it beforehand for us, and an ill resting place it is!'

They shall say, 'Our Lord! whoso prepared this beforehand for us, give him double torment in the Fire!' And they shall say, 'What ails us that we do not see men whom we used to think amongst the wicked? whom we used to take for mockery? have our eyes escaped them?'

Verily, that is the truth; the contention of the people of the Fire.

[65] Say, 'I am only a warner; and there is no god but Allah, the one, the victorious, the Lord of the heavens and the earth, and what is between the two, the mighty, the forgiving!'

Say, 'It is a grand story, and yet we turn from it'! I had no knowledge of the exalted chiefs when they contended.

[70] I am only inspired that I am a plain warner. When thy Lord said to the angels, 'Verily, I am about to create a mortal out of clay; and when I have fashioned him, and breathed into him of my spirit, then fall ye down before him adoring.' And the angels adored all of them, save Iblîs,

who was too big with pride, and was of the misbelievers.

[75] Said He, 'O Iblîs! what prevents thee from adoring what I have created with my two hands? Art thou too big with pride? or art thou amongst the exalted?' Said he, 'I am better than he, Thou hast created me from fire, and him Thou hast created from clay.' Said He, 'Then go forth therefrom, for, verily, thou art pelted, and, verily, upon thee is my curse unto the day of judgement.'

[80] Said he, 'My Lord! then respite me until the day when they are raised.' Said He, 'Then thou art amongst the respited until the day of the stated time.' Said he, 'Then, by Thy might! I will surely seduce them all together, except Thy servants amongst them who are sincere!' [85] Said He, 'It is the truth, and the truth I speak; I will surely fill Hell with thee and with those who follow thee amongst them all together.'

Say, 'I do not ask thee for it any hire, nor am I of those who take too much upon myself. It is but a reminder to the servants, and ye shall surely know its story after a time.'

THE CHAPTER OF THE TROOPS

XXXIX (*Mecca*)

In the name of the merciful and compassionate Allah.

The sending down of the Book from Allah, the mighty, the wise.

Verily, we have sent down to thee the Book in truth, then serve Allah, being sincere in religion unto Him. Aye!

Allah's is the sincere religion: and those who take beside Him patrons—'We do not serve them save that they may bring us near to Allah—' Verily, Allah will judge between them concerning that whereon they do dispute.

[5] Verily, Allah guides not him who is a misbelieving liar.

Had Allah wished to take to Himself a child, He would have chosen what He pleased from what He creates;— celebrated be His praises! He is Allah, the one, the victorious. He created the heavens and the earth in truth! It is He who clothes the day with night; and clothes the night with day; and subjects the sun and the moon, each one runs on to an appointed time; aye! He is the mighty, the forgiving! He created you from one soul; then He made from it its mate; and He sent down upon you of the cattle four pairs!¹ He creates you in the bellies of your mothers,—creation after creation, in three darknesses.² That is Allah for you! His is the kingdom, there is no god but He; how then can ye be turned away?

If ye be thankless, yet is Allah independent of you. He is not pleased with ingratitude in His servants; but if ye give thanks, He is pleased with that in you. But no burdened soul shall bear the burden of another; then unto your Lord is your return, and He will inform you of that which ye have done. [10] Verily, He knows the natures of men's breasts!

And when distress touches a man he calls his Lord, turning repentant to Him; then when He confers on him a favour from Himself he forgets what he had called upon Him for before, and makes peers for Allah to lead astray from His way! Say, 'Enjoy thyself in thy misbelief a little, verily, thou art of the fellows of the Fire.'

Shall he who is devout throughout the night, adoring and standing, cautious concerning the hereafter, and hoping for the mercy of his Lord . . .? Say, 'Shall those who know be deemed equal with those who know not? Only those will remember, who are endowed with minds!'

Say, 'O my servants who believe! fear your Lord! for those who do well in this world are good, and Allah's earth is spacious; verily, the patient shall be paid their hire without count!'

Say, 'Verily, I am bidden to serve Allah, being sincere in religion to Him; and I am bidden that I be the first of those resigned.'

[15] Say, 'Verily, I fear, if I rebel against my Lord, the torment of a mighty day.' Say, 'Allah do I serve, being sincere in my religion to Him; serve then what ye will beside Him!' Say, 'Verily, the losers are those who lose themselves and their families on the resurrection day. Aye, that is the obvious loss.'

They shall have over them shades of fire, and under them shades; with that does Allah frighten His servants: O my servants! then fear me.

But those who avoid Tâghût[3] and serve them not, but turn repentant unto Allah, for them shall be glad tidings. Then give glad tidings to my servants who listen to the word and follow the best thereof; they it is whom Allah guides, and they it is who are endowed with minds. [20] Him against whom the word of torment is due,—canst thou rescue him from the Fire?

But for those who fear their Lord for them are upper chambers, and upper chambers above them built, beneath which rivers flow; Allah's promise! Allah does not fail in His promise.

Hast thou not seen that Allah sends down from the heaven water, and conducts it into springs in the earth? Then He brings forth therewith corn varied in kind, then it dries up, and ye see it grow yellow; then He makes it grit;—verily, in that is a reminder for those endowed with minds.

Is he whose breast Allah has expanded for Islam, and who is in light from his Lord . . .? And woe to those whose hearts are hardened against a remembrance of Allah! Those are in obvious error.

Allah has sent down the best of legends, a book uniform and repeating; whereat the skins of those who fear their Lord do creep! then their skins and their hearts soften at the remembrance of Allah. That is the guidance of Allah! He guides therewith whom He will. But he whom Allah leads astray there is no guide for him.

[25] Shall he who must screen himself with his own face from the evil torment on the resurrection day . . .? And it shall be said of those who do wrong, taste what ye have earned.

Those before them called the (prohets) liars, and the torment came to them from whence they perceived it not; and Allah made them taste disgrace in the life of this world. But surely the torment of the hereafter is greater, if they did but know. We have struck out for men in this Qur'ân every sort of parable, haply they may be mindful.

An Arabic Qur'ân with no crookedness therein; haply they may fear!

[30] Allah has struck out a parable, a man who has partners who oppose each other; and a man who is wholly given up to another; shall they be deemed equal in similitude? Praise be to Allah! Nay, but most of them know not!

Verily, thou shalt die, and, verily, they shall die; then, verily, on the resurrection day before your Lord shall ye dispute.

And who is more unjust than he who lies against Allah, and calls the truth a lie when it comes to him? Is there not in Hell a resort for those who misbelieve? But whoso brings the truth and believes in it, these are they who fear.

[35] For them is what they please with their Lord, that is the reward of those who do well; that Allah may cover for them their offences which they have done, and may reward them with their hire for the best of that which they have done.

Is not Allah sufficient for His servants? and yet they would frighten thee with those beside Him.[4] But he whom Allah leads astray there is no guide for him; and he whom Allah guides there is none to lead him astray: is not Allah mighty, the Lord of vengeance?

And if thou shouldst ask them who created the heavens and the earth, they will surely say, 'Allah!' Say, 'Have ye considered what ye call on beside Allah? If Allah wished me harm,[5] could they remove His harm? or did He wish me mercy, could they withhold His mercy?' Say, 'Allah is enough for me, and on Him rely those who rely.'

[40] Say, 'O my people! act according to your power; I too am going to act; and ye shall know.'

He to whom the torment comes it shall disgrace him, and there shall alight upon him lasting torment.

Verily, we have sent down to thee the Book for men in truth; and whosoever is guided it is for his own soul: but whoso goes astray it is against them, and thou art not a guardian for them.

Allah takes to Himself souls at the time of their death; and those which do not die (He takes) in their sleep; and He holds back those on whom He has decreed death, and sends others back till their appointed time;—verily, in that are signs unto a people who reflect.

Do they take besides Allah intercessors? Say, 'What! though they have no control over anything and have no sense.'

[45] Say, 'Allah's is the intercession, all of it; His is the kingdom of the heavens and the earth; then unto Him shall ye be sent back.'

And when Allah alone is mentioned the hearts of those who believe not in the hereafter quake, and when those beside Him are mentioned, lo, they are joyful!

Say, 'O Allah! originator of the heavens and the earth, who knowest the unseen and the visible, thou wilt judge between thy servants concerning that whereon they do dispute!'

And had those who do wrong all that is in the earth, and the like thereof with it, they would ransom themselves therewith from the evil of the torment on the resurrection day! But there shall appear to them from Allah that which they had not reckoned on; and the evils of what they have earned shall appear to them; but that shall close in on them at which they mocked!

[50] And when harm touches man he calls on us; then, when we grant him favour from us, he says, 'Verily, I am given it through knowledge!' Nay, it is a trial,—but most of them do not know!

Those before them said it too, but that availed them not which they had earned, and there befell them the evil deeds of what they had earned: and those who do wrong of these (Meccans), there shall befall them too the evil deeds of what they had earned, nor shall they frustrate Him.

Have they not known that Allah extends His provision to whom He pleases, or doles it out? Verily, in that are signs unto a people who believe.

Say, 'O my servants! who have been extravagant against their own souls!' be not in despair of the mercy of Allah; verily, Allah forgives sins, all of them; verily, He is forgiving, merciful.

[55] But turn repentant unto your Lord, and resign yourselves to Him, before there comes on you torment! then ye shall not be helped: and follow the best of what has been sent down to you from your Lord, before there come on you the torment suddenly, ere ye can perceive!

Lest a soul should say, 'O my sighing! for what I have neglected towards Allah! for, verily, I was amongst those who did jest!' or lest it should say, 'If Allah had but guided me, I should surely have been of those who fear!'

or lest it should say, when it sees the torment, 'Had I another turn I should be of those who do well!'

[60] 'Yea! there came to thee my signs and thou didst call them lies, and wert too big with pride, and wert of those who misbelieved!'

And on the resurrection day thou shalt see those who lied against Allah, with their faces blackened. Is there not in Hell a resort for those who are too big with pride?

And Allah shall rescue those who fear Him, into their safe place; no evil shall touch them, nor shall they be grieved.

Allah is the creator of everything, and He is guardian over everything; His are the keys of the heavens and the earth; and those who misbelieve in the signs of Allah, they it is who lose!

Say, 'What! other than Allah would you bid me serve, O ye ignorant ones? [65] When He has inspired thee and those before thee that, "If thou dost associate aught with Him, thy work will surely be in vain, and thou shalt surely be of those who lose!" Nay, but Allah do thou serve, and be of those who do give thanks!'

And they do not value Allah at His true value; while the earth all of it is but a handful for Him on the resurrection day, and the heavens shall be rolled up in His right hand! Celebrated be His praise! and exalted be He above what they associate with Him! And the trumpet shall be blown, and those who are in the heavens and in the earth shall swoon, save whom Allah pleases. Then it shall be blown again, and, lo! they shall stand up and look on. And the earth shall beam with the light of its Lord, and the Book shall be set forth, and the prophets and martyrs[6] shall be brought; and it shall be decreed between them in truth, and they shall not be wronged! [70] And every soul shall be paid for what it has done, and He knows best that which they do; and those who misbelieve shall be driven to Hell in troops; and when they come there, its doors shall be opened, and its keepers shall say to them, 'Did not apostles from amongst yourselves come to you to recite to you the signs of your Lord, and to warn you of the meeting of this day of yours?' They shall say, 'Yea, but the sentence of torment was due against the misbelievers!' It shall be said, 'Enter ye the gates of Hell, to dwell therein for aye! Hell is the resort of those who are too big with pride!'

But those who fear their Lord shall be driven to Paradise in troops; until they come there, its doors shall be opened, and its keepers shall say to them, 'Peace be upon you, ye have done well! so enter in to dwell for aye!' and they shall say, 'Praise be to Allah, who hath made good His promise to us, and hath given us the earth to inherit! We establish ourselves in Paradise wherever we please; and goodly is the reward of those who work!'

[75] And thou shalt see the angels circling round about the throne, celebrating the praise of their Lord; and it shall be decided between them in truth; and it shall be said, 'Praise be to Allah, the Lord of the worlds!'

THE CHAPTER OF THE BELIEVER

XL (*Mecca*)

In the name of the merciful and compassionate Allah.

'H. M. The sending down of the Book from Allah, the mighty, the knowing, the forgiver of sin and accepter of repentance, keen at punishment, long-suffering! there is no god but He! to whom the journey is!

None wrangle concerning the signs of Allah but those who misbelieve; then let not their going to and fro in the cities deceive thee.

[5] The people of Noah before them called the prophets liars; and the confederates after them; and every nation schemed against their Apostle to catch him. And they wrangled with falsehood that they might refute the truth thereby, but I seized them, and how was my punishment!

Thus was the sentence of thy Lord due against those who misbelieved, that they are the fellows of the Fire!

Those who bear the throne and those around it celebrate the praise of their Lord, and believe in Him, and ask pardon for those who believe: 'Our Lord! thou dost embrace all things in mercy and knowledge, then pardon those who turn repentant and follow thy way, and guard them from the torment of Hell! Our Lord! make them enter into gardens of Eden which thou hast promised to them, and to those who do well of their fathers, and their wives, and their seed; verily, thou art the mighty, the wise! and guard them from evil deeds, for he whom thou shalt guard from evil deeds on that day, thou wilt have had mercy on, and that is mighty bliss!'

[10] Verily, those who misbelieve shall be cried out to, 'Surely, Allah's hatred is greater than your hatred of each other when ye were called unto the faith and misbelieved!' They shall say, 'Our Lord! Thou hast killed us twice, and Thou hast quickened us twice;[1] and we do confess our sins: is there then a way for getting out?'

That is because when Allah alone was proclaimed ye did disbelieve; but when partners were joined to Him ye did believe; but judgement belongs to Allah, the high, the great! He it is who shows you His signs, and sends down to you from heaven provision; but none is mindful except him who turns repentant; then call on Allah, being sincere in your religion to Him, averse although the misbelievers be! [15] Exalted of degrees! The Lord of the throne! He throws the spirit by His bidding upon whom He will of His servants, to give warning of the day of meeting. The day when they shall be issuing forth, naught concerning them shall be hidden from Allah. Whose is the kingdom on that day?—Allah's, the one, the dominant! Today shall every soul be recompensed for that which it has earned. There is no wrong today; verily, Allah is quick at reckoning up!

And warn them of the day that approaches, when hearts are choking in the gullets; those who do wrong shall have no warm friend, and no intercessor who shall be obeyed. [20] He knows the deceitful of eye and what men's breasts conceal, and Allah decides with truth; but those they call on beside Him do not decide at all: verily, Allah, He both hears and looks.

Have they not journeyed on in the earth and seen how was the end of those who journeyed on before them? They were stronger than them in might, and their vestiges are in the land; but Allah caught them up in their sins, and they had none to guard them against Allah.

That is for that their apostles did come to them with manifest signs, and they misbelieved, and Allah caught them up; verily, He is mighty, keen to punish!

And we did send Moses with our signs, and with obvious authority, [25] unto Pharaoh and Hâmân and Qarûn. They said, 'A lying sorcerer!' and when they came to them with truth from us, they said, 'Kill the sons of those who believe with him, and let their women live!' but the stratagem of the misbelievers is only in error!

And Pharaoh said, 'Let me kill Moses; and then let him call upon his Lord! Verily, I fear that he will change your religion, or that he will cause evil doing to appear in the land.'

And Moses said, 'Verily, I take refuge in my Lord and your Lord from every one who is big with pride and believes not on the day of reckoning.'

And a believing man of Pharaoh's people, who concealed his faith, said, 'Will ye kill a man for saying, "My Lord is Allah", when he has come to you with manifest signs from your Lord? and if he be a liar, against him is his lie; and if he be truthful, there will befall you somewhat of that which he threatens you; verily, Allah guides not him who is an extravagant liar. [30] O my people! yours is the kingdom today, ye are eminent in the land, but who will help us against the violence of Allah, if it comes upon us?'

Said Pharaoh, 'I will only show you what I see, and I will only guide you into the way of right direction.'

And he who believed said, 'O my people! verily, I fear for you the like of the day of the confederates, the like of the wont of the people of Noah and 'Âd and Hâmân, and of those after them; for Allah desires not injustice for His servants. O my people! verily, I fear for you the day of crying out,—[35] the day when ye shall turn your backs, fleeing, with no defender for you against Allah; for he whom Allah leads astray, for him there is no guide!

And Joseph came to you before with manifest signs, but ye ceased not to doubt concerning what he brought you, until, when he perished, ye said, "Allah will not send after him an apostle"; thus does Allah lead astray him who is extravagant, a doubter.

'Those who wrangle concerning the signs of Allah without authority having come to them are greatly hated by Allah and by those who believe; thus does Allah set a stamp upon the heart of every tyrant too big with pride!'

And Pharaoh said, 'O Hâmân! build for me a tower, haply I may reach the tracts,—the tracts of heaven, and may mount up to the Allah of Moses, for, verily, I think him a liar.'

[40] And thus was his evil deed made seemly to Pharaoh, and he was turned from the way; but Pharaoh's stratagem ended only in ruin, and he who believed said, 'O my people! follow me, I will guide you to the way of the right direction. O my people! verily, the life of this

world is but a provision, but, verily, the hereafter, that is
the abode of stability! Whoso does evil, he shall only be
recompensed with the like thereof; and whoso does right,
be it male or female and a believer, these shall enter into
Paradise; they shall be provided therein without count. O
my people! why should I call you to salvation, and you call
me to the Fire? [45] Ye call on me to disbelieve in Allah,
and to join with Him what I have no knowledge of; but I
call you to the mighty forgiving One! No doubt that what
ye call me to ought not to be called on in this world or in
the hereafter, and that we shall be sent back to Allah, and
that the extravagant, they are the fellows of the Fire!

'But ye shall remember what I say to you; and I
entrust my affair to Allah, verily, Allah looks upon His
servants!'

And Allah guarded him from the evils of what they
plotted, and there closed in upon Pharaoh evil woe.

The Fire—they shall be exposed to it morning and
evening; and 'on the day the Hour shall arise', enter, O
people of Pharaoh! into the keenest torment.

[50] And when they argue together in the Fire, and the
weak say to those who were big with pride, 'Verily, we
were followers of yours, can ye then avail us against a
portion of the Fire?'

Those who were big with pride shall say, 'Verily, we are
all in it; verily, Allah has judged between His servants.'

And those who are in the Fire shall say unto the keepers
of Hell, 'Call upon your Lord to lighten from us one day
of the torment.' They shall say, 'Did not your apostles
come to you with manifest signs?' They shall say, 'Yea!'

They shall say, 'Then, call!'—but the call of the misbelievers is only in error.

Verily, we will help our apostles, and those who believe, in the life of this world and on the day when the witnesses shall stand up: [55] the day when their excuse shall not avail the unjust; but for them is the curse, and for them is an evil abode.

And we did give Moses the guidance; and we made the children of Israel to inherit the Book, as a guidance and a reminder to those endowed with minds.

Be thou patient, then; verily, Allah's promise is true: and ask thou forgiveness for thy sins, and celebrate the praise of thy Lord in the evening and in the morn.

Verily, those who wrangle concerning the signs of Allah without authority having come to them, there is naught in their breasts but pride; but they shall not attain it: do thou then seek refuge in Allah; verily, He both hears and looks!

Surely the creation of the heavens and the earth is greater than the creation of man: but most men know it not.

[60] The blind and the seeing shall not be deemed alike, nor those who believe and do right and the evil-doer; little is it that they remember.

Verily, the Hour will surely come; there is no doubt therein; but most men do not believe!

And your Lord said, 'Call upon me, I will answer you; verily, those who are too big with pride to worship shall enter into Hell, shrinking up.'

Allah it is who has made for you the night to repose therein, and the day to see by; verily, Allah is Lord of grace to men, but most men give no thanks!

There is Allah for you! your Lord! the creator of everything! There is no god but He, how then can ye lie?² [65] Thus did those lie who gainsaid the signs of Allah.

Allah it is who has made for you the earth as a resting place, and a heaven as building, and has formed you and made excellent your forms; and has provided you with good things! There is Allah for you!—your Lord! Then blessed be Allah, the Lord of the worlds!

He is the living One, there is no god but He! Then call on Him, being sincere in your religion to Him; praise be to Allah, the Lord of the worlds!

Say, 'Verily, I am forbidden to serve those whom ye call on beside Allah, since there have come to me manifest signs from my Lord, and I am bidden to be resigned unto the Lord of the worlds.'

He it is who created you from the earth, then from a clot, then from congealed blood, then He brings you forth a child; then ye reach to puberty; then do ye become old men,—though of you there are some who are taken away before,—that ye may reach an appointed time, and haply ye may have some sense.

[70] He it is who quickens and kills, and when He decrees a matter, then He only says to it, 'BE', and it is.

Hast thou not seen those who wrangle concerning the signs of Allah how they are turned away? Those who call the Book, and what we have sent our apostles with, a lie, soon shall know—when the fetters are on their necks and the chains, as they are dragged into Hell!—then in the Fire shall they be baked.

Then it shall be said to them, 'Where is what ye did associate beside Allah?' They shall say, 'They have strayed away from us; nay, we did not call before upon anything!'—thus does Allah lead the misbelievers astray.

[75] There! for that ye did rejoice in the land without right; and for that ye did exult; enter ye the gates of Hell, to dwell therein for aye; for evil is the resort of those who are too big with pride!

But be thou patient; verily, the promise of Allah is true; and whether we show thee a part of what we promised them, or whether we surely take thee to ourself, unto us shall they be returned.

And we did send apostles before thee: of them are some whose stories we have related to thee, and of them are some whose stories we have not related to thee; and no apostle might ever bring a sign except by the permission of Allah; but when Allah's bidding came it was decided with truth, and there were those lost who deemed it vain!

Allah it is who has made for you cattle, that ye may ride on some of them;—and of them ye eat, [80] and ye have in them advantages;—and that ye may attain thereon a want which is in your breasts; upon them and upon ships are ye borne.

He shows you His signs; which sign then of your Lord do ye deny?

Have they not journeyed on in the land and seen how was the end of those before them, who were more numerous than they and stronger in might, and in their vestiges which are still in the land? but of no avail to them was that which they had earned.

And when there came to them their apostles with manifest signs they rejoiced in what knowledge they had; but there closed in upon them that whereat they had mocked.

And when they saw our violence they said, 'We believe in Allah alone, and we disbelieve in what we once associated with Him.'

[85] But their faith was of no avail to them when they saw our violence—the course of Allah with His servants in time past, and there the misbelievers lose!

THE CHAPTER 'DETAILED'

XLI (*Mecca*)

In the name of the merciful and compassionate Allah.

'H. M. A revelation from the merciful, the compassionate; a book whose signs are detailed; an Arabic Qur'ân for a people who do know; a herald of glad tidings and a warning. But most of them turn aside and do not hear, and say, 'Our hearts are veiled from what thou dost call us to, and in our ears is dulness, and between us and thee there is a veil. Act thou; verily, we are acting too!' [5] Say, 'I am but a mortal like yourselves, I am inspired that your Allah is one Allah; then go straight to Him, and ask forgiveness of Him; and woe to the idolaters, who give not alms, and in the hereafter disbelieve!'

Verily, those who believe and do right, for them is a hire that is not grudged.

Say, 'What! do ye really misbelieve in Him who created the earth in two days, and do ye make peers for Him?—that is the Lord of the worlds!'

And He placed thereon¹ firm mountains above it and blessed it, and apportioned therein its foods in four days alike for those who ask. [10] Then He made for the heaven and it was but smoke, and He said to it and to the earth, 'Come, ye two, whether ye will or no!' They said, 'We come willingly!'

And He decreed them seven heavens in two days, and inspired every heaven with its bidding: and we adorned the lower heaven with lamps and guardian angels; that is the decree of the mighty, the knowing One.

But if they turn aside, then say, 'I have warned you of a thunderclap like the thunderclap of 'Âd and Thamûd; when their apostles came to them from before them and from behind them (saying), "Serve ye none but Allah." ' They said, 'If our Lord pleased He would send down angels; so we in what ye are sent with disbelieve.'

And as for 'Âd, they were big with pride in the land, without right, and said, 'Who is stronger than us in might?' Did they not see that Allah who created them He was stronger than they in might? But they did gainsay our signs. [15] And we sent upon them a cold blast in unfortunate days, that we might make them taste the torment of disgrace in the life of this world;—but the torment of the hereafter is more disgraceful, and they shall not be helped.

And as for Thamûd we guided them; but they preferred blindness to guidance, and the thunderclap of the torment of abasement caught them for what they had earned; but we saved those who believed and who did fear.

And the day when the enemies of Allah shall be gathered together into the Fire, marshalled along; until when they come to it, their hearing and their eyesight and their skins shall bear witness against them of that which they have done. [20] And they shall say to their skins, 'Why have ye borne witness against us?' They shall say, 'Allah gave us speech who has given speech to everything; He created you at first, and unto Him shall ye be returned; and ye could not conceal yourselves that your hearing and your eyesight should not be witness against you, nor your skins; but ye thought that Allah did not know much of what ye do. And that thought of yours which ye thought concerning your Lord has destroyed you, and ye have now become of those who lose!'

And if they are patient, still the Fire is a resort for them; and if they ask for favour again, they shall not be taken into favour.

We will allot to them mates,[2] for they have made seemly to them what was before them and what was behind them; and due against them was the sentence on the nations who passed away before them; both of jinns and of mankind; verily, they were the losers!

[25] Those who misbelieve say, 'Listen not to this Qur'ân, but talk foolishly about it, haply ye may gain the upper hand.'[3] But we will make those who misbelieve taste keen torment; and we will recompense them with the worst of that which they have done. That is, the

recompense of the enemies of Allah,—the Fire! for them is an eternal abode therein: a recompence for that they did gainsay our signs.

And those who misbelieved say, 'Our Lord, show us those who have led us astray amongst the jinns and mankind; we will place them beneath our feet, and they shall both be amongst those who are put down!' [30] Verily, those who say, 'Our Lord is Allah,' and then go straight, the angels descend upon them—'Fear not and be not grieved, but receive the glad tidings of Paradise which ye were promised; we are your patrons in the life of this world and in the next, and ye shall have therein what your souls desire, and ye shall have therein what ye call for,—an entertainment from the forgiving, the merciful!'

And who speaks better than he who calls to Allah and does right, and says, 'Verily, I am of those resigned'?

Good and evil shall not be deemed alike; repel (evil) with what is best, and lo! He between whom and thyself was enmity is as though he were a warm patron. [35] But none shall meet with it save those who are patient; and none shall meet with it save those who are endowed with mighty good fortune.

And if an incitement from the devil incites you, then seek refuge in Allah; verily, He both hears and knows.

And of His signs are the night and the day, and the sun and the moon. Adore ye not the sun, neither the moon; but adore Allah who created you, if it be Him ye serve.

But if they be too big with pride—yet those who are with thy Lord celebrate His praises by night and day, and they are never weary.

And of His signs (is this), that thou mayest see the earth drooping, and when we send down water upon it it stirs and swells; verily, He who quickens it will surely quicken the dead; verily, He is mighty over all.

[40] Verily, those who are inclined to oppose our signs are not hidden from us. Is he who is cast into the Fire better, or he who comes safe on the resurrection day? Do what ye will: verily, He on what ye do doth look.

Verily, those who misbelieve in the reminder when it comes to them—and, verily, it is a glorious Book! Falsehood shall not come to it, from before it, nor from behind it—a revelation from the wise, the praise worthy One. Naught is said to thee but what was said to the apostles before thee, 'Verily, thy Lord is Lord of forgiveness and Lord of grievous torment!'

And had we made it a foreign Qur'ân, they would have said, 'Unless its signs be detailed. . . . What! foreign and Arabic?'4 Say, 'It is, for those who believe, a guidance and a healing. But those who believe not, in their ears is dulness, and it is blindness to them; these are called to from a far-off place.'

[45] And we gave Moses the Book, and it was disputed about; but had it not been for thy Lord's word already passed it would have been decided between them, for, verily, they were in hesitating doubt thereon.

Whoso does right it is for his soul, and whoso does evil it is against it, for thy Lord is not unjust towards His servants.

To Him is referred the knowledge of the Hour: and no fruits come forth from their husks, and no female conceives, or is delivered, save with His knowledge.

And the day when He shall call to them, 'Where are the partners ye did join with me?' they shall say, 'We do own to thee there is no witness amongst us!' and that on which they used to call before shall stray away from them, and they shall think there is no escape for them. Man is never tired of praying for good, but if evil touch him, then he is despairing and hopeless.

[50] But if we make him taste mercy from us after distress has touched him he will surely say, 'This is for me, and I do not think the Hour is imminent; and if I be brought back to my Lord, verily, I shall surely have good with Him;'⁵ but we will inform those who misbelieve of what they have done, and we will surely make them taste wretched torment.

And when we have been gracious to man, he turns away and goes aside; but when evil touches him he is one of copious prayer.

Say, 'Let us see now! if it be from Allah and ye disbelieve in it, who is more in error than he who is in a remote schism?'

We will show them our signs in the regions and in themselves, until it is plain to them that it is the truth. Is it not enough for thy Lord that He is witness over all? Ay, verily, they are in doubt about the meeting of their Lord! Ay, verily, He encompasses all!

THE CHAPTER OF COUNSEL

XLII (*Mecca*)

In the name of the merciful and compassionate Allah.

'H. M. 'H. S. Q. Thus does Allah, the mighty, the wise, inspire thee and those before thee.

His is what is in the heavens and what is in the earth, and He is the high, the mighty!

The heavens well-nigh cleave asunder from above them; and the angels celebrate the praises of their Lord, and ask forgiveness for those who are on the earth. Ay, verily, Allah, He is the forgiving and merciful! but those who take beside Him patrons, Allah watches over them, and thou hast not charge over them.

[5] Thus have we revealed an Arabic Qur'ân, that thou mayest warn the Mother of cities¹ and all around it; and warn them of a day of gathering, there is no doubt therein;—a part in Paradise and a part in the blaze.

But had Allah pleased He would have made them one nation; but He makes whom He will enter into His mercy; and the unjust have neither patron nor help. Do they take other patrons besides Him, when Allah He is the patron, and He quickens the dead and He is mighty over all?

But whatsoever ye dispute about, the judgement of it is Allah's. There is Allah for you!—my Lord! upon Him do I rely, and unto Him I turn repentant. The originator of the heavens and the earth, He has made for you from yourselves wives; and of the cattle mates; producing you thereby. There is naught like Him, for He both hears and sees.

[10] His are the keys of the heavens and the earth, He extends provision to whom He will, or doles it out; verily, He knows everything.

He has enjoined upon you for religion what He prescribed to Noah and what we inspired thee with, and what we inspired Abraham and Moses and Jesus,—to be steadfast in religion, and not to part into sects therein—a great thing to the idolaters is that which ye call them to! Allah elects for Himself whom He pleases and guides unto Himself him who turns repentant.

But they did not part into sects until after the knowledge had come to them, through mutual envy; and had it not been for thy Lord's word already passed for an appointed time, it would surely have been decided between them; but, verily, those who have been given the Book as an inheritance after them, are in hesitating doubt concerning it.

Wherefore call thou, and go straight on as thou art bidden, and follow not their lusts; and say, 'I believe in the Book which Allah has sent down; and I am bidden to judge justly between you. Allah is our Lord and your Lord; we have our works and ye have your works; there is no argument between us and you. Allah will assemble us together and unto Him the journey is.'

[15] But those who argue about Allah after it has been assented to,² their arguments shall be rebutted before their Lord; and upon them shall be wrath, and for them shall be keen torment.

Allah it is who has sent down the Book with truth, and the balance;[3] and what shall make thee know whether haply the Hour be nigh? Those who believe not would hurry it on; and those who believe shrink with terror at it and know that it is true. Ay, verily, those who dispute concerning the Hour are in remote error!

Allah is kind to His servants; He provides whom He will, and He is the mighty, the glorious.

He who wishes for the tilth of the next world, we will increase for him the tilth; and he who desires the tilth of this world, we will give him thereof: but in the next he shall have no portion.

[20] Have they associates who have enjoined any religion on them which Allah permits not?—But were it not for the word of decision[4] it would have been decreed to them. Verily, the unjust,—for them is grievous woe. Thou shalt see the unjust shrink with terror from what they have gained as it falls upon them; and those who believe and do right, in meads of Paradise, they shall have what they please with their Lord;—that is great grace!

That is what Allah gives glad tidings of to His servants who believe and do righteous acts.

Say, 'I do not ask for it a hire—only the love of my kinsfolk.' And he who gains a good action we will increase good for him thereby; verily, Allah is forgiving and grateful!

Or will they say he has forged against Allah a lie? But if Allah pleased He could set a seal upon thy heart; but Allah will blot out falsehood and verify truth by His word; verily, He knows the nature of men's breasts!

He it is who accepts repentance from His servants and pardons their offences and knows that which ye do. [25] And He answers the prayer of those who believe and do right, and gives them increase of His grace; but the misbelievers,—for them is keen torment.

And if Allah were to extend provision to His servants they would be wanton in the earth. But He sends down by measure what He pleases; verily, of His servants He is well aware and sees.

He it is who sends down the rain after they have despaired; and disperses His mercy, for He is the praiseworthy patron.

And of His signs is the creation of the heavens and the earth, and what He hath spread abroad therein of beasts; and He is able to collect them when He will.

And what misfortunes befall you it is for what your hands have earned; but He pardons much; [30] yet ye cannot make Him helpless in the earth, nor have ye, besides Allah, either a patron or a helper.

And of His signs are the ships that sail like mountains in the sea. If He will, He calms the wind, and they become motionless on the back thereof: verily, in that are signs to every patient, grateful person:—or He makes them founder for what they have earned; but He pardons much. But let those who wrangle about our signs know that they shall have no escape!

And whatever ye are given it is but a provision of the life of this world; but what is with Allah is better and more lasting for those who believe and who upon their Lord rely, [35] and those who avoid great sins and abominations, and who when they are wroth forgive, and who assent to their Lord, and are steadfast in prayer, and whose affairs go by counsel amongst themselves, and who of what we have bestowed on them give alms, and who, when wrong befalls them, help themselves.

For the recompence of evil is evil like unto it; but he who pardons and does well, then his reward is with Allah; verily, He loves not the unjust. And he who helps himself after he has been wronged, for these—there is no way against them. [40] The way is only against those who wrong men and are wanton in the earth without right; these—for them is grievous woe.

But surely he who is patient and forgives,—verily, that is a determined affair.[5]

But whomsoever Allah leads astray he has no patron after Him; and thou mayest see the unjust when they see the torment say, 'Is there no way to avert this?'[6] and thou mayest see them exposed to it, humbled with abasement, looking with a stealthy glance. And those who believe shall say, 'Verily, the losers are they who have lost themselves and their families upon the resurrection day!' Ay, verily, the unjust are in lasting torment!

[45] And they shall have no patrons to help them beside Allah, and whomsoever Allah leads astray, there is no way for him.

Assent to your Lord before the day comes of which there is no averting from Allah; there is no refuge for you on that day; and for you there is no denial.

But if they turn aside, we have not sent thee to them as a guardian, thou hast only thy message to preach.

And, verily, when we have made man taste of mercy from us he rejoices therein; but if there befall them an evil for what their hands have done before—then, verily, man is ungrateful!

Allah's is the kingdom of the heavens and the earth, He creates what He pleases, He grants to whom He pleases females, and He grants to whom He pleases males, or He gives them in pairs, males and females; and He makes whom He pleases barren; verily, He is knowing, powerful!

[50] It is not for any mortal that Allah should speak to him, except by inspiration, or from behind a veil, or by sending an apostle and inspiring, by His permission, what He pleases; verily, He is high and wise!

And thus have we inspired thee by a spirit[7] at our bidding; thou didst not know what the Book was, nor the faith: but we made it a light whereby we guide whom we will of our servants. And, verily, thou shalt surely be guided into the right way,—the way of Allah, whose is what is in the heavens and what is in the earth. Ay, to Allah affairs do tend!

THE CHAPTER OF GILDING

XLIII (*Mecca*)

In the name of the merciful and compassionate Allah.

'H. M. By the perspicuous Book, verily, we have made it an Arabic Qur'ân; haply ye will have some sense. And it is in the Mother of the Book with us,—high and wise.[1]

Shall we then push aside from you the Reminder, because ye are a people who are extravagant?

[5] How many prophets have we sent amongst those of yore? And there never came to them a prophet but they did mock at him; then we destroyed them—more valiant than these;[2] and the example of those of yore passed away.

And if thou shouldst ask them who created the heavens and the earth, they will surely say, 'The mighty, the knowing One created them', who made for you the earth a couch and placed for you therein roads, haply ye may be guided: [10] and who sent down from the heaven water in due measure; and we raised up thereby a dead country; thus shall ye too be brought forth; and who has created all species; and has made for you the ships and the cattle whereon to ride that ye may settle yourselves on their backs; then remember the favour of your Lord when ye settled thereon, and say, 'Celebrated be the praises of Him who hath subjected this to us! We could not have got this ourselves; and, verily, unto our Lord shall we return!'

Yet they make for Him of His servants offspring; verily, man is surely obviously ungrateful.

[15] Has He taken of what He creates daughters, and chosen sons for you?

Yet when the tidings[3] are given any one of that which he strikes out as a similitude for the Merciful One, his face grows black and he is choked. What! one brought up amongst ornaments, and who is always in contention without obvious cause?[4]

And have they made the angels, who are the servants of the Merciful Ones, females? Were they witnesses of their creation? Their witness shall be written down, and they shall be questioned; and they say, 'Had the Merciful pleased we should never have worshipped them.' They have no knowledge of that, they only conjecture.

[20] Have we given them a book[5] before it to which they might hold?

Nay; they say, 'We found our fathers (agreed) upon a religion, and, verily, we are guided by their traces.'

Thus, too, did we never send before thee to a city any warner, but the affluent ones thereof said, 'Verily, we found our fathers (agreed) upon a religion, and, verily, we are led by their traces.'

Say, 'What! if I come to you with what is a better guide than what ye found your fathers agreed upon?' and they will say, 'Verily, we in what ye are sent with disbelieve!'

Then we took vengeance on them, and see how was the end of those who called the (apostles) liars.

[25] When Abraham said to his father and his people, 'Verily, I am clear of all that ye serve, except Him who created me; for, verily, He will guide me:' and he made it a word remaining among his posterity, that haply they might return.

Nay; but I let these (Meccans) and their fathers have enjoyment until the truth came to them, and an apostle. And when the truth came to them they said, 'This is magic, and we therein do disbelieve!' [30] And they say, 'Unless this Qur'ân were sent down to a man great in the two cities. . . .'[6]

Is it they who distribute the mercy of thy Lord? We distribute amongst them their livelihood in the life of this world, and we exalt some of them above others in degrees, that some may take others into subjection; but the mercy of thy Lord is better than that which they amass.

And but that men would then have been one nation, we would have made for those who misbelieve in the Merciful One roofs of silver for their houses, and steps up thereto which they might mount; and to their houses doors, and bedsteads on which they might recline; and gilding,—for, verily, all that is a provision of the life of this world, but the hereafter is better with thy Lord for those who fear!

[35] And whosoever turns from the reminder of the Merciful One, we will chain to him a devil, who shall be his mate; and, verily, these shall turn them from the path while they reckon that they are guided; until when he comes to us he shall say, 'O, would that between me and thee there were the distance of the two orients,[7] for an evil mate (art thou)!' But it shall not avail you on that day, since ye were unjust; verily, in the torment shall ye share!

What! canst thou make the deaf to hear, or guide the blind, or him who is in obvious error?

[40] Whether then we take thee off we will surely take vengeance on them; or whether we show thee that which we have promised them; for, verily, we have power over them.

Say, 'Dost thou hold to what is inspired thee?' Verily, thou art in the right way, and, verily, it is a reminder to thee and to thy people, but in the end they shall be asked.

And ask those whom we have sent before thee amongst the prophets, 'Did we make gods beside the Merciful One for them to serve?'

[45] We did send Moses with our signs to Pharaoh and

his chiefs, and he said, 'Verily, I am the apostle of the Lord of the worlds; but when he came to them with our signs, lo, they laughed at them!'

And we did not show them a sign, but it was greater than its fellow; and we seized them with the torment, haply they might turn.

And they said, 'O thou magician! pray for us to thy Lord, as He has engaged with thee: verily, we are guided.'

And when we removed from them the torment, behold they broke their word.

[50] And Pharaoh proclaimed amongst his people; said he, 'O my people! is not the kingdom of Egypt mine? and these rivers that flow beneath me? What! can ye then not see? Am I better than this fellow, who is contemptible, who can hardly explain himself?[8] Unless then bracelets of gold be cast upon him, or there come with him angels as his mates . . .!'

And he taught his people levity; and they obeyed him: verily, they were an abominable people.

[55] And when they had annoyed us we took vengeance on them, and we drowned them all together, and we made them a precedent and an example to those after them.

And when the son of Mary was set forth as a parable, behold thy people turned away from him and said, 'Are our gods better, or is he?' They did not set it forth to thee save for wrangling. Nay, but they are a contentious people.[9]

He is but a servant whom we have been gracious to, and we have made him an example for the children of Israel. [60] And if we please we can make of you angels in the earth to succeed you.[10] And, verily, he is a sign of the Hour.[11] Doubt not then concerning it, but follow this right way; and let not the devil turn you away; verily, he is to you an open foe!

And when Jesus came with manifest signs he said, 'I am come to you with wisdom, and I will explain to you something of that whereon ye did dispute, then fear Allah, obey me; verily, Allah, He is my Lord and your Lord, serve Him then, this is the right way.'

[65] But the confederates disputed amongst themselves; and woe to those who are unjust from the torment of a grievous day!

Do they expect aught but that the Hour will come upon them suddenly while they do not perceive? Friends on that day shall be foes to each other, save those who fear.

O my servants! there is no fear for you on that day; nor shall ye be grieved who believe in our signs and who are resigned. [70] Enter ye into Paradise, ye and your wives, happy!

Dishes of gold and pitchers shall be sent round to them; therein is what souls desire, and eyes shall be delighted, and ye therein shall dwell for aye; for that is Paradise which ye are given as an inheritance for that which ye have done. Therein shall ye have much fruit whereof to eat.

Verily, the sinners are in the torment of Hell to dwell for aye. [75] It shall not be intermitted for them, and they therein shall be confused. We have not wronged them, but it was themselves they wronged.

And they shall cry out, 'O Mâlik![12] let thy lord make an

end of us'; he shall say, 'Verily, ye are to tarry here.'

We have brought you the truth, but most of you are averse from the truth. Have they arranged the affair? then will we arrange it too![13]

[80] Or do they reckon that we did not hear their secrets and their whispering? Nay, but our messengers are with them writing down.[14]

Say, 'If the Merciful One has a son then am I the first to worship him. Celebrated be the praise of the Lord of the heavens and the earth! the Lord of the throne, above all they attribute to Him!'

But leave them to ponder and to play until they meet that day of theirs which they are promised.

He it is who is in the heaven a Allah and in the earth a Allah! and He is the wise, the knowing. [85] And blessed be he whose is the kingdom of the heavens and the earth, and what is between both, and His is the knowledge of the Hour, and unto Him shall ye be brought back!

And those they call on beside Him shall not possess intercession except those only who bear witness for the truth and who do know.

And if thou shouldst ask them who created them they shall surely say, 'Allah!' How then can they lie?

And what he[15] says, 'O Lord, verily, these are a people who do not believe; shun them then and say, "Peace!" for they at length shall know!'

THE CHAPTER OF SMOKE

XLIV (*Mecca*)

In the name of the merciful and compassionate Allah.

'H. M. By the perspicuous Book! verily, we have sent it down on a blessed night;—verily, we had given warning—wherein is decided every wise affair, as an order from us. Verily, we were sending (apostles)— [5] a mercy from thy Lord; verily, He both hears and knows: from the Lord of the heavens and the earth and what is between the two, if ye were but sure. There is no god but He, He quickens and He kills—your Lord and the Lord of your fathers of yore! Nay, they in doubt do play!

But expect thou the day when the heaven shall bring obvious smoke [10] to cover men—this is grievous torment!

Our Lord! remove from us the torment; verily, we are believers.

How can they have the reminder (now), when they have had a plain apostle, and when they turned their backs away from him and said, 'Taught! Mad!' Verily, we will remove the torment a little, (but) ye will surely return!

[15] On the day when we will assault with the great assault, verily, we will take vengeance.

And we already tried the people of Pharaoh when there came to them a noble apostle: 'Send back to me Allah's servants; verily, I am to you a faithful apostle'; and, 'Exalt not yourselves above Allah; verily, I come to you with obvious authority. And, verily, I seek refuge in my Lord and your Lord, that ye stone me not. [20] And if ye believe not in me then let me alone!'

Then he called upon his Lord, 'Verily, these are a sinful people.' So journey with my servants by night—verily, ye will be pursued. But leave the sea in quiet—verily, they are a host to be drowned! How many gardens and springs have they left, [25] and corn lands and a noble place, and comfort wherein they did enjoy themselves!

Thus—and we gave them for an inheritance to another people. And the heaven wept not for them, nor the earth, nor were they respited.

But we saved the children of Israel from shameful woe!—[30]—from Pharaoh; verily, he was haughty, one of the extravagant! And we did choose them, wittingly, above the worlds; and we gave them signs wherein was an obvious trial!

Verily, these[1] say, 'It is but our first death,[2] so bring our fathers, if ye do speak the truth!'

[35] Are they better than the people of Tubbâ'h,[3] and those before them? We destroyed them—verily, they were sinners!

Nor did we create the heavens and the earth, and what is between the two in sport: we did but create them in truth, though most of them know it not!

[40] Verily, the day of separation is their appointed term; the day when master shall not avail client at all, nor shall they be helped; save whomsoever Allah shall have mercy on; verily, He is the mighty, the merciful!

Verily, the Zaqqûm tree (shall be) the food of the sinful: [45] as it were melting,[4] shall it boil in their bellies like the boiling of hot water!—'Take him and hale him into the midst of Hell! Then pour over his head the torment of hot water!—Taste! Verily, thou art the mighty, the honourable! [50] Verily, this is that whereon ye did dispute!'

Verily, the pious shall be in a safe place! in gardens and springs, they shall be clad in satin and stout silk face to face. Thus!—and we will wed them to bright and large-eyed maids! [55] They shall call therein for every fruit in safety. They shall not taste therein of death save their first death, and we will keep them from the torment of Hell! Grace from the Lord, that is the grand bliss!

And we have only made it easy for thy tongue, that haply they may be mindful. Then watch thou; verily, they are watching too!

THE CHAPTER OF THE KNEELING

XLV (*Mecca*)

In the name of the merciful and compassionate Allah.

'H. M. A revelation of the Book from Allah, the mighty, the wise. Verily, in the heavens and the earth are signs to those who believe; and in your creation and the beasts that are spread abroad are signs to a people who are sure; and in the alternation of night and day, and the provision that Allah has sent down from heaven and quickened thereby the earth after its death, and in the veering of the winds are signs unto a people who have sense.

[5] These are the signs of Allah which we recite to thee

in truth; and in what new story after Allah and His signs will they believe?

Woe to every sinful liar who hears Allah's signs sent to him, then persists in being big with pride as though he heard them not—so give him the glad tidings of grievous woe—and when he knows something of our signs takes them for a jest! These,—for them is shameful woe, behind them is Hell, and what they have earned shall not avail them aught, nor what they have taken besides Allah for patrons; and for them is mighty woe.

[10] This is a guidance, and those who misbelieve in the signs of their Lord, for them is torment of a grievous plague.

Allah it is who subjects to you the sea that the ships may sail thereon at his bidding, and that ye may crave of His grace, and that haply ye may give thanks; and He has subjected to you what is in the heavens and what is in the earth,—all from Him; verily, in that are signs unto a people who reflect.

Say to those who believe that they pardon those who hope not for Allah's days,[1] that He may reward a people for that which they have earned.

Whosoever acts aright it is for his own soul, and whosoever does evil is against it; then unto your Lord shall ye be returned.

[15] And we did bring the children of Israel the Book and judgement and prophecy, and we provided them with good things, and preferred them above the worlds. And we brought them manifest proofs of the affair, and they disputed not until after knowledge had come to them,

through mutual envy. Verily, thy Lord will decide between them on the resurrection day concerning that whereon they did dispute.

Then we did set thee[2] over a law concerning the affair: follow it then, and follow not the lusts of those who do not know. Verily, they shall not avail thee against Allah at all; and, verily, the wrongdoers are patrons of each other, but Allah is the patron of those who fear.

This is an insight for men and a guidance and a mercy to a people who are sure.

[20] Do those who commit evil deeds count that we will make them like those who believe and work righteous deeds, equal in their life and their death?—ill it is they judge.

And Allah created the heavens and the earth in truth; and every soul shall be recompensed for that which it has earned, and they shall not be wronged.

Hast thou considered him who takes his lusts for his god, and Allah leads him astray wittingly, and has set a seal upon his hearing and his heart, and has placed upon his eyesight dimness? Who then shall guide him after Allah? Will they not then mind?

They say, 'It is only our life in this world, we die and we live, and naught destroys us but time!' But they have no knowledge of this; they do but suspect.

And when our signs are rehearsed to them with evidences their only argument is to say, 'Bring our fathers, if ye speak the truth.'

[25] Say, 'Allah quickens you, then He kills you, then He will gather you unto the resurrection day, there is no

doubt therein; but most men do not know.'

Allah's is the kingdom of the heavens and the earth, and on the day when the Hour shall arise on that day shall those who call it³ vain be losers! And thou shalt see each nation kneeling, each nation summoned to its Book, 'To-day are ye rewarded for that which ye have done.'

This is our Book that speaketh to you with truth; verily, we have written down what ye have done.

But as to those who believe and do righteous deeds their Lord will make them enter into His mercy: that is the obvious bliss.

[30] And as for those who misbelieve,—were not my signs recited to you and ye were too big with pride and ye were a sinful people? And when it was said, 'Verily, the promise of Allah is true, and the Hour there is no doubt therein'; ye said, 'We know not what the Hour is, we only suspect, and we are not sure.'

But there shall appear to them the evils of what they have done, and that shall encompass them at which they have been mocking. And it shall be said, 'Today will we forget you as ye forgot the meeting of this day of yours, and your resort shall be the Fire, and ye shall have no helpers. That is because ye took the signs of Allah for a jest and the life of this world deceived you; wherefore to-day ye shall not be brought forth therefrom, neither shall ye be taken back into favour.'

[35] Allah's then is the praise, the Lord of the heavens and the Lord of the earth, the Lord of the worlds! His is the grandeur in the heavens and the earth, and He is the mighty and the wise!

THE CHAPTER OF EL A'HQÂF[1]

XLVI (*Mecca*)

In the name of the merciful and compassionate Allah.

'H. M. The revelation of the Book from Allah the mighty, the wise.

We have only created the heavens and the earth and what is between the two in truth and for an appointed time; but those who misbelieve from being warned do turn aside.

Say, 'Have ye considered what ye call on beside Allah?' Show me what they have created of the earth?' or have they share in the heavens? Bring me a book before this or a vestige of knowledge, if ye do tell the truth!

But who is more in error than he who calls beside Allah on what will never answer him until the resurrection day and who are heedless of their calling, [5] and when men are gathered together are enemies of theirs and do deny their service?

And when our evident signs are recited to them, those who misbelieve say of the truth when it comes to them, 'This is obvious magic.'

Or do they say, 'He has forged it?' Say, 'If I have forged ye cannot obtain for me aught from Allah; He knows best what ye utter concerning it; He is witness enough between me and you, and He is the forgiving, the merciful.'

Say, 'I am not an innovator among the apostles; nor do I know what will be done with me or with you if I follow aught but what I am inspired with; nor am I aught but a plain warner.'

Say, 'Have ye considered, if it is from Allah and ye have disbelieved therein, and a witness from the children of Israel testifies to the conformity of it, and he believes while ye are too big with pride? Verily, Allah guides not the unjust people.'

[10] And those who misbelieve say of those who believe, 'If it had been good, they would not have been beforehand with us therein'; and when they are not guided thereby, then will they say, 'This is an old-fashioned lie.'

But before it was the Book of Moses, a model and a mercy; and this is a book confirming it in Arabic language, to warn those who do wrong and as glad tidings to those who do well.

Verily, those who say, 'Our Lord is Allah', and then keep straight, there is no fear for them, and they shall not be grieved. These are the fellows of Paradise to dwell therein for aye, a recompence for that which they have done.

We have prescribed for man kindness towards his parents. His mother bore him with trouble and brought him forth with trouble; and the bearing of him and the weaning of him is thirty months; until, when he reaches puberty, and reaches forty years, he says, 'Lord! stir me up that I may be thankful for thy favours wherewith thou hast favoured me and my parents; and that I may do right to please Thee; and make it right for me in my offspring; verily, I turn repentant unto Thee, and, verily, I am of those resigned.'

[15] There are those from whom we accept the best of what they have done, and we pass over their offences—

amongst the fellows of Paradise; the promise of truth which they have been promised.

But he who says to his parents, 'Fie upon you! Do ye promise me that I shall be brought forth² when generations have passed away before me?'—then shall they both cry to Allah for help. Woe to thee! Believe! Verily, the promise of Allah is true. Then says he, 'This is but old folks' tales.'

There are those against whom the sentence was due amongst the nations who have passed away before them of jinns and men; verily, they have been the losers; and for all are degrees of what they have done, so that He may repay them their works, and they shall not be wronged.

And the day when those who misbelieve shall be exposed to the Fire: 'Ye made away with your good things in your worldly life, and ye enjoyed them; wherefore to-day shall ye be rewarded with the torment of disgrace, for that ye were big with pride in the earth without the right, and for that ye did abomination.'

[20] Remember too the brother of 'Âd³ when he warned his people at El A'hqâf,—though warners have passed away before him and after him,—'Serve not other than Allah; verily, I fear for you the torment of a mighty day!'

They said, 'Hast thou come to us to turn us from our gods? Then bring us what thou dost threaten us with, if thou art of those who speak the truth!' Said he, 'Knowledge is only with Allah: but I will preach to you that which I am sent with, though I see you are a people who are ignorant.' And when they saw a traversing cloud approaching their valleys they said, 'This is a cloud to give us rain.' 'Nay, but it is what ye sought to hasten on—a wind in which is grievous torment; it will destroy everything at the order of its Lord!' And in the morning naught was seen save their dwellings. Thus do we reward the sinful people!

[25] We had established them in what we have established you,[4] and we made for them hearing and eyesight and hearts; but neither their hearing nor their eyesight nor their hearts availed them aught, since they did gainsay the signs of Allah, and that encompassed them whereat they had mocked.

And we destroyed the cities that are around you:—and we turned about the signs that haply they might return.

Why did not those help them, whom beside Allah they took for gods that could draw nigh to Him? Nay! they strayed away from them; for that was their lie and what they had forged.

And when we turned towards thee some of the jinn listening to the Qur'ân, and when they were present at (the reading of) it, they said, 'Be silent!' and when it was over they turned back to their people, warning them.

Said they, 'O our people! verily, we have heard a book sent down after Moses, verifying what came before it, guiding to the truth, and unto the right way. [30] O our people! respond to Allah's crier and believe in Him, and He will pardon you your sins and will deliver you from grievous woe.'

And whoso responds not to Allah's crier shall not frustrate Him in the earth, and shall not have any patrons beside Him:—these are in obvious error!

Did they not see that Allah who created the heavens and the earth, and was not wearied with creating them, is able to quicken the dead?—nay, verily, He is mighty over all!

And the day when those who misbelieve shall be exposed to the Fire,—'Is not this the truth?' they shall say, 'Yea, by our Lord!' He shall say, 'Then taste the torment for that ye did misbelieve!'

Then do thou[5] be patient, as the apostles endowed with a purpose were patient, and hasten not on (their punishment). It shall be to them, on the day they see what they are threatened with, as though they [35] had tarried but an hour of the day. A preaching this! Shall any perish but the people who work abomination?

THE CHAPTER OF MOHAMMED, ALSO CALLED FIGHT

XLVII (*Medina*)

In the name of the merciful and compassionate Allah.

Those who misbelieve and turn folk from Allah's way, He will make their works go wrong. But those who believe and do right and believe in what is revealed to Mohammed,—and it is the truth from their Lord,—He will cover for them their offences and set right their mind.

That is because those who misbelieve follow falsehood, and those who believe follow the truth from their Lord. Thus does Allah set forth for men their parables.

And when ye meet those who misbelieve—then striking off heads until ye have massacred them, and bind fast the bonds!

[5] Then either a free grant (of liberty) or a ransom until the war shall have laid down its burdens. That!—but if Allah please He would conquer them—but (it is) that He may try some of you by the others. And those who are slain in Allah's cause, their works shall not go wrong; He will guide them and set right their mind; and will make them enter into Paradise which He has told them of.

O ye who believe! if ye help Allah, He will help you, and will make firm your footsteps.

But as for those who misbelieve—confound them! and He will make their works go wrong.

[10] That is because they were averse from what Allah has revealed; but their works shall be void!

Have they not journeyed through the land and seen how was the end of those before them? Allah destroyed them; and for the misbelievers is the like thereof.

That is because Allah is the patron of those who believe, and because the misbelievers have no patron.

Verily, Allah causes those who believe and do right to enter into gardens beneath which rivers flow; but those who misbelieve enjoy themselves and eat as the cattle eat; but the Fire is the resort for them!

How many a city, stronger than thy city which has driven thee out, have we destroyed, and there was none to help them!

[15] Is he who rests upon a manifest sign from his Lord

like him, the evil of whose works is made seemly to him, and who follow their lusts?

The similitude of Paradise which is promised to the pious,—in it are rivers of water without corruption, and rivers of milk, the taste whereof changes not, and rivers of wine delicious to those who drink; and rivers of honey clarified; and there shall they have all kinds of fruit and forgiveness from their Lord! (Is that) like him who dwells in the Fire for aye? And who are given to drink boiling water that shall rend their bowels asunder?

Some of them there are who listen to thee, until when they go forth from thee they say to those who have been given the knowledge,[1] 'What is this which he says now?' These are those on whose hearts Allah has set a stamp and who follow their lusts.

But those who are guided, He guides them the more, and gives them the due of their piety.

[20] Do they wait for aught but the Hour, that it should come to them suddenly? The conditions thereof have come already; how, when it has come on them, can they have their reminder?

Know thou that there is no god but Allah; and ask pardon for thy sin and for the believers, men and women; for Allah knows your return and your resort!

Those who misbelieve say, 'Why has not a surah been revealed?' But when a decisive surah is revealed and fighting is mentioned therein, thou mayest see those in whose heart is sickness looking towards thee with the look of one fainting in death. Preferable for them were obedience and a reasonable speech! But when the matter is determined on, then if they believed Allah it were better for them.

Would ye perhaps, if ye had turned back, have done evil in the land and severed the bonds of kinship?

[25] It is these whom Allah has cursed, and has made them deaf, and has blinded their eyesight! Do they not peruse the Qur'ân? or are there locks upon their hearts?

Verily, those who turn their backs after the guidance that has been manifested to them—Satan induces them, but (Allah) lets them go on for a time!

That is for that they say to those who are averse from what Allah has revealed, 'We will obey you in part of the affair!' but Allah knows their secrets! How will it be when the angels² take their souls, smiting their faces and their backs?

[30] This is because they follow what angers Allah and are averse from His goodwill; and their works are void.

Do those in whose hearts is sickness reckon that Allah will not bring their malice forth?

But did we please we would show thee them, and thou shouldst know them by their cognizances. But thou shalt know them by their distorting their speech, and Allah knows their works!

But we will try you until we know those among you who fight strenuously and the patient; and we will try the reports concerning you.

Verily, those who misbelieve and turn folks off Allah's path, and break with the Apostle after the guidance that has been manifested to them, cannot harm Allah at all, and their works shall be void!

[35] O ye who believe! obey Allah, and obey the

Apostle; and make not your works vain.

Verily, those who misbelieve and turn folks off Allah's path, and then die misbelievers, Allah will not pardon them.

Then faint not, nor cry for peace while ye have the upper hand; for Allah is with you and will not cheat you of your works!

The life of this world is but a play and a sport; but if ye believe and fear Allah, He will give you your hire.

He does not ask you for (all) your property; if He were to ask you for it and to press you, ye would be niggardly, and he would bring your malice out.

[40] Here are ye called upon to expend in Allah's cause, and among you are some who are niggardly; and he who is niggardly is but niggardly against his own soul: but Allah is rich and ye are poor, and if ye turn your backs He will substitute another people in your stead, then they will not be like you.

THE CHAPTER OF VICTORY

XLVIII (*Medina*)

In the name of the merciful and compassionate Allah.

Verily, we have given thee an obvious victory! that Allah may pardon thee thy former and later sin,[1] and may fulfil His favour upon thee, and guide thee in a right way, and that Allah may help thee with a mighty help.

It is He who sent down His *shechina*[2] into the hearts of the believers that they might have faith added to their faith;—and Allah's are the hosts of the heavens and the earth, and Allah is knowing, wise—[5] to make the believers, men and women, enter into gardens beneath which rivers flow, to dwell therein for aye; and to cover for them their offences; for that with Allah is a grand bliss: and to torment the hypocrites, men and women, and the idolaters, men and women, who think evil thoughts of Allah;—over them is a turn of evil fortune, and Allah will be wroth with them and curse them, and has prepared for them Hell, and an evil journey shall it be!

Allah's are the hosts of the heavens and the earth, and Allah is mighty, wise!

Verily, we have sent thee as a witness, and a herald of glad tidings, and a warner;—that ye may believe in Allah and His Apostle, and may aid Him and revere Him and celebrate His praises morning and evening!

[10] Verily, those who swear allegiance to thee do but swear allegiance to Allah;—Allah's hand is above their hands! and whoso perjures himself does but perjure himself against himself; but he who fulfils what he has covenanted with Allah, Allah shall bring him mighty hire.

The desert Arabs who were left behind³ shall say, 'Our wealth and our people occupied us; ask pardon then for us!'—they speak with their tongues what is not in their hearts!

Say, 'Who can control for you aught from Allah, if He wish you harm or wish you advantage?' Nay, Allah of what ye do is well aware!

Nay, ye thought that the Apostle and the believers would not ever return again to their families; that was made seemly in your hearts! and ye thought evil thoughts, and ye were a corrupt people.

Whoso believes not in Allah and His Apostle—we have prepared for the unbelievers a blaze!

Allah's is the kingdom of the heavens and of the earth. He pardons whom He pleases, and torments whom He pleases; and Allah is forgiving, merciful.

[15] Those who were left behind[4] shall say when ye have gone forth to spoils that ye may take, 'Let us follow you'; they wish to change Allah's words. Say, 'Ye shall by no means follow us; thus did Allah say before!'

They will say, 'Nay! but ye envy us!' Nay! they did not understand save a little.

Say to those desert Arabs who were left behind, 'Ye shall be called out against a people endowed with vehement valour,[5] and shall fight them or they shall become Muslims. And if ye obey, Allah will give you a good hire; but if ye turn your backs, as ye turned your backs before, He will torment you with grievous woe!'

There is no compulsion on the blind, and no compulsion on the lame, and no compulsion on the sick, but whoso obeys Allah and His Apostle, He will make him enter gardens beneath which rivers flow; but whoso turns his back He will torment with grievous woe.

Allah was well pleased with the believers when they did swear allegiance to thee beneath the tree;[6] and He knew what was in their hearts, and He sent down His *shechina*[7] upon them and rewarded them with a victory nigh at hand,[8] and many spoils for them to take; for Allah is mighty, wise!

[20] Allah promised you many spoils and hastened this on for you, and restrained men's hands from you; and it may be a sign for the believers and guide you in a right way;—and other (spoils) which ye could not gain; but Allah has encompassed them; for Allah is mighty over all.

And had those who misbelieved fought you, they would have turned their backs; then they would have found neither patron nor helper!—Allah's course which has been followed before, and thou shalt find no change in the course of Allah!

He it was who restrained their hands from you, and your hands from them in the mid valley of Mecca[9] after He had given you the victory over them; for Allah on what ye do doth look!

[25] Those who misbelieved and turned (you) away from the Sacred Mosque, and (turned away) the offering, kept from arriving at its destined place;[10] and had it not been for believing men and believing women whom ye knew not, whom ye might have trampled on, and so a crime might have occurred to you on their account without your knowledge—that Allah may make whomsoever He pleases enter into His mercy. Had they been distinct from one another, we would have tormented those of them who misbelieved with grievous woe.

When those who misbelieved put in their hearts pique—the pique of ignorance[11]—and Allah sent down His *shechina* upon His Apostle and upon the believers, and obliged them to keep to the word of piety,[12] and they were most worthy of it and most suited for it; for Allah all things doth know.

Allah truly verified for His Apostle the vision[13] that ye shall verily enter the Sacred Mosque, if Allah please, in safety with shaven heads or cut hair, ye shall not fear; for He knows what ye know not, and He has set for you, beside that, a victory nigh at hand.[14]

He it is who sent His Apostle with guidance and the religion of truth to set it above all religion; for Allah is witness enough!

Mohammed is the Apostle of Allah, and those who are with Him are vehement against the misbelievers,—compassionate amongst themselves; thou mayest see them bowing down, adoring, craving grace from Allah and His goodwill,—their marks are in their faces from the effects of adoration;—that is their similitude in the law[15] and their similitude in the gospel; as a seedling puts forth its sprouts and strengthens it, and grows stout, and straightens itself upon its stem, delighting the sower!—that the misbelievers may be angry at them;—Allah has promised those of them who believe and do right—forgiveness and a mighty hire.

THE CHAPTER OF THE INNER CHAMBERS

XLIX (Medina)

In the name of the merciful and compassionate Allah.

O ye who believe! do not anticipate Allah and His Apostle, but fear Allah; verily, Allah both hears and knows.

O ye who believe! raise not your voices above the voice

of the prophet, and do not speak loud to him as ye speak loud to one another,¹ lest your works become vain, while ye do not perceive.

Verily, those who lower their voice before the Apostle of Allah, they are those whose hearts Allah has proved for piety, for them is forgiveness and a mighty hire.

Verily, those who cry out to thee from behind the inner chambers,² most of them have no sense; [5] but did they wait until thou come out to them, it were better for them;—but Allah is forgiving, merciful.

O ye who believe! if there come to you a sinner with an information, then discriminate, lest ye fall upon a people in ignorance and on the morrow repent of what ye have done.³

And know that among you is the Apostle of Allah; if he should obey you in many a matter ye would commit a sin;⁴ Allah has made faith beloved by you, and has made it seemly in your hearts, and has made misbelief and iniquity and rebellion hateful to you.—These are the rightly directed—grace from Allah and favour! and Allah is knowing, wise.

And if the two parties of the believers quarrel,⁵ then make peace between them; and if one of the twain outrages the other, then fight the party that has committed the outrage until it return to Allah's bidding; and if it do return then make peace between them with equity, and be just; verily, Allah loves the just.

[10] The believers are but brothers, so make peace between your two brethren and fear Allah, haply ye may obtain mercy!

O ye who believe! let not one class ridicule another who are perchance better than they; nor let women ridicule other women who are perchance better than they; and do not defame each other, nor call each other bad names—an ill name is iniquity after faith![6]

O ye who believe! carefully avoid suspicion; verily, some suspicion is a sin. And do not play the spy, nor backbite each other; would one of you like to eat his dead brother's flesh?—why! ye would abhor it! Then fear Allah; verily, Allah is relentant, compassionate.

O ye folk! verily, we have created you of male and female, and made you races and tribes that ye may know each other.

Verily, the most honourable of you in the sight of Allah is the most pious of you; verily, Allah is knowing, aware!

The desert Arabs say, 'We believe.' Say, 'Ye do not believe; but say, "We have become Muslims"; for the faith has not entered into your hearts: but if ye obey Allah and His Apostle He will not defraud you of your works at all: verily, Allah is forgiving, compassionate!'

[15] The believers are only those who believe in Allah and His Apostle, and then doubt not, but fight strenuously with their wealth and persons in Allah's cause—these are the truth tellers!

Say, 'Will ye teach Allah your religion?' when Allah knows what is in the heavens and what is in the earth, and Allah all things doth know!

They deem that they oblige thee by becoming Muslims. Say, 'Nay! deem not that ye oblige me by your becoming

Muslims! Allah obliges you, by directing you to the faith, if ye do speak the truth!'

Verily, Allah knows the unseen things of the heavens and the earth, and Allah on what ye do doth look.

THE CHAPTER OF Q.

L (*Mecca*)

In the name of the merciful and compassionate Allah.

Q. By the glorious Qur'ân! nay, they wonder that there has come to them a warner from amongst themselves; and the misbelievers say, 'This is a wondrous thing! What, when we are dead and have become dust?—that is a remote return!'

We well know what the earth consumes of them, for with us is a book that keeps (account).

[5] Nay, they call the truth a lie when it comes to them, and they are in a confused affair.[1]

Do not they behold the heaven above them, how we have built it and adorned it, and how it has no flaws?

And the earth, we have stretched it out and thrown thereon firm mountains, and caused to grow thereon every beautiful kind.

An insight and a reminder to every servant who repents!

And we sent down from the heaven water as a blessing, and caused to grow therewith gardens and the harvest grain!

[10] And the tall palm trees having piled up spathes, for a provision to (our) servants; and we quickened thereby

a dead land; thus shall the resurrection be!

Before them the people of Noah and the fellows of ar Rass² and Thamûd and ʿÂd and Pharaoh called the apostles liars; and the brethren of Lot and the fellows of the Grove³ and the people of Tubbâ'h⁴ all called the prophets liars, and the threat was duly executed.

Were we then fatigued with the first creation? Nay! but they are in obscurity concerning the new creation.

[15] But we created man, and we know what his soul whispers; for we are nigher to him than his jugular vein!

When the two meeters meet,⁵ sitting the one on the right and the other on the left, not a word does he utter, but a watcher is by him ready!

And the agony of death shall come in truth!—'that is what thou didst shun!'

And the trumpet shall be blown!—that is the threatened day!

[20] And every soul shall come—with it a driver and a witness!

'Thou wert heedless of this, and we withdrew thy veil from thee, and today is thine eyesight keen!'⁶

And his mate shall say, 'This is what is ready for me (to attest).

'Throw into Hell every stubborn misbeliever!⁷—who forbids good, a transgressor, a doubter! [25] who sets other gods with Allah—and throw him, ye twain, into fierce torment!'

His mate shall say, 'Our Lord! I seduced him not, but he was in a remote error.'

He shall say, 'Wrangle not before me; for I sent the

threat to you before. The sentence is not changed with me, nor am I unjust to my servants.'

On the day we will say to Hell, 'Art thou full?' and it will say, 'Are there any more?'

[30] And Paradise shall be brought near to the pious, —not far off.

This is what ye are promised, to every one who turns frequently (to Allah) and keeps His commandments: who fears the Merciful in secret and brings a repentant heart.

'Enter into it in peace: this is the day of eternity!'

They shall have what they wish therein, and increase from us!

[35] How many a generation have we destroyed before them, mightier than they in prowess!

Pass through the land, is there any refuge?⁸ Verily, in that is a reminder to whomsoever has a heart, or gives ear, and is a witness thereto.

We did create the heavens and the earth and what is between the two in six days, and no weariness touched us.⁹

Be thou patient then of what they say, and celebrate the praises of thy Lord before the rising of the sun and before the setting. And through (some) of the night celebrate His praise and the additional adorations.¹⁰

[40] And listen for the day when the crier shall cry from a near place;¹¹—the day when they shall hear the shout¹² in truth—that is the day of coming forth!

Verily, we quicken and we kill, and unto us the journey is!

On the day when the earth shall be cleft asunder from them swiftly;—that is a gathering together which is easy to us!

We know what they say; nor art thou over them one to compel.

[45] Wherefore remind, by the Qur'ân, him who fears the threat.

THE CHAPTER OF THE SCATTERERS

LI (*Mecca*)

In the name of the merciful and compassionate Allah.

By the scatterers[1] who scatter! and by those pregnant[2] with their burden! and by those running on[3] easily! and by the distributors[4] of affairs!—[5] verily, what ye are threatened with is surely true!

And, verily, the judgement will surely take place!

By the heaven possessed of paths; verily, ye are at variance in what ye say!

He is turned from it who is turned.

[10] Slain be the liars, who are heedless in a flood (of ignorance).

They will ask, 'When is the day of judgement?' The day when at the Fire they shall be tried.—'Taste your trial! This is what ye wished to hasten on!'

[15] Verily, the pious are in gardens and springs, taking what their Lord brings them. Verily, they before that did well. But little of the night they slept; and at the dawn

they asked forgiveness. And in their wealth was what was due to him who asked, and him who was kept back from asking.

[20] And in the earth are signs to those who are sure, and in yourselves,—what! do ye not then see?

And in the heaven is your provision and that which ye are promised.[5]

But by the Lord of the heaven and the earth! verily, it is the truth,—like that which ye do utter![6]

Has the tale of Abraham's honoured guests reached thee?[7] [25] When they entered in unto him and said, 'Peace!' he said, 'Peace—a people unrecognized.'

And he went aside unto his people and fetched a fat calf, and brought it nigh unto them; said he, 'Will ye then not eat?'

And he felt a secret fear of them: said they, 'Fear not.' And they gave him glad tidings of a knowing boy.

And his wife approached with a noise, and smote her face, and said, 'An old woman, barren!'

[30] Said they, 'Thus says thy Lord, He is knowing, wise.' Said he, 'And about what is your errand, O ye messengers?'

They said, 'Verily, we are sent unto a sinful people, to send upon them stones of clay, marked from thy Lord for the extravagant.'[8]

[35] And we sent out therefrom such as were in it of the believers; but we only found therein one house of Muslims.

And we left therein a sign to those who fear the grievous woe.

And in Moses; when we sent him to Pharaoh with obvious authority.

But he turned his back towards his column,⁹ and said, 'A sorcerer or mad!'

[40] And we seized him and his hosts and hurled them into the sea; for he was to be blamed.

And in 'Âd, when we sent against them a desolating wind, that left naught on which it came without making it ashes!

And in Thamûd, when it was said to them, 'Enjoy yourselves for a season.' But they revolted against the bidding of their Lord; and the noise caught them as they looked on. [45] And they could not stand upright, and they were not helped!

And the people of Noah of yore; verily, they were an abominable people.

And the heaven—we have built it with might, and, verily, we do surely give it ample space!

And the earth—we have spread it out; and how well we lay it out!

And of everything have we created pairs, haply ye may be mindful.

[50] Flee then to Allah; verily, I am a plain warner from Him to you!

And do not set with Allah another god; verily, I am a plain warner from Him to you!

Thus there came no apostle to those before them, but they said, 'A sorcerer, mad!

Do they bequeath it¹⁰ to each other?

Yea, they are an outrageous people!

So turn thy back upon them, so thou wilt not be to blame.

[55] And remind; for, verily, the reminder shall profit the believers.

And I have not created the jinn and mankind save that they may worship me.

I do not desire any provision from them, and I do not wish them to feed me.

Verily, Allah, He is the provider, endowed with steady might.

Verily, for those who injure (the Apostle) shall be a portion like the portion of their fellows,¹¹ but let them not hurry Me!

[60] Then woe to those who misbelieve from their day which they are threatened.

THE CHAPTER OF THE MOUNT

LII (*Mecca*)

In the name of the merciful and compassionate Allah.

By the mount! by the Book inscribed upon an outstretched vellum! by the frequented house!¹ [5] by the elevated roof!² by the swelling sea! verily, the torment of thy Lord will come to pass;—there is none to avert it!

The day when the heavens shall reel about, [10] and the mountains shall move about,—then woe upon that day to those who call (the apostles) liars, who plunge into discussion for a sport!

On the day when they shall be thrust away into the Fire of Hell,—'This is the Fire, the which ye used to call a lie!—[15] Is it magic, this? or can ye not see?—broil ye therein, and be patient thereof or be not patient, it is the same to you: ye are but rewarded for that which ye did do!'

Verily, the pious (shall be) in gardens and pleasure, enjoying what their Lord has given them; for their Lord will save them from the torment of Hell.

'Eat and drink with good digestion, for that which ye have done!'

[20] Reclining on couches in rows; and we will wed them to large-eyed maids.

And those who believe and whose seed follows them in the faith, we will unite their seed with them; and we will not cheat them of their work at all;—every man is pledged for what he earns.³

And we will extend to them fruit and flesh such as they like. They shall pass to and fro therein a cup in which is neither folly nor sin.

And round them shall go boys of theirs, as though they were hidden pearls.

[25] And they shall accost each other and ask questions, and shall say, 'Verily, we were before amidst our families shrinking with terror,⁴ but Allah has been gracious to us and saved us from the torment of the hot blast.

'Verily, we used to call on Him before; verily, He is the righteous, the compassionate!'

Wherefore do thou⁵ remind them: for thou art, by the favour of thy Lord, neither a soothsayer nor mad!

Will they say, 'A poet; we wait for him the sad accidents of fate?'

[30] Say, 'Wait ye then; for I too am of those who wait!'

Do their dreams bid them this? or are they an outrageous people?

Or will they say, 'He has invented it?'—nay, but they do not believe!

But let them bring a discourse like it, if they tell the truth!

[35] Or were they created of nothing, or were they the creators? Or did they create the heavens and the earth?—nay, but they are not sure!

Or have they the treasures of thy Lord? or are they the governors supreme?

Or have they a ladder whereon they can listen?[6]—then let their listener bring obvious authority.

Has He daughters, while ye have sons?

[40] Or dost thou ask them a hire, while they are borne down by debt?

Or have they the unseen, so that they write it down?

Or do they desire a plot?—but those who misbelieve it is who are plotted against!

Or have they a god beside Allah? Celebrated be Allah's praises above what they join with Him!

But if they should see a fragment of the sky falling down, they would say, 'Clouds in masses!'

[45] But leave them till they meet that day of theirs whereon they shall swoon;[7] the day when their plotting shall avail them naught, and they shall not be helped!

And, verily, there is a torment beside that[8] for those

who do wrong; but most of them do not know!

But wait thou patiently for the judgement of thy Lord, for thou art in our eyes. And celebrate the praises of thy Lord what time thou risest, and in the night, and at the fading of the stars!

THE CHAPTER OF THE STAR

LIII (*Mecca*)

In the name of the merciful and compassionate Allah.

By the star when it falls, your comrade errs not, nor is he deluded! nor speaks he out of lust! It is but an inspiration inspired! [5] One mighty in power[1] taught him, endowed with sound understanding, and appeared, he being in the loftiest tract.

Then drew he near and hovered o'er! until he was two bows' length off or nigher still! [10] Then he inspired his servant what he inspired him; the heart belies not what he saw! What, will ye dispute with him on what he saw?

And he saw him another time, by the lote tree none may pass; [15] near which is the garden of the Abode! When there covered the lote tree what did cover it! The sight swerved not nor wandered. He saw then the greatest of the signs of his Lord.

Have ye considered Allât and Al 'Huzzâ, [20] and Manât the other third?[2] Shall there be male offspring for Him and female for you? That were an unfair division! They are but names which ye have named, ye and your fathers!

Allah has sent down no authority for them! They do but follow suspicion and what their souls lust after!—And yet there has come to them guidance from their Lord.

Shall man have what he desires? [25] But Allah's is the hereafter and the present!

How many an angel in the heaven!—their intercession avails not at all, save after Allah has given permission to whomsoever He will and is pleased with!

Verily, those who believe not in the hereafter do surely name after Allah the angels with female names!—but they have no knowledge thereof; they do but follow suspicion, and, verily, suspicion shall not avail against the truth at all!

[30] But turn aside from him who turns his back upon our remembrance and desires naught but this world's life! This is their sum of knowledge; verily, thy Lord knows best who has erred from His way, and He knows best who is guided!

Allah's is what is in the heavens and what is in the earth, that He may reward those who do evil for what they have done; and may reward those who do good with good! Those who shun great sins and iniquities,—all but venial faults,—verily, thy Lord is of ample forgiveness; He knows best about you, when He produced you from the earth, and when ye were embryos in the wombs of your mothers.

Make not yourselves out, then, to be pure; He knows best who it is that fears.

Hast thou considered him who turns his back? who gives but little [35] and then stops?³ Has he then the knowledge of the unseen, so that he can see?

Has he not been informed of what is in the pages of Moses and Abraham who fulfilled his word?—that no burdened soul shall bear the burden of another? [40] and that man shall have only that for which he strives; and that his striving shall at length be seen? Then shall he be rewarded for it with the most full reward; and that unto thy Lord is the limit; [45] and that it is He who makes men laugh and weep; and that it is He who kills and makes alive; and that He created pairs, male and female, from a clot when it is emitted; and that for Him is the next production;⁴ and that he enriches and gives possession; [50] and that He is the Lord of the Dog Star,⁵ and that He it was who destroyed 'Âd of yore, and Thamûd, and left none of them; and the people of Noah before them,—verily, they were most unjust and outrageous!

And the overthrown (cities)⁶ He threw down; [55] and there covered them what did cover them!

Which then of your Lord's benefits do ye dispute?

This is a warner, one of the warners of yore!

The approaching day approaches; there is none to discover it but Allah.

At this new discourse then do ye wonder? [60] and do ye laugh and not weep? and ye divert yourselves the while!

But adore Allah and serve (Him).⁷

THE CHAPTER OF THE MOON

LIV (*Mecca*)

In the name of the merciful and compassionate Allah.

The Hour draws nigh, and the moon is split asunder.[1] But if they see a sign they turn aside and say, 'Magic, continuous!'[2]

And they call it a lie and follow their lusts; but every matter is settled!

There has come to them some information[3] with restraint in it—[5] wisdom far-reaching—but warners avail not!

But turn thy back on them!

The day when the caller[4] shall call to an awkward thing.[5]

Humbly casting down their looks shall they come forth from their graves, as though they were locusts scattered abroad!

Hurrying forwards to the caller! the misbelievers shall say, 'This is a difficult day!'

Noah's people before them called (the apostles) liars; they called our servant a liar; and they said, 'Mad!' and he was rejected.

[10] And he called upon his Lord, 'Verily, I am overcome, come then to my help!'

And we opened the gates of heaven with water pouring down!

And we made the earth burst forth in springs, and the waters met at a bidding already decreed.

But we bore him on the thing of planks and nails; sailing on beneath our eyes, a reward for him who had been disbelieved!

[15] And we left it a sign;—but is there any one who will mind?

'Âd called the apostles liars, and how was my punishment and my warning?

Verily, we sent on them a cold storm wind on a day of continuous ill luck!

[20] It reft men away as though they had been palm stumps torn up!

We have made the Qur'ân easy as a reminder—but is there any one who will mind?

Thamûd called the warnings lies, and said, 'A mortal, one of us, alone, shall we follow him? Then indeed were we in error and excitement!⁶

[25] 'Is the warning cast on him alone among us? Nay, he is an insolent liar!

'They shall know tomorrow about the insolent liar!

'Verily, we are about to send the she-camel as a trial for them, then watch them and have patience! and inform them that the water is shared between them (and her); each draught shall be sought by turns.'

Then they called their companion, and he plied (a knife) and hamstrung her.

[30] Then how was my punishment and my warning? Verily, we sent against them one noise, and they were like the dry sticks of him who builds a fold.

We have made the Qur'ân easy as a reminder—but is there any one who will mind?

Lot's people called the apostles liars; verily, we sent against them a heavy sandstorm; all, save Lot's family, we saved them at the dawn. [35] As a favour from us; so do we reward him who gives thanks!

He indeed had warned them of our assault, but they doubted of the warning.

And they desired his guest, and we put out their eyes.—

'So taste ye my torment and warning!'

And there overtook them on the morning a settled punishment!—

'So taste ye my torment and warning!'

[40] We have made the Qur'ân easy as a reminder—but is there any one who will mind?

The warning came to Pharaoh's people; they called our signs all lies, and we seized on them with the seizing of a mighty powerful one.

Are your misbelievers better than they? or have ye an exemption in the Scriptures? Or do they say we are a victorious company?

[45] The whole shall be routed and shall turn their backs in flight.[7]

Nay, the Hour is their promised time! and the Hour is most severe and bitter!

Verily, the sinners are in error and excitement. On the day when they shall be dragged to the Fire upon their faces!—'Taste ye the touch of Hell.'

Verily, everything have we created by decree, [50] and our bidding is but one (word), like the twinkling of an eye!

We have destroyed the like of you—but is there any who will mind?

And everything they do is in the books,[8] and everything small and great is written down.

Verily, the pious shall be amid gardens and rivers, [55] in the seat of truth, with the powerful king.

THE CHAPTER OF THE MERCIFUL

LV (*Mecca*)

In the name of the merciful and compassionate Allah.
The Merciful taught the Qur'ân;
He created man, taught him plain speech.
The sun and the moon have their appointed time;
[5] The herbs and the trees adore;
And the heavens, He raised them and set the balance, that
    ye should not be outrageous in the balance;
But weigh ye aright, and stint not the balance.
And the earth He has set it for living creatures;
    [10] therein are fruits and palms, with sheaths; and
    grain with chaff and frequent shoots;
Then which of your Lord's bounties will ye twain deny?
He created men of crackling clay like the potters.
And He created the jinn from smokeless fire.
[15] Then which of your Lord's bounties will ye twain
    deny?
The Lord of the two easts[1] and the Lord of the two wests!
Then which of your Lord's bounties will ye twain deny?
He has let loose the two seas that meet together;
    [20] between them is a barrier they cannot pass!

Then which of your Lord's bounties will ye twain deny?

He brings forth from each pearls both large and small!

Then which of your Lord's bounties will ye twain deny?

His are the ships which rear aloft in the sea like mountains.

[25] Then which of your Lord's bounties will ye twain deny?

Every one upon it² is transient, but the face of thy Lord endowed with majesty and honour shall endure.

Then which of your Lord's bounties will ye twain deny?

Of Him whosoever is in the heaven and the earth does beg; every day He is in (some fresh) business!

[30] Then which of your Lord's bounties will ye twain deny?

We shall be at leisure for you, O ye two weighty ones!³

Then which of your Lord's bounties will ye twain deny?

O assembly of jinns and mankind! If ye are able to pass through the confines of heaven and earth then pass through them!—ye cannot pass through save by authority!

Then which of your Lord's bounties will ye twain deny?

[35] There shall be sent against you a flash of fire, and molten copper, and ye shall not be helped!

Then which of your Lord's bounties will ye twain deny?

And when the heaven is rent asunder and become rosy red⁴—(melting) like grease!

Then which of your Lord's bounties will ye twain deny?

On that day neither man nor jinn shall be asked about his crime!

[40] Then which of your Lord's bounties will ye twain deny?

The sinners shall be known by their marks, and shall be
    seized by the forelock and the feet!
Then which of your Lord's bounties will ye twain deny?
'This is Hell, which the sinners did call a lie! They shall
    circulate between it and water boiling quite!'
[45] Then which of your Lord's bounties will ye twain
    deny?
But for him who fears the station of his Lord are gardens
    twain!
Then which of your Lord's bounties will ye twain deny?
Both furnished with branching trees.
Then which of your Lord's bounties will ye twain deny?
[50] In each are flowing springs.
Then which of your Lord's bounties will ye twain deny?
In each are, of every fruit, two kinds.
Then which of your Lord's bounties will ye twain deny?
Reclining on beds the linings of which are of brocade,
    and the fruit of the two gardens within reach to cull.
[55] Then which of your Lord's bounties will ye twain
    deny?
Therein are maids of modest glances whom no man nor
    jinn has deflowered before.
Then which of your Lord's bounties will ye twain deny?
As though they were rubies and pearls.
Then which of your Lord's bounties will ye twain deny?
[60] Is the reward of goodness aught but goodness? Then
    which of your Lord's bounties will ye twain deny?
And besides these, are gardens twain,[5]
Then which of your Lord's bounties will ye twain deny?
With dark green foliage.

[65] Then which of your Lord's bounties will ye twain
deny?

In each two gushing springs.

Then which of your Lord's bounties will ye twain deny?

In each fruit and palms and pomegranates.

Then which of your Lord's bounties will ye twain deny?

[70] In them maidens best and fairest!

Then which of your Lord's bounties will ye twain deny?

Bright and large-eyed maids kept in their tents.

Then which of your Lord's bounties will ye twain deny?

Whom no man nor jinn has deflowered before them.

[75] Then which of your Lord's bounties will ye twain
deny?

Reclining on green cushions and beautiful carpets.

Then which of your Lord's bounties will ye twain deny?

Blessed be the name of thy Lord possessed of majesty and
honour!

THE CHAPTER OF THE INEVITABLE

LVI (*Mecca*)

In the name of the merciful and compassionate Allah.

When the inevitable[1] happens; none shall call its
happening a lie!—abasing—exalting!

When the earth shall quake, quaking! [5] and the
mountains shall crumble, crumbling, and become like
motes dispersed!

And ye shall be three sorts;

And the fellows of the right hand—what right lucky
    fellows!
And the fellows of the left hand—what unlucky fellows!
[10] And the foremost foremost![2]
These are they who are brought nigh,
In gardens of pleasure!
A crowd of those of yore,
And a few of those of the latter day!
[15] And gold-weft couches, reclining on them face to face.
Around them shall go eternal youths, with goblets and
    ewers and a cup of flowing wine; no headache shall
    they feel therefrom, nor shall their wits be dimmed!
[20] And fruits such as they deem the best;
And flesh of fowl as they desire;
And bright and large-eyed maids like hidden pearls;
A reward for that which they have done!
They shall hear no folly there and no sin;
[25] Only the speech, 'Peace, Peace!'
And the fellows of the right—what right lucky fellows!
Amid thornless lote trees.
And tal'h[3] trees with piles of fruit;
And outspread shade,
[30] And water outpoured;
And fruit in aboundance, neither failing nor forbidden;
And beds upraised!
Verily, we have produced them[4] a production.
[35] And made them virgins, darlings of equal age (with
    their spouses) for the fellows of the right!
A crowd of those of yore, and a crowd of those of the
    latter day!

[40] And the fellows of the left—what unlucky fellows!
In hot blasts and boiling water;
And a shade of pitchy smoke,
Neither cool nor generous!

Verily, they were affluent ere this, [45] and did persist in
mighty crime; and used to say, 'What, when we die and
have become dust and bones, shall we then indeed be
raised? or our fathers of yore?'

Say, 'Verily, those of yore and those of the latter day
[50] shall surely be gathered together unto the tryst of
the well-known day.'

Then ye, O ye who err! who say it is a lie! shall eat of the
Zaqqûm tree! and fill your bellies with it! and drink
thereon of boiling water! [55] and drink as drinks the
thirsty camel.

This is their entertainment on the judgement day!
We created you, then why do ye not credit?
Have ye considered what ye emit?
Do ye create it, or are we the creators?

[60] We have decreed amongst you death; but we are not
forestalled from making the likes of you in exchange,
or producing you as ye know not of.

Ye do know the first production—why then do ye not
mind?

Have ye considered what ye till?
Do ye make it bear seed, or do we make it bear seed?

[65] If we pleased we could make it mere grit, so that ye
would pause to marvel:

'Verily, we have got into debt⁵ and we are excluded.'⁶
Have ye considered the water which ye drink?

Do ye make it come down from the clouds, or do we make it come down?

If we pleased we could make it pungent—why then do ye not give thanks?

[70] Have ye considered the fire which ye strike?

Do ye produce the tree that gives it,[7] or do we produce it?

We have made it a memorial and a chattel for the traveller of the waste!

Then celebrate the grand name of thy Lord!

So I will not swear by the positions of the stars; [75] and, verily, it is a grand oath if ye did but know— that, verily, this is the honourable Qur'ân—in the laid-up Book!

Let none touch it but the purified!

A revelation from the Lord of the worlds.

[80] What! this new discourse will ye despise?

And make for your provision, that you call it a lie?

Why then—when it[8] comes up to the throat, and ye at that time look on, though we are nearer to him than you are, but ye cannot see,—[85] why, if ye are not to be judged, do ye not send it back, if ye do tell the truth?

But either, if he be of those brought nigh to Allah,—then rest and fragrance and the garden of pleasure!

Or, if he be of the fellows of the right! [90] then 'Peace to thee!' from the fellows of the right!

Or, if he be of those who say it is a lie,—who err! then an entertainment of boiling water! and broiling in Hell!

[95] Verily, this is surely certain truth!

So celebrate the grand name of thy Lord!

THE CHAPTER OF IRON

LVII (*Mecca*)

In the name of the merciful and compassionate Allah.

Whatever is in the heavens and the earth celebrates the praises of Allah, for He is the mighty, the wise!

His is the kingdom of the heavens and the earth: He quickens and He kills, and He is mighty over all!

He is the first and the last; and the outer and the inner; and He all things doth know!

He it is who created the heavens and the earth in six days, then He made for the throne; and He knows what goes into the earth and what goes forth therefrom, and what comes down from the sky and what goes up therein, and He is with you wheresoe'er ye be: for Allah on what ye do doth look!

[5] His is the kingdom of the heavens and the earth, and unto Allah affairs return. He makes the night succeed the day, and makes the day succeed the night; and He knows the nature of men's breasts.

Believe in Allah and His Apostle, and give alms of what He has made you successors of. For those amongst you who believe and give alms—for them is mighty hire.

What ails you that ye do not believe in Allah and His Apostle? He calls on you to believe in your Lord; and He has taken a compact from you, if ye be believers.

He it is who sends down upon His servants manifest signs, to bring you forth from the darkness into the light; for, verily, Allah to you is kind, compassionate!

[10] What ails you that ye give not alms in Allah's cause? for Allah's is the inheritance of the heavens and the earth. Not alike amongst you is he who gives alms before the victory and fights,—they are grander in rank than those who give alms afterwards and fight. But to all does Allah promise good; and Allah of what ye do is well aware!

Who is there who will lend a good loan to Allah? for He will double it for him, and for him is a generous reward.

On the day when thou shalt see believers, men and women, with their light running on before them and on their right hand,[1]—'Glad tidings for you today.—Gardens beneath which rivers flow, to dwell therein for aye; that is the grand bliss!'

On the day when the hypocrites, men and women, shall say to those who believe, 'Wait for us that we kindle at your light.' It will be said, 'Get ye back, and beg a light.' And there shall be struck out between them a wall with a door; within it shall be mercy, and outside before it torment. They shall cry out to them, 'We were not with you!' They shall say, 'Yea, but ye did tempt yourselves, and did wait, and did doubt; and your vain hopes beguiled you; and the beguiler beguiled you about Allah.

'Wherefore today there shall not be taken from you a ransom, nor from those who misbelieved. Your resort is the Fire; it is your sovereign, and an ill journey will it be!'

[15] Is the time come to those who believe, for their hearts to be humbled at the remembrance of Allah, and of what He has sent down in truth? And for them not to be like those who were given the Scriptures before, and

over whom time was prolonged, but their hearts grew hard, and many of them were workers of abomination?

Know that Allah quickens the earth after its death!—we have manifested to you the signs; haply ye may have some sense!

Verily, those who give in charity, men and women, who have lent to Allah a goodly loan,—it shall be doubled for them, and for them is a generous hire.

And those who believe in Allah and His Apostle, they are the confessors and the martyrs with their Lord; for them is their hire and their light! But those who misbelieve and call our signs lies, they are the fellows of Hell!

Know that the life of this world is but a sport, and a play, and an adornment, and something to boast of amongst yourselves; and the multiplying of children is like a rain growth, its vegetation pleases the misbelievers; then they wither away, and thou mayest see them become yellow; then they become but grit.

But in the hereafter is a severe woe, [20] and forgiveness from Allah and His goodwill; but the life of this world is but a chattel of guile.

Race towards forgiveness from your Lord and Paradise, whose breadth is as the breadth of the heavens and the earth, prepared for those who believe in Allah and His apostles! And Allah's grace, He gives it to whom He pleases, for Allah is Lord of mighty grace!

No accident befalls in the earth, or in yourselves, but it was in the Book, before we created them; verily, that is easy unto Allah.

That ye may not vex yourselves for what ye miss, nor

be overjoyed at what He gives you; for Allah loves no arrogant boasters, who are niggardly and bid men be niggardly: but whoso turns his back,[2] verily, Allah is rich, praiseworthy.

[25] We did send our apostles with manifest signs; and we did send down among you the Book and the balance, that men might stand by justice; and we sent down iron in which is both keen violence and advantages to men; and that Allah might know who helps Him and His apostles in secret; verily, Allah is strong and mighty!

And we sent Noah and Abraham; and placed in their seed prophecy and the Book; and some of them are guided, though many of them are workers of abomination!

Then we followed up their footsteps with our apostles; and we followed them up with Jesus the son of Mary; and we gave him the gospel; and we placed in the hearts of those who followed him kindness and compassion.—But monkery, they invented it; we only prescribed to them the craving after the goodwill of Allah, and they observed it not with due observance. But we gave to those who believe amongst them their hire; though many amongst them were workers of abomination!

O ye who believe! fear Allah, and believe in His Apostle: He will give you two portions of His mercy, and will make for you a light for you to walk in, and will forgive you; for Allah is forgiving, compassionate.

That the people of the Book may know that they cannot control aught of Allah's grace; and that grace is in Allah's hands, He gives it to whom He will; for Allah is Lord of mighty grace!

THE CHAPTER OF THE WRANGLER

LVIII (*Medina*)

Allah had heard the speech of her who wrangled with you about her husband,¹ and complained to Allah; and Allah hears your gossip; verily, Allah both hears and sees.

Those among you who back out of their wives² they are not their mothers: their mothers are only those who gave them birth; and, verily, they speak a wrong speech and false.

Verily, Allah both pardons and forgives. But those who back out of their wives and then would recall their speech,—then the manumission of a captive before they touch each other; that is what ye are admonished, and Allah of what ye do is well aware!

[5] But he who finds not (the means):—then a fast for two months consecutively, before they touch each other; and he who cannot endure that:—then the feeding of sixty poor folk. That is that ye may believe in Allah and His Apostle; and these are the bounds of Allah; and for the misbelievers is grievous woe!

Verily, those who oppose Allah and His Apostle shall be upset, as those before them were upset.

We have sent down manifest signs: for the misbelievers is shameful woe on the day when Allah shall raise them all together, and shall inform them of what they have done. Allah has taken account of it, but they forget it; for Allah is witness over all!

Dost thou not see that Allah knows what is in the

heavens and what is in the earth? And that there cannot be a privy discourse of three but He makes the fourth? nor of five but He makes the sixth? nor less than that nor more, but that He is with them wheresoe'er they be? Then He will inform them of what they have done upon the resurrection day; verily, Allah all things doth know!

Dost thou not look at those who were prohibited from privy talk, and then returned to that they were forbidden? And they too discourse together with sin and enmity and rebellion against the Apostle; and when they come to thee they greet thee with what Allah greets thee not;[3] and they say in themselves, Why does not Allah torment us for what we say? Hell is enough for them! They shall broil therein, and an ill journey shall it be!

[10] O ye who believe! when ye discourse together, then discourse not in sin and enmity and rebellion against the Apostle; but discourse together in righteousness and piety; and fear Allah, for unto Him ye shall be gathered!

Privy talk is only from the devil, and those who do believe may grieve: it cannot hurt them at all, except by the permission of Allah: and upon Allah let the believers rely.

O ye who believe! when it is said to you, 'Make room in your assemblies', then make room; Allah will make room for you; and when it is said to you, 'Rise up', then rise up; Allah will raise all you who believe, as well as those who are given knowledge, in rank; for Allah of what ye do is well aware!

O ye who believe! when ye address the Apostle, then give in charity before addressing him; that is better for you, and more pure. But if ye find not the means,—then

Allah is forgiving, compassionate. What! do ye shrink from giving in charity before addressing him? Then if ye do it not, and Allah relents towards you, then be steadfast in prayer, and give alms, and fear Allah and His Apostle; for Allah is well aware of what ye do!

[15] Dost thou not look at those who take for patrons a people[4] Allah is wrath with? They are neither of you nor of them, and they swear to you a lie the while they know; for them Allah has prepared severe torment; verily, evil is it they have done!

They take their faith for a cloak; and they turn men aside from the path of Allah; and for them is shameful woe!

Their wealth shall not avail them, nor their children at all, against Allah; they are the fellows of the Fire, and they shall dwell therein for aye!

On the day when Allah raises them all together, then will they swear to Him as they swore to you; and they will think that they rest on somewhat.—Ay, verily, they are liars!

[20] Satan hath overridden them, and made them forget the remembrance of Allah: they are the crew of Satan; ay, the crew of Satan, they are the losers!

Verily, those who oppose Allah and His Apostle are amongst the most vile.

Allah has written, 'I will surely prevail, I and my apostles'; verily, Allah is strong and mighty!

Thou shalt not find a people who believe in Allah and the last day loving him who opposes Allah and His Apostle, even though it be their fathers, or their sons, or their brethren, or their clansmen.

He has written faith in their hearts, and He aids them with a spirit from Him; and will make them enter into gardens beneath which rivers flow, to dwell therein for aye! Allah is well pleased with them, and they well pleased with Him: they are Allah's crew; ay, Allah's crew, they shall prosper!

THE CHAPTER OF THE EMIGRATION

LIX (*Medina*)

In the name of the merciful and compassionate Allah.

What is in the heavens and in the earth celebrates Allah's praises; He is the mighty, the wise!

He it was who drove those of the people of the Book who misbelieved forth from their houses, at the first emigration;[1] ye did not think that they would go forth, and they thought that their fortresses would defend them against Allah; but Allah came upon them from whence they did not reckon, and cast dread into their hearts! They ruined their houses with their own hands and the hands of the believers; wherefore take example, O ye who are endowed with sight!

Had it not been that Allah had prescribed for them banishment, He would have tormented them in this world;[2] but for them in the next shall be the torment of the Fire! That is because they opposed Allah and His Apostle: and whoso opposes Allah, verily, Allah is keen to punish!

[5] What palm trees ye did cut down or what ye left standing upon their roots was by Allah's permission, and to disgrace the workers of abomination; and as for the spoils that Allah gave to His Apostle from these (people) ye did not press forward after them with horse or riding camel; but Allah gives His Apostle authority over whom He pleases, for Allah is mighty over all![3]

What Allah gave as spoils to His Apostle of the people of the cities is Allah's, and the Apostle's, and for kinsfolk, orphans, and the poor, and the wayfarer, so that it should not be circulated amongst the rich men of you.

And what the Apostle gives you, take; and what he forbids you, desist from; and fear Allah, verily, Allah is keen to punish!

And (it is) for the poor who fled,[4] who were driven forth from their houses and their wealth, who crave grace from Allah and His goodwill, and help Allah and the Apostle; they are the truthful.

And those who were settled in the abode[5] and the faith before them, love those who fled to them;[6] and they do not find in their breasts a need of what has been given to them; preferring them to themselves, even though there be poverty amongst them; and whoso is preserved from his own covetousness, these are the prosperous!

[10] And those who came after them say, 'Our Lord, forgive us and our brethren who were beforehand with us in the faith, and place not in our hearts ill will towards those who believe—our Lord! verily, thou art kind, compassionate!'

Dost thou not look on those who were hypocritical,

saying to their brethren who misbelieved amongst the people of the Book,[7] 'If ye be driven forth we will go forth with you; and we will never obey any one concerning you; and if ye be fought against we will help you.' But Allah bears witness that they are surely liars!

If they be driven forth, these will not go forth with them; and if they be fought against, these will not help them; or if they do help them, they will turn their backs in flight;—then shall they not be helped!

Ye indeed are a keener source of fear in their hearts than Allah; that is because they are a people who do not understand! They will not fight against you in a body save in fortified cities, or from behind walls; their valour is great amongst themselves;—thou dost reckon them as one body, but their hearts are separated. This is because they are a people who have no sense!

[15] Like unto those before them, recently;[8] they tasted the evil result of their affair, and for them is grievous woe.

Like unto the devil when he said to man, 'Disbelieve.' But when he disbelieved, he said, 'Verily, I am clear of thee! Verily, I fear Allah the Lord of the worlds!' And the end of them both shall be that they shall both be in the Fire, to dwell therein for aye! for that is the reward of the unjust!

O ye who believe! fear Allah; and let each soul look to what it sends on for the morrow; and fear Allah; verily, Allah is well aware of what ye do!

And be ye not like those who forget Allah, and He makes them forget themselves; they are the workers of abomination!

[20] Not deemed alike shall be the fellows of the Fire and the fellows of Paradise: the fellows of Paradise they are the blissful!

Had we sent down this Qur'ân upon a mountain, thou wouldst have seen it humbling itself, splitting asunder from the fear of Allah! These parables do we strike out for men; haply they may reflect!

He is Allah than whom there is no god; who knows the unseen and the visible; He is the merciful, the compassionate! He is Allah than whom there is no god; the King, the Holy, the Peace Giver, the Faithful, the Protector, the Mighty, the Repairer, the Great!—celebrated be the praises of Allah above what they join with Him.

He is Allah, the Creator, the Maker, the Fashioner; His are the excellent names! His praises, whatever are in the heavens and the earth do celebrate; for Allah is the mighty, the wise!

THE CHAPTER OF THE TRIED

LX (*Medina*)

In the name of the merciful and compassionate Allah.

O ye who believe! take not my enemy and your enemy for patrons, encountering them with love for they misbelieve in the truth that is to come to you; they drive out the Apostle and you for that ye believe in Allah your Lord![1]

If ye go forth fighting strenuously in my cause and

craving my good pleasure, and secretly show love for them, yet do I know best what ye conceal and what ye display! and he of you who does so has erred from the level path.

If they find you they will be enemies to you, and they will stretch forth against you their hands and their tongues for evil, and would fain that ye should disbelieve; neither your kindred nor your children shall profit you upon the resurrection day; it will separate you! but Allah on what ye do doth look!

Ye had a good example in Abraham and those with him, when they said to their people, 'Verily, we are clear of you and of what ye serve beside Allah. We disbelieve in you: and between us and you is enmity and hatred begun for ever, until ye believe in Allah alone!'

But not² the speech of Abraham to his father, 'Verily, I will ask forgiveness for thee, though I cannot control aught from Allah!' O our Lord! on thee do we rely! and unto thee we turn! and unto thee the journey is!

[5] Our Lord! make us not a trial for those who misbelieve; but forgive us! Our Lord! verily, thou art mighty, wise!

Ye had in them a good example for him who would hope in Allah and the last day. But whoso turns his back, verily, Allah, He is rich and to be praised.

Mayhap that Allah will place love between you and between those of them ye are hostile towards:³ for Allah is powerful, and Allah is forgiving, compassionate.

Allah forbids you not respecting those who have not fought against you for religion's sake, and who have not driven you forth from your homes, that ye should act righteously and justly towards them; verily, Allah loves the just!

He only forbids you to make patrons of those who have fought against you for religion's sake, and driven you forth from your homes, or have aided in your expulsion; and whoever makes patrons of them, they are the unjust!

[10] O ye who believe! when there come believing women who have fled, then try them: Allah knows their faith. If ye know them to be believers do not send them back to the misbelievers;—they are not lawful for them, nor are the men lawful for these;—but give them⁴ what they have expended,⁵ and it shall be no crime against you that ye marry them, when ye have given them their hire. And do not ye retain a right over misbelieving women; but ask for what ye have spent, and let them ask for what they have spent. That is Allah's judgement: He judges between you, for Allah is knowing, wise!

And if any of your wives escape from you to the misbelievers, and your turn comes, then give to those whose wives have gone away the like of what they have spent; and fear Allah, in whom it is that ye believe.

O thou prophet! when believing women come to thee and engage with thee that they will not associate aught with Allah, and will not steal, and will not fornicate, and will not kill their children, and will not bring a calumny which they have forged between their hands and feet,⁶ and that they will not rebel against thee in what is reasonable, then engage with them and ask forgiveness for them of Allah;—verily, Allah is forgiving, compassionate.

O ye who believe! take not for patrons a people whom Allah is wroth against; they despair of the hereafter, as the misbelievers despair of the fellows of the tombs![7]

THE CHAPTER OF THE RANKS

LXI (*Mecca*)

In the name of the merciful and compassionate Allah.

What is in the heavens and what is in the earth celebrates the praises of Allah, for He is the mighty, the wise!

O ye who believe! say not what ye do not. It is most hateful to Allah that ye say what ye do not.

Verily, Allah loves those who fight in His cause in ranks as though they were a compact building.[1]

[5] When Moses said to his people, 'O my people! why do ye hurt me, when ye know that I am the apostle of Allah to you?' And when they swerved, Allah made their hearts to swerve; for Allah guides not the people who work abomination!

And when Jesus the son of Mary said, 'O children of Israel! verily, I am the apostle of Allah to you, verifying the law that was before me and giving you glad tidings of an apostle who shall come after me, whose name shall be A'hmed!'[2]—but when he did come to them with manifest signs, they said, 'This is manifest sorcery!'

And who is more unjust than he who forges against Allah a lie when called unto Islam? But Allah guides not the unjust people.

They desire to put out the light of Allah with their mouths; but Allah will perfect His light, averse although the misbeliever be!

He it is who sent His Apostle with guidance and the religion of truth to set it above all religion; averse although the idolaters may be.

[10] O ye who believe! shall I lead you to a merchandise which will save you from grievous woe?

To believe in Allah and His Apostle, and to fight strenuously in Allah's cause with your property and your persons; that is better for you if ye did but know!

He will pardon you your sins, and bring you into gardens beneath which rivers flow, and goodly dwellings in gardens of Eden;—that is the mighty bliss!

And other things which ye love,—help from Allah and victory nigh! so do thou give the glad tidings unto the believers!

O ye who believe! be ye the helpers³ of Allah! as Jesus son of Mary said to the apostles, 'Who are my helpers for Allah?' Said the apostles, 'We are Allah's helpers!'⁴

And a party of the children of Israel believed, and a party misbelieved. And we aided those who believed against their enemies, and they were on the morrow superior!

THE CHAPTER OF
THE CONGREGATION

LXII (*Medina*)

In the name of the merciful and compassionate Allah.

What is in the heavens and what is in the earth celebrates the praises of Allah the King, the holy, the mighty, the wise!

He it is who sent unto the Gentiles[1] a prophet amongst themselves to recite to them His signs and to purify them, and to teach them the Book and the wisdom, although they were before in obvious error.

And others of them have not yet overtaken them;[2] but He is the mighty, the wise!

That is Allah's grace, He gives it to whomsoever He will; for Allah is Lord of mighty grace.

[5] The likeness of those who were charged with the law and then bore it not is as the likeness of an ass bearing books: sorry is the likeness of the people who say Allah's signs are lies! but Allah guides not an unjust people.

Say, 'O ye who are Jews! if ye pretend that ye are the clients of Allah, beyond other people; then wish for death if ye do speak the truth!'

But they never wish for it, through what their hands have sent before! but Allah knows the unjust.

Say, 'Verily, the death from which ye flee will surely meet you; then shall ye be sent back to Him who knows the unseen and the visible, and He will inform you of that which ye have done!'

O ye who believe! when the call to prayer is made upon the Congregation Day,[3] then hasten to the remembrance of Allah, and leave off traffic; that is better for you, if ye did but know!

[10] And when prayer is performed, then disperse abroad in the land, and crave of Allah's grace; and remember Allah much; haply ye may prosper!

But when they see merchandise or sport they flock to it and leave thee standing![4] Say, 'What is with Allah is better than sport and than merchandise, for Allah is the best of providers!'

THE CHAPTER OF THE HYPOCRITES[1]

LXIII (*Medina*)

In the name of the merciful and compassionate Allah.

When the hypocrites come to thee, they say, 'We bear witness that thou art surely the Apostle of Allah'; but Allah knows that thou art His Apostle: and Allah bears witness that the hypocrites are liars!

They take their faith[2] for a cloak, and then they turn folks from Allah's way:—evil is that which they have done! That is because they believed and then disbelieved, wherefore is a stamp set on their hearts so that they do not understand!

And when thou seest them, their persons please thee;[3] but if they speak, thou listenest to their speech: they are like timber propped up:[4] they reckon every noise against them! They are the foe, so beware of them!—Allah fight against them, how they lie!

[5] And when it is said to them, 'Come, and the Apostle of Allah will ask forgiveness for you!' they turn away their heads, and thou mayest see them turning away since they are so big with pride!

It is the same to them whether thou dost ask forgiveness for them, or whether thou dost not ask forgiveness for them,—Allah will not forgive them; verily, Allah guides not a people who work abomination!

They it is who say, 'Expend not in alms upon those who are with the Apostle of Allah, in order that they may desert him!'—but Allah's are the treasures of the heavens and the earth; but the hypocrites have no sense!

They say, 'If we return to el Medina, the mightier will surely drive out the meaner therefrom'; but to Allah belongs the might, and to His Apostle and to the believers; but the hypocrites do not know!

O ye who believe! let not your property nor your children divert you from the remembrance of Allah,—for whosoever does that, they are those who lose!

[10] But expend in alms of what we have bestowed upon you before death come on any one of you, and he says, 'My Lord! wouldst thou but have respited me till an appointed time nigh at hand, then would I surely give in charity and be among the righteous!' But Allah will never respite a soul when its appointed time has come: and Allah of what ye do is well aware.

THE CHAPTER OF CHEATING

LXIV (*Place of origin doubtful*)

In the name of the merciful and compassionate Allah.

What is in the heavens and what is in the earth celebrates Allah's praises; His is the kingdom, and His is the praise, and He is mighty over all!

He it is who created you, and of you is (one) a misbeliever and (one) a believer; and Allah on what ye do does look.

He created the heavens and the earth in truth; and has formed you and made excellent your forms; and unto Him the journey is!

He knows what is in the heavens and the earth, and knows what ye conceal and what ye display; for Allah knows the nature of men's breasts!

[5] Has there not come to you the story of those who misbelieved before, and tasted the evil result of their affair, and for them was grievous woe?

That is because their apostles came to them with manifest signs, and they said, 'Shall mortals guide us?' and they misbelieved and turned their backs. But Allah was independent of them; for Allah is rich and to be praised!

Those who misbelieve pretend that they shall surely not be raised: say, 'Yea! by my Lord! ye shall surely be raised: then ye shall be informed of that which ye have done'; for that is easy unto Allah.

So believe in Allah and His Apostle and the light which we have sent down; for Allah of what ye do is well aware!

On the day when he shall gather you to the day of gathering, that is the day of cheating![1] but whoso believes in Allah and acts aright, He will cover for him his offences, and will bring him into gardens beneath which rivers flow, to dwell therein for aye! That is the mighty bliss!

[10] But those who misbelieve and say our signs are lies, they are the fellows of the Fire, to dwell therein for aye! and evil shall the journey be!

No calamity befalls but by the permission of Allah: and whoso believes in Allah, He will guide his heart; for Allah all things doth know!

So obey Allah and obey the Apostle:[2] but if ye turn your backs—our Apostle has only his plain message to preach!

Allah, there is no god but He; and upon Him let the believers rely!

O ye who believe! verily, among your wives and children are foes of yours: so beware of them! But if ye pardon, and overlook it, and forgive,—verily, Allah is forgiving, compassionate!

[15] Your property and your children are but a trial; and Allah, with Him is mighty hire!

Then fear Allah as much as ye can! and hear, and obey, and expend in alms: it is better for yourselves. But whosoever is saved from his own covetousness—these are the prosperous!

If ye lend to Allah a goodly loan, He will double it for you, and will forgive you; for Allah is grateful, clement!

He knows the unseen and the visible; the mighty, the wise!

THE CHAPTER OF DIVORCE

LXV (*Medina*)

In the name of the merciful and compassionate Allah.

O thou prophet! when ye divorce women, then divorce them at their term,[1] and calculate the term and fear Allah your Lord. Do not drive them out of their houses unless they have committed manifest adultery. These are Allah's bounds, and whoso transgresses Allah's bounds has wronged himself. Thou knowest not whether haply Allah may cause something fresh to happen after that.[2]

And when they have reached their appointed time, then retain them with kindness, or separate from them with kindness; and bring as witnesses men of equity from among you; and give upright testimony to Allah. That is what He admonishes him who believes in Allah and the last day; and whosoever fears Allah, He will make for him a (happy) issue, and will provide for him from whence he reckoned not.

And whosoever relies on Allah, He is sufficient for him: verily, Allah will attain His purpose:—Allah has set for everything a period.

And such of your women as despair of menstruation, —if ye doubt, then their term is three months; and such as have not menstruated too.

And those who are heavy with child their appointed time is when they have laid down their burden; and whosoever fears Allah, He will make for him an easy affair.

[5] That is Allah's command, He has sent it down to

you; and whosoever fears Allah He will cover for him his offences and will make grand for him his hire.

Let them[3] dwell where ye dwell, according to your means, and do not harm them, to reduce them to straits; and if they be heavy with child, then pay for them until they lay down their burdens; and if they suckle (the child) for you, then give them their hire, and consult among yourselves in reason; but if ye be in difficulties, and another woman shall suckle the child for him, let him who has plenty expend of his plenty; but he whose provision is doled out, let him expend of what Allah has given him; Allah will not compel any soul beyond what He has given it;—Allah will make after difficulty ease!

How many a city has turned away from the bidding of its Lord and His apostles; and we called them to a severe account, and we tormented them with an unheard of torment!

And they tasted the evil results of their conduct; and the end of their conduct was loss!

[10] Allah prepared for them severe torment;—then fear Allah, ye who are endowed with minds!

Ye who believe! Allah has sent down to you a reminder;—an apostle to recite to you Allah's manifest signs;—to bring forth those who believe and act aright from darkness into light! And whoso believes in Allah and acts right He will bring him into gardens beneath which rivers flow, to dwell therein for ever and for aye! Allah has made goodly for him his provision!

Allah it is who created seven heavens, and of the earth the like thereof. The bidding descends between them, that ye may know that Allah is mighty over all, and that Allah has encompassed all things with His knowledge!

THE CHAPTER OF PROHIBITION[1]

LXVI (*Medina*)

In the name of the merciful and compassionate Allah.

O thou prophet! wherefore dost thou prohibit what Allah has made lawful to thee, craving to please thy wives? But Allah is forgiving, compassionate!

Allah has allowed you to expiate your oaths; for Allah is your sovereign, and He is the knowing, the wise!

And when the prophet told as a secret to one of his wives a recent event, and when she gave information thereof and exposed it, he acquainted her with some of it and avoided part of it. But when he informed her of it, she said, 'Who told thee this?' he said, 'The wise one, the well aware informed me.

'If ye both turn repentant unto Allah,—for your hearts have swerved!—but if ye back each other up against him,—verily, Allah, He is the sovereign; and Gabriel and the righteous of the believers, and the angels after that, will back him up.

[5] 'It may be that his Lord if he divorce you will give him in exchange wives better than you, Muslims, believers, devout, repentant, worshipping, given to fasting—such as have known men and virgins too.'

O ye who believe! save yourselves and your families

from the Fire, whose fuel is men and stones;—over it are angels stout and stern; they disobey not Allah in what He bids them, but they do what they are bidden!

O ye who disbelieve! excuse not yourselves today;—ye shall only be rewarded for that which ye have done.

O ye who believe! turn repentant to Allah with sincere repentance; it may be that thy Lord will cover for you your offences and will bring you into gardens beneath which rivers flow!—the day Allah will not disgrace the Prophet nor those who believe with him; their light shall run on before them, and at their right hands! they shall say, 'Our Lord! perfect for us our light and forgive us; verily, Thou art mighty over all!'

O thou prophet! fight strenuously against the misbelievers and hypocrites and be stern towards them; for their resort is Hell, and an evil journey shall it be!

[10] Allah strikes out a parable to those who misbelieve: the wife of Noah and the wife of Lot; they were under two of our righteous servants, but they betrayed them: and they availed them nothing against Allah; and it was said, 'Enter the Fire with those who enter.'

And Allah strikes out a parable for those who believe: the wife of Pharaoh, when she said, 'My Lord, build for me a house with Thee in Paradise, and save me from Pharaoh and his works, and save me from the unjust people!'

And Mary, daughter of Imrân, who guarded her private parts, and we breathed therein of our spirit and she verified the words of her Lord and His books, and was of the devout.

THE CHAPTER OF THE KINGDOM

LXVII (*Mecca*)

In the name of the merciful and compassionate Allah.

Blessed be He in whose hand is the kingdom, for He is mighty over all!

Who created death and life, to try you, which of you does best; for He is the mighty, the forgiving!

Who created seven heavens in stories; thou canst not see any discordance in the creation of the Merciful!

Why, look again! canst thou see a flaw? Then look again twice!—thy look shall return to thee driven back and dulled!

[5] And we have adorned the lower heaven with lamps; and set them to pelt the devils with;¹ and we have prepared for them the torment of the blaze!

And for those who disbelieve in their Lord is the torment of Hell, and an evil journey shall it be!

When they shall be cast therein they shall hear its braying² as it boils—it will well-nigh burst for rage!

Whenever a troop of them is thrown in, its treasurers shall ask them, 'Did not a warner come to you?'

They shall say, 'Yea! a warner came to us, and we called him liar, and said, "Allah has not sent down aught; ye are but in great error!" '

[10] And they shall say, 'Had we but listened or had sense we had not been amongst the fellows of the blaze!'

And they will confess their sins; but 'Avaunt to the fellows of the blaze!'

Verily, those who fear their Lord in secret, for them is forgiveness and a great hire!

Speak ye secretly or openly, verily, He knows the nature of men's breasts!

Ay! He knows who created! for He is the subtle, the well aware!

[15] He it is who made the earth flat for you; so walk in the spacious sides thereof and eat of His provision; for unto Him the resurrection is!

Are ye sure that He who is in the heaven will not cleave the earth with you, and that it then shall quake?

Or are ye sure that He who is in the heaven will not send against you a heavy sandstorm, and that ye then shall know how the warning was?

But those before them did call the apostles liars, and what a change it was!

Or have they not looked at the birds above them expanding their wings or closing them?—none holds them in except the Merciful One; for He on everything doth look.

[20] Or who is this who will be a host for you, to help you against the Merciful?—the misbelievers are only in delusion!

Or who is this who will provide you if He hold back His provision?—Nay, but they persist in perverseness and aversion!

Is he who walks prone upon his face more guided than he who walks upright upon a straight path?

Say, 'It is He who produced you and made for you hearing and sight and hearts'—little is it that ye give thanks.

Say, 'It is He who sowed you in the earth, and unto Him shall ye be gathered!'

[25] They say, 'When shall this threat be, if ye do speak the truth?'

Say, 'The knowledge is only with Allah; and I am but a plain warner!'

And when they see it nigh, sorry shall be the faces of those who misbelieve; and it shall be said, 'This is that for which ye used to call!'

Say, 'Have ye considered, whether Allah destroy me and those with me, or whether we obtain mercy, yet who will protect the misbelievers from grievous torment?'

Say, 'He is the Merciful; we believe in Him, and upon Him do we rely; and ye shall shortly know who it is that is in obvious error!'

[30] Say, 'Have ye considered if your waters on the morrow should have sunk, who is to bring you flowing water?'

THE CHAPTER OF THE PEN

LXVIII (*Mecca*)

In the name of the merciful and compassionate Allah.

N.[1] By the pen, and what they write, thou art not, by Allah's grace, mad! and, verily, thine is a hire that is not grudged! [5] and, verily, thou art of a grand nature![2]

But thou shalt see and they shall see which of you is the infatuated.

Verily, thy Lord He knows best who errs from His way; and He knows best those who are guided.

Then obey not those who call thee liar; they would fain that thou shouldst be smooth with them, then would they be smooth with thee!

[10] And obey not any mean swearer,³ a backbiter, a walker about with slander; a forbidder of good, a transgressor, a sinner; rude, and base born too; though he have wealth and sons!

[15] When our signs are recited to him he says, 'Old folks' tales!'

We will brand him on the snout!

Verily, we have tried them as we tried the fellows of the garden when they swore, 'We will cut its fruit at morn!'

But they made not the exception;⁴ and there came round about it an encompassing calamity from thy Lord the while they slept; [20] and on the morrow it was as one the fruit of which is cut.

And they cried to each other in the morning, 'Go early to your tilth if ye would cut it!'

So they set off, saying privily to each other, 'There shall surely enter it today unto you no poor person!'

[25] And they went early deciding to be stingy.⁵

And when they saw it they said, 'Verily, we have erred! Nay, we are forbidden (its fruit)!'

Said the most moderate of them, 'Said I not to you, "unless ye celebrate Allah's praises!"'

Said they, 'Celebrated be the praises of our Lord! Verily, we were unjust!'

[30] And they approached each other with mutual blame.

Said they, 'O woe to us! verily, we have been outrageous! Haply our Lord may give us instead a better than it; verily, we unto our Lord do yearn.'

Thus is the torment, but, verily, the torment of the hereafter is greater, if ye did but know!

Verily, for the pious with their Lord are gardens of pleasure!

[35] Shall we then make the Muslims like the sinners? What ails you? How ye judge!

Or have ye a book in which ye can study, that ye are surely to have what ye may choose?

Or have ye oaths binding on us until the judgement day that ye are surely to have what ye may judge?

[40] Ask them, which of them will vouch for this? Or have they partners, then let them bring their partners if they do speak the truth?

On the day when the leg shall be bared;[6] and they shall be called to adore and shall not be able!

Lowering their looks, abasement shall attack them, for they were called to adore while yet they were safe!

But let me alone with him who calls this new discourse a lie. We will surely bring them down by degrees from whence they do not know.

[45] And I will let them have their way! for my device is sure.

Or dost thou ask them a hire for it while they are burdened with debts?

Or have they the knowledge of the unseen, so that they write?

But wait patiently for the judgement of thy Lord, and be not like the fellow of the fish,[7] when he cried out as he was choking with rage.

Had it not been that grace from his Lord reached him, he would have been cast out on the naked (shore) and blamed the while!

[50] But his Lord elected him, and made him of the pious.

The misbelievers well-nigh upset thee with their looks when they hear the reminder, and they say, 'Surely he is mad!'

And yet it is but a reminder to the worlds!

THE CHAPTER OF THE INFALLIBLE

LXIX (*Mecca*)

In the name of the merciful and compassionate Allah.

The Infallible, what is the Infallible? and what should make thee know what the Infallible is?

Thamûd and 'Âd called the Striking[1] Day a lie; [5] but as for Thamûd they perished by the shock; and as for 'Âd they perished with the violent cold blast of wind, which He subjected against them for seven nights and eight days consecutively. Thou mightest see the people therein prostrate as though they were palm stumps thrown down, and canst thou see any of them left?

And Pharaoh and those before him of the overturned cities[2] committed sins, [10] and they rebelled against the apostle of their Lord, and He seized them with an excessive punishment.

Verily, we, when the water surged, bore you on it in a sailing ship, to make it a memorial for you, and that the retentive ear might hold it.

And when the trumpet shall be blown with one blast, and the earth shall be borne away, and the mountains too, and both be crushed with one crushing; [15] on that day shall the inevitable happen; and the heaven on that day shall be cleft asunder, for on that day shall it wane! and the angels upon the sides thereof; and above them on that day shall eight bear the throne of thy Lord!

On the day when ye shall be set forth no hidden thing of yours shall be concealed.

And as for him who is given his book in his right hand, he shall say, 'Here! take and read my book. [20] Verily, I thought that I should meet my reckoning'; and he shall be in a pleasing life, in a lofty garden, whose fruits are nigh to cull—'Eat ye and drink with good digestion, for what ye did aforetime in the days that have gone by!'

[25] But as for him who is given his book in his left hand he shall say, 'O, would that I had not received my book! I did not know what my account would be. O, would that it[3] had been an end of me! My wealth availed me not! My authority has perished from me!' [30] 'Take him and fetter him, then in Hell broil him! then into a chain whose length is seventy cubits force him! Verily, he believed not in the mighty Allah, nor was he particular to feed the poor: [35] therefore he has not here today any warm

friend, nor any food except foul ichor, which none save sinners shall eat!'

I need not swear by what ye see or what ye do not see, [40] verily, it is the speech of a noble apostle; and it is not the speech of a poet:—little is it ye believe!

And it is not the speech of a soothsayer,—little is it that ye mind!—a revelation from the Lord of the worlds.

Why if he had invented against us any sayings, [45] we would have seized him by the right hand, then we would have cut his jugular vein; nor could any one of you have kept us off from him.

Verily, it is a memorial to the pious; and, verily, we know that there are amongst you those who say it is a lie; [50] and, verily, it is a source of sighing to the misbelievers; and, verily, it is certain truth!

Therefore celebrate the name of thy mighty Lord!

THE CHAPTER OF THE ASCENTS

LXX (*Mecca*)

In the name of the merciful and compassionate Allah.

An asker[1] asked for torment that must befall, for the unbelievers; there is no repelling it; from Allah the Lord of the ascents,[2] whereby ascend the angels and the Spirit unto Him in a day whose length is fifty thousand years.[3]

[5] Wherefore be patient with fair patience; verily, they see it as afar off, but we see it nigh!

The day when the heaven shall be as molten brass, and

the mountains shall be like flocks of wool; [10] when no warm friend shall question friend; they shall gaze on each other, and the sinner would fain give as a ransom from the torment of that day his sons and his mate, and his brother and his kin who stand by him, and all who are in the earth, that yet it might rescue him!

[15] Nay, verily, it is a flame,—dragging by the scalp! it shall call those who retreated and turned their backs and who amassed and hoarded!

Verily, man is by nature rash![4] [20] when evil touches him, very impatient; when good touches him, niggardly; all save those who pray, who remain at their prayers, and in whose wealth is a reasonable due (set aside) [25] For him who asks and him who is kept from asking, and those who believe in a day of judgement, and those who shrink in terror from the torment of their Lord;—verily, the torment of their Lord is not safe;—and those who guard their private parts, [30] except for their wives or the (slave girls) whom their right hands possess, for they are not to be blamed; but whoso craves beyond this, they are the transgressors; and those who observe their trusts and their compacts, and those who are upright in their testimonies, and those who keep their prayers, [35] these shall dwell in gardens honoured.

What ails the misbelievers that they hurry on before thee, crowding together on the right and on the left?[5] Does every man of them wish to enter the garden of pleasure?

Nay, we created them of what they know!

[40] And I need not swear by the Lord of the easts and

the wests;[6] verily, we are able to change them for others better, nor are we prevented!

So leave them to plunge in discussion, and to play until they meet that day of theirs which they are threatened with, the day when they shall come forth in haste from the graves, as though they flock to a standard! with their looks abashed; meanness shall cover them! That is the day which they were promised!

THE CHAPTER OF NOAH

LXXI (*Mecca*)

In the name of the merciful and compassionate Allah.

Verily, we sent Noah to his people, 'Warn thy people before there come to them a grievous torment!'

Said he, 'O my people! verily, I am to you an obvious warner, that ye serve Allah and fear Him and obey me. He will pardon you your sins, and will defer you unto an appointed time; verily, Allah's appointed time when it comes will not be deferred, did ye but know!'

[5] Said he, 'My Lord! verily, I have called my people by night and day, and my call did but increase them in flight; and, verily, every time I called them, that Thou mightest pardon them, they placed their fingers in their ears and tried to cover themselves with their garments and persisted, and were very big with pride. Then I called them openly; then I published to them and I spoke to them in secret, and I said, "Ask forgiveness of your Lord,

verily, He is very forgiving. [10] He will send the rain upon you in torrents, and will extend to you wealth and children, and will make for you gardens, and will make for you rivers. What ails you that ye hope not for something serious from Allah, when He has created you by steps?[1] Do ye not see how Allah has created the seven heavens in stories, [15] and has set the moon therein for a light, and set the sun for a lamp? And Allah has made you grow out of the earth, and then He will make you return thereto, and will make you come forth therefrom; and Allah has made for you the earth a carpet that ye may walk therein in broad paths." '

[20] Said Noah, 'My Lord! verily, they have rebelled against me, and followed him whose wealth and children have but added to his loss, and they have plotted a great plot, and said, "Ye shall surely not leave your gods: ye shall surely neither leave Wadd, nor Suwâ'h, nor Yaghûth, nor Ya'ûq, nor Nasr, and they led astray many." ' And thou (Mohammed) wilt only increase the unjust in their error—[25] because of their sins they were drowned and made to enter into the Fire, and they found no helpers against Allah!

And Noah said, 'My Lord! leave not upon the earth one dweller of the misbelievers. Verily, Thou, if Thou shouldst leave them, they will lead astray Thy servants, and they will only bear for children sinners and misbelievers. My Lord! pardon me and my two parents, and whomsoever enters my house believing, and (pardon) the believers men and women—but Thou shalt only increase the unjust in loss.'

THE CHAPTER OF THE JINN

LXXII (*Mecca*)

In the name of the merciful and compassionate Allah.

Say, 'I have been inspired that there listened a company of the jinn,[1] and they said, "We have heard a marvellous Qur'ân that guides to the right direction; and we believe therein, and we join no one with our Lord, for, verily, He—may the majesty of our Lord be exalted!—has taken to Himself neither consort nor son.

' "And, verily, a fool among us spake against Allah wide of the mark!

' "[5] And we thought that men and jinn would never speak a lie against Allah.

' "And there are persons amongst men who seek for refuge with persons amongst the jinn;[2] but they increase them in their perverseness. And they thought, as ye thought, that Allah would not raise up any one from the dead.

' "But we touched the heavens and found them filled with a mighty guard and shooting stars; and we did sit in certain seats thereof to listen; but whoso of us listens now finds a shooting star for him on guard.

' "[10] And, verily, we know not whether evil be meant for those who are in the earth, or if their Lord means right by them.

' "And of us are some who are pious, and of us are some who are otherwise: we are in separate bands.

' "And we thought that we could not frustrate Allah in the earth, and could not frustrate Him by flight.

' "But, verily, when we heard the guidance we believed therein, and he who believes in his Lord shall fear neither diminution nor loss.

' "And, verily, of us are some who are Muslims, and of us some are trespassers; but those of us who are Muslims they strive after right direction; [15] and as for the trespassers they are fuel for Hell." '

And if they[3] will go right upon the way, we will irrigate them with copious water to try them thereby; and whoso turns from the remembrance of his Lord He will drive him to severe torment.

And (say) that the mosques are Allah's, and that ye should not call on any one with Allah, and that when Allah's servant[4] stood up to pray they[5] called out to him and well-nigh crowded upon him. [20] Say, 'I only call upon my Lord, and I join no one with Him.'

Say, 'Verily, I cannot control for you either harm, or right direction.'

Say, 'Verily, as for me none can protect me against Allah, nor do I find any refuge beside Him,—except delivering the message from Allah and His errands: and whoso rebels against Allah and His Apostle, verily, for him is the Fire of Hell for them to dwell therein for ever and for aye!'

[25] Until when they see what they are threatened with, then shall they surely know who is most weak at helping and fewest in numbers!

Say, 'I know not if what ye are threatened with be nigh, or if my Lord will set for it a term. He knows the unseen, and He lets no one know His unseen, save such apostle as He is well pleased with: for, verily, He sends marching before him and behind him a guard!'

That He may know that they have delivered the errands of their Lord, for He compasses what they have, and reckons everything by number.

THE CHAPTER OF THE ENWRAPPED
LXXIII (*Mecca*)

In the name of the merciful and compassionate Allah.

O thou who art enwrapped! rise by night except a little—the half, or deduct therefrom a little, or add thereto, and chant the Qur'ân chanting. [5] Verily, we will cast on thee a heavy speech.

Verily, the early part of the night is stronger in impressions and more upright in speech!

Verily, thou hast by day a long employment; but mention the name of thy Lord and devote thyself thoroughly to Him, the Lord of the east and the west; there is no god but He; then take Him for a guardian!

[10] And endure patiently what they say, and flee from them with a decorous flight.

And leave me and those who say it is a lie, who are possessed of comfort; and let them bide for a while.

Verily, with us are heavy fetters and hellfire, and food that chokes, and mighty woe!

On the day when the earth and the mountains shall tremble and the earth shall be as a crumbling sand hill!

[15] Verily, we have sent unto you an apostle bearing witness against you, as we sent an apostle unto Pharaoh.

But Pharaoh rebelled against the apostle, and we seized him with an overpowering punishment.

Then how will ye shield yourselves if ye misbelieve from the day which shall make children grey headed, whereon the heaven cleaves—its promise shall be fulfilled!

Verily, this is a memorial, and whose will, let him take unto his Lord a way.[1]

[20] Verily, thy Lord knows that thou dost stand up to pray nearly two-thirds of the night, or the half of it or the third of it, as do part of those who are with thee; for Allah measures the night and the day; He knows that ye cannot calculate it, and He turns relentant towards you.

So read what is easy of the Qur'ân. He knows that there will be of you some who are sick and others who beat about in the earth craving the grace of Allah, and others who are fighting in the cause of Allah. Then read what is easy of it and be steadfast in prayer, and give alms, and lend to Allah a goodly loan, for what ye send forward for yourselves of good ye will find it with Allah. It is better and a greater hire; and ask ye pardon of Allah: verily, Allah is forgiving, merciful!

THE CHAPTER OF THE 'COVERED'[1]

LXXIV (*Mecca*)

In the name of the merciful and compassionate Allah.

O thou who art covered! rise up and warn!

And thy Lord magnify!

[5] And thy garments purify!

And abomination shun!

And grant not favours to gain increase!

And for thy Lord await!

And when the trump is blown,—for that day is a difficult day! [10] for the misbelievers aught but easy!

Leave me alone with him I have created, and for whom I have made extensive wealth,[2] and sons that he may look upon, and for whom I have smoothed things down. [15] Then he desires that I should increase! Nay, verily, he is hostile to our signs! I will drive him up a hill! Then he reflected and planned! May he be killed,—how he planned! [20] Again, may he be killed,—how he planned! Then he looked; then he frowned and scowled; then he retreated and was big with pride and said, 'This is only magic exhibited! [25] This is only mortal speech!'—I will broil him in hellfire! and what shall make thee know what hellfire is? It will not leave and will not let alone. It scorches the flesh; [30] over it are nineteen (angels).

We have made only angels guardians of the Fire, and we have only made their number a trial to those who misbelieve; that those who have been given the Book may be certain, and that those who believe may be increased in faith; and that those who have been given the Book and the believers may not doubt; and that those in whose hearts is sickness, and the misbelievers may say, 'What does Allah mean by this as a parable?'

Thus Allah leads astray whom He pleases, and guides him He pleases: and none knows the hosts of thy Lord save Himself; and it is only a reminder to mortals!

[35] Nay, by the moon!

And the night when it retires!

And the morning when it brightly dawns!

Verily, it is one of the greatest misfortunes; a warning to mortals; [40] for him amongst you who wishes to press forward or to tarry!

Every soul is pledged[3] for what it earns; except the fellows of the right: in gardens shall they ask each other about the sinners!—'What drove you into hellfire?'

They shall say, 'We weren't[4] of those who prayed; [45] we didn't feed the poor; but we did plunge into discussion with those who plunged, and we called the judgement day a lie until the certainly[5] did come to us!'

But there shall not profit them the intercession of the intercessors.

[50] What ailed them that they turned away from the memorial as though they were timid asses fleeing from a lion?

Nay, every man of them wished that he might have given him books spread open!

Nay, but they did not fear the hereafter!

Nay, it is a memorial! and let him who will remember it; [55] but none will remember it except Allah please. He is most worthy of fear; and he is most worthy to forgive!

THE CHAPTER OF
THE RESURRECTION

LXXV (*Mecca*)

In the name of the merciful and compassionate Allah.

I need not swear by the resurrection day!

Nor need I swear by the self-accusing soul!

Does man think that we shall not collect his bones? Able are we to arrange his finger tips!

[5] Nay, but man wishes to be wicked henceforth! He asks, "When is the resurrection day?"

But when the sight shall be dazed, and the moon be eclipsed, and the sun and the moon be together, [10] and man shall say upon that day, 'Where is a place to flee to?'—nay, no refuge! and to thy Lord that day is the sure settlement: He will inform man on that day of what He has sent forward or delayed!

Nay, man is an evidence against himself, [15] and even if he thrusts forward his excuses—.

Do not move thy tongue thereby to hasten it.[1] It is for us to collect it and to read it; and when we read it then follow its reading. And again it is for us to explain it.

[20] Nay, indeed, but ye love the transient life, and ye neglect the hereafter!

Faces on that day shall be bright, gazing on their Lord!

And faces on that day shall be dismal!

[25] Thou wilt think that a back-breaking calamity has happened to them!

Nay, but when the [soul] comes up into the throat, and it is said, 'Who will charm it back?' and he will think that it is his parting [hour]. And leg shall be pressed on leg;[2] [30] unto thy Lord on that day shall the driving be.

For he did not believe[3] and did not pray; but he said it was a lie, and turned his back! Then he went to his people haughtily—woe to thee, and woe to thee! again woe to thee, and woe to thee!

Does man think that he shall be left to himself?

Wasn't[4] he a clot of emitted seed? Then he was congealed blood, and (Allah) created him, and fashioned him, and made of him pairs, male and female.

[35] Is not He able to quicken the dead?

THE CHAPTER OF MAN

LXXVI (*Mecca*)

In the name of the merciful and compassionate Allah.

Does there not come on man a portion of time when he is nothing worth mentioning?[1]

Verily, we created man from a mingled clot, to try him; and we gave him hearing and sight. Verily, we guided him in the way, whether he be grateful or ungrateful.

Verily, we have prepared for those who misbelieve chains and fetters and a blaze!

[5] Verily, the righteous shall drink of a cup tempered with Kâfûr,[2] a spring from which Allah's servants shall drink and make it gush out as they please!

They who fulfil their vows, and fear a day, the evil which shall fly abroad, and who give food for His love to the poor and the orphan and the captive. 'We only feed you for Allah's sake; we desire not from you either reward or thanks; [10] we fear from our Lord a frowning, calamitous day!'

And Allah will guard them from the evil of that day and will cast on them brightness and joy; and their reward for their patience shall be Paradise and silk! Reclining therein upon couches they shall neither see therein sun nor piercing cold;[3] and close down upon them shall be its shadows; and lowered over them its fruits to cull; [15] and they shall be served round with vessels of silver and goblets that are as flagons—flagons of silver which they shall mete out! and they shall drink therein a cup tempered with *zinjabîl*,[4] a spring therein named Silsabîl! and there shall go round about them eternal boys; when thou seest them thou wilt think them scattered pearls; [20] and when thou seest them thou shalt see pleasure and a great estate! On them shall be garments of green embroidered satin and brocade; and they shall be adorned with bracelets of silver; and their Lord shall give them to drink pure drink! Verily, this is a reward for you, and your efforts are thanked.

Verily, we have sent down upon thee the Qur'ân. Wherefore wait patiently for the judgement of thy Lord, and obey not any sinner or misbeliever amongst them. [25] But remember the name of thy Lord morning, and evening, and through the night, and adore Him, and celebrate His praises the whole night long.

Verily, these love the transitory life, and leave behind them a heavy day!

We created them and strengthened their joints; and if we please we can exchange for the likes of them in their stead. Verily, this is a memorial, and whoso will, let him take unto his Lord a way.

[30] But ye will not please except Allah please! Verily, Allah is knowing, wise.

He makes whomsoever He pleases to enter into His mercy; but the unjust He has prepared for them a grievous woe!

THE CHAPTER OF THOSE SENT

LXXVII (*Mecca*)

In the name of the merciful and compassionate Allah.
By those sent in a series!¹
And by those who speed swiftly!
And by the dispensers abroad!
And by the separators apart!
[5] And by those who instil the reminder, as an excuse or warning!
Verily, what ye are threatened with shall surely happen!
And when the stars shall be erased!
And when the heaven shall be cleft!
[10] And when the mountains shall be winnowed!
And when the apostles shall have a time appointed for them!

For what day is the appointment made?

For the day of decision! And what shall make thee know what the decision is?

[15] Woe on that day for those who say it is a lie!

Have we not destroyed those of yore, and then followed them up with those of the latter day? Thus do we with the sinners.

Woe on that day for those who say it is a lie!

[20] Did we not create you from contemptible water, and place it in a sure depository unto a certain decreed term? For we are able and well able too!

Woe on that day for those who say it is a lie!

[25] Have we not made for them the earth to hold the living and the dead? and set thereon firm mountains reared aloft? and given you to drink water in streams?

Woe on that day for those who say it is a lie!

Go off to that which ye did call a lie! [30] Go off to the shadow of three columns, that shall not shade nor avail against the flame! Verily, it throws off sparks like towers,—as though they were yellow camels!

Woe on that day for those who say it is a lie!

[35] This is the day when they may not speak,—when they are not permitted to excuse themselves!

Woe on that day for those who say it is a lie!

This is the day of decision! We have assembled you with those of yore; if ye have any stratagem employ it now!

[40] Woe on that day for those who say it is a lie!

Verily, the pious are amid shades and springs and fruit such as they love.—'Eat and drink with good digestion, for that which ye have done!'

Verily, thus do we reward those who do well.

[45] Woe on that day for those who say it is a lie! 'Eat and enjoy yourselves for a little; verily, ye are sinners!'

Woe on that day for those who say it is a lie!

And when it is said to them bow down, they bow not down.

Woe on that day for those who say it is a lie!

[50] And in what new discourse after it will they believe?

THE CHAPTER OF THE INFORMATION

LXXVIII (*Mecca*)

In the name of the merciful and compassionate Allah.

Of what do they ask each other?—Of the mighty information whereon they do dispute?¹ Nay, they shall know too well! [5] Again, nay, they shall know too well!

Have we not set the earth as a couch, and the mountains as stakes, and created you in pairs, and made your sleep for rest, [10] and made the night a garment, and made the day for livelihood, and built above you seven solid (heavens), and set a burning lamp, and sent down from the rain-expressing clouds water pouring forth, [15] to bring out thereby the grain and herb and gardens thickly planted?

Verily, the day of decision is an appointed time; and the day when the trumpet shall be blown, and ye shall come in troops, and the heavens shall be opened, and shall be all doors, [20] and the mountains shall be moved, and shall be like a mirage!

Verily, Hell is an ambuscade; a reward for the outrageous, to tarry therein for ages. They shall not taste therein cool nor drink, [25] but only boiling water and pus;—a fit reward!

Verily, they did not hope for the account; but they ever said our signs were lies.

Everything have we remembered in a book.

[30] 'Then taste, for we will only increase your torment!'

Verily, for the pious is a blissful place,—gardens and vineyards, and girls with swelling breasts of the same age as themselves, and a brimming cup; [35] they shall hear therein no folly and no lie;—a reward from thy Lord, a sufficient gift! The Lord of the heavens and the earth, and what is between them both,—the Merciful,—they cannot obtain audience of Him!

The day when the Spirit and the angels shall stand in ranks, they shall not speak save to whom the Merciful permits, and who speaks aright.

That is the true day; and whoso pleases let him take to a resort unto his Lord!

[40] Verily, we have warned you of a torment that is nigh: on a day when man shall see what his two hands have sent forward; and the misbeliever shall say, 'Would that I were dust!'

THE CHAPTER OF
THOSE WHO TEAR OUT

LXXIX (*Mecca*)

In the name of the merciful and compassionate Allah.

By those who tear out violently!

And by those who gaily release![1]

And by those who float through the air!

And the preceders who precede![2]

[5] And those who manage the affair!

On the day when the quaking[3] quakes which the following one shall succeed! Hearts on that day shall tremble; eyes thereon be humbled!

[10] They say, 'Shall we be sent back to our old course?—What! when we are rotten bones?' they say, 'That then were a losing return!'

But it will only be one scare, and lo! they will be on the surface!

[15] Has the story of Moses[4] come to you? When his Lord addressed him in the holy valley of Tuvâ, 'Go unto Pharaoh, verily, he is outrageous; and say, "Hast thou a wish to purify thyself, and that I may guide thee to thy Lord, and thou mayest fear?"'

[20] So he showed him the greatest signs; but he called him a liar and rebelled. Then he retreated hastily, and gathered, and proclaimed, and said, 'I am your Lord most High!' [25] but Allah seized him with the punishment of the future life and of the former.

Verily, in that is a lesson to him who fears!

Are ye harder to create or the heaven that He has built? He raised its height and fashioned it; and made its night to cover it, and brought forth its noonday light; [30] and the earth after that He did stretch out. He brings forth from it its water and its pasture.

And the mountains He did firmly set, a provision for you and for your cattle.

And when the great predominant calamity shall come, [35] on the day when man shall remember what he strove after, and Hell shall be brought out for him who sees!

And as for him who was outrageous and preferred the life of this world, verily, Hell is the resort!

[40] But as for him who feared the station of his Lord, and prohibited his soul from lust, verily, Paradise is the resort!

They shall ask thee about the Hour, for when it is set. Whereby canst thou mention it? Unto thy Lord its period belongs.

[45] Thou art only a warner to him who fears it.

On the day they see it, it will be as though they had only tarried an evening or the noon thereof.

THE CHAPTER 'HE FROWNED'
LXXX (*Mecca*)

In the name of the merciful and compassionate Allah.

He frowned and turned his back, for that there came to him a blind man![1]

But what should make thee know whether haply he

may be purified? or may be mindful and the reminder profit him?

[5] But as for him who is wealthy, thou dost attend to him; and thou dost not care that he is not purified; but as for him who comes to thee earnestly fearing the while, [10] from him thou art diverted!

Nay! verily, it is a memorial; and whoso pleases will remember it.

In honoured pages exalted, purified, [15] in the hands of noble, righteous scribes!

May man be killed! How ungrateful he is!

Of what did He create him? Of a clot. He created him and fated him; [20] then the path He did make easy for him; then He killed him, and laid him in the tomb; then when He pleases will He raise him up again.

Nay, he has not fulfilled his bidding!

But let man look unto his foods. [25] Verily, we have poured the water out in torrents: then we have cleft the earth asunder, and made to grow therefrom the grain, and the grape, and the hay, and the olive, and the palm, [30] and gardens closely planted, and fruits, and grass,— a provision for you and for your cattle!

But when the stunning noise shall come, on the day when man shall flee from his brother [35] and his mother and his father and his spouse and his sons! Every man among them on that day shall have a business to employ him.

Faces on that day shall be bright,—laughing, joyous! [40] and faces shall have dust upon them,—darkness shall cover them! Those are the wicked misbelievers!

THE CHAPTER OF THE FOLDING UP

LXXXI (*Mecca*)

In the name of the merciful and compassionate Allah.
When the sun is folded up,
And when the stars do fall,
And when the mountains are moved,
And when the she-camels ten months' gone with young
    shall be neglected,[1]
[5] And when the beasts shall be crowded together,[2]
And when the seas shall surge up,
And when souls shall be paired with bodies,
And when the child who was buried alive shall be asked
    for what sin she was slain,[3]
[10] And when the pages shall be spread out,
And when the heavens shall be flayed.
And when Hell shall be set ablaze,
And when Paradise shall be brought nigh,
The soul shall know what it has produced!
[15] I need not swear by the stars that slink back, moving
    swiftly, slinking into their dens!
Nor by the night when darkness draws on!
Nor by the morn when it first breathes up!
Verily, it is the speech of a noble apostle, [20] mighty, standing
    sure with the Lord of the throne, obeyed and trusty too!
Your comrade is not mad; he saw him[4] on the plain horizon,[5]
    nor does he grudge to communicate the unseen.[6]
[25] Nor is it the speech of a pelted devil.[7]
Then whither do ye go?

It is but a reminder to the worlds, to whomsoever of you pleases to go straight:—but ye will not please, except Allah, the Lord of the world, should please.

THE CHAPTER OF
THE CLEAVING ASUNDER

LXXXII (*Mecca*)

In the name of the merciful and compassionate Allah.
When the heaven is cleft asunder,
And when the stars are scattered,
And when the seas gush together,
And when the tombs are turned upside down,
[5] The soul shall know what it has sent on or kept back!

O man! what has seduced thee concerning thy generous Lord, who created thee, and fashioned thee, and gave thee symmetry, and in what form He pleased composed thee?

Nay, but ye call the judgement a lie! [10] but over you are guardians set,[1]—noble, writing down! They know what ye do!

Verily, the righteous are in pleasure, and, verily, the wicked are in Hell; [15] they shall broil therein upon the judgement day; nor shall they be absent therefrom!

And what shall make thee know what is the judgement day? Again, what shall make thee know what is the judgement day? A day when no soul shall control aught for another; and the bidding on that day belongs to Allah!

THE CHAPTER OF
THOSE WHO GIVE SHORT WEIGHT

LXXXIII (*Mecca*)

In the name of the merciful and compassionate Allah.

Woe to those who give short weight! who when they measure against others take full measure; but when they measure to them or weigh to them, diminish!

Do not these think that they shall be raised again [5] at the mighty day? The day when men shall stand before the Lord of the worlds!

Nay, verily, the book of the wicked is in Sijjîn;[1] and what shall make thee know what Sijjîn is?—a book inscribed!

[10] Woe on that day for those who say it is a lie!

Who call the judgement day a lie! but none shall call it a lie except every sinful transgressor, who, when our signs are read to him, says, 'Old folks' tales!'

Nay, but that which they have gained has settled upon their hearts.

Nay, verily, [15] from their Lord on that day are they veiled; and then, verily, they shall broil in Hell; then it shall be said, 'This is what ye once did call a lie!'

Nay, verily, the book of the righteous is in 'Illiyûn;[2] and what shall make thee know what 'Illiyûn is?— [20] a book inscribed! Those nigh to Allah shall witness it.

Verily, the righteous shall be in pleasure; upon couches shall they gaze; thou mayest recognize in their faces the brightness of pleasure; [25] they shall be given to drink wine that is sealed, whose seal is musk; for that then let the aspirants aspire!—and it shall be tempered with Tasnîm,[3]—a spring from which those nigh to Allah shall drink.

Verily, those who sin do laugh at those who believe; [30] and when they pass by they wink at one another, and when they return to their family they return ridiculing them; and when they see them they say, 'Verily, these do go astray!'—but they are not sent as guardians over them!

But today those who believe shall at the misbelievers laugh! [35] Upon couches shall they gaze; are the misbelievers rewarded for what they have done?

THE CHAPTER OF THE RENDING ASUNDER

LXXXIV (*Mecca*)

In the name of the merciful and compassionate Allah.

When the heaven is rent asunder and gives ear unto its Lord, and is dutiful!

And when the earth is stretched out and casts forth what is in it, and is empty, [5] and gives ear unto its Lord, and is dutiful!

O man! verily, thou art toiling after thy Lord, toiling; wherefore shalt thou meet Him!

And as for him who is given his book in his right hand, he shall be reckoned with by an easy reckoning; and he shall go back to his family joyfully.

[10] But as for him who is given his book behind his back,[1] he shall call out for destruction, but he shall broil in a blaze! Verily, he was amongst his family joyful. Verily, he thought that he should never return to Allah.

[15] Yea, verily, his Lord on him did look!

I need not swear by the evening glow,

Or by the night, and what it drives together,

Or by the moon when it is at its full,

Ye shall be surely transferred from state to state![2]

[20] What ails them that they do not believe? and, when the Qur'ân is read to them, do not adore? Nay, those who misbelieve do say it is a lie, but Allah knows best the (malice) that they hide.

So give them the glad tidings of grievous woe! [25] save those who believe and act aright, for them is hire that is not grudged!

THE CHAPTER OF
THE ZODIACAL SIGNS

LXXXV (*Mecca*)

In the name of the merciful and compassionate Allah.

By the heaven with its zodiacal signs![1]

And the promised day!

And the witness and the witnessed![2]

The fellows of the pit were slain;

[5] And the Fire with its kindling,

When they sat over it

And witnessed the while what they were doing with those who believed.[3]

And they took not vengeance on them save for their belief in Allah,

The mighty, the praiseworthy,

Whose is the kingdoms of the heavens and the earth;

For Allah is witness over all!

[10] Verily, those who make trial of the believers, men and women, and then do not repent, for them is the torment of Hell, and for them is the torment of the burning!

Verily, those who believe and act aright, for them are gardens beneath which rivers flow,—that is the great bliss!

Verily, the violence of thy Lord is keen!

Verily, He produces and returns, and He is the forgiving, the loving, [15] the Lord of the glorious throne; the doer of what He will!

Has there come to thee the story of the hosts of Pharaoh and Thamûd?

Nay, those who misbelieve do say it is a lie; [20] but Allah is behind them—encompassing!

Nay, it is a glorious Qur'ân in a preserved tablet.[4]

THE CHAPTER OF THE NIGHT STAR
LXXXVI (*Mecca*)

In the name of the merciful and compassionate Allah.

By the heaven and by the night star! And what shall make thee know what the night star is?—The star of piercing brightness.

Verily, every soul has a guardian over it.

[5] Then let man look from what he is created: he is created from water poured forth, that comes out from between the loins and the breast bones.[1]

Verily, He is able to send him back again, on the day when the secrets shall be tried, [10] and he shall have no strength nor helper.

By the heaven that sends back the rain!

And the earth with its sprouting!

Verily, it is indeed a distinguishing speech, and it is no frivolity!

[15] Verily, they do plot a plot!

But I plot my plot too! Let the misbelievers bide; do thou then let them bide awhile!

THE CHAPTER OF THE MOST HIGH
LXXXVII (*Mecca*)

In the name of the merciful and compassionate Allah.

Celebrated be the name of thy Lord most High, who created and fashioned, and who decreed and guided, and who brings forth the pasture, [5] and then makes it dusky stubble!

We will make thee recite, and thou shalt not forget,¹ save what Allah pleases. Verily, He knows the open and what is concealed; and we will send thee easily to ease; wherefore remind, for, verily, the reminder is useful.

[10] But he who fears will be mindful; but the wretch will avoid it; he who will broil on the great Fire, and then therein shall neither die nor live!

Prosperous is he who purifies himself, [15] and remembers the name of his Lord and prays!

Nay! but ye prefer the life of this world, while the hereafter is better and more lasting.

Verily, this was in the books of yore,—the books of Abraham and Moses.

THE CHAPTER OF
THE OVERWHELMING¹

LXXXVIII (*Mecca*)

In the name of the merciful and compassionate Allah.

Has there come to thee the story of the overwhelming?

Faces on that day shall be humble, labouring, toiling,— shall broil upon a burning fire; [5] shall be given to drink from a boiling spring! No food shall they have save from the foul thorn, which shall not fatten nor avail against hunger!

Faces on that day shall be comfortable, content with their past endeavours,—[10] in a lofty garden wherein they shall hear no foolish word; wherein is a flowing fountain; wherein are couches raised on high, and goblets set down, [15] and cushions arranged, and carpets spread!

Do they not look then at the camel how she is created?²

And at the heaven how it is reared?

And at the mountains how they are set up?

[20] And at the earth how it is spread out?

But remind: thou art only one to remind; thou art not in authority over them; except such as turns his back and misbelieves, for him will Allah torment with the greatest torment.

[25] Verily, unto us is their return, and, verily, for us is their account!

THE CHAPTER OF THE DAWN

LXXXIX (*Mecca*)

In the name of the merciful and compassionate Allah.

By the dawn and ten nights!¹

And the single and the double!

And the night when it travels on!

Is there in that an oath for a man of sense?

[5] Hast thou not seen how thy Lord did with 'Âd?— with Irem of the columns?² the like of which has not been created in the land?

And Thamûd when they hewed the stones in the valley?

And Pharaoh of the stakes?³

[10] Who were outrageous in the land, and did multiply wickedness therein, and thy Lord poured out upon them the scourge of torment.

Verily, thy Lord is on a watch tower! and as for man, whenever his Lord tries him and honours him and grants him favour, then [15] he says, 'My Lord has honoured me'; but whenever he tries him and doles out to him his subsistence, then he says, 'My Lord despises me!'

Nay, but ye do not honour the orphan, nor do ye urge each other to feed the poor, [20] and ye devour the inheritance (of the weak) with a general devouring,[4] and ye love wealth with a complete love!

Nay, when the earth is crushed to pieces, and thy Lord comes with the angels, rank on rank, and Hell is brought on that day,—on that day shall man be reminded! but how shall he have a reminder?

[25] He will say, 'Would that I had sent something forward for my life!'

But on that day no one shall be tormented with a torment like his, and none shall be bound with bonds like his!

O thou comforted soul! return unto thy Lord, well pleased and well pleased with!

And enter amongst my servants, [30] and enter my Paradise!

THE CHAPTER OF THE LAND

XC (*Mecca*)

In the name of the merciful and compassionate Allah.

I need not swear by the Lord of this land,[1] and thou a dweller in this land![2]

Nor by the begetter and what he begets!

We have surely created man in trouble.

[5] Does he think that none can do aught against him?

He says, 'I have wasted wealth in plenty'; does he think that no one sees him?

Have we not made for him two eyes and a tongue, and two lips? [10] and guided him in the two highways? But he will not attempt the steep!

And what shall make thee know what the steep is? It is freeing captives, or feeding on the day of famine, [15] an orphan who is akin, or a poor man who lies in the dust; and again (it is) to be of these who believe and encourage each other to patience, and encourage each other to mercy,—these are the fellows of the right![3]

But those who disbelieve in our signs, they are the fellows of the left, [20] for them is fire that closes in!

THE CHAPTER OF THE SUN

XCI (*Mecca*)

In the name of the merciful and compassionate Allah.

By the sun and its noonday brightness!

And the moon when it follows him!

And the day when it displays him!

And the night when it covers him!

[5] And the heaven and what built it!

And the earth and what spread it!

And the soul and what fashioned it, and taught it its sin and its piety!

Prosperous is he who purifies it!

[10] And disappointed is he who corrupts it!

Thamûd called the apostle a liar¹ in their outrage, when their wretch rose up and the apostle of Allah said to them, 'Allah's she-camel! so give her to drink.'

But they called him a liar, and they hamstrung her; but their Lord destroyed them in their sins, and served them all alike; [15] and He fears not the result thereof!

THE CHAPTER OF THE NIGHT

XCII (*Mecca*)

In the name of the merciful and compassionate Allah.

By the night when it veils!

And the day when it is displayed!

And by what created male and female!

Verily, your efforts are diverse!
[5] But as for him who gives alms and fears Allah,
And believes in the best,
We will send him easily to ease!
But as for him who is niggardly,
And longs for wealth,
And calls the good a lie,
[10] We will send him easily to difficulty!
And his wealth shall not avail him
When he falls down (into Hell)!
Verily, it is for us to guide;
And, verily, ours are the hereafter and the former life!
And I have warned you of a fire that flames!

[15] None shall broil thereon, but the most wretched,
who says it is a lie and turns his back.

But the pious shall be kept away from it, he who gives
his wealth in alms, and who gives no favour to any one
for the sake of reward, [20] but only craving the face of
his Lord most High; in the end he shall be well pleased!

THE CHAPTER OF THE FORENOON

XCIII (*Mecca*)

In the name of the merciful and compassionate Allah.
By the forenoon!
And the night when it darkens!
Thy Lord has not forsaken thee, nor hated thee! and
surely the hereafter is better for thee than the former;

[5] and in the end thy Lord will give thee, and thou shalt be well pleased!

Did He not find thee an orphan, and give thee shelter? and find thee erring, and guide thee? and find thee poor with a family, and nourish thee?

But as for the orphan oppress him not; [10] and as for the beggar drive him not away; and as for the favour of thy Lord discourse thereof.

THE CHAPTER OF
'HAVE WE NOT EXPANDED?'

XCIV (*Mecca*)

In the name of the merciful and compassionate Allah.

Have we not expanded for thee thy breast?[1] and set down from thee thy load which galled thy back? and exalted for thee thy renown?

[5] Verily, with difficulty is ease! Verily, with difficulty is ease!

And when thou art at leisure then toil, and for thy Lord do thou yearn!

THE CHAPTER OF THE FIG

XCV (*Place of origin doubtful*)

In the name of the merciful and compassionate Allah.

By the fig!

And by the olive!

And by Mount Sinai!

And by this safe land![1]

We have indeed created man in the best of symmetry.

[5] Then we will send him back the lowest of the low; save those who believe and act aright; for theirs is a hire that is not grudged.

But what shall make thee call the judgement after this a lie!

Is not Allah a most just of judges?

THE CHAPTER OF CONGEALED BLOOD[1]

XCVI (*Mecca*)

In the name of the merciful and compassionate Allah.

Read, in the name of thy Lord!

Who created man from congealed blood!

Read, for thy Lord is most generous!

[5] Who taught the pen!

Taught man what he did not know!

Nay, verily, man is indeed outrageous at seeing himself get rich!

Verily, unto thy Lord is the return!

Hast thou considered him who forbids [10] a servant² when he prays?³

Hast thou considered if he were in guidance or bade piety?

Hast thou considered if he said it was a lie and turned his back?

Did he not know that Allah can see?

[15] Nay, surely, if he do not desist we will drag him by the forelock!—the lying sinful forelock!

So let him call his counsel: we will call the guards of Hell!

Nay, obey him not, but adore and draw nigh!

THE CHAPTER OF POWER¹

XCVII (*Place of origin doubtful*)

In the name of the merciful and compassionate Allah.

Verily, we sent it down on the Night of Power!

And what shall make thee know what the Night of Power is?—the Night of Power is better than a thousand months!

The angels and the Spirit descend therein, by the permission of their Lord with every bidding.

[5] Peace it is until rising of the dawn!

THE CHAPTER OF
THE MANIFEST SIGN

XCVIII (*Place of origin doubtful*)

In the name of the merciful and compassionate Allah.

Those of the people of the Book and the idolaters who misbelieve did not fall off until there came to them the manifest sign,—

An apostle from Allah reading pure pages wherein are right scriptures:

Nor did those who were given the Book divide into sects until after there came to them the manifest sign.

But they were not bidden aught but to worship Allah, being sincere in religion unto Him as *hanîfs*, and to be steadfast in prayer, and to give alms: for that is the standard religion.

[5] Verily, those who disbelieve amongst the people of the Book and the idolaters shall be in the Fire of Hell, to dwell therein for aye; they are wretched creatures!

Verily, those who believe and act aright, they are the best of creatures; their reward with their Lord is gardens of Eden, beneath which rivers flow, to dwell therein for aye; Allah shall be well pleased with them, and they with Him! That is for him who fears his Lord!

THE CHAPTER OF THE EARTHQUAKE

XCIX (*Place of origin doubtful*)

In the name of the merciful and compassionate Allah.

When the earth shall quake with its quaking!

And the earth shall bring forth her burdens, and man shall say, 'What ails her!'

On that day she shall tell her tidings, [5] because thy Lord inspires her.

On the day when men shall come up in separate bands to show their works: and he who does the weight of an atom of good shall see it! and he who does the weight of an atom of evil shall see it!

THE CHAPTER OF THE CHARGERS

C (*Mecca*)

In the name of the merciful and compassionate Allah.

By the snorting chargers!

And those who strike fire with their hoofs!

And those who make incursions in the morning,

And raise up dust therein,

[5] And cleave through a host therein!

Verily, man is to his Lord ungrateful; and, verily, he is a witness of that.

Verily, he is keen in his love of good.

Does he not know when the tombs are exposed, [10] and what is in the breasts is brought to light?

Verily, thy Lord upon that day indeed is well aware.

THE CHAPTER OF THE SMITING
CI (*Mecca*)

In the name of the merciful and compassionate Allah.

The smiting!

What is the smiting?

And what shall make thee know what the smiting is?

The day when men shall be like scattered moths; and the mountains shall be like flocks of carded wool!

[5] And as for him whose balance is heavy, he shall be in a well-pleasing life.

But as for him whose balance is light, his dwelling shall be the pit of Hell.[1]

And who shall make thee know what it is?—a burning fire!

THE CHAPTER OF
THE CONTENTION ABOUT NUMBERS
CII (*Place of origin doubtful*)

In the name of the merciful and compassionate Allah.

The contention about numbers deludes you till ye visit the tombs![1]

Not so! In the end ye shall know! And again not so! In the end ye shall know!

[5] Not so! Did ye but know with certain knowledge!

Ye shall surely see Hell! And again ye shall surely see it with an eye of certainty.

Then ye shall surely be asked about pleasure![2]

THE CHAPTER OF THE AFTERNOON[1]

CIII (*Mecca*)

In the name of the merciful and compassionate Allah.

By the afternoon! verily, man is in loss! save those who believe and do right, and bid each other be true, and bid each other be patient.

THE CHAPTER OF THE BACKBITER

CIV (*Mecca*)

In the name of the merciful and compassionate Allah.

Woe to every slanderous backbiter, who collects wealth and counts it.

He thinks that his wealth can immortalize him.

Not so! He shall be hurled into El 'Hutamah!

[5] And what shall make thee understand what El 'Hutamah is?—the fire of Allah kindled; which rises above the hearts. Verily, it is an archway over them on long-drawn columns.

THE CHAPTER OF THE ELEPHANT

CV (*Mecca*)

In the name of the merciful and compassionate Allah.

Hast thou not seen what thy Lord did with the fellows of the elephant?[1]

Did He not make their stratagem lead them astray, and send down on them birds in flocks, to throw down on them stones of baked clay, [5] and make them like blades of herbage eaten down?

THE CHAPTER OF THE QURÂIS

CVI (*Mecca*)

In the name of the merciful and compassionate Allah.

For the uniting of the Qurâis; uniting them for the caravan of winter and summer.

So let them serve the Lord of this house who feeds them against hunger and makes them safe against fear.[1]

THE CHAPTER OF 'NECESSARIES'

CVII (*Place of origin doubtful*)

In the name of the merciful and compassionate Allah.

Hast thou considered him who calls the judgement a lie?
He it is who pushes the orphan away; and urges not
(others) to feed the poor.

But woe to those who pray [5] and who are careless in
their prayers,

Who pretend and withhold necessaries.[1]

THE CHAPTER OF EL KÂUTHAR

CVIII (*Mecca*)

In the name of the merciful and compassionate Allah.
Verily, we have given thee El Kâuthar;[1]
So pray to thy Lord and slaughter (victims).
Verily, he who hates thee shall be childless.[2]

THE CHAPTER OF MISBELIEVERS

CIX (*Mecca*)

In the name of the merciful and compassionate Allah.

Say, 'O ye misbelievers! I do not serve what ye serve;
nor will ye serve what I serve; nor will I serve what ye
serve; [5] nor will ye serve what I serve;—ye have your
religion, and I have my religion!'

THE CHAPTER OF HELP

CX (*Mecca*)

In the name of the merciful and compassionate Allah.

When there comes Allah's help and victory,

And thou shalt see men enter into Allah's religion by troops.

Then celebrate the praises of thy Lord, and ask forgiveness of Him, verily, He is relentant!

THE CHAPTER OF ABU LAHEB[1]

CXI (*Mecca*)

In the name of the merciful and compassionate Allah.

Abu Laheb's two hands shall perish, and he shall perish!

His wealth shall not avail him, nor what he has earned!

He shall broil in a fire that flames,[2] and his wife carrying faggots!—[5] on her neck a cord of palm fibres.

THE CHAPTER OF UNITY[1]
CXII (*Place of origin doubtful*)

In the name of the merciful and compassionate Allah.
Say, 'He is Allah alone!
Allah the Eternal!
He begets not and is not begotten!
Nor is there like unto Him any one!'

THE CHAPTER OF THE DAYBREAK
CXIII (*Place of origin doubtful*)

In the name of the merciful and compassionate Allah.
Say, 'I seek refuge in the Lord of the daybreak, from the evil of what He has created; and from the evil of the night when it cometh on;[1] and from the evil of the blowers upon knots;[2] [5] and from the evil of the envious when he envies.'

THE CHAPTER OF MEN
CXIV (*Place of origin doubtful*)

In the name of the merciful and compassionate Allah.
Say, 'I seek refuge in the Lord of men, the King of men, the Allah of men, from the evil of the whisperer,[1] who slinks off, [5] who whispers into the hearts of men!—from jinns and men!'

NOTES

CHAPTER II

1 The mysterious letters which are placed at the beginning of
   certain chapters of the Qur'ân are explained in various ways by
   the Muslim commentators. Some suppose them to be part of the
   revelation itself, and to conceal sublime and inscrutable
   mysteries; others think that they stand for the names of Allah,
   Gabriel, Mohammed, and so on.

   Nöldeke has the ingenious theory that they were monograms of
   the names of the persons from whom Zâid and his companions
   obtained the portions to which they are prefixed; thus, A.L.R.
   would stand for Ez-zubâir, A.L.M.R. for Al-Mughâirah, T.H. for
   Tal'hah, and so on. A comparison of the Arabic letters themselves
   with the names suggested makes the hypothesis a very probable
   one. They may have been mere numerical or alphabetical labels for
   the boxes of scraps on which the original was written; the authors
   of the Commentary known as *El Jelâlâin*, however, give the
   prevailing opinion amongst Muslim scholars when they say, 'Allah
   alone knows what He means by these letters.'

2 Although the Arabic demonstrative pronoun means '*that*', the
   translators have hitherto always rendered it '*this*', forgetting
   that it is not an address to the *reader*, but supposed to be
   Gabriel's words of inspiration to Mohammed while showing him
   the *Umm al Kitâb*—the 'Eternal original of the Qur'ân'; cf.
   Chapter X.

3 This change of number is of frequent occurrence in the Qur'ân,
   and is not incompatible with the genius of the Arabic language.

4 That is, the idols.

5 The vagueness is in the original; it is variously interpreted 'fruits
   like each other', or 'like the fruits of earth'.

6 This is in answer to the objections that had been taken against the
   mention of such small things as the 'spider' and the 'bee', which
   give their names to two of the chapters of the Qur'ân.

7 That is, truthful in their implied suggestion that man would be inferior to themselves in wisdom and obedience. The whole tradition here alluded to of the creation accords with the Talmudic legends, and was probably current among the Jewish Arab tribes.

8 Cf. Exodus xxxii: 24, 26, 27.

9 According to some commentators, Jerusalem; and according to others, Jericho.

10 The word means Remission, or laying down the burden (of sins).

11 Some say the expression they used was *habbah fi sha'hîrah*, 'a grain in an ear of barley', the idea being apparently suggested by the similarity between the words '*hittah*, as given above, and '*hintah*, 'a grain of wheat'. The commentators add that they crept in in an indecent posture instead of entering reverently as they were bidden.

12 The Mohammedan legend is that this was done by the angel Gabriel to terrify the people into obedience.

13 The tradition is that some inhabitants of Elath (Akabah) were transformed into apes for catching fish on the Sabbath in David's time. Other commentators say that the expression is only figurative.

14 The legend embodied in this passage and what follows appears to be a distorted account of the heifer ordered by the Mosaic law to be slain in expiation of a murder, the perpetrator of which had not been discovered. Deut. xxi: 1–9.

15 A constant charge against the Jews is that of having corrupted the Scriptures.

16 A superstition of certain Jews.

17 Alluding to some quarrels among the Jewish Arabs.

18 The Qur'ân.

19 Exodus xxxii: 20.

20 The Jews objected to Mohammed's assertion that the archangel Gabriel revealed the Qur'ân to him, saying that he was an avenging angel, and that had it been Michael, their own guardian angel (Dan. xii: 1), they would have believed.

21 Solomon's acts of disobedience and idolatry are attributed by Muslim tradition to the tricks of devils, who assumed his form.

22 Two angels who having fallen in love with daughters of men
(Gen. vi: 2) were condemned to hang in chains in a pit at Babylon,
where they teach men magic.

23 The Jewish Arabs used the first of these two words derisively. In
Arabic it merely means 'observe us', but the Jews connected it
with the Hebrew root *rû'há*, 'to be mischievous'. *Unthurnâ*
signifies 'behold us'.

24 The word *resignation* (Islam) is that by which Mohammed's
religion is known and by which it is spoken of in the Qur'ân.

25 Probably alluding to the occasion on which the Meccans
prevented Mohammed from using the Kaabah, in the sixth year of
the Hijrah.

26 i.e. Allah forbid!

27 Imam, the name given to the priest who leads the prayer; it is
equivalent to *Antistes*.

28 The Kaabah or square temple at Mecca is spoken of as *Bâit Allah*
= Bethel, 'the house of Allah'.

29 The *Muqâm Ibrahîm*, in the Kaabah enclosure, where a so-called
footprint of the patriarch is shown.

30 The last sentence might be rendered 'until ye become Muslims'.

31 The sentence might be rendered 'until ye become Muslims'.

32 The sentence might be rendered 'until ye become Muslims'.

33 The word means in Arabic 'inclining to what is right'; it is often
used technically for one who professes El Islam.

34 The metaphor is derived from dyeing cloth, and must not be
translated by the technical word *baptism*, as in Sale's version.

35 The point to which they turn in prayer, from qabala, 'to be before'.

36 At first Mohammed and his followers adopted no point of
adoration. After the Hijrah, or flight from Mecca to Medina,
however, he bade them turn their face, as did the Jews, to the
temple at Jerusalem; but in the second year of the Hijrah he
resumed the ancient Arab plan, and turned to the Kaabah at
Mecca when he prayed.

37 i.e. at Mecca.

38 i.e. know Mohammed from the prophecies the Scriptures are
alleged to contain about him.

39 On the last day.

40 Or rather be not grateful, the word *Kufr* implying negation of benefits received as well as of faith.

41 i.e. in the cause of religion.

42 This formula is always used by Mohammedans in any danger and sudden calamity, especially in the presence of death.

43 Two mountains near Mecca, where two idols used to stand.

44 Or, 'respited', as some interpret it.

45 Variously interpreted 'idols' and 'chiefs'.

46 Chiefs of sects and founders of false religions.

47 i.e. their mutual relations.

48 i.e. on earth.

49 i.e. as cattle hear the sound of the drover without understanding the meaning of his words, so the infidels fail to comprehend the meaning and importance of the words that are preached to them.

50 At the time of slaughtering an animal the Muslims always repeat the formula *bismi'llâh*, in the name of Allah.

51 i.e. the wayfarer.

52 The relations of a murdered man are always allowed to choose the fine instead of the blood revenge.

53 The legacy.

54 i.e. able to fast but do not.

55 i.e. who is at home during the month Ramadan and not on a journey, or in a place where it is impossible to keep the fast.

56 The Arabs before Mohammed's time had a superstition that it was unlucky to enter their houses by the doors on their return from Mecca, so they made holes in the hinder walls to enter in by instead.

57 Or, 'cause', see p. 31, note 41.

58 By beginning the fight yourselves.

59 The other Arabs had attacked them during the month *Dhu'lqa'hdah*, which was one of their sacred months; the Moslems therefore are bidden to attack them if necessary in the sacred month of Ramadan.

60 If a breach of their sanctity be committed.

61 i.e. going to the visitation at once without waiting for the month of the pilgrimage to come round.

62 By trading during the Hajj pilgrimage.

63 A'hnas ibn Surâiq eth thaqafî, a fair spoken man of pleasant appearance, who pretended to believe in Mohammed.

64 Zuhâib ibn Sinân er Rûmî, who being threatened at Mecca with death unless he apostatized from Islam, said, 'I am an old man, who cannot profit you if he be with you, nor hurt you if he be against you,' and was allowed to escape to Medina.

65 Here used as a synonym for resignation, i.e. Islam.

66 In the Arabic *hâjarû*, i.e. who fled with Mohammed in his Hijrah or expatriation to Medina, from which the Muslim era dates.

67 The jihad, or general war of extermination against infidels, to threaten or preach which is a favourite diplomatic weapon with Mohammedan nations.

68 *'Hamr*, which is rendered 'wine', includes all alcoholic and intoxicating drinks.

69 *El mâisar* was a game of chance, played with arrows, the prize being a young camel, which was slaughtered and given to the poor, the price of it being paid by the losers. This distribution to the poor Mohammed speaks of as useful, but the quarrels and extravagance to which the game gave rise, he considers, overbalanced the profit.

70 i.e. if ye wrong orphans.

71 Either wishing for a child, or saying, 'in the name of Allah', *Bâidhâvî*.

72 The confusion of numbers and persons is in the original. The meaning of the passage is that 'divorce is allowed twice only, and that on each occasion the man may take the woman back if pregnant during the next four months; that if a woman be retained after divorced she is to be treated kindly, but if she be sent away she is not to be deprived of her dowry. If, however, they feel that they cannot live together, the woman may give up a part of her dowry to induce her husband to part with her'.

73 i.e. with honest intentions.

74 Until the time prescribed by the Qur'ân be fulfilled.

75 That is, unless the wife choose to give up a part of the half which

she could claim, or the husband do the same on his part, in which case an unequal partition is lawful.

76 Interpreted to mean either the middle or the odd one of the five.

77 That is, if ye are in danger, say your prayers, as best you can, on foot or horseback, not staying so as to endanger your lives.

78 The legend to which this alludes is variously told, but the most usually accepted version is that a number of the Israelites fled from their homes to avoid a jihad or 'religious war', and were struck dead, and afterwards revived by the prophet Ezekiel's intervention. The story is apparently a distorted version of Ezekiel's vision of the dry bones. Ezek. xxxvii: 1–10.

79 Samuel.

80 Saul.

81 The commentators do not understand that the word, *sakînah*, which is in the original, is identical with the Hebrew, *shechina*, and render it 'repose' or 'tranquillity'.

82 1 Samuel iv, v, vi.

83 Gideon and Saul are here confused; this portion of the story is taken from Judges vi.

84 Goliath.

85 Moses, called Kalîmu 'llâh, 'He with whom Allah spake'.

86 This the famous *âyatu 'l kursîy*, or 'verse of the throne', considered as one of the finest passages in the Qur'ân, and frequently found inscribed in mosques and the like.

87 The idols and demons of the ancient Arabs are so called.

88 Nimrod, who persecuted Abraham, according to the eastern legend; see Chapter XXI, verses 52–69.

89 According to the Arabic commentators, 'Huzair (Esdras) ibn Sara'hyâ or Al 'Hizr (Elias) is the person alluded to; and the 'village' Jerusalem after its destruction by Ba'htnazr, Nebuchadnezzar. The legend probably refers to Nehemiah ii: 13.

90 Cf. Genesis xv: 9.

91 i.e. by a mutual understanding between seller and buyer.

92 i.e. Mohammed.

93 I must remind the reader that the language of the Qur'ân is really rude and rugged, and that although the expressions employed in

it are now considered as refined and elegant, it is only because all literary Arabic has been modelled on the style of the Qur'ân. The word which I have ventured to translate by this somewhat inelegant phrase (*dharban*) means literally, 'to beat or knock about', and as colloquial English affords an exact equivalent I have not hesitated to use it.

94 i.e. his former conduct shall be pardoned.

CHAPTER III

1 i.e. the fundamental part of it.

2 On the occasion of the battle of Bedr.

3 The word also means 'illiterate', and refers here to the Pagan Arabs in Mohammed's time. He seems to have borrowed the expression from the Jews, *ummîyûn*, having the same signification as the Hebrew *goyîm*.

4 The sentence might be rendered 'until ye became Muslims'.

5 Amram, who, according to the Mohammedans, was the father of the Virgin Mary (Miriam). A confusion seems to have existed in the mind of Mohammed between Miriam 'the Virgin Mary', and Miriam the sister of Moses.

6 The Mohammedan superstition is that the devils listen at the gate of heaven for scraps of the knowledge of futurity, and when detected by the angels are pelted with shooting stars. The expression may also refer to the ceremony of 'pelting the devil', as performed by Hajj pilgrims at Minâ, in memory, it is said, of Abraham's having driven Iblîs away with stones when tempted by him to disobey Allah and refuse to sacrifice Isaac.

7 The legend is that the priests threw lots by casting arrows into the river Jordan. The word used for arrows means simply unfeathered and unpointed arrows, and is the same as that used in the Arab game *mâisar*, referred to on page 40, note 69.

8 The Arabic expression is '*Havârîyûn*, which means 'fullers', and is explained by the commentators either as referring to their 'trade' or to their 'sincerity and candour'. The word is really derived from an Ethiopic root signifying 'to send'.

9 See page 25, note 24.

10 The Mohammedans believe that it was an *eidolon* and not Jesus himself who was crucified.

11 This word dhikr is used by Mohammedans for the recitation of the Qur'ân, and is also applied to the religious celebrations of the dervishes.

12 See p. 28, note 33.

13 This is said to allude to some Jews who professed Islam in the morning and recanted at night, saying that they had in the meantime consulted their books and found nothing to confirm it, hoping by this stratagem to raise doubts in the believers' minds.

14 A 'talent', *qintâr*, is used for any very large sum, a dinar ('denarius') was a gold coin worth about 10s.

15 i.e. pervert it.

16 In the original Rabbânîyîn, an expression identical with Rabboni, cf. John xx: 16.

17 The legend, borrowed from Talmudic sources, is that Allah assembled all past, present, and future prophets on Mount Sinai and entered into the compact mentioned in the text.

18 Another name of Mecca.

19 Alluding to an occasion in which the ancient rivalry between the two tribes of El Aus and El 'Hazraj, which had been reconciled by Islam, was on the point of breaking out again.

20 i.e. only a slight hurt.

21 That is, unless they enter into either the spiritual or temporal dominion of Islam, by professing the Mohammedan creed, or by paying a tribute.

22 This refers to the battle of Ohod, when Mohammed experienced a severe check, and lost two teeth by a shot from an arrow.

23 Or 'battles'.

24 Or 'martyrs'.

25 Plunder.

26 This word is always used for the pagan Arabs.

27 He means that the loss at Ohod was more than counterbalanced by their previous success at Bedr.

28 Mohammed, in his message to the Jewish tribe of Kainûka, used the words of the Qur'ân, and bade them 'lend to Allah at good

interest', when Phineas Ibn Azûra mockingly said, 'Surely, Allah is poor since they try to borrow for him!' Whereupon Abu Bekr, who had brought the letter, smote him on the face and said that, but for the truce between them, he would have smitten off his head. On complaint being made of this conduct to Mohammed the above verse was revealed.

29 The commentators say that the Jewish Rabbis demanded of Mohammed this proof of his prophetic mission, having regard, probably, to the contest between Elijah and the priests of Baal on Mount Carmel.

30 This passage was revealed in answer to the objection of Umm Salmâ, one of Mohammed's wives, when the women who fled with him were not mentioned as well as the men in the promised reward of the future life.

31 That is, with their enemies.

CHAPTER IV

1 That is, fear Allah, and pay respect to your mothers and wives.

2 That is, female slaves.

3 The Arabic idiom for the enjoyment of property being to eat it up, Mohammed here gives the men permission to enjoy such portion of their wives' dowries as the latter might be pleased to remit, and adds, with a sort of humour, the colloquial expression used by the Arabs when any one is eating. The sentence might be paraphrased 'and if they are kind enough to remit any portion of it of their own accord, then enjoy it, and much good may it do you!'

4 To idiots or persons of weak intellect.

5 The word in the original is that always used to express this relationship.

6 i.e. to the heirs.

7 Women taken in adultery or fornication were at the beginning of Islam literally immured.

8 The commentators are not agreed as to the nature of the offence here referred to. The text, however, speaks of two of the masculine gender. The punishment to be inflicted is also the

subject of dispute, the original merely saying, as I have translated it, 'hurt them'.

9 That is, from marrying again.

10 That is, a large dowry.

11 This question is ironical, and intended as a warning against bringing a false accusation of infidelity against a wife for the sake of keeping her dowry when divorced.

12 Man and wife.

13 i.e. slaves.

14 The abbreviated form *taku* (for *takun*) is used in the Arabic.

15 See p. 24, note 23.

16 See Chapter II, verse 61.

17 The word in the original means a fibre in the cleft of a date stone, or the rush wick of a candle.

18 Idols of the ancient Arabs; see p. 47.

19 Literally, a dent or cleft in a date stone.

20 See p. 47, note 87.

21 Mecca.

22 Captive.

23 Because a believer might not be attacked and plundered as an infidel might be.

24 Alluding to some half-hearted Muslims, slain at Bedr.

25 The pagan Arabs used to cut off the ears of cattle, and mutilate their slaves by branding and filing their teeth, partly that they might recognize them and partly as a superstitious ceremony. See p. 114, note 15.

26 Chap. VI, v. 67, which chronologically precedes the present.

27 See p. 19, note 14.

28 See p. 59, note 10.

29 This may allude to the time of his death after his second advent, when he shall slay the Antichrist.

30 See p. 77, note 5.

CHAPTER V

1 Mu'harram.

2 The Qurâish, who sent to meet Mohammed with 1,400 men at 'Hudâibîyeh to prevent him from approaching Mecca, A.H. 6.

3 Literally, 'stones set up', Dolmens and the like, which are so common throughout Arabia.

4 By the game of *mâisar*, see p. 40, note 69.

5 Referring to the oath of fidelity which Mohammed's adherents took at 'Akabah.

6 Various stories are told in explanation of this passage, but they are all obviously apocryphal, the angel Gabriel intervening to prevent some mischief either to the Apostle or his followers.

7 That is, the text foretelling the coming of Mohammed.

8 See p. 61, note 16.

9 The time before the Mohammedan dispensation is always so called.

10 i.e. to take his place.

11 The ancient Arabs always lit a beacon fire as a proclamation of war, or a notice of the approach of an enemy.

12 i.e. from the yoke of captivity.

13 See p. 40, note 69.

14 This has been thought by strict Mussulmans to exclude the game of chess. Sunni, however, play the game with plain pieces like draughts, though Persians and Indians are not so scrupulous.

15 These were the names given to certain animals which were marked and allowed to graze at liberty. *Ba'hîrah* was the name given to a camel which had had ten young ones; her ear was then slit and she was turned loose to feed. When she died her flesh was eaten by the men only, the women being forbidden to touch it. There were, however, cases in which any she-camel was so called and treated. *Sâibah* signifies merely a camel turned loose; her being so turned out was generally in fulfilment of a vow. *Wazîlah* was a term applied to any cattle, including sheep and goats, and generally meant a beast who had brought forth a male and female at the seventh parturition. *'Hâmî* was a stallion camel which, after begetting ten young ones, was turned loose.

As all these customs were connected with the idolatrous superstitions of the pagan Arabs, and tended to keep alive the rites and beliefs of paganism, Mohammed forbade them, with other similar superstitions.

CHAPTER VI

1 So called from the mention which it contains of the superstitious customs of the Arabs with regard to their cattle.

2 Said to be a protest against the dualistic doctrine that Light and Darkness were two co-eternal principles.

3 i.e. a term for your life and another for your resurrection.

4 By good or evil works.

5 i.e. the prophet.

6 i.e. their innate propensities to good and their reason.

7 Mohammed.

8 Most of the Mohammedan commentators say this word means 'treasuries'. The allusion, however, is obviously to the Rabbinical tradition of the three keys, in the hands of Allah.

9 In sleep.

10 The Hebrew *Terah* is in Arabic *Târah*. Eusebius gives the form *Athar*, which may in some measure account for the name here given.

11 The Jews are here, as frequently in the Qur'ân, accused of suppressing and altering those parts of their scriptures which referred, according to the Mussulman theory, to the mission of Mohammed.

12 Mecca.

13 This refers to Abdallah ibn Sa'hd ibn Abî Sar'h, who acted as amanuensis to Mohammed, and when he came to the words 'We have created man from an extract of clay . . ., then we produced it another creation', he said, 'and blessed be Allah, best of creators', and Mohammed told him to write that down too; whereupon he boasted that he also had been inspired with this sentence which Mohammed acknowledged to be part of the Qur'ân.

14 This word is nearly always used for the verses of the Qur'ân.

15 That is, partners with Allah, *idols*; to *associate* being the usual phrase in the Qur'ân for idolatry.

16 In the womb.

17 Supernatural beings created, like the devils, of fire instead of clay, and possessed of miraculous powers. They are devoutly believed in by Muslims, and are supposed to be subject to the same controlling laws as mankind, and to have also had prophets sent to them. They are probably a survival of some old worship of the powers of nature. The word *jinn* is the same as that which in the old translation of the Arabian Nights is rendered 'genie'.

18 This word may also be rendered 'before them' or 'a surety' (for the truth of the revelation).

19 That is, makes him appear as one who would attempt some great but impossible thing and fails therein.

20 i.e. the idols.

21 The pagan Arabs used to set apart certain of the produce of their fields to Allah, the chief allah, and other portions to minor deities of their pantheon. The fruits of the portion of the latter were reserved for the priests, who were careful to restore to their lot anything that might have fallen into that of Allah, but seldom troubled themselves to do the converse. This custom survives to a certain extent in the desert to the present day, where one tree in every district is devoted to patron saints, and allowed to grow untouched, although the others in the neighbourhood are hacked to pieces as food for camels.

22 Alluding both to human sacrifices to idols and the cruel custom of burying female children alive.

23 That is, to obscure what little trace it had of the original faith of Abraham the Hanîf.

24 Trailed over an 'Arîsh, that is, a sort of hut made of boughs.

25 That is, spread out when slaughtered, or from the hides and wool, &c., of which a bed (*farsh*) is made.

26 The Arabs alternately made it unlawful to eat the males, and then the young of these four kinds of cattle. Mohammed in this passage shows the absurdity of their custom by pointing out the difficulty of deciding which is lawful and unlawful in the case of eight pairs.

27 That is, commit no homicide unless it be by legal execution or the slaying of infidels in war.

28 Signs of the approach of the day of judgement.

29 Not receive the recompense of other than persons' evil actions.

CHAPTER VII

1 The name of the bridge between heaven and hell described in this chapter.

2 i.e. fine dresses.

3 That is, wear your best apparel in the mosque.

4 Whereas now idolaters share in the good things of this world; but on the day of judgement those only shall enjoy them who were believers here.

5 That is, they shall have whatever portion of good or evil is written for them in the book of their fate.

6 See p. 129, note 17.

7 Literally, his sister.

8 The fruits of Paradise.

9 The highest heaven is so called.

10 An extinct tribe of the ancient Arabs.

11 Hûd and Thamûd, both mentioned in the works of Ptolemy, were two tribes of the ancient Arabs, extinct in Mohammed's time, whose disappearance had been attributed, by popular tradition, to divine vengeance.

12 Referring to the numerous excavated rock dwellings in Idumaea.

13 All that has been hitherto written about the legend Zâli'h and his camel is pure conjecture; the native commentators add nothing but a few marvellous details to the story as given in the Qur'ân, and the European annotators can only suggest possible identifications for Zâli'h himself, such as the Schelah of Gen. xi: 13. My own view of the matter is of course an hypothesis too, but it has at least some circumstantial evidence in its favour; it is embodied in the following extract from my 'Desert of the Exodus', p. 50: 'Near El Watiyeh is situated the tomb of Nebi Sáleh, a wretched little building, but accounted by the Bedawin

one of the most sacred spots on the Peninsula (of Sinai). Hither they resort in great numbers at certain seasons of the year to perform ceremonies and sacrificial rites. Who and what was Nebi Sáleh, "the Prophet Sáleh", or, as his name implies, "the Righteous Prophet"? A great saint with the Bedawin, perhaps the ancestor of the Sawáliheh tribe, who are named after him; but this explanation is vague and unsatisfactory, and in the absence of any certain information on the subject I will venture to propound a theory. I must premise that near the summit of Jebel Musa is a peculiar mark in the stone which has a strong resemblance to the imprint of a camel's foot. It is regarded by the Bedawin with great veneration, and the girls, when tending their flocks on the mountains, often milk their goats into it as a sure means of obtaining increase and prosperity. This mark is called Athar Nágat en Nebí, "the footprint of the Prophet's she-camel". It is generally taken for granted that the Prophet in question is Mohammed, but to my mind there are several circumstances which seem to connect the Nebi Sáleh of the tomb with the prophet of the legend. A Bedawin's notions of the separate identity of Moses, Elias, and Sáleh are of the vaguest kind, and if asked to which of his national saints the camel belonged you will find that he has never even thought of the question at all. There is no point in attributing the mysterious footprint to the camel of Mohammed, for the celebrated "night journey" to heaven, the Prophet's only recorded aeronautic trip, was performed on Borák, a creature with the feet of a mule. But Mohammed has a legend in the Qur'ân of a certain "Nebi Sáleh", who was sent as a prophet to the people of Thamúd, and whose divine mission was attested by the production of a *she-camel* from the rock. The author of "El Islam" certainly did visit the Sinaitic mountains, and may in all probability have taken the story from the national traditions of the Peninsula. The origin and history of Nebi Sáleh is quite unknown to the present Bedawin inhabitants, but they nevertheless regard him with more *national* veneration than even Moses himself. I should therefore conclude that the Nebi Sáleh of the tomb in Wády es Sheikl, the prophet of the camel's footprint, and the Sáleh of the Qur'ân are identical, and that the "people of Thamúd" are the Saracen inhabitants of Sinai, who preceded the Mohammedan invasion. Who then *was* Nebi Sáleh? Looking at the veneration in which his memory is held, and at the character of the miracle attributed to him—the rock smitten with a rod, and a live camel, the greatest of Bedawin blessings, miraculously produced therefrom—with the subsequent rebellion of the people for whom the Prophet worked the sign, I fancy we may recognize in the tradition a distorted reminiscence of the Israelitish law-giver himself.'

14 The Jethro of the Bible.

15 That is, 'give us a chance', the idiom is still current in modern parlance. A shopkeeper, for instance, who has not sold anything all day, or who refuses a bargain, always says, '*yefta'h'allah*', 'never mind! Allah will give me a chance of selling it.'

16 The word is used of an arrow that hits a mark, and hence of any sudden calamity that falls on a man.

17 Or, cause us to die Moslems.

18 The word *y'arishûn* is properly used of making wooden huts, but is here applied to any structures, especially the massive temples and other piles of Egyptian buildings.

19 This is also a Talmudic legend.

20 Or, the apostle of the Gentiles.

21 Cf. Chapter II, 61.

22 Said to refer to Balaam, but also to several pretenders of prophecy amongst the Arabians. By some it is referred to 'Omâiyyat ibn Abi Zalt, or to a certain Jewish Rabbi, who had prophesied the coming of a prophet about Mohammed's time, but would not acknowledge the latter as such.

23 The word *vul'hidûna* is used in the later Arabic for any form of atheism. The expression in the text means the perversion, as Mohammed called it, of the name Allah in the names of the other allahs, such as Allat, the feminine form of the same word.

24 Mohammed.

25 Literally, under the influence of the jinn.

26 This story is said to refer to Adam and Eve; the act of idolatry mentioned being the naming of their first son, at the instigation of Satan, 'Abd el 'Hareth, 'servant of 'Hareth', instead of 'servant of Allah', 'Hareth being Satan's name among the angels. The legend arose probably from a misunderstanding of the title given

to Cain in the Bible, 'Obed Adâma, 'a tiller of the ground', which would read word for word in Arabic 'Abd el 'Hareth.

27 i.e. if an evil suggestion occurs to them, they mention Allah's name and immediately see the folly and wickedness thereof.

28 That is, a verse in the Qur'ân.

CHAPTER VIII

1 At Medina.

2 The occasion alluded to was one when Mohammed had made preparations for attacking an unarmed caravan on its way from Syria to Mecca, when Abu Sufiân, who was in charge of it, sent to Mecca and obtained an escort of nearly a thousand men; many of Mohammed's followers wished to attack the caravan only, but the prophet and his immediate followers were for throwing themselves on the escort.

3 The Muslims were fewer in number than the enemy, and the latter had command of the water, at both of which circumstances their hearts sank. In the night, however, rain fell, refreshed them and supplied their wants.

4 Alluding to the alleged miracle of the gravel thrown into the eyes of the Qurâis at the battle of Bedr, to which the Muslim victory was due.

5 An address to the Meccans who, when threatened with an attack from Mohammed, took sanctuary in the Kaabah, and prayed to Allah that if they were right He would help them, but that if Mohammed was in the right He would help him.

6 Here used in the sense of victory.

7 That is, they have the doom of former people as a warning and an example.

8 That is, had ye agreed to attack them.

9 The angels who were fighting on the Muslim side.

10 i.e. beguiled them into attacking a force superior in numbers.

11 That is, make them an example to all future opponents by the severity of thy dealing with them.

12 Mohammed here blames them for having accepted ransom from

the captives which they took at the Battle of Bedr; but acknowledges that previously revealed passages of the Qur'ân did in the strict letter allow of such ransom being taken.

13 To the prophet.

14 The Ansârs and Muhâjerîn, that is, those who lent aid to, and those who fled with, Mohammed were at first regarded as next of kin and heirs to each other's property to the exclusion of blood relationship, until the above passage was abrogated by the last words of this chapter.

CHAPTER IX

1 This chapter is without the initial formula 'In the name of Allah', &c. The Caliph Othman said that the omission arose from its having been revealed shortly before Mohammed's death, who left no instructions on the subject. But some commentators assert that it arises from its having originally formed part of the previous chapter.

2 Abu 'l 'Abbâs, Mohammed's uncle, when taken prisoner and reproached with his unbelief, appealed to his having performed these duties as entitling him to as much consideration as if he had professed Islam.

3 'Honein is the name of a valley about three miles to the north-east of Mecca, where, in the eighth year of the Flight, a battle took place between Mohammed and his followers with an army of twelve thousand men, and two tribes of idolatrous Arabs. Too confident in their numbers the Moslems at first received a check, but were rallied by Mohammed and his immediate followers and kindred.

4 See p. 45, note 81.

5 That is, from the stoppage of traffic and merchandise.

6 The Moslem tradition is that Ezra, after being dead 100 years, was raised to life, and dictated from memory the whole of the Jewish Scriptures which had been lost during the captivity, and that the Jews said he could not have done this unless he had been the son of Allah. There is no Jewish tradition whatever in support of this accusation of Mohammed's, which probably was entirely due to his own invention or to misinformation. Bâidhâvî, the well-

known commentator, says that it must have been true because the Jews themselves, to whom the passage was read, did not deny it.

7 Alluding to the word *rabbi*, which in Arabic is applied to Allah alone.

8 The pagan Arabs used to put off the observance of a sacred month when it was inconvenient to them and observe another instead; this Mohammed deprecates.

9 The prophet.

10 That is, with only one companion, namely Abubekr.

11 That is, excuse me from the fighting in the cause of religion.

12 i.e. victory or martyrdom.

13 i.e. in collecting or distributing them.

14 Reconciled, that is, to Islam.

15 That is, reproach or quarrel with the prophet; I have used the old fashion English expression in order to preserve the pun upon the word *ear* which exists in the original.

16 Chapter of the Qur'ân.

17 i.e. are niggardly and refuse to give alms.

18 Sodom and Gomorrah.

19 A plot had been set afoot at Medina to kill Mohammed, and was only abandoned because of the increased trade and prosperity which Mohammed's residence then brought.

20 At the battle of Tabûk.

21 The Muhâjerîn, or those who fled with Mohammed from Mecca.

22 The Ansârs who helped him while at Medina.

23 The Mosque of Qubâ', about two miles from Medina, the foundation stone of which was laid by Mohammed four days before he entered Medina on his flight from Mecca, was the first place of public prayer in Islam. The Beni Ghanm had built another mosque to rival this, at the instigation of Abu 'Hâmir, a monk who was opposed to Mohammed, and wished the prophet to consecrate it.

24 The Beni Ghanm.

25 i.e. they will feel compunctions about it till the day of their death.

26 Three of the Ansârs who refused to accompany Mohammed to Tabûk.

27 A wady is the bed of a torrent, which in Arabia is generally dry, but occasionally after a storm is filled with the torrent.

CHAPTER X

1 Of Mecca.
2 i.e. a reward awaiting them for their sincerity.
3 The recording angels.
4 An instance of the frequent abrupt changes of persons with which the Qur'ân abounds.
5 i.e. Mohammed.
6 A portion of the Qur'ân. The word means *reading*.
7 Your idols.
8 Noah's people.
9 i.e. adapt them by their position and construction to become places in which prayer may be performed.
10 This is supposed to be the taunting reply of the angel Gabriel.
11 Compare Exodus xiv: 30. The Mohammedan legend is that as some of the children of Israel doubted whether Pharaoh was really drowned, the angel Gabriel caused the naked corpse to swim that they might see it.
12 See p. 28, note 33.

CHAPTER XI

1 That is, before the creation; see Genesis i: 2.
2 That is, of the idolater.
3 The Qur'ân.
4 *Tannûr* (oven) signifies also a reservoir of water. Its use in this passage has, however, given rise to some ridiculous superstitions amongst the Mohammedans as to the origin of the deluge.
5 This story and the further allusion to Noah's son in the next page were probably suggested by Genesis ix: 20–25.
6 The ark.

7 Jûdî is a corruption apparently for Mount Giordi, the Gordyæi of the Greeks, situated between Armenia and Mesopotamia.

8 i.e. upon some of the nations who are to form the posterity of thyself and the members of thy family saved with thee.

9 See p. 146, note 13.

10 i.e. he was powerless to help them.

11 i.e. some support, such as a powerful clan or chieftain.

12 That is, overturned the cities of the plain.

13 The Abyssinians, who had invaded Mecca some years before, are mentioned in the Chapter of the Elephant (CV) as being destroyed in a similar manner by flocks of birds, who threw down such missiles upon them.

14 The legend is that they each contained the name of the person for whom they were destined; so the old saying, 'every bullet has its billet'.

15 i.e. the same punishment is likely to overtake other wrongdoers, the threat being especially directed against the unbelieving inhabitants of Mecca.

16 See Chapter VII.

17 A little which Allah leaves you after paying every one his due.

18 The word used is that always applied by desert Arabs to going to a spring for water.

19 i.e. unless He please to increase their happiness.

CHAPTER XII

1 The word means a band of between twenty and forty persons.

2 This is a prophetic intimation to Joseph of his future interview with his brethren in Egypt.

3 The age of puberty.

4 The angel Gabriel in the form of his father appeared with a warning gesture, according to the Muslim commentators.

5 In their sudden emotion at his beauty.

6 Of his innocence.

7 In a dream.

8 The application of the pronoun is vague in the text of this passage, which is variously interpreted, either that Satan made the butler forget to mention Joseph to his lord Pharaoh, or that Satan made Joseph forget for the moment his Lord Allah, and place his trust on the man rather than on Him.

9 i.e. press wine and oil.

10 The goods which they had brought to barter, or the money they had paid for the corn.

11 Commentators differ as to whether this means that what they had brought was insufficient, or whether the additional measure was a small quantity for Pharaoh to bestow, or whether Jacob utters the words meaning that it is not enough to induce him to part with his son.

12 By some unavoidable hindrance.

13 i.e. by the law of Egypt it was not lawful for Joseph to take his brother for a bondsman as a punishment for theft.

CHAPTER XIII

1 Guardian angels.

2 i.e. hope of rain; lightning is always hailed with joy by the Arabs as a precursor of rain.

3 They would not believe.

4 The word used in the original, *yâi'as*, means 'despair', but in the patois of the Na'ha'h tribe signifies 'know', and is so interpreted by the native commentators on this passage.

5 See p. 13, note 2.

6 Alluding to the conquests of Islam.

CHAPTER XIV

1 This may, according to the Arab idiom, mean either 'battles' in which Allah had given victory to the believers; or simply 'days' on which Allah has shown them favour.

2 Easterns, when annoyed, always bite their hands; see Chapter III, verse 115.

3 Sale and Rodwell have softened down this filthy expression, one
  rendering it 'filthy water' and the other 'tainted water'; the
  Arabic, however, will not bear this rendering. The first word
  meaning 'water' or 'liquid', and the second, in apposition with it,
  'pus', or purulent matter oozing from a corpse or a sore.
4 Mecca and its neighbourhood.
5 The Kaabah at Mecca.
6 i.e. with their looks fixed straight in front of them through terror.

CHAPTER XV

1 El 'Hajr, literally, 'the rock': the Petra of Strabo, and the
  traditional habitation of 'the people of Thamûd'.
2 Verses.
3 See p. 25, note 24.
4 See p. 57, note 6.
5 i.e. the winds that bring the rain clouds and fertilize the earth.
6 Because to turn their backs on each other would appear
  contemptuous.
7 i.e. thy people.
8 i.e. to protect.
9 Addressed to Mohammed.
10 On the road from the territory of the Qurâis to Syria.
11 The Midianites, who are spoken of as dwelling in a grove, and to
  whom Jethro, or, as he is called in the Qur'ân, Sho'hâib, was sent
  as an apostle; see p. 147.
12 i.e. both Sodom and Midian.
13 The tribe of Thamûd, see p. 145.
14 The Opening Chapter, which contains seven verses, and is named
  the Seven of Repetition (sab'h al Mathânî), from this passage, and
  because it is to be repeated on so many occasions.
15 The unbelievers.
16 Behave with humility and gentleness.
17 Probably referring to the Jews and Christians who are here and
  elsewhere accused of mutilating and altering the Scriptures.

CHAPTER XVI

1 Said to refer to the building and overthrow of the tower of Babel.

2 The Pentateuch and Gospels.

3 See p. 133, note 21.

4 The Arabs used to call the angels 'daughters of Allah'. They, however, objected strongly (as do the modern Bedawîn) to female offspring, and used to bury their infant daughters alive. This practice Mohammed elsewhere reprobates. See p. 133, note 22.

5 The Arab writers mention several varieties of honey differing in colour, and some of which are used as medicine.

6 Their slaves.

7 'Tents' are called 'houses of hair' or 'of hide' by the desert Arabs.

8 Of mail.

9 The Meccans.

10 The Arabs, like most half-savage tribes, used to consider superior numerical strength as entitling them to disregard a treaty.

11 See p. 57, note 6.

12 Gabriel.

13 See p. 25, note 24.

14 The Ansârs.

15 Any town, but Mecca in particular.

16 Literally, 'taste'.

17 See p. 135.

18 Some commentators take this word *ummatan* as equivalent to *imâman*, 'antistes', and this interpretation I have followed. Others take it in its ordinary sense of 'nation'; but the use of the other epithets seems to favour the former interpretation.

19 This passage refers to the killing of 'Hamzah, Mohammed's uncle, at the battle of O'hod, and the subsequent mutilation of his corpse by the Meccans, and is a protest against taking too severe a revenge.

CHAPTER XVII

1 Also called 'The Children of Israel'.

2 The Kaabah at Mecca.

3 The Temple at Jerusalem.

4 The Mohammedan commentators interpret this as referring the first to either Goliath, Sennacherib, or Nebuchanezzar, and the latter to a second Persian invasion. The two sins committed by the Jews, and for which these punishments were threatened and executed, were, first, the murder of Isaiah and the imprisonment of Jeremiah, and the second, the murder of John the Baptist. Mohammedan views of ancient history are, however, vague.

5 Supply, 'we sent foes'.

6 i.e. 'fortune' or 'fate', literally, 'bird'; the Arabs, like the ancient Romans, having been used to practise divination from the flight of birds.

7 Bade them obey the Apostle.

8 i.e. if you are compelled to leave them in order to seek your livelihood; or if your present means are insufficient to enable you to relieve others.

9 See p. 246, note 4.

10 i.e. they are not to provoke the idolaters by speaking too roughly to them so as to exasperate them.

11 Sale interprets this to mean 'the angels and prophets'. Rodwell remarks that it is an 'obvious allusion to the saint worship of the Christians'. As, however, precisely the same expression is used elsewhere in the Qur'ân for the false allahs of the Arabs, and the existence of those jinns and angels whom they associated with Allah is constantly recognized, their divinity only being denied, I prefer to follow the Moslem commentators, and refer the passage to the allahs of the Arabian pantheon at Mecca; cf. p. 129, note 17.

12 The Zaqqûm; see Chapter XXXVII, verse 60. The vision referred to is the night journey to heaven, although those commentators who believe this to have been an actual fact suppose another vision to account for this passage.

13 The commentators say that this refers to a treaty proposed by the tribe of Thaqîf, who insisted, as a condition of their submission, that they should be exempt from the more irksome duties of Muslims, and should be allowed to retain their idol Allat for a certain time, and that their territory should be considered sacred, like that of Mecca.

14 According to some, the soul generally; but according to others, and more probably, the angel Gabriel as the agent of revelation.

15 As occasion required.

16 The Arabs whom Mohammed addressed seem to have imagined that he meant by Allah and Ar-ra'hmân (the Merciful One) two separate deities. The various epithets which are applied to Allah in the Qur'ân, such as 'kind', 'seeing', 'knowing', &c., are called by the Muslims *al 'asmâ'u 'l'husnâ*, 'the best of names', and are repeated in telling the beads of their rosary.

17 This command is obeyed by the Muslims frequently pronouncing the phrase *Allâhu akbar*, especially as an expression of astonishment. It is the same expression as that used by the Egyptian women concerning Joseph, in Chapter XII, verse 31.

CHAPTER XVIII

1 This is the well-known story of the Seven Sleepers of Ephesus. What is meant by Er-raqîm no one knows. The most generally accepted Mohammedan theory is that it was a dog belonging to the party; though some commentators take it to be the name of the valley or mountain in which the cave was situated; others again say that it was a metal plate inscribed with the name of the Sleepers.

2 That is, the youths themselves or the people they met on their awakening.

3 That is, the Christians.

4 Mohammed being asked by the Jews concerning the number of the Seven Sleepers, had promised to bring them a revelation upon the subject on the morrow: this verse is a rebuke for his presumption.

5 This expression Sale takes to be ironical, and translates, 'make thou him to see and hear'; Rodwell renders it, 'look thou and hearken unto him': both translators having missed both the force of the idiom and the explanation given by the commentators Al Bâidhâvî and Jalâlâin, to whom Sale refers. The meaning is that which I have given, and the idiom is equivalent to that which occurs in a passage of Harîrî, Maqâmah 3 (p. 30, De Sacy's first

edition), *akrim bihi*, 'how noble it is!' *abzar bihi* being equivalent to *mâ abzarahu*, 'how observant He is!'

6 Said to refer to Ommâiyet ibn 'Half, who had requested Mohammed to give up his poorer followers to please the Qurâis; see Chapter VI, verse 52.

7 In the original *Mâ sâ' allâh*; this is the usual formula for expressing admiration among Muslims.

8 i.e. *wrung his hands*.

9 In the hand of each.

10 This passage is aimed at the Qurîs. The 'course of those of yore' is the punishment inflicted on the 'people of Noah, Lot', &c. for similar acts of misbelief, and 'the torment' is said to refer to their losses at the battle of Bedr.

11 The word used signifies a space of eighty years and upwards.

12 Literally, 'of their intermediate space'.

13 See p. 273, note 17.

14 That is, *embarked*. All nautical metaphors in Arabic being taken from camel riding. The Arabs do not call the camel 'the ship of the desert', but they call a ship 'the riding camel of the sea'.

15 The expression *wanted to fall* is colloquial in Arabic as well as in English. Bâidhâvî says, 'the expression *wanting to* is in this case figuratively used for *being on the point of*'.

16 That is, every whole or sound ship.

17 For this legend there appears to be no ancient authority whatever; the Mohammedan commentators merely expand it, and say that El 'Hidhr (a mythical personage, who is identified with the prophet Elias, St. George, and the prime minister of Alexander the Great) had disappeared in search of the water of immortality. Moses was inspired to search for him, and told that he would find him by a rock where two seas met, and where he should lose a fish which he was directed to take with him. Moses' servant in the legend is Joshua, and the mysterious young man who guided him is generally supposed to be El 'Hidhr himself, rendered immortal and supernaturally wise by having found and drunk of the water of life.

18 Literally, 'the two horned'; this personage is generally supposed to be Alexander the Great, who is so represented on his coins. The

Mohammedan histories of him, however, contain so many gross anachronisms, making him, for instance, a contemporary with Moses, Abraham, &c., that it is probable they may have confused him with some much more ancient traditional conqueror.

19 Probably, as Bâidhâvî suggests, the ocean, which, with its dark waters, would remind an Arab of such a pool.

20 Gog and Magog. The people referred to appear to be tribes of the Turkomans, and the rampart itself has been identified with some ancient fortifications extending from the west coast of the Caspian to the Pontus Euxinus. The word translated *mountains* is the same as that translated *rampart* a little further on. I have, in rendering it mountains, followed the Mohammedan commentators, whose view is borne out by the subsequent mention of mountain sides.

21 The process here described for repressing the incursions of Gog and Magog is the building of a wall of pig iron across the opening between the two mountains, fusing this into a compact mass of metal, and strengthening it by pouring molten brass over the whole.

22 Gog and Magog.

23 On the day of judgement, or, as some think, a little before it.

24 Here the Persian word Firdâus is used, which has supplied the name to the abode of the blessed in so many languages.

CHAPTER XIX

1 Cf. Luke i: 61, where, however, it is said that *none of Zachariah's kindred* was ever before called by that name. Some commentators avoid the difficulty by interpreting the word *samîyyun* to mean 'deserving of the name'.

2 Either the infant himself or the angel Gabriel; or the expression 'beneath *her*' may be rendered 'beneath *it*', and may refer to the palm tree.

3 See p. 56, note 5.

4 See p. 267, note 5.

5 That is, 'gave them great renown'.

6 Generally identified with Enoch.

7 Amongst various conjectures the one most usually accepted by
the Mohammedan commentators is that these are the words of the
angel Gabriel, in answer to Mohammed's complaint of long
intervals elapsing between the periods of revelation.

8 This is interpreted by some to mean that all souls, good and bad,
must pass through Hell, but that the good will not be harmed.
Others think it merely refers to the passage of the bridge of el
Aarâf.

9 'Hâsîy ibn Wâil, being indebted to 'Habbâb, refused to
pay him unless he renounced Mohammed. This 'Habbâb said he
would never do alive or dead, or when raised again at the last day.
El 'Hâsîy told him to call for his money on the last day, as he
should have wealth and children then.

10 That is, the false allahs.

CHAPTER XX

1 The Arabs used to light fires to guide travellers to shelter and
entertainment. These fires, 'the fire of hospitality', 'the fire of
war', &c. are constantly referred to in the ancient Arabic poetry.
No less than thirteen fires are enumerated by them.

2 This may be also rendered, 'I almost conceal it (from myself)';
i'hfâ'un having, like many words in Arabic, two meanings directly
opposite to each other. This probably arose from words being
adopted into the Quarâis idiom from other dialects.

3 The Muslim legend is that Moses burnt his tongue with a live coal
when a child. This incident is related at length, together with
other Mohammedan legends connected with Moses and the
Exodus, in my 'Desert of the Exodus', Appendix C. p. 533. Transl.

4 Literally, vizîr, 'vizier', 'one who bears the burden' of office.

5 i.e. 'strengthen me'. The idiom is still in common use amongst the
desert Arabs.

6 i.e. the festival.

7 In order that they might all see.

8 Or, 'your most eminent men', as some commentators interpret it,
i.e. the children of Israel.

9 Pharaoh.

10 i.e. the Samaritan; some take it to mean a proper name, in order to avoid the anachronism.

11 A handful of dust from the footprint of the angel Gabriel's horse, which, being cast into the calf, caused it to become animated and to low.

12 The idea conveyed seems to be that he should be regarded as a leper, and obliged to warn people from coming near him. The reference is no doubt to the light in which the Samaritans (see p. 288, note 10) were regarded by the Jews.

13 Because 'blue eyes' were especially detested by the Arabs as being characteristic of their greatest enemies, the Greeks. So they speak of an enemy as 'black-livered', 'red-whiskered', and 'blue-eyed'. The word in the text may also mean 'blear-eyed', or 'blind'.

14 That is, the angel who is to summon them to judgement, and from whom none can escape, or who marches straight on.

15 Cf. p. 267, note 4.

16 The Meccans.

17 Literally, 'pairs'.

CHAPTER XXI

1 Or, child, since the passage refers both to the Christian doctrine and to the Arab notion that the angels are daughters of Allah.

2 Mohammed.

3 Literally, 'they turned upside down upon their heads', the metaphor implying that they suddenly changed their opinion and relapsed into belief in their idols.

4 See p. 27, note 27.

5 This case, say the commentators, being brought before David and Solomon, David said that the owner of the field should take the sheep in compensation for the damage; but Solomon, who was only eleven years old at the time, gave judgement that the owner of the field should enjoy the produce of the sheep—that is, their milk, wool, and lambs —until the shepherd had restored the field to its former state of cultivation, and this judgement was approved by David.

6 This legend, adopted from the Talmud, arises from a too literal interpretation of Psalm cxlviii.

7 The legend of Solomon, his seal inscribed with the holy name by which he could control all the powers of nature, his carpet or throne that used to be transported with him on the wind wherever he pleased, his power over the jinns, and his knowledge of the language of birds and beasts are commonplaces in Arabic writings.

8 That is, Elias, or, as some say, Joshua, and some say Zachariah, so called because he had a *portion* from Allah Most High, and guaranteed his people, or because he had double the work of the prophets of his time and their reward; the word *Kifl* being used in the various senses of 'portion', 'sponsorship', and 'double'.— Bâidhâvî.

9 Literally, 'he of the fish', that is, Jonah.

10 See p. 276.

11 The word 'ummatun' is here used in the sense rather of 'religion', regarding the various nations and generations as each professing and representing a particular faith, and means that the religion preached to the Meccans was the same as that preached to their followers by the various prophets who are mentioned in this chapter.

12 See p. 274.

13 'Hadab, some read jadath, 'grave'.

14 See p. 15, note 4.

15 Es-Sijill is the name of the angel who has charge of the book on which each human being's fate is written, which book he rolls up at a person's death. The word, however, may mean a scroll or register, and the passage may be rendered, 'like the rolling up of a scroll for writings'.

16 Psalm xxxvii: 29.

CHAPTER XXII

1 The word may also be rendered 'sky'.

2 Namely, the believers and the misbelievers.

3 The first ten days of Dhu 'l 'Hijjeh, or the tenth day of that month, when the sacrifices were offered in the vale of Minâ, and the three following days.

4 Such as not shaving their heads and other parts of their bodies, or cutting their beards and nails, which are forbidden the pilgrim from the moment he has put on the *I'hrâm*, or pilgrim garb, until the offering of the sacrifice at Minâ.

5 This means by presenting fine and comely offerings.

6 Waiting to be sacrificed.

7 Some say that the word *tamannâ* means 'reading', and the passage should then be translated, 'but that when he read Satan threw something into his reading'; the occasion on which the verse was produced being that when Mohammed was reciting the words of the Qur'ân, Chapter LIII, verses 19, 20, 'Have ye considered Allat and Al 'Huzzâ and Manât the other third?' Satan put it into his mouth to add, 'they are the two high-soaring cranes, and, verily, their intercession may be hoped for'; at this praise of their favourite idols the Qurâis were much pleased, and at the end of the recitation joined the prophet and his followers in adoration. Mohammed, being informed by the angel Gabriel of the reason for their doing so, was much concerned until this verse was revealed for his consolation. The objectionable passage was of course annulled, and the verse made to read as it now stands.

8 Either 'the day of resurrection', as giving birth to no day after it, or 'a day of battle and defeat', that makes mothers childless, such as the infidels experienced at Bedr.

9 As it will do at the last day. The words of the text might also be rendered 'withholds the rain', though the commentators do not seem to notice this sense.

CHAPTER XXIII

1 See p. 127, note 13.

2 That is, 'seven heavens'.

3 Or, 'religion'.

4 Literally, 'into Scriptures', i.e. into sects, each appealing to a particular book.

5 i.e. their works are far different to the good works just described.

6 At their possession of the Kaabah. The Qurâis are meant.

7 The famine which the Meccans suffered; and which was attributed to Mohammed's denunciations.

8 Their defeat at Bedr.

9 i.e. by doing good for evil, provided that the cause of Islam suffers nothing from it.

10 i.e. back to life. The plural is used 'by way of respect', say the commentators.

11 To our evil ways.

12 That is, the recording angels.

CHAPTER XXIV

1 He would punish you.

2 This passage and what follows refers to the scandal about Mohammed's favourite wife Ayesha, who, having been accidentally left behind when the prophet and his followers were starting at night on an expedition, in the sixth year of the Hijrah, was brought on to the camp in the morning by Zafwân ibn de Mu'hattal: this gave rise to rumours derogatory to Ayesha's character, which these verses are intended to refute. Ayesha never forgave those who credited the reports against her innocence, and 'Ali, who had spoken in a disparaging manner of her on the occasion, so seriously incurred her displeasure that she contrived to bring about the ruin of his family, and the murder of his two sons Hasan and Husein; the principal parties concerned in the actual spread of the calumny were punished with the fourscore stripes above ordained, with the exception of the ringleader, Abdallah ibn Ubbâi, who was too important a person to be so treated.

3 Abu bekr had sworn not to do anything more for a relation of his, named Mista'h, who had taken part in spreading the reports against Ayesha.

4 Or, according to some, of deficient intellect.

5 i.e. they are not to tinkle their bangles or ankle rings.

6 i.e. a document allowing them to redeem themselves on payment of a certain sum.

7 Abdallah ibn Ubbâi, mentioned on p. 318, note 2, had six slave girls whom he compelled to live by prostitution. One of them complained to Mohammed, whence this passage.

8 i.e. like the stories of Joseph, p. 214, and the Virgin Mary, p. 278, both of whom, like Ayesha, were accused of incontinence, and miraculously proved innocent.

9 i.e. masses of cloud as large as mountains.

10 The construction of the original is vague, and the commentators themselves make but little of it. The most approved rendering, however, seems to be that obedience is the reasonable course to pursue, and not the mere swearing to obey.

11 i.e. at the times when persons are undressed, namely, to rise in the morning, to sleep at noon, and to retire for the night, their attendants and children must not come in without first asking permission.

12 The Arabs in Mohammed's time were superstitiously scrupulous about eating in any one's house but their own.

13 That is, do not address the prophet without some respectful title.

CHAPTER XXV

1 In Arabic *Al Furqân*, which is one of the names of the Qur'ân.

2 Another reading of the text is, 'ye cannot'.

3 The ancient Arabs used this formula when they met an enemy during a sacred month, and the person addressed would then abstain from hostilities. The sinners in this passage are supposed to use it to the angels, but without effect. Some commentators take it to mean that the 'glad tidings' are 'rigorously forbidden', and that the angels are the speakers.

4 See Chapter III, verse 115.

5 That is, followed him.

6 Like the Pentateuch and Gospels, which were revealed all at once, according to the Mohammedan tradition.

7 Or it may be rendered, 'slowly and distinctly'; the whole revelation of the Qur'ân extends over a period of twenty-three years.

8 The commentators do not know where to place ar Rass; some say it was a city in Yamâmah, others that it was a well near Midian, and others that it was in 'Hadhramaut.

9 That is, the idolatrous Meccans; see p. 239, note 10.

10 That is, either the Qur'ân, cf. p. 257, line 27; or the words may be rendered, 'We distribute it' (the rain), &c.

11 That is, that if a man chose to expend anything for the cause of Allah he can do so.

12 For prayer.

13 See p. 136, note 27.

14 In Paradise.

CHAPTER XXVI

1 That he may be my minister.

2 The slaying of the Egyptian.

3 Pharaoh.

4 See p. 239, note 11.

5 The Qur'ân.

6 The angel Gabriel.

7 The Qur'ân.

8 Infidelity.

9 See p. 57, note 6.

10 See p. 240, note 16.

11 Or, it may be thy going to and fro among believers, as Mohammed is reported to have done one night, to see what they were about, and he found the whole settlement 'buzzing like a hornet's nest with the sound of the recitation of the Qur'ân and of their prayers'.

12 That is, by listening at the door of heaven; see p. 57, note 6.

13 That is, in what condition they shall be brought before Allah.

CHAPTER XXVII

1 The Sebâ of the Bible, in the south of the Arabian peninsula.
2 The commentators are uncertain as to whether this was 'Âzaf, Solomon's prime minister, or whether it was the prophet 'Hidhr, or the angel Gabriel, or, indeed, Solomon himself.
3 Commentators differ as to whether the last words are to be taken as the conclusion of the Queen of Sebâ's speech, or as Solomon's comment upon it.

CHAPTER XXVIII

1 Hâmân, according to the Qur'ân, is made out to be the prime minister of Pharaoh.
2 Either devoid of patience, according to some, or of anxiety, according to others, or it may be to everything but the thought of Moses.
3 That is, Moses was made to refuse the breast of the Egyptian woman before his sister came to offer her services, and point out a nurse who would rear him.
4 See p. 276, note 1.
5 That is, the Pentateuch and Qur'ân.
6 In Arabic Qârûn. The legend based upon Talmudic tradition of Korah's immense wealth appears to be also confused with that of Crœsus.

CHAPTER XXIX

1 i.e. if you are pressed in Mecca, there are plenty of places where you can take shelter, as Mohammed himself and a few of his followers did at Medina.

CHAPTER XXX

1 In Arabic Rûm, by which is meant the Byzantine or eastern Roman empire.

2 About the beginning of the sixth year before the Hijrah the Persians conquered Syria, and made themselves masters also of Palestine, and took Jerusalem. The Greeks were so distressed by their defeat that there appeared little likelihood of their being able to retrieve their fortune, and in the following year the Persians proceeded to lay siege to Constantinople itself. In the year 625 AD, however, the fourth year before the Hijrah, the Greeks gained a signal victory over the Persians, and not only drove them out of the borders of the Byzantine empire, but carried the war into Persian territory, and despoiled the city of Medayen. It is the defeat which is alluded to in this passage, and the subsequent victory that is prophesied, the date of the chapter being ascribed to the period when the Persians took Jerusalem.

3 Or, according to another reading, 'unto those who know'; cf. p. 363, line 1.

4 i.e. as they, the Meccans, do not consider their slaves their equals, still less does Allah hold the false allahs they associate with Him to be His equals, it being always remembered that these partners or false allahs were not spoken of in the Qur'ân as non-existent, but as supernatural beings, to whom divinity has been wrongly ascribed.

5 In Paradise.

6 i.e. see the young corn parched.

7 i.e. a verse.

CHAPTER XXXI

1 This sage is generally identified with the Aesop of the Greeks. The legends current in the East concerning him accord exactly with those of the Greek fabulist.

2 An Nadhr ibn al 'Hareth had purchased in Persia some of the old legends of Rustam and Isfendiâr, which were afterwards embodied in the *Shâh-nâmeh* of Firdausî. These he read to the Qurâis as being more wonderful than the Qur'ân.

CHAPTER XXXII

1 i.e. the torment of this world as well as that of the next.

2 This may refer to the alleged meeting of Mohammed and Moses in heaven during the 'night journey'; or it may be translated, 'the reception of it', i.e. the Qur'ân, the expression in Chapter XXVII, 6, being derived from the same root in Arabic, which means 'to meet'. The native commentators are divided in opinion as to these two interpretations. It is quite possible, however, that it may mean, 'be not in doubt as to a meeting with Him', and be a mere reiteration of the sentiment so often expressed, that Muslims are to be certain of a meeting with their Lord.

CHAPTER XXXIII

1 When this surah was written Medina was besieged by a confederation of the Jewish tribes with the Arabs of Mecca, Nejd and Tehâmah, at the instigation of the Jewish tribe of Nadhîr, whom Mohammed had expelled from Mecca the year before. The event took place in the fifth year of the Hijrah.

2 The Arabs were in the habit of divorcing their wives on certain occasions with the words, 'Thy back is to me as my mother's back', after which they considered it as unnatural to approach them as though they were their real mothers. This practice Mohammed here forbids. They used also to consider their adopted children in the same light as real children of their body; in forbidding this practice also, Mohammed legalized his marriage with Zâinab, the divorced wife of his freedman Zâid, who was also his adopted son.

3 The Muhâjerîn.

4 See p. 62, note 17.

5 Of angels.

6 On the approach of the confederate army, to the number of 12,000, Mohammed, by the advice of Selmân the Persian, ordered a deep trench to be dug round Medina, and himself went out to defend it with 3,000 men. The two forces remained for nearly a month in their respective camps without coming to an actual

conflict: until one night a piercing east wind blew so violently, and made such disorder in the camp of the besiegers, that a panic seized upon them, and they retired precipitately. Some of them had been encamped on the heights to the east of the town, the others in the lower part of the valley.

7 The ancient name of the city; it was only called 'El Medina, 'the city', after it had become famous by giving shelter to Mohammed.

8 In the trenches.

9 i.e. if the confederates had effected an entry, these half-hearted persons would have listened to their proposals, and have deserted the prophet.

10 i.e. chary of helping you, but greedy of the spoils.

11 i.e. the best share of the spoils.

12 i.e. their vow to fight till they obtained martyrdom.

13 i.e. changed their mind.

14 i.e. who had helped the confederates.

15 The Quraithah Jews, whom Mohammed attacked after the siege of Medina had been raised, and punished for their treachery in having joined the confederates although in league with him at the time.

16 Mohammed being annoyed by the demands made by his wives for costly dresses and the like, offered them the choice of divorce or of being content with their usual mode of living. They chose the latter.

17 Here the pronoun is changed from feminine to masculine, and the passage is appealed to by the Shiahs as showing the intimate relations that existed between Mohammed and 'Alî, for they say that by 'his household' are particularly meant *Fatimah* and ' *Alî*. In the next paragraph the feminine is again used.

18 i.e. Muslims; see p. 25, note 24.

19 i.e. divorced her.

20 Zâid was Mohammed's freedman and adopted son. Mohammed had seen and admired Zâid's wife Zâinab, and her husband at once offered to divorce her: this Mohammed dissuaded him from until the transaction was sanctioned by the verse. The relations of the Arabs to their adopted children were, as has been remarked before, p. 378, note 2, very strict; and Mohammed's marriage with

Zâinab occasioned much scandal among his contemporaries. This
passage and those at the commencement of the chapter abrogate
all these inconvenient restrictions. Zâid and Abu Laheb, Surah
CXI, are the only two persons of Mohammed's acquaintance who
are mentioned in the Qur'ân by name.

21 The same word is used as is rendered 'pray' in all the other
passages in the Qur'ân, though the commentators interpret it here
as meaning 'bless'. So, too, in the formula which is always used
after Mohammed's name, *zalla 'llâhu 'alâihi wa sallam*, 'may
Allah bless and preserve him!'

22 Either, 'do not ill-treat them', or, 'take no notice of their ill-
treating thee'.

23 i.e. dowry.

24 Slave girls.

25 i.e. from her turn of conjugal rights.

26 i.e. divorced.

27 He would be reluctantly obliged to ask you to leave.

28 The tent of an Arab chief is looked upon as a place of general
entertainment, and is always besieged by visitors. The advent of a
stranger, or indeed any occasion that demands the preparation of
food or any form of entertainment, is the signal for every adult
male of the encampment to sit round it, and wait for an invitation
to partake of the meal. This becomes a very serious tax upon the
sheikh, as the laws of Arab hospitality imperatively require every
person present to be invited to join in the repast. The translator
has often witnessed scenes—especially among the Arabs of Edom
and Moab—which gave a very living significance to these words
of the Qur'ân. Mohammed's exceptionally prominent position
exposed him in a peculiar manner to these irruptions of unbidden
guests. Another saying bearing upon the point is traditionally
ascribed to him, *zur ghibban tazdâd 'hubban*, 'visit seldom and
you will get more love.'

29 The prophet's wives.

30 The women to the present day always remain behind a curtain
which screens off their part of the tent from the rest, but freely
converse with their husband and his guests, and hand over the
dishes and any other articles that may be required by the company.

31 The prophet's wives.

32 See p. 383, note 21.

33 The occasion of the revelation of this verse is said to have been that Mohammed being accused of unfairly dividing certain spoils, said, 'Allah, have mercy on my brother Moses; he was wronged more than this, and bore it patiently.'

34 That is, 'the faith'.

CHAPTER XXXIV

1 A city of Yemen which was also called Mârab; it was about three days' journey from Sanâ'h. The bursting of the dyke of Mârab and the destruction of the city by a flood are historical facts, and happened in about the first or second century of our era.

2 The Mohammedan legend is that Solomon had employed the jinns to construct the temple of Jerusalem for him, and perceiving that he must die before it was completed, he prayed Allah to conceal his death from them lest they should relinquish the work when no longer compelled to keep to it by fear of his presence. This prayer was heard, and Solomon, who died while resting on his staff, remained in this position for a year without his death being suspected, until a worm having eaten away his staff it broke, and the corpse fell to the ground, thus revealing the fact of his death. The shameful torment which the jinns might have avoided is their forced labour in building the temple.

3 The *Rhamnus Nabeca* of Forshål, the *Rhamnus Nabeca Spina Christi* of Linnæus; its fruit, which is called Nebuk, is a small round berry, in taste something like the jargonelle pear, and is a great favourite with the Bedawîn. It grows freely in the Sinaitic peninsula.

4 A great trade used formerly to exist between Sebâ and Syria. The Mohammedan commentators suppose that the cessation of traffic, which naturally caused the gradual ruin of the intermediate towns, and the subsequent destruction of Sebâ or Mârab itself by the flood, was a punishment for the covetous wish of the people of the city, that the distances which traders had to pass over were longer, so that they themselves might earn more money by providing them with camels and escorts.

5 In Paradise.
6 See p. 129, note 17.
7 That is, the Meccans.
8 That he, Mohammed, is not possessed by a jinn.

CHAPTER XXXV

1 Also called 'of the Originator'.
2 Literally, the husk of a date stone.
3 The word is here used in its geological sense, and is applied to the various coloured streaks which are so plainly to be seen in the bare mountain sides of Arabia. The Arabs of the desert to this day call them by the same name as is here used in the Qur'ân.
4 The earth.

CHAPTER XXXVI

1 The *Umm al Kitâb*. See p. 13, note 2.
2 The legend is that Jesus sent two of His disciples to the city of Antioch, none believing them but one 'Habîb en Najjâr, that is, ''Habîb the carpenter', and all three were thrown into prison. Simon Peter was subsequently sent to their rescue; a great many were converted, and the rest were destroyed by a shout from the angel Gabriel. The shrine of 'Habîb en Najjâr at Antioch is still a favourite place of pilgrimage for Mohammedans.
3 There is a various reading here, 'and has no place of rest'.
4 Some take this to refer to Noah's ark.
5 That is, the punishment of this world and the next.
6 Mohammed.
7 i.e. they are ready to defend their false allahs.

CHAPTER XXXVII

1 Driving the clouds or 'scaring the devils'.
2 See p. 57, note 6.

3 The people of Mecca.

4 That is, with a good omen.

5 See Chapter XV, verse 47.

6 Ez Zaqqûm is a foreign tree with an exceedingly bitter fruit, the name of which is here used for the infernal tree.

7 The unbelievers objected that the tree could not grow in Hell, where the very stones (see p. 15, note 4) were fuel for the fire.

8 Mohammedan commentators say that he pretended to a knowledge of astrology and made as though he saw a presage of coming sickness for himself in the stars, whereupon the others fled for fear of contagion, and Abraham took the opportunity of absenting himself from the festival which was being held in honour of the idols.

9 The people of the city.

10 The Mohammedan theory is that it was Ishmael and not Isaac who was taken as a sacrifice.

11 Supposed by the Mohammedans to be the same as Al 'Hidhr and Idrîs.

12 This is probably another form of the word Elyâs, on the model of many Hebrew words which have survived in the later Arabic dialect. The Mohammedan commentators however conjecturally interpret it in various ways, some consider it to be a plural form, including Elias and his followers; others divide the word and read it Âl-ya-sîn, i.e. 'the family of Ya-sin', namely, Elias and his father. Others imagine it to mean Mohammed or the Qur'ân. Most probably however the final syllable *în* was nothing more than a prolonged utterance of the case ending, here improperly used in order to preserve the rhyme or final cadence of the verse. The modern Bedawîn frequently do the same, and I have heard them singing a song commencing 'Zaidûn, Zaidûn, Zaidûn', when they should say, 'Zaidu, 'O Zaid!' &c.

13 The word used in the text is always applied to runaway slaves.

14 The Meccans.

15 See p. 246, note 4.

16 This speech is supposed to be the words of the angel Gabriel.

17 i.e. in the Qur'ân.

CHAPTER XXXVIII

1 The Arabic commentators say of this title, 'Allah only knows what He means by it.' All the explanations given of it are purely conjectural. See p. 1 for this and the other mysterious letters used throughout the Qur'ân.

2 Some say this refers to the punishment which Pharaoh used to inflict upon those who had offended him, whom he used to tie to four stakes and then torture. Others take the expression to refer to the stability of Pharaoh's kingdom. The word in the original is applied to the pegs with which Arabs fasten their tents.

3 The Meccans.

4 The word in Arabic signifies a horse that stands on three legs and just touches the ground with the fore part of the hoof of the fourth. The story is that Solomon was so lost in the contemplation of his horses one day that he forgot the time of evening prayer, and was so smitten with remorse on discovering his negligence that he sacrificed them all except a hundred of the best. Allah however recompensed him by giving him dominion over the winds instead.

5 The Mohammedan legend, borrowed from the Talmud, is that having conquered the king of Sidon and brought away his daughter Jerâdeh, he made her his favourite. She however so incessantly mourned her father that Solomon commanded the devils to make an image of him to console her, and to this she and her maids used to pay divine honours. To punish him for encouraging this idolatry, a devil named Sakhar one day obtained possession of his ring, which he used to entrust to a concubine named Amînah when he went out for any necessary purpose. As the whole secret of his power lay in this ring, which was engraved with the Holy Name, the devil was able to personate Solomon, who, being changed in form, was not recognized by his subjects, and wandered about for the space of forty days, the time during which the image had been worshipped in his house. After this Sakhar flew away and threw the signet into the sea, where it was swallowed by a fish, which was afterwards caught and brought to Solomon, who by this means recovered his kingdom and power.

6 The Mohammedan legend is that when Job was undergoing his

trials, the devil appeared to his wife and promised, if she would worship him, to restore their former prosperity; this she asked her husband to allow her to do. Job was so enraged at her conduct that he swore if he recovered to give her a hundred stripes. When Job had uttered the prayer recorded on page 299, line 3, Gabriel appeared and bade him in the words of the text to strike the ground with his feet. A fountain at once gushed forth, in which he washed and was healed, his wife also becoming young and beautiful again. In order not to break his oath he was commanded to strike her with a bundle of palm leaves, giving her a hundred painless blows at once.

7 See page 299.

CHAPTER XXXIX

1 Camel, oxen, sheep, and goats.
2 i.e. the belly, the womb, and the placenta.
3 See p. 47, note 87.
4 By their idols.
5 The pronoun in Arabic is feminine, and refers to the false allahs, especially to the favourite allahdesses of the Qurâis.
6 Or witnesses.

CHAPTER XL

1 Referring to the absence of life before birth and the deprivation of it at death, and to the being quickened at birth and raised again after death.
2 Or 'turn away'.

CHAPTER XLI

1 On the earth.
2 Devils, opposed to the guardian angels of the believers.
3 i.e. interrupt the reading of the Qur'ân by talking, in order to overpower the voice of the reader.

4 i.e. they would have said, 'What! is the revelation in a foreign tongue, and we who are expected to read it Arabs?' This is paraphrased by Sale: 'If we had revealed the Qur'ân in a foreign language, they had surely said, "Unless the signs thereof be distinctly explained we will not receive the same: is the Book to be written in a foreign tongue, and the person unto whom it is directed an Arabian?" '

5 Or the words may be rendered, 'There is good with him still due to me.'

CHAPTER XLII

1 Mecca.

2 i.e. after the faith of Islam had been accepted by them, or after Allah had assented to the prophet's prayer and supported the faith, or after the Jews and Christians had assented to the teaching of Mohammed, for the commentaries are uncertain as to the exact meaning of the phrase.

3 i.e. the law contained in the Qur'ân.

4 i.e. were it not that Allah has promised that those things shall be decided at the day of judgement.

5 i.e. it is a duty laid down by law.

6 Or 'to return (to the world)', Bâidhâvî.

7 Gabriel.

CHAPTER XLIII

1 See p. 13, note 2.

2 i.e. the Meccans.

3 i.e. of the birth of a daughter, see p. 246, note 4.

4 i.e. what! do they assign children of this kind, viz. daughters, to Allah?

5 i.e. a scripture authorizing the practice of their religion, such as the worship of angels and the ascribing of daughters to Allah.

6 i.e. had it been sent down to some man of influence and importance in Mecca and Tâ'if we would have received it.

7 i.e. the east and west, though some understand it between the two solstices.

8 See p. 284, note 3.

9 The Arabs objected that Jesus was worshipped by Christians as an Allah, and that when Mohammed cursed their false allahs, the ban must apply equally to him.

10 Just as Jesus was miraculously conceived, so can miraculously conceived offspring be produced among the Meccans themselves.

11 Some read, 'a sign', which is perhaps better. The reference is to the predicted second advent of the Messiah, which is to precede the end of the world. Some commentators, however, read 'it', instead of 'he', referring to the Qur'ân, instead of to Jesus.

12 Mâlik is the keeper of Hell, and presides over the tortures of the damned.

13 The word used signifies twisting up the strands of a rope.

14 i.e. the recording angel.

15 Mohammed.

CHAPTER XLIV

1 The Meccans.

2 i.e. we shall only die once.

3 The Himyarite Arabs, whose kings were called Tubbâ'h, i.e. 'successors'.

4 Or 'like the dregs of oil'.

CHAPTER XLV

1 That is, the successful battles against the infidels, 'battles' being always spoken of by the ancient Arabs as 'days'.

2 Mohammed.

3 The Qur'ân.

CHAPTER XLVI

1 Name of a tract of land in Si'hr in Yemen.
2 i.e. from the grave.
3 The prophet Hûd.
4 i.e. the Meccans.
5 Addressed to Mohammed.

CHAPTER XLVII

1 To the more learned amongst the prophet's companions, such as Ibn 'Abbâs.
2 Munkir and Nakîr.

CHAPTER XLVIII

1 Some of the commentators take this to mean sins committed by Mohammed before his call and after; others refer the word to the liaison with the Coptic handmaiden Mary, and to his marriage with Zâinab the wife of his adopted son Zâid.
2 Or tranquillity; see p. 45, note 81.
3 Alluding to certain tribes who held aloof from the expedition of 'Hudâibîyeh.
4 In an expedition against the Jews of Khâibar, which Mohammed undertook shortly after his return from 'Hudâibîyeh, and obtained considerable booty, which he shared only with those who had accompanied him on the previous occasion.
5 The followers of Musâilimah, Mohammed's rival, and the tribes that had apostatized from Islam. Some think it refers to the Greeks and Persians.
6 At 'Hudâibîyeh.
7 See p. 45, note 81.
8 Either the success at Khâibar or the taking of Mecca.
9 Alluding to the truce concluded at 'Hudâibîyeh.
10 Mohammed having only set out with the intention of peaceably performing the pilgrimage, carried cattle with him to sacrifice in

the valley of Minâ, but was obliged by the Qurâis to turn back.

11 Suhail ibn 'Amr, who concluded the truce with Mohammed at 'Hudâibîyeh, objected to the formula 'In the name of the merciful and compassionate Allah', with which the prophet ordered 'Alî to commence the document, and insisted on the heathen formula 'In Thy name, O Allah!' He also refused to admit the words 'Mohammed, the Apostle of Allah', saying, that if they had granted so much they would not have opposed him; the words 'Mohammed the son of Abdallah' were therefore substituted. These objections were so annoying to the Muslims, that it was with difficulty that Mohammed could restrain them from an immediate breach of the peace.

12 The Mohammedan profession of faith, 'There is no allah but Allah, and Mohammed His servant is the Apostle.' Or it may be the initial formula which the unbelieving Meccans rejected.

13 Mohammed dreamed that he would accomplish the pilgrimage to Mecca with all its rites; the affair at 'Hudâibîyeh disappointed his followers, but in the following year it was fulfilled.

14 i.e. that of Khâibar.

15 Or the Pentateuch.

CHAPTER XLIX

1 Said to refer to a dispute between Abu Bekr and 'Omar, in the course of which they came to high words in the presence of the prophet.

2 Two of the Arabs wishing to speak with Mohammed when he was sleeping at noon in his harem, cried out rudely to him, 'Mohammed, come out to us!' See p. 325, note 13.

3 Al Walîd ibn 'Hugbâ was sent by Mohammed to collect the zakât from the tribe of Mustaleq, with whom he had had a feud in the time preceding Islam. Seeing them coming out to meet him in large numbers, he grew apprehensive, and returned hastily with the information that the tribe had refused the tribute. Mohammed thereupon sent 'Halîd ibn Walîd to reduce them by force, when it was found that the former messenger's fears had been quite groundless.

4 i.e. ye would mislead him.

5 Alluding to one of the frequent disputes between the tribes of Aus and 'Hazraj at Medina.

6 i.e. it is defamation to charge a person who has embraced the faith with iniquity. The passage is said to have been revealed on account of Zafîyah bint 'Huyâi, one of the prophet's wives, who complained to him that she had been taunted by the other women with her Jewish origin. Mohammed answered her, 'Canst thou not say, "Aaron is my father, Moses my uncle, and Mohammed my husband"?'

CHAPTER L

1 Alluding to the various opinions expressed by the unbelievers with reference to the Qur'ân; some calling it sorcery or divination, others poetry, and some asserting it to be 'old folks' tales' or mere invention.

2 See p. 329, note 8.

3 See p. 239, note 11.

4 See Chapter XLIV, verse 35, p. 450, note 3.

5 The two recording angels, who accompany every man and note down his every word and action.

6 These words are supposed to be addressed by the 'driver' to the unbelieving soul.

7 These words are spoken by Allah.

8 i.e. from the vengeance of Allah.

9 A protest against the assertion that Allah *rested* on the seventh day.

10 Two *sijdahs* used at the evening prayers, but not incumbent on the worshipper.

11 i.e. a place from which all men may hear; generally supposed by Muslims to be the temple at Jerusalem.

12 The sound of the last trumpet.

CHAPTER LI

1 The winds.
2 The clouds.
3 The ships.
4 Angels or winds.
5 i.e. rain, which produces material sustenance, and there too is the promise of the future life.
6 i.e. unreserved and plain as ye yourselves affirm truths to each other.
7 See pp. 206–7.
8 See p. 206, note 11.
9 Either Pharaoh's forces, or one of his nobles, or something else on which he relied. See p. 206, note 11.
10 i.e. this taunt.
11 i.e. like the fate of those who wronged the apostles of old.

CHAPTER LII

1 i.e. either the Kaabah itself or the model of it, said to exist in the heavens and to be frequented by the angels.
2 i.e. of heaven.
3 Every man is pledged to Allah for his conduct, and, if he does well, redeems himself.
4 At the thought of the next life.
5 Addressed to Mohammed.
6 i.e. a ladder reaching to the gates of heaven, upon which they may stand and listen to the angels discoursing, as the devils do. See p. 57, note 6.
7 At the sound of the last trumpet.
8 i.e. beside the torment of the judgement day they shall be punished with defeat and loss here.

CHAPTER LIII

1 The angel Gabriel, who appeared twice to Mohammed in his natural form, namely, on the occasion of the 'Night Journey', to which this passage refers, and on the first revelation of the Qur'ân.

2 See p. 307, note 7.

3 This passage refers to one El Walîd ibn Mughâirah, who being abused for following Mohammed and forsaking the religion of the Qurâis, answered that he had done so to escape divine vengeance. Thereupon an idolater offered to take on himself El Walîd's sin for a certain sum of money. The offer was accepted, and Walîd apostatized from El Islam, paying down a portion of the amount agreed upon at the time. Later on he refused to pay the balance on the ground that he had already paid enough.

4 i.e. the resurrection.

5 Sirius, or the Dog Star, was an object of worship amongst the ancient Arabs.

6 Sodom, Gomorrah, &c.

7 At this verse the Qurâis, who were present at the first reading of this chapter when their allahs were spoken well of, fell down adoring with Mohammed.

CHAPTER LIV

1 According to a tradition this refers to a miracle: the unbelievers having asked for a sign, the moon appeared to be cloven in twain. The tradition is, however, supported by very doubtful authority, and is directly opposed to the teaching of the Qur'ân elsewhere, for the power to comply with the demand for a sign is always distinctly disclaimed. The more usual explanation is the natural one, that the expression merely refers to one of the signs of the day of judgement.

2 The word is interpreted by some to mean 'transient', by others 'powerful'.

3 The Qur'ân.

4 The angel Isrâfîl.

5 The last judgement.

6 Or madness.

7 This is appealed to by Muslims as a prophecy fulfilled at the battle of Bedr.

8 The books kept by the recording angels.

CHAPTER LV

1 See p. 445, note 7.

2 The earth.

3 i.e. mankind and the jinn; the meaning is, that Allah will have leisure to judge them both.

4 The word is also said to mean red leather.

5 For the inferior inhabitants of Paradise.

CHAPTER LVI

1 i.e. the day of judgement.

2 i.e. the foremost in professing the faith on earth shall be the foremost then.

3 The mimosa gummifera is generally so called in Arabia; but the banana is said to be meant in this passage.

4 The celestial damsels.

5 i.e. for seed and labour.

6 From reaping the fruits of it.

7 The ancient Arabs produced fire by the friction of a stick in a hollow piece of wood. Cf. p. 402, line 24.

8 The soul of a dying man.

CHAPTER LVII

1 i.e. guiding them to Paradise.

2 i.e. from alms giving.

CHAPTER LVIII

1 Khâulah bint Tha'labah being divorced from her husband by the formula mentioned below, and which was always considered to be a final separation, appealed to Mohammed, who said he could not alter the custom. Afterwards, on the woman praying to Allah, this passage was revealed, abolishing the objectionable form of divorce.

2 i.e. divorce them by the formula 'Thou art to me as my mother's back!' See p. 50, note 93.

3 Instead of saying, *Es salâm 'halaika*, 'peace be upon thee!' they used to say, *Es sâm 'halaika*, 'mischief be upon thee!'

4 The Jews.

CHAPTER LIX

1 The Jews of en Nadhîr, near Medina, who at first promised to stand neuter between him and the idolaters. After his success at Bedr they came over to his side, but turned again after the defeat of Ohod. For this offence they were forced to leave the country.

2 Like those of Qurâidhah, who were slaughtered.

3 The Muslims did not use cavalry on the occasion, Mohammed himself being the only mounted member of the expedition. For this reason the spoils were assigned to the prophet alone, and not divided in the usual manner as prescribed in Chapter VIII, verse 42, pp. 164–5.

4 The poorer Muhâjerîn were allowed to participate in the spoils, but not the Ansârs.

5 The Ansârs at Medina.

6 The Muhâjerîn.

7 The Jews.

8 Either the idolaters slain at Bedr, or the Jews of Qâinuqâh, or those of Nadhîr.

CHAPTER LX

1 'Hâtîb ibn abi Balta'hah had given the Meccans warning of an intended surprise by Mohammed, and on his letter being intercepted, excused himself by saying that he had only done so in order to make terms for his family, who were at Mecca, and that he knew that the information would be of no avail. Mohammed pardoned him, but the verse in the text prohibits such conduct for the future.

2 i.e. they are not to imitate Abraham's speech to his father, and ask forgiveness for their infidel friends. Cf. p. 184, verse 115.

3 i.e. by their becoming converted to Islam.

4 i.e. to their infidel husbands.

5 The dowries.

6 This is said by some commentators to mean foisting spurious children on to their husbands.

7 i.e. of the resurrection of the dead.

CHAPTER LXI

1 Who fight in close and unbroken lines.

2 A'hmed is equivalent in meaning to Mohammed, and means 'Praised', 'Laudable'. The allusion is to the promise of the Paraclete in John xvi. 7, the Muslims declaring that the word *paráklhtoF* has been substituted in the Greek for *periklqtóF*, which would mean the same as A'hmed.

3 Ansâr.

4 See pp. 58–9 (Chapter III, verse 45).

CHAPTER LXII

1 See p. 154, note, 20.

2 i.e. by embracing Islam.

3 Friday, called before this 'Harûbah. It was the day on which Mohammed entered Medina for the first time.

4 It is said that one Friday a caravan entered the town while

Mohammed was conducting the public prayers, and the congregation hearing the drums beat rushed out to see the sight, with the exception of about twelve of them.

CHAPTER LXIII

1 The disaffected portion of the inhabitants of Medina.
2 Or, by a various reading, 'their oaths'.
3 Abdallah ibn Ubai, the leader of the 'Hypocrites', was a man of fine presence and eloquent address.
4 i.e. though of tall and imposing presence, they are really like mere logs.

CHAPTER LXIV

1 i.e. both the righteous and the wicked will disappoint each other by reversing their positions, the wicked being punished while the righteous are in bliss.
2 This expression seems to indicate that this verse at least was revealed at Medina.

CHAPTER LXV

1 When they have had three periods of menstruation; or, if they prove with child, after their delivery. See p. 42.
2 i.e. whether Allah may not reconcile them again.
3 The divorced women.

CHAPTER LXVI

1 This chapter was occasioned by Mohammed's liaison with the Coptic girl Mary, with whom he lay on the day due to 'Âyeshah or 'Hafsah. The latter was greatly enraged, and Mohammed to pacify her swore never to touch the girl again, and enjoined 'Hafsah to keep the matter secret from the rest of his wives. She, however, revealed it in confidence to 'Âyeshah; when

Mohammed, annoyed at finding his confidence betrayed, not only divorced her, but separated himself from his other wives for the space of a month, which time he passed in Mary's apartment. The chapter is intended to free him from his oath respecting Mary, and to reprove his wives for their conduct.

CHAPTER LXVII

1 See p. 57, note 6.
2 Cf. Chapters XXV, verse 12, and XXXI, verse 18.

CHAPTER LXVIII

1 The Arabic name of the letter *nûn* signifies both 'a fish' and 'an inkstand'; the symbol is by some supposed to refer to Jonah, mentioned in verse 48, and by others to writing on the eternal tablets (see p. 13, note 2), to which the first words of the chapter apply.
2 For bearing so meekly the insults of the misbelievers.
3 The person meant is, probably, Walîd ibn Mughâirah, the inveterate enemy of the prophet.
4 i.e. they did not add, 'If Allah please!'
5 Or, according to another interpretation, 'with a determined purpose'.
6 An expression signifying any great calamity or battle, because the non-combatants gird up their loins to be ready for flight.
7 Jonah.

CHAPTER LXIX

1 Cf. Chapter XIII, verse 31, p. 227.
2 Sodom and Gomorrah; cf. p. 178, note 18.
3 i.e. death.

CHAPTER LXX

1 The person referred to is said to have been either Abu Jahl, who challenged Mohammed to cause a portion of the heaven to fall on them, see Chapter XXVI, verse 187, p. 339, or one Nadhr ibn el 'Hâreth, who said of Islam, 'If this be the truth from Thee, then rain down on us stones from heaven!'

2 Either steps by which the prayers of the righteous or the angels ascend to heaven; or the word may refer to the various degrees of the angels, or to the seven heavens themselves.

3 Cf. Chapter XXXII, verse 4, p. 375.

4 Cf. Chapter XVII, verse 12, p. 255.

5 Cf. p. 488.

6 i.e. of the east and the west; or of the various points of the horizon at which the sun rises and sets in the course of the year.

CHAPTER LXXI

1 See Chapter XXII, verse 5, p. 301.

CHAPTER LXXII

1 The occasion of Mohammed's preaching to the jinn was on his returning from his unsuccessful errand to Tâ'if.

2 The pagan Arabs when they found themselves in a lonely place, such as they supposed the jinn to haunt, used to say, 'I take refuge in the Lord of this valley from the foolish among his people!'

3 The Meccans.

4 Mohammed.

5 The jinn.

CHAPTER LXXIII

1 From verse 20 the rest of the surah seems from its style to belong to the Medina period; and there is a tradition ascribed to

'Âyeshah that it was revealed a year later than the earlier part of the chapter.

CHAPTER LXXIV

1 The first five verses of this chapter form the second revelation by the angel Gabriel in person, and the first after the *Fatrah*, or period of 'Intermission'.
2 The person meant is generally supposed to be Walîd ibn Mughâirah, one of the chiefs of the Qurâis.
3 See Chapter LII, verse 21, p. 477, note 3.
4 See p. 82, note 14.
5 i.e. death.

CHAPTER LXXV

1 i.e. the revelation; see p. 267, note 4, and p. 290, note 15. The words are addressed to Mohammed by the angel Gabriel.
2 i.e. in the death struggle.
3 Or did not give in charity.
4 See p. 82, note 14.

CHAPTER LXXVI

1 While in the womb.
2 Name of a river in Paradise, so called because it is white, cool, and sweet smelling, as camphor is.
3 *Zamharîr*, the word here rendered 'piercing cold', is by some authorities interpreted to mean 'the moon'.
4 *Zinjabîl* signifies 'ginger'.

CHAPTER LXXVII

1 Either angels or winds, or as some interpret the passage, the verses of the Qur'ân.

CHAPTER LXXVIII

1 i.e. the news of the resurrection.

CHAPTER LXXIX

1 Referring to the angel of death and his assistants, who tear away the souls of the wicked violently, and gently release the souls of the good.

2 The angels who precede the souls of the righteous to Paradise.

3 The trumpet blast at the last day, which shall make the universe quake.

4 See Chapter XX, verse 12, p. 283.

CHAPTER LXXX

1 One Abdallah ibn Umm Maktûm, a poor blind man, once interrupted Mohammed while the latter was in conversation with Walîd ibn Mughâirah and some others of the Qurâis chiefs. The prophet taking no notice of him, the blind man raised his voice and earnestly begged for religious instruction, but Mohammed, annoyed at the interruption, frowned and turned away. This passage is a reprimand to the prophet for his conduct on the occasion. Afterwards, whenever he saw the blind Abdallah, Mohammed used to say, 'Welcome to him on whose account my Lord reproved me!' and subsequently made him governor of Medina.

CHAPTER LXXXI

1 Such camels being among the most valuable of an Arab's possessions, neglect of them must imply some terribly engrossing calamity.

2 The terrors of the judgement day will drive all the wild beasts together for mutual shelter.

3 See p. 133, note 22, and p. 246, note 4.

4 Gabriel.
5 See Chapter LIII, verses 1–19, pp. 479.
6 Some copies have a various reading, 'suspicious of'.
7 See p. 57, note 6.

CHAPTER LXXXII

1 See p. 471, note 5.

CHAPTER LXXXIII

1 Sijjîn, the 'prison' of Hell, whence the register of the wicked is named.
2 'Illiyûn means 'high places'.
3 Name of a fountain in Paradise, so called because it is conveyed to the highest apartments there.

CHAPTER LXXXIV

1 i.e. in the left hand, which will be chained behind the back, the right hand being fettered to the neck.
2 From life to death, and from death to the future life.

CHAPTER LXXXV

1 Literally, 'towers'.
2 Various interpretations are given of these words, the most probable perhaps being that 'the witness' is Mohammed, and 'the witnessed' the faith.
3 Alluding to the persecution of the Christians at Nejrân by Dhu 'n Navvâs, king of Yemen, who had embraced the Jewish religion, and who commanded all his subjects who would not do the same to be flung into a pit filled with fire, and burnt to death.
4 See p. 13, note 2.

CHAPTER LXXXVI

1 From the loins of the man and the breast bones of the woman—
Al Bâidhâvî.

CHAPTER LXXXVII

1 See Chapter II, verse 100, p. 25.

CHAPTER LXXXVIII

1 Another name of the last day.
2 So useful an animal as a camel being to an Arab a singular
instance of divine wisdom.

CHAPTER LXXXIX

1 The first ten nights of the sacred months of Dhu 'l Hejjeh.
2 Sheddâd, the son of 'Âd, is related to have ordered the
construction of a terrestrial paradise in the desert of Aden,
ostensibly in rivalry of the celestial one, and to have called it
Irem, after the name of his great-grandfather Irem (Aram). On
going to take possession of it, he and all his people were struck
dead by a noise from heaven, and the paradise disappeared.
Certain Arab travellers are declared to have come across this
mysterious garden.
3 Cf. p. 410, note 2.
4 Cf. p. 76, note 1.

CHAPTER XC

1 i.e. the sacred territory of Mecca.
2 Or, 'art at liberty to act as thou pleasest'.
3 See pp. 488–9.

CHAPTER XCI

1 See p. 146, note 13.

CHAPTER XCIV

1 i.e. expanded it for the reception of the truth. Taking the words literally some Muslims have supposed it to refer to the legend, that the angel Gabriel appeared to Mohammed while he was a child, and having cut open his breast took out his heart, and cleansed it from the black drop of original sin. This explanation is, however, rejected by the more sensible of the orthodox Muslim divines.

CHAPTER XCV

1 Alluding to the inviolable character of the sacred territory of Mecca.

CHAPTER XCVI

1 The five opening verses of the chapter are generally allowed to have been the first that were revealed.
2 i.e. Mohammed.
3 The allusion is to Abu Jahl, who threatened to set his foot on Mohammed's neck if he caught him in the act of adoration.

CHAPTER XCVII

1 The word *el Qadr* signifies 'power,' 'worth', 'measure', and 'the divine decree'.

CHAPTER CI

1 El Hâwiyeh.

CHAPTER CII

1 The commentators say that in one of the frequent contentions
   about the respective nobility of the Arab tribes, the Abu Menaf
   clan disputed with that of Sahm, which was the most numerous,
   and the latter, having lost many men in battle, declared that their
   dead should be taken into account as well as the living.
2 That is, the pleasures of this life.

CHAPTER CIII

1 Or, 'the age'.

CHAPTER CV

1 Abrahat el Asram, an Abyssinian Christian, and viceroy of the
   King of Sanaa in Yemen in the year in which Mohammed was
   born, marched with a large army and some elephants upon Mecca,
   with the intention of destroying the Kaabah. He was defeated and
   his army destroyed in so sudden a manner as to have given rise to
   the legend embodied in the text. It is conjectured that smallpox
   broke out amongst his men.

CHAPTER CVI

1 Some connect the first sentence with the last chapter.

CHAPTER CVII

1 Or, 'alms'. The word might be rendered 'resources'.

CHAPTER CVIII

1 The word signifies 'abundance'. It is also the name of a river in Paradise.

2 This is directed against Âs ibn Wail, who, when Mohammed's son El Qâsim died, called him *abtar*, which means 'dock tailed', i.e. childless.

CHAPTER CXI

1 Abu Laheb, 'the father of the flame', was the nickname of 'Abd el 'Huzzâ, uncle of Mohammed, and a bitter opponent of Islam.

2 A pun upon his name.

CHAPTER CXII

1 The chapter is generally known in Arabic by the name of El I'hlâs, 'clearing oneself', i.e. of belief in any but one Allah.

CHAPTER CXIII

1 Or, according to a traditional explanation given by the prophet to 'Âyeshah, 'the moon when it is eclipsed'.

2 Witches who make knots in string and blow upon them, uttering at the same time some magical formula and the name of the persons they wish to injure.

CHAPTER CXIV

1 The devil.